THE AUTOBIOGRAPHY AND CORRESPONDENCE

OF

MARY GRANVILLE,

MRS. DELANY:

WITH INTERESTING REMINISCENCES OF

KING GEORGE THE THIRD AND QUEEN CHARLOTTE.

EDITED

BY THE RIGHT HONOURABLE

LADY LLANOVER.

THREE VOLUMES,

VOL. II.

LONDON:
RICHARD BENTLEY, NEW BURLINGTON STREET,
Publisher in Ordinary to Her Majesty.
1861.

This scarce antiquarian book is included in our special *Legacy Reprint Series*. In the interest of creating a more extensive selection of rare historical book reprints, we have chosen to reproduce this title even though it may possibly have occasional imperfections such as missing and blurred pages, missing text, poor pictures, markings, dark backgrounds and other reproduction issues beyond our control. Because this work is culturally important, we have made it available as a part of our commitment to protecting, preserving and promoting the world's literature.

THE

LIFE AND CORRESPONDENCE

OF

MARY GRANVILLE.

(MRS. DELANY.)

Mrs. Pendarves to Mrs. Cath. Collingwood, in New Bond Street, next door to the Coke.[1]

Friday morning.

I am much obliged to my dear Miss Collingwood for both her letters; but let me tell you, you exult too soon, *I cannot yet own my wager lost.*[2] *Designing* and *acting* are two things, but if I do lose it, I will pay it honestly, and contrive a way for you to receive it on the spot it was lost. I have done a thousand things since I saw you, and well I may (for it is a thousand years) modestly speaking. I was in London for twenty minutes, but it being devotion-time I would not attempt calling on you. I have had some company with me; been at Isleworth, Twickenham, Whitton, Hounslow; seen Mr. Wingfield,

---

[1] "*Coke.*" This word is meant for the *Cock*, but is spelt in various ways in different letters.

[2] The "*Wager*" probably was that Miss Collingwood instead of going into a convent would be married before the "*Strawberry season*" was over.

his lady, and Mr. Pope's gardens; almost finished a history piece and a portrait; worked hard at my grotto, (undone as much as I have done,) am to dine to-day at Osterley, Sr Francis Child's, and will do my utmost to smite the old knight. But tell me who your rapturous lord was? there is but one in the world I could have *suspected* for such a speech, and he is over the hills and far away! My brother is returned from Tunbridge. Yesterday he and the Wingfields dined with me; to-morrow I shall have a house full. Expect a challenge for some day next week, and if you wish to see me as much as I wish to see you, my scheme will succeed. I am Mrs. Collingwood's humble servant, and dear Colly's

Most faithful
M. PEN.

Don't think me saucy; this is a hasty dab, but the coach waits.

Lysons says that Osterley House "was rebuilt by Sir Thomas Gresham, and was completed in 1577. In the year 1578 Queen Elizabeth visited Osterley, where Sir Thomas Gresham entertained her in a very magnificent manner. Lord Chief Justice Coke inhabited it after Lady Gresham's death, and George Earl of Desmond and his Countess resided at Osterley many years. Sir William Waller, the Parliamentary general, lived there from 1657 to his death in 1668.

"In the early part of the 18th century, Osterley became the property of Sir Francis Child, a citizen of great opulence and eminence. He was Lord Mayor of London in 1699, as was his son, Sir Francis, in 1732. The house was again rebuilt by Francis Child, Esq., about 1760; the ancient ground-plan was, for the most part, preserved, and the turrets at the corners remain, having been newly cased: the inside was fitted up with taste and magnificence, and was finished by Robert Child, who succeeded his brother Francis, in 1763; the staircase is ornamented with a fine painting by Rubens, of the apotheosis of William I. Prince of Orange, brought from Holland by Sir Francis Child. The most remarkable rooms are a noble gallery, containing a good collection of pictures by the old masters, and some valuable portraits; the state bedroom, very magnificently furnished; and a drawing-room hung with beautiful tapestry, procured from the Gobelins manufactory in 1775; the library contains a large and valuable collection of books. In the garden was a menagerie containing a large collection of rare birds."

Walpole says, in 1773: "On Friday we went to see—oh, the palace of palaces!—and yet a palace *sans crown, sans coronet;* but such expense! such taste! such profusion! and yet half an acre produces all the rents that furnish such magnificence. It is a jaghire got without a crime; in short, a shop is the estate, and Osterley Park is the spot. The old house I have often seen, which was built by Sir Thomas Gresham; but it is so improved and enriched, that all the Percies and Seymours of Sion must die of envy; there is a double portico that fills the space between the towers in front, and is as noble as the Propyleum of Athens. There is a hall, library, breakfast-room, eating-room, all chefs-d'œuvre of Adam; a gallery one hundred-and-thirty feet long, and a drawing-room worthy of Eve before the Fall. Mrs. Child's dressing-room is full of pictures, gold filigree, china and japan. So is all the house; the chairs are taken from antique lyres, and make charming harmony; there are Salvators, Gaspar Poussins, and to a beautiful staircase, a ceiling by Rubens; not to mention a *kitchen-garden* that costs 1400*l.* a year, a menagerie full of birds that come from a thousand islands which Mr. Banks has not discovered; and then, in the drawing-room I mentioned, there are door-cases, and a crimson and gold frieze, that I believe were borrowed from the Palace of the Sun, and then the park is the ugliest spot of ground in the universe, and so I returned comforted to Strawberry! You shall see these wonders the first time you come to Twickenham."

Mrs. Pendarves to Mrs. Ann Granville.

Northend, 10 Oct., 1737.

I dedicate this hour to tell you how well everything here looks, from the generous lord of the place down to cross squawling Patch, the thing in the house least in my favour. We came on Saturday as you know, if you are with Sally; the day proved so wet, that I could only take one walk round the garden; but having Sir John Stanley to converse with, you'll say I had not much reason to complain of my confinement. Yesterday the weather was very agreeable—a soft air and no rain; I walked almost two hours without resting. The trees and grass were so green, and the flowers so sweet, that I was, deceived for some time, and *took it for spring*; my happy imagination led me to a train of delights, the chief of which was the hopes of seing my dearest sister in a month or two! I walked from one flower-plot to another, till I composed a nosegay of anemonies, carnations, roses, honeysuckles, sweet williams, jessamine, sweet briar, and myrtle, full of pleasing reflections, till unluckily I turned down the lime walk, where the fluttering of the brown leaves about my ears, and the feuille-mort carpet under my feet, led me back to the latter end of October, destroyed every pleasing thought, and left me six months further from you than I was the moment before. What a transition!

I must talk to you now of the *only person* who can make up in any degree that change to me—our dear

Sir John: he looks and is as well as you and I can wish him to be, and so entertaining that I am sorry when ten o'clock comes, the hour we walk to our chambers. He has given me for you nine red and white cambric handkerchiefs, which I will send you when you please, they are made up; he has given me a pair of pretty white china babies for my cupboard, and a bowl for a ladle in china, in the shape of an Indian leaf.

I find no considerable alteration in Northend, some trees have danced, and shelves filled with books are put up in the closet within the calico room. We have talked about my brother's building, but nothing can be determined till we know more particularly the dimensions of the ground where it is to be placed. Sir John approves very well of the *thatched temple;* Dapper is here, and happy to meet with so many playfellows. To-morrow I return to *Fairy Castle,* and must think of making visits. Leonora has taken a little house in Audley Street unfurnished; I don't understand how the interest of £4000 will afford that, and maintain two maids and a man; she must have good friends to help, and I believe will. Your last dear letter I received the night before I came here—I was then at Lady Sunderland's; Lady Frances Eliot[1] was there, who enquired after you, and I made your compliments as due.

Miss Sutton is grown very tall and thin, and looks pale, not having quite recovered the disorder she had before I came to town. She is an agreeable girl, and has

---

[1] Lady Frances Nassau d'Auverquerque, eldest daughter of the 1st Earl of Grantham, married in June, 1737, to Captain Elliot, was niece to the Lady Frances Nassau before mentioned, who married the Earl of Bellamont.

something in her manner solid and sensible; she is a different turn from any girl I have ever met with, and continues her love to reading; she goes to bed at her usual hour, nine o'clock, and sups between seven and eight upon spoonmeat or roots, and I hope that regularity will make her healthy. She desired me to make her compliments to you. I am glad you saw our poor old woman once more; no circumstance that happened last summer gave me so much true satisfaction as our visit to Foxot. Friday was so fine a day that I conclude you marched as you designed; I shall be glad to have an account of your travels as leisure offers; when you have time, tell me how many pieces of cross-stitch I have left with you, and what grounds the borders have? I am determined, if possible, to finish my set of chairs against next year. Don't work at that which is wrong traced, I design it for a screen, and shall want the chairs first. Mr. Stanley is come to town, and next week I will get him to take out the lottery tickets. Pray let me know as soon as you can what money I desired you to pay for me at Gloucester; I am going to settle all my accounts in a regular way, and must know that particularly; I have got the laces, and the suit of nightclothes[1] I have pitched on for you are charming—it is grounded Brussels. I hope Mrs. Percival will not insist on having both?

The lottery is frequently mentioned in the course of this correspondence, and according to Smollett, " the whole nation was infected with the spirit of stock-jobbing to an astonishing degree.

---

[1] " *Night clothes* "—clothes to be worn *at night*, when dressed, not clothes to be worn in bed.

All distinctions of party, religion, sect, character, and circumstances, were swallowed up. Exchange Alley was filled with a strange concourse of statesmen and clergymen, churchmen and dissenters, Whigs and Tories, physicians and lawyers, tradesmen, and even females; all other professions and employments were utterly neglected." In fact, a spirit of gambling pervaded the nation, and more especially the upper classes of society, during the whole of the 18th century, and it would have been very extraordinary if any fashionable lady in the early days of Mary Granville had not taken tickets in the frequent lotteries. A very curious History of Lotteries may be found in Beckman.

The Editor does not possess any letters from Mrs. Pendarves, or Ann Granville, from October 10th, 1737, till November 8th, 1738, when Mrs. Pendarves writes from Gloucester to Lady Throckmorton.[1] The sisters must have been together during that year either in London, at Gloucester, or visiting friends and relations in the country; Mr. Granville was at that time in possession of Calwich, and it is very probable that some months were spent there.

The Honble G. Granville[2] to Mrs. Ann Granville.

Windsor, Nov. 1st, 1738.

It was no loss to dear Miss Granville my letter being so long before it came to her hand, yet fear it might make me appear neglectful in returning you my thanks for the favour of your letter, but I think daily experience learns us that we must not always judge by outward experience. I return you a thousand thanks for your last favour; I was very much pleased to hear of your flight

---

[1] "*Lady Throckmorton*" was the "*fair Kitty*" and the "*dear Collyflower*" of the Duchess of Portland, Mrs. Pendarves, and Ann Granville, who put an end to the alarm of her friends, lest she should enter a convent, by marrying Sir Robert Throckmorton, January 1738.

[2] The Honourable Grace Granville, daughter of George Lord Lansdowne.

into Gloucestershire, as I know it prevented you a parting, which is always disagreable to you. We are in hopes your next expedition will be to visit your friends in this part of the world.

According to your desire, I have enquired after our "*new star of righteousness;*" he does deserve in every particular the character you give of him. His name is Thorold, he has a very plentiful fortune — three thousand a year at present, and will have ten after his father's death, a married man and five children. He preaches twice a week, Monday and Fridays, reads a chapter out of the Bible, and then explains every verse of it. He has got a young gentleman from Oxford to live with him, who follows his example: they leave this country very soon, and don't return hither till spring. The Mr. Murray[1] Lady Betty Finch has married is the same Pope celebrates, and I believe he is by everybody that knows him well spoken of; I hear there is to be *no finery* at the Birthday, by his Majesty's desire. Princess Amelia has a stuff of 30 shillings a yard, without either gold or silver; this news I had from Lady Hertford. Mentioning her, puts me in mind of a love-tale Lady Pomfret has wrote her word of from Paris, which I must tell you; I did not think such a story could be met with but in a romance, but this is *really fact,* and happened very lately.

---

[1] William Murray, third son of David, 5th Viscount Stormont, born at Scone, March 2, 1705. Called to the English Bar in 1730. Was Solicitor-General in 1742, and Attorney-General in 1754, and Lord Chief Justice of the Court of King's Bench, Nov. 8, 1756; he was created Earl of Mansfield, Oct. 19, 1776, and married, in 1738, Elizabeth, daughter of Daniel, Earl of Winchelsea and Nottingham. Died, *s. p.*, March 20, 1793. The earldom devolved on his nephew, Viscount Stormont.

Mr. Middleton, a young gentleman of no fortune, and younger brother to the Irish Lord Midleton, went into France, where he got into the French army. The man of the house where he boarded had an extremely handsome daughter, with whom Mr. Middleton was very much enamoured, and made his addresses to her: her father perceived it, and knowing his daughter to be much inferiour to the young gentleman, told him he found he did his daughter the honour to make his addresses to her, but as her birth was much too low to be his wife, and much above being his mistress, he begged him not to persevere in his addresses to her, for it might prove a disadvantage to them both, and in particular to his daughter, who had nothing but her character to depend on. The young gentleman replied that he loved his daughter too well to have a thought of her but what was honourable, and he should be a most miserable man if he would not consent to their having a contract of marriage pass between them. The father most honourably endeavoured as much as possible to persuade him to the contrary, but all to no purpose. At last the contract was drawn; but unluckily for the lovers, the young man was obliged to go to Paris, where he met with his general, a Lord Clair, and distant relation of his (a very officious person, as you'll find by the end of my story). He was informed of this affair, and thought himself obliged to send post-haste to acquaint all Mr. Middleton's relations of his amour, which alarmed them very much; upon which they wrote to him letters of advice, endeavouring if possible to demonstate to him how disadvantageous a match it would be to him to marry a woman without either birth or fortune, and if he really and truly loved her he would not persist in his resolution, for with his narrow fortune they could have no view of happiness; and that as for his friends and relations, they were *determined*, if he persisted, never to have anything to say to him, and his wisest way of proceeding would be to set the young woman at liberty, by desiring the contract to be returned. At last they prevailed with him to write to her. In his letter he told her he should never love any woman except herself, but that he was so unhappy as not to have a fortune which could any ways contribute to their happiness, therefore would be miserable himself (as he must be without her) rather than make her in the least unhappy, and desired to set her free by begging she would return him the contract. Her answer was,—she willingly granted his request, and never should have consented to the contract had it not been to have satisfied him for the present, knowing *how improper* a match *it was for him*; as for her affections, they were not in her power to change, being too strongly fixed in his favour, but she wished him all happiness this world could afford. The poor young woman took this so much to heart that she fell into a consumption and died within the twelvemonth. Mr. Middleton, who was all life and spirit, and fond of the gaieties of the world, forsook them all upon hearing of this news, was seized with a fever, and *died in a few days!*

After having told my dear cousin so long a history and so extraordinary one, I believe she would wish me to conclude, but I must add my compliments to Mrs. Granville and Madam Pen; my sisters are very much humble servants to you all. The Duchess of Portland breakfasted here yesterday morning: we talked of our friends at Gloucester, and you are often thought of by, dear Miss Granville,

    Your most affectionate and faithful

                        G. GRANVILLE.

Mrs. Kingdom is not yet gone to Bath; I believe she don't think of going till Xtmas, being, thank God, much better in health.

Mrs. Pendarves to Lady Throckmorton.[1]

                        Glocester, 8 Nov. 1738.

I shall make no apology to dear Lady Throck. for leaving her so long in repose. Report informs me you will soon be under a confinement that will make letters for some time very improper visiters, and I am willing, you should know that my best wishes attend you on this occasion, as they have done on all others. Your Ladyship's last letter was a great joy to me; I began to fear you had cast me off, and was just upon the brink of reproaching Sir Robert as the cause of my unhappiness and your infidelity! These thoughts I confess perplexed me greatly: when I grew calmer and considered how much reason you had to like one another, I was not surprized you should not be permitted to bestow your time elsewhere, or that you should grow indifferent to the rest of your friends. Possessed of one you rate so highly, I was not a little pleased to find after all my reasonings I was no outcast, but still favoured with your remembrance and friendship;

---

[1] Miss Catherine Collingwood.

and you must change wonderfully, when I can be negligent of a distinction I wish so much to preserve. Gloucester affords so little variety, that I can send you no accounts from hence worthy your notice; we have assemblies once a week, such as they are, and we go because we would not be thought churlish. They are made up of an odd mixture, and if my sister and myself loved pulling people to pieces, we should find material enough, to exercise our wits upon—at least excellent food for ill nature.

You have left Bath to the possession of their Royal Highness's, who make no small racket. As you have no doubt accounts from the fountain-head of all that passes, I will not trouble you with my second-hand news. It is impossible to take Weston in the way to Bulstrode, without altering the geography of the country—an undertaking by no means suited to my genius. 'Tis well at this time your Ladyship is out of my way, for I might call on you at an improper time, and I wish that may not be my brother's case: he is still at Calwich, but proposes going to town some time this month, and I know promises himself great pleasure in paying his respects to the happy pair, but if a visit this month should prove mal-a-propos, pray let me give him notice. This leads me to beg some account from any friendly or charitable hand as soon as you are brought to bed: my sister joins earnestly in the petition with me, for as we both sincerely love you, you may imagine how necessary it is we should have that satisfaction; perhaps I may at that time be at Bulstrode, for I go the last week of this month; my sister therefore desires, she may particularly be informed. Her most faithful and kind service attends you

and Sir Robert. I almost had forgot to thank you for delivering my letter to Mr. Hook; I had an answer from him, and I dropt there, for fear my letters might prove as bad a persecution to him as an easterly wind. I was charmed with the life you lead at Holt, and what pleased me most in it was the sympathy there was between your way of spending your time and ours at Calwich, where we enjoyed every rural delight. I am impatient to be acquainted with Miss Birch—my sister must bring that about as soon as she comes to town. She stays with my mother till spring, but I hope you will pave the way for me, and if that ingenious lady is so happy as to be with you now, assure her of the great desire I have of being introduced to her. There is no end of my prating to you, my dear lady Throck.! When shall we meet? Is London so detestable and so miserable as never to receive your footsteps? Wherever you are, depend upon the affectionate wishes of
Your most faithful
M. PENDARVES.

Mrs. Pendarves to Mrs. Ann Granville.
Bulstrode, 12 Dec., 1738.

I think you idle folks at Gloucester that have nothing to do but to go to church and to assemblies, might compose a romance, and lay the principal scene at Bulstrode. I rejoice at your coming off so well after your raking; since it agreed with you, I advise a repetition. I own if dancing was added to our entertainments here I should be glad, but we are not numerous enough! The character you give me of the *Inferencer* has raised my esteem of him; I wish he could meet with friends that would be of real use to him, but so singular a way of thinking in an attorney will hardly prove a profitable one. My mama is *very kind* in inviting Mrs. Elstob.[1] I almost fancy she will not accept of it, because of having been there in a disguised way; the Duchess has now a thousand fears, least my Lord and Lady Oxford should have any objections against taking her, but I hope they will all prove false; she can't very conveniently take her till next summer, that she comes to Bulstrode (that will be about six months hence), because in town they have not at present any convenient room for her. Mrs. Elstob seems, out of modesty and diffidence of herself, to decline coming, but it would be most imprudent for her to refuse such an offer, when no fatigue will be imposed upon her, but all imaginable care will be taken of her. I own I long to have *you see her*, that I may really know what sort of woman she is. My Lord Oxford objects to her not speaking French, but the Duchess answers she shall have a master for that, or a maid to talk, and all she requires and hopes of Mrs. Elstob is to instruct her children in the principles of religion and virtue, to teach them to speak, read, and understand English well, to cultivate their minds as far as their capacity will allow, and to keep them company in the house,

---

[1] "After the decease of Queen Caroline Mrs. Elstob was again brought into difficulties, and though mistress of *eight languages* besides her own, was obliged to seek for employment as a preceptress of children; but she might be considered as having been very fortunate in the situation which she obtained in this capacity, as in 1739 she was taken into the family of the Duchess of Portland, where she continued till her death, which happened on May 30, 1756, when she was buried at St. Margaret's, Westminster."— *Biographia Britannica.*

and when her strength and health will permit to take the
air with them. All this surely she is well qualified to do,
and it would be a sincere joy to me to have our worthy
Duchess possest of so valuable a person; but don't speak
of her coming here till 'tis more confirmed.

I made your compliments in your own words at breakfast yesterday morning, every one was pleased with your
obliging compliments, and volleys have been shot off
in return this afternoon, when I said I was coming to my
room to write to you. This morning I had a letter from
Sally, who is quite dispirited at her disappointment of
not spending the Xtmas holidays; I think it would have
been cruel to let her, though she was hardy enough to
venture; but she has now turned her thoughts another
way, and *perplexed me extremely*—she *proposes to me*
coming to spend a week with me at Bulstrode, to introduce her to the Duchess! Alas! how wild is imagination when let loose, and not trimmed by a *little knowledge
of the world?* She has worked herself up to a belief
that it *may be done* easily, and is so eager, that if I did
not know she always judges kindly of our actions, I
should fear the refusing her would make an eternal breach.
I have written her plainly *the impossibility* of putting such
a scheme in practice, and hope she will be convinced of
her error without taking anything ill of me, for surely
I always mean her well! You know from the Duchess
and our cousins of my having been at Old Windsor.

From Mrs. Elstob to Mrs Ann Granville, in Gloucester.

Bath, Dec. 14, 1738.

DEAR MADAM,

The favour of your most charming letter I received with the greatest joy and pleasure imaginable, It gives me both courage and assurance to address myself to you, as you there command me, with the freedom of an old friend. I wish you don't repent your obliging invitation to a correspondence, for though I am not one of the greatest talkers in the world, I am an everlasting scribbler; a proof of this truth you will have when I tell you, that I have written two long letters to your excellent sister, Mrs. Pendarves, since Thursday last, on which day I received one from her, which so transported me with admiration of her goodness towards me, that I verily think for some time I was hardly sensible, nor am I yet able to express myself as I ought upon the subject of it, and fear I nevershall. Though I am commanded to reveal it to nobody, I believe I may be certain she will not take it ill if I communicate it to you; it was the honour of an offer from their Graces the Duke and Duchess of Portland to teach their children, with the promise of a generous allowance. The charming character Mrs. Pendarves gives me of those noble persons would not suffer me to think twice whether I should accept it, notwithstanding the true sense I have of my own unworthiness of so great an honour.

I beg ten thousand pardons, dear madam, that I did not deliver your letter to Mrs. Bendon[1] with my own hand, but I was so extremely ill that I was not able to

---

[1] Query Bindon?

go abroad; my bad health and great weakness deprives me of the happiness of waiting on the worthy ladies I know in Bath. I have had the happiness of seeing Mrs. Bendon but once since I came; and according to my weak judgment she answers the character you give her. I have seen Lady Cocks twice, the first time she sent for me to wait on Lady Codrington; her Ladyship was then very ill with a cold she had got coming to Bath. Since that she invited me to dine with her: she then seemed pretty cheerful; our conversation was upon indifferent things, which is certainly best for persons inclined to melancholy. My obligations to Dr. Oliver are very great, which increases the vast number upon me of yours and Mrs. Pendarves's. I think it is now high time to take my leave, and to assure you that I am, with the highest value and esteem for the worthy Mrs. Granville and yourself,[1]

Dear madam,
Your most grateful and affectionate
Humble servant,
ELIZABETH ELSTOB.

Mrs. Pendarves to Mrs. Ann Granville, at Gloucester.

Bulstrode, Dec. 22, 1738.

Though the bright celestial sun has put on all his charms, and adorned with sword and belt, shines with the utmost splendor, and as I passed by the window of

---

[1] It is evident from the above letter to Ann Granville that she *had* made the personal acquaintance of Mrs. Elstob some time before, and, therefore, that the words of Mrs. Pendarves, expressing her desire that her sister should "*see her*," must have meant at her mother's house, that she might the better judge of her character, before she went to the Duchess of Portland.

assignation twinkled upon me to call me to a conference, I resist all his allurements! I have your last dear letters now before me. I turn over *another* leaf, *another*, *another* and *another!* I would indeed be your *chief* delight, but not your *only* one, and you add to my own particular happiness by making that of so many agreeable friends that know how to value you. I hope my poor Fo. has had my letter; I grieve for all her sorrows. Our queen of a Duchess *truly loves you*, and admires your letters excessively; she was in raptures with that she received last post, the Elstobian affair is *quite fixed*, and she expressed the utmost satisfaction at having secured such a worthy woman to educate her children; I wrote last post to Mrs. Elstob to tell her the Duchess looked on her as engaged to her, and that her salary should begin on Xtmas Day next, though she could not conveniently take her into her family till Midsummer; I hope she will write to the Duchess, and suppose she will of course; I gave her a little hint, but would not have it mentioned that I did. I agree with you in what you say about our cousins; but you and I have often agreed, though we have a perfect reliance on Providence, that we are to make use of all reasonable methods for our advancement, and, as far as our short-sightedness will allow, to provide against the common accidents of life. I think your advise to Mrs. Elstob quite right about *paying debts;* a person of such principles as hers cannot enjoy any advantages without doing that justice when it is in her power to do it.

I wish prosperity to the convocation; may it meet weekly and produce much edification, not only to the present members but to the absent one, who hopes to reap much fruit at a distance from its ingenious and *sprightly conferences*. You diverted me extreamly with the discretion of the Miller, I have a little of the fairy disposition, and like to have my favours concealed. I think your plot *against* Quadrille a good one, but Gloucester is not worthy, nor are people who only love snapping noses formed to receive such entertainment, 'twould be (saving their presence) " throwing pearl before swine:" but if you would *compile* a *journal* in the dressing-room, and call in to your assistance the Inferencer and his cousin elect, there *are* souls at Bulstrode could relish such an entertainment.

I missed the occultation of Aldebaran and the moon; the nights have been so cold of late, and Mr. Achard so grunting that I have not peeped much at the heavenly bodies, but I have had two or three lectures of cosmography in the library. This morning, as my master and I were drawing and examining circles, who should come in but Mr. Robert Harley; I blushed and looked excessive silly to be caught in the fact, but the affair, which I have endeavoured to keep secret, is discovered, and I must bear the reflection of those who think me very presuming in *attempting to be wise*. I am much obliged to my master; he takes a great deal of pains with me, and has a clear way of instructing me. I shall never aim at talking upon subjects of that kind, but the little I may gain by these lectures will make me take more pleasure in hearing others talk.

I am sorry for my Lady Cox, and lament the want of judgment in a woman of such excellent virtues; but a warm heart, with excess of good nature, will lead people into error without a *proper resolution* and very *discerning judgment* to keep the balance even. You forgot in your last to enclose Mrs. Elstob's letter, though you said you had.

Yesterday morning, at breakfast, the Duchess said she had "had a charming letter from her dear Pip." "Pip," says Lord Dup. "must write long letters, she has such a flow of spirits and of wit that if it were not for frequent explosions, they would prey upon and destroy her constitution; she is by much the most spirituelle creature I ever met with. I shall never forget the last conversation we had: why does not she come to town? She must!" He ran on saying much more than I can remember. At dinner to-day Mrs. Pipkin's health was drank to Cousin *Pots*[1] and all the young Pipperkins, which made the youth blush abundantly. Lord Oxford came here last Tuesday, and brought with him a pretty kind of man (Mr. Robert Harley[2]) : his manner sensible and agreeable, his person something like my Lord Foley, but the Duchess won't allow that he is better. Lord Oxford and I talked of books and pictures.

Pray tell me if you recollect the name of the ruins I sketched in my book, and who the place belonged to? I took care of all your letters. The King has given Lady Bateman[3] lodgings in Windsor Castle, which will be great joy to Miss Granville, for they are very intimate.

---

[1] Cousin Pots. Query Lord Dupplin.

[2] "*Mr. Robert Harley*," son of Edward Harley of Eywood, first cousin of Edward, 2nd Earl of Oxford, and brother to Edward, 3rd Earl of Oxford.

[3] Sir James Bateman was M.P. for Ilchester in 1712; in 1717 he was Lord Mayor of London; in 1718 he was Governor of the South Sea Company, and in the same year he died. His wife was Anne, daughter and co-heir of John Searle, Esq., of Finchley. Their son William was created a Viscount in 1725, and married Lady Anne Spencer, eldest daughter, by the second

Donnellan talks of getting to Bath by February; I own her very ill state of health quite damps the joy of seeing her; she bids me tell you she takes you into her scheme there and in all her healthy designs. She writes me a short letter, and says even that's a pain to her to write. Adieu, my dearest sister; my affectionate duty to my mother, kind service to all friends.

Mrs. Pendarves to Mrs. Ann Granville, at Gloucester.

Bulstrode, Dec. 29, 1738.

Two of your letters are spread before me; but how well I shall discharge the debt I cannot guess, for my Lord Oxford has lent me some curious drawings of Stonehenge to copy, that if I don't finish by Monday next, I shall never more get possession of. They have employed me two mornings, and will two mornings more, so that my writing-hour is drove down to the evening. Well, I must drink coffee at five, and play with the little jewels—it is the ceremony of the house: then says the Duchess, "Don't go, Penny, till I have net one row in my cherry net," which proves a hundred meshes, then comes some prater, asks her Grace a question; the arm suspended in the air forgets its occupation; she answers, and asks some other question in return—ten to one but a laugh is hatched, and once in a quarter of an hour the netting-work is remembered! With patience I await her solemn motions, and by half-an-hour after six we are in the dressing-room, armed with pen and ink, and the fair

---

marriage, of Charles, 3rd Earl of Sunderland. The date of death of Lady Bateman is not given, nor the date of the Viscount's marriage, but one or other of these ladies must have had the rooms at Windsor, probably the latter.

field prepared to receive the attack. Then comes Lady Elizabeth, Lady Harriot, and the noble Marquis; after half an hour's jumping, they are dismissed, and we soberly say, " Now we will write our letters." In comes the Duke, "*the tea stays for the ladies:*" well, we must go, for there's no living at Bulstrode without four meals a-day; then when the beaux esprits are met, the fumes of inspiring tea begin to operate, 'till eight of the clock strikes; then we start up, run away, and here I am, brimful of a thousand things to say to you, but have no time to write them, and that you know is a sad case. You and I perfectly agree in what you say of Sir John Stanley and my brother.

We leave Bulstrode next Saturday se'night; I shall sigh when I turn my back upon it, for I have passed my time as happily as it is possible for me in your absence. 'Tis not to be told how many pretty engaging ways our dear friend has to gain the love and admiration of those she honours with her friendship, and this you well know, but I love to repeat it.

I am seriously alarmed about the panics you take in the *Prelate's* company: "*aw'd by a thousand tender fears, tell me—tell me, my heart, if this be love?*" Ah, ma chère! what, caught in a *purple rope?* but I would not have you despair; I will give a hint to Lord Dup. to speak a favourable word for you, if his political conversations will allow him to talk of anything but Parliamentary affairs, etc. I will give him to understand that you are an excellent housewife, can raise paste, feed poultry, keep accounts, and talk very prettily to the young parsons, that you will indulge your Lord in *his* ways, and with a gentle sway pursue *your own!*

Much more I had to say, but the Duchess is so provokingly witty, and my *Lady Waw* seconds the motion so strongly, with the help of her fingers tickling me wherever she can catch me, that I can scrawl no more. So farewell; and if my letter is unintelligible and freakish, 'tis owing to my mad companions, who have made such confusion in my brain. I can think distinctly but in one particular, and that is, that in all my humours, whether grave or merry, I am,

With the most tender and constant affection,

Yours.

Lady Waw may look as pretty as she pleases, and say as many civil things as words can express; I won't tell you a tittle in her favour to-night.

Mrs. Pendarves to Mrs. Ann Granville.

9th January, 1738-9.

I am arrived at the land of hurry and impertinence, and have left the gentle delights of Bulstrode; much I lament the change, though I have had the great pleasure of finding all our good friends in very good health and glad to see me.

We set out from Bulstrode at eleven, and were in town by half an hour after two, over hills of snow and heaps of ice; but our horses flew as if each had been a Pegasus —four coaches and six, with twelve horsemen attending, besides apothecaries, bakers, butchers, that joined in the procession to escort us part of the way. The Duchess of Portland and all her train are very well after their journey.

Yesterday I dined with Sir John Stanley; he looks

and is very well: he says he was determined to use me very ill, but he has not kept to his resolution. He has given me an excessively pretty English pebble bottle with a gold top, which is an absolute beauty, and has put into my hands for you two black and gold japan cups and saucers, which I am sure you will like. Yesterday, in the afternoon, I went to my Lady Sunderland: she looks charminly, though she has had a bad cold, attended by a sore throat. Miss Sutton is very tall—is thin, but grows more and more agreeable: she asked after all her friends at Gloucester, and wishes to see you in town soon. I staid with the Countess till nearly twelve: the *Dragon* was abroad; all the boys are at home, so there is noise enough you may believe. I called yesterday morning on Lady Sarah Cowper, she was so ill with a violent headache, she could hardly speak. Your letter to my brother has given me a little comfort on Mrs. Duncomb's account; I have been very much grieved about her, but hope she will now soon get the better of her disorder.

To-day I dine at my brother's, and come home in the afternoon to see folks. To-morrow I go to hear Mr. Handel's oratorio rehearsed, and in the afternoon am to have our amiable Duchess snug to myself; for though we passed so many weeks together, she and I had but *one* tête-à-tête the whole time, for Lady W. is a sort of *an idle body*, and *never retired to her room* for one moment, for she drest as soon as she was up—so she had no call from us. On Thursday I am to go to Lady North's,[1] and Friday stay at home for Mrs. Cary,

---

[1] Francis Lord North, married, secondly, in 1736, Elizabeth, Viscountess Dowager of Lewisham, daughter of Sir Arthur Kaye.

Lady Wallingford, and anybody that comes.—Thus is my time cut out for this week; and now it is time for me to thank my dearest sister for her most sprightly letter, with Binikin's enclosed, which diverted me extremely. Mrs. Delahay and a thousand Mrs. Fiddlefaddles to plague me. Three gowns have I tried on; yesterday I bespoke a hoop petticoat, of the exact dimensions of my old one; the fashionable hoops are made of the richest damask, trimmed with gold and silver, fourteen guineas a hoop. Would you have me bespeak you such a one against you come?

Last night I received a very entertaining letter, and some excellent verses from the Miller of Mansfield. The prose I will answer as soon as I can find time (a most precious and rare thing). Poor Mrs. Greville! I shall rejoice to hear of her having finished her painful task. The newspapers, I suppose, informed you of the unhappy end of one of the Duchess of Portland's maids, who was thrown out of the waggon;[1] the wheels ran over her, and she lived three hours in exquisite misery: this melancholy accident damped all our spirits extremely. Bunny is gone this morning to Whitehall; he looks very well, but is rather fatter: he desired me to make his compliments and excuse for not writing. Young Monck is in town, and the *finest of beaux*; I asked him if he heard that Miss Usher was going to be married? He said, "*No*;" I wish your news of her may be true. I believe Donnellan will be in England in a month, and

---

[1] Dean Swift, when a young man, used to travel by a stage-waggon from Moor Park into Leicestershire to see his mother. Some of the "flying waggons" of the middle of the eighteenth century vied with each other in accommodations for passengers.

I hope you will give her the meeting: my brother and I have contrived that between our two houses we shall accomodate you both very cleverly; you and I are one, Phil may have George's room, and two of our maids may lie at my brother's. I own I have but little joy at the thought of seing poor Don, for were she not in a very bad way she would not take such a voyage and journey at this time of the year.

I must entreat you to make my excuse to Mrs. Viney and her daughters. I am ashamed of not having answered their kind letters, but will soon make my own apology. My very kind wishes attend her and hers.

Mrs. Pendarves to Mrs. Ann Granville.

Brook Street, 23 Jan. 1738-9.

I have gone through infinite vanity and bustle since my last visit to you, but shall think my toils well recompensed, if I can draw any entertainment out of them for you. I wrote to you last Thursday; dined that day at Sir John Stanley's, came home to receive our cousins, (three of the Carteret race,) and went afterwards to Lady Strafford's[1] with Lady Wallingford,[2] who I am sure will be extremely pleased with your letter. Lady Straff's, you

---

[1] Anne, sole daughter and heir of Sir Henry Johnson, married, on Sept. 6, 1711, Thomas Wentworth, Earl of Strafford. The Earl died in November, 1739.

[2] Lord Viscount Wallingford, M.P. for Banbury, died in June, 1740. Lady Wallingford is said by Walpole to be the daughter of John Law, the speculator, and Lady Catherine, his wife. In 1783 he speaks of seeing her frequently at the Duchess of Montrose's, and mentions that " she has by no means a look of the age to which she had arrived." John Law, the Mississippi projector, married Catherine, daughter of Nicholas Knolles, Earl of Banbury,

know, is but a muzzy place; I met nothing to chatter with that gave me any pleasure, except our *sprightly Duchess*, who came in just as I was going away with Lady Lucy Manners[1] from the play.

Friday was appointed for our meeting Lord Oxford at Mr. Virtue's the engraver's,[2] where I saw nothing extraordinary, but an old picture which belongs to my Lord Digby's family, of Queen Elizabeth being carried under a canopy of state in honour of Lord Hunsdon's marriage with a Lady Mary ——'s daughter. There are six men of quality that carry the Queen, and Knights of the Garter attending the bride, her mother and sisters all on foot; all the figures are supposed to be portraits, but none are known now but Lord Hunsdon's, Lord Burleigh's, and Lord Leicester's. Virtue is copying it in miniature for my Lord Oxford, I dined that day at Whitehall, and came home to Mr. Hambden, who was to introduce his two nieces. Lady Catherine Hanmer spent the whole afternoon with me; Misses Kempthorns seem to be modest, well-behaved young women, nothing remarkable in their persons, handsome or otherwise, which is all I can judge from a first visit. After much persuasion and many debates within myself, I consented to go with Lady Dysart to the Prince's birthday, humbly drest in my

---

and had a son, John, who died at Maestricht in 1734; and a daughter, married to William, Viscount Wallingford, who died in 1790, aged 80. John Law died at Venice in 1729.

[1] Lady Lucy Manners, youngest daughter of John, 2nd Duke of Rutland, by his second wife, Lucy, daughter of Bennet, Baron Sherard. She married, in 1742, William, 2nd Duke of Montrose.

[2] George Vertue, the eminent engraver and antiquary, born in London, in 1684. He was patronized by the Earl of Oxford and Sir Godfrey Kneller, and soon rose into note. The works of Vertue are numerous, and valuable on account of their accuracy, though sometimes deficient in spirit.

pink damask, white and gold handkerchief, plain green ribbon, and Lady Sunderland's buckles for my stays.[1] I was a *good foil* for those that were there. I never saw so much finery without any mixture of trumpery in my life. Lady Huntingdon's,[2] as the most extraordinary, I must describe first:—her petticoat was black velvet embroidered with chenille, the pattern a *large stone vase* filled with *ramping flowers* that spread almost over a breadth of the petticoat from the bottom to the top; between each vase of flowers was a pattern of gold shells, and foliage embossed and most heavily rich; the gown was white satin embroidered also with chenille mixt with gold ornaments, *no vases* on the *sleeve*, but *two or three on the tail*; it was a most laboured piece of finery, the pattern much properer for a stucco staircase than the apparel of a lady,—a mere shadow that tottered under every step she took under the load. The next fine lady was Mrs. Spencer; her clothes, green paduasoy covered all over, the gown as well as petticoat, with a very fine and very pretty trimming; it was well made; she looked genteel and easy, and had all the dowager Duchess of M.'s jewels, which made her look quite magnificent. Lady

---

[1] "*My stays.*" Straps from the gown, the stays were white silk covered with a lacing through which a handkerchief was passed.

[2] Theophilus, Earl of Huntingdon, married June 3, 1728, Lady Selina Shirley, second daughter of Washington Earl Ferrers, celebrated after the Earl's decease (which took place in 1746) by the leading part she took in religious matters. Availing herself of her privilege as a peeress, she nominated chaplains, and had services performed wherever she was; one of her chaplains was Whitfield. She built chapels in various places, which are still called by her name, and, after the death of Whitfield, his followers were called "*Lady Huntingdon's people.*" She espoused the principles of the Calvinistic Methodists, and founded the College of Trevecca in South Wales. Lady Huntingdon died 1791.

Dysart was white gold, and looked as handsome as ever I saw her; Miss Carteret in an uncut blue velvet, and *all* my Lady Carteret's jewels; Lady Carteret in the same clothes she made for the Prince's wedding, white and gold and colours; the Princess was in white satin, the petticoat covered with a gold trimming like embroidery, faced and robed with the same. Her head and stomacher a rock of diamonds and pearls; her looks pleased me better than her dress; there appeared in them such strong marks of contentment and good-humour. She spoke *to everybody*, and so did the Prince. The ball began at eight; I never saw a ball at Court well managed before. The Prince and Princess sat under the State, their attendants on stools on the right and left hand; benches were placed for the rest of the company, the first row of which was kept for the dancers. The best dancers were Lady Catherine Hanmer, Lady Dysart, and Miss Wyndham; nothing extraordinary among the men; much finery, chiefly brown with gold or silver embroidery, and rich waistcoats. Lord Carteret was there morning and night.

'Tis now strongly reported that there is going to be a reconciliation between the King and Prince, but the truth of that is doubted. Lord Townshend has thrown up, nobody knows why. The Prince began the ball with the Duchess of Bedford; after one minuet he sat down. When two country-dances were over the Princess went to quadrille with Lady Archibald Hamilton, Lady Westmoreland, and Lady Chesterfield; the Prince in another room to whisk with Lord Baltimore, Lady Blandford, and Lady Carteret. At half an hour after eleven the Prince and Princess gave over cards and went away.

The dancing broke up at the same time, and all the company I believe was gone by half an hour after twelve; which I think was very orderly, considering how many people there were to get at their equipages. I got home a little after twelve, eat my supper, told George[1] all I had seen, was in bed soon after one, and slept happily for I dreamt of you, and next morning, was up and ready to receive my Lord Dupplin and Mr. Wotton, who came to breakfast with me; talked much of my favourite art,— Mr. Wotton encourages me to go on. Went to church at eleven; your humble servant Mr. Stillingfleet, I believe is chaplain to the Bishop of Durham; he comes constantly to church with him and sits in his seat. Should I not ask him to come and see me? Mr. Harbin and my brother eat part of the Glocester chine; a thousand thanks for it.

Mrs. Pendarves to Mrs. Ann Granville.

27th January, 1738-9.

I was yesterday at dinner at Lord Oxford's when I received your last letter, which, with the permission of the company, I skimmed over to satisfy myself of your health: at my return home I indulged myself with a more particular perusal, and dwelt upon each line with true delight. The enclosed letter I sent this morning by Jo to Mr. Hooker's for my chairs according to your advise; I would have sent a porter, but Jo *begged* he might go to see the town. He

---

[1] George was a waiting woman, and very probably a gentlewoman, as was very common in those days, when the daughters of clergymen or decayed gentlemen became "*waiting women*," a term now lost in that of "lady's maid."

behaves very well, and is thus far the best servant I ever had.

To return to Mr. N.'s manuscript. I think it worthy of the author, and hope it will answer the good design it was wrote with, but alas, those that will read it with attention and approbation are those that *don't* want it! I will speak to the Duchess to take the paper; I should be very glad Mr. Newton met with any encouragement or advantage, as I have a very just opinion of his worth.

I am delighted that my mother approves so well of the Irish flax; I will send the pattern of thread to Mrs. Donnellan, but it seems to be so strong, I can't think it is too fine, it will be a work when finished more precious than that Arachne wove when she enraged Pallas by her excelling! I lost one cold at Lady Stratford's, and caught another last Wednesday at Norfolk House, which makes me cough, but not bad. I really was glad to hear of poor Mrs. Greville's death, I never could think of her alive and in misery without pain.

When I see the Duchess of Portland I shall have Sally's historical epistle. I rejoice to hear she is alive. I wrote to her a huge folio just before I left Bulstrode, and she has not so much as afforded me a small duodecimo in return! I should be glad to see any of Mrs. Elstob's works, and will enquire after the translation you mention. I shall be glad when she is safe with you at Gloucester. I gave you an account in my last of Lady Sun.'s kindness to Mr. Gwinnet, she begged her name might not be mentioned.

How shall I return the money to you?

Mrs. Cocks is still with Lady Mary Colley, sometimes scolding, sometimes friends; they rub on pretty well.

She is unhealthy, which is what Lady Mary complains of. I fully designed writing to-day to Mrs. Viney, but this letter will be as much as I can possibly compass this morning, for I dine at the Squire's, am to meet the Westcomb's, every moment expect Goupy, and in the afternoon meet Lady Sarah Cowper at Mrs. Claverin's. The Duchess of Marlborough was brought to bed yesterday at eleven o'clock of a son,[1] a great joy!

Lady Anne Lumley[2] one of Princess Amelia's ladies, is to be married to Mr. Franklyn; she asked leave yesterday. She is well pleased too I believe, for her charms are in their decline, and Mr. Franklyn is a very good match for her.

Next Monday, at the Thatched House[3] in St. James's Street, there is to be an assembly—dancing and cards. Lady Egmont[4] presides: she has ask'd my brother to be of the party; men you know, especially unmarried, are valuable commoditys. I am not to be there, nor do I know who is besides, nor upon what occasion this grand affair is set on foot, but I believe it is some charity business. I hope you have got Swift's poem safe—I long to know how you like it. Mr. Nugent,[5] that married Mrs. Knight, has lately wrote two odes, one to Mr. Pulteney on his changing his religion; they are much

---

[1] George, afterwards 3rd Duke of Marlborough.
[2] Lady Anne Lumley, third daughter of Richard, 1st Earl of Scarborough, married, in February 1739, Frederic Frankland, Esq., M.P. for Thirsk. Lady Anne died in February, 1740.
[3] The Thatched House, St. James's Street, stood originally on the site of the present Conservative Club.
[4] Catherine, wife of the 1st Earl of Egmont.
[5] Mr. Nugent, afterwards Earl Nugent, wrote several poems, and an ode "upon his own conversion from popery."

commended, but thought too fine to be the production of the person named to be the author.

The Duchess of Portland, Dash, and the Duke drank tea and picked shells for me last Thursday. Yesterday I dined at Lord Oxford's; we went at twelve to look over prints of Hollar, and drawings from antiquities and reliques at Rome. There remains so much more to see, that we are to go there next Friday at nine o'clock in the morning to finish.

Mrs. Pendarves to Mrs. Ann Granville.

[The commencement of this letter is lost.]

Query (Bulstrode, 1739).

Lady Betty is rather too young, being but three years old, to have a preceptor, but as Mrs. Elstob has no settled home to go to, I dare say the Duchess will consent to take her before the time of her being wanted. I much fear her being in so bad a state of health will make her incapable of application, but being settled in a good family where she will have no cares, may be more beneficial to her than the skill of all the physicians. I desire you will make my particular compliments to Mrs. Viney; it was a sincere concern to me to leave her with her affairs in so perplexed a way, and heartily wish her better success. Remember me kindly to her pretty children and all friends. George calls to me, "Madam, remember to tell Miss Granville, Dapper killed a hare yesterday in the garden." She begs her humble duty, and is thoroughly sensible of all your favours. Adieu till after breakfast.

The following story I picked up at the tea-table, and hope I shall be beforehand with the Gloucester journal:—

A lady came into Birmingham with a handsome equipage, and "desired the landlord of the inn to get her a husband, being determined to marry somebody or other before she left the town." The man bowed, and supposed her ladyship to be in a facetious humour, but being made sensible how much she was in earnest, he went out in search of a man that would marry a fine lady without asking questions! After many repulses from poor fellows who were not desperate enough for such a venture, he met with an exciseman, who said he "*could not be in a worse condition than he was,*" and accordingly went with the innkeeper, and made a tender of himself, which was all he had to bestow on the lady, who immediately went with him to one who gave them a license, and made them man and wife, on which the bride gave her spouse *two hundred pounds*, and without more delay left the town and the bridegroom to find out who she was or unriddle this strange adventure. Soon after she was gone, two gentlemen came into the town in full pursuit of her: they had traced her so far upon the road, and finding the inn where she had put up, they examined into all the particulars of her conduct, and on hearing she *was married* gave over their pursuit, and returned back! perhaps our little Yorkshire Tanner may in time furnish us with as good a story? 'Tis supposed the young lady in a desperate fit, for fear of being married where she did not like, chose this unaccountable way of preventing it. Don't think that though I have wrote you so long a letter, my eye has suffered from it, for it feels perfectly easy, and if I had time I could without any prejudice to it add another page, but as this letter is of a reasonable length I will now retire, though thought rises on thought and urges me to indulge myself.

Lady Wal. is continually engaging me by the obliging things she says of you; she improves on acquaintance, and is gentle, sensible, and modest; my Lord is the counterpart of Jack Lewson the elder. The Duke of Portland is very sorry not to be able to grant a scarf[1] to our acquaintance—his are *all filled up*, and the first two that fall have been promised these four years: when I go to town if I can make interest to get one I will. I bespoke six pair of *cut fingered* gloves of the man at Gloucester, send them directed to me here to be left at Gerrard's Cross, and give me notice when they are sent. The drawing may be rolled on a smooth stick and sent at the same time; have you heard lately of Mrs. Wells?

I had a letter to-day from Donnellan, she complains much, and says she is forbid writing, but as soon as her spirits will admit of it she will write to her dear namesake. I am glad Jack Yate behaved generously to the poor disconsolate widow.

P.S. Wrote by Lord Bathurst in 1727—

"Bathurst remembers what the Psalmist sings,
And *finds*, that princes *are the sons of kings*."

Now answered that what

"Bathurst forgets the Psalmist writ
Was strictly true, and once again *is bit*."

---

[1] "*Grant a scarf to our acquaintance.*"—This possibly might have alluded to an application for Mr. Chapon to be appointed one of the Duke of Portland's chaplains.

Mrs. Pendarves to Mrs. Ann Granville.

13th Feb. 1738-9.

I was at the oratorio last Saturday with Lady Dysart, and (*oh wonderful*) Lord Carteret: he met with two patriot ladies that took up his attention more than the music, but it was triumph enough to *get him there,* and what will more increase your wonder, *he treated* his ladies with their tickets! Lady Carteret is very much out of order with a feverish disorder, which has not yet intermitted enough to give the bark, but she has been blooded and blistered; she was something better yesterday; Dr. Hollins attends her, and proposed giving her the bark last night. She holds up pretty well all day, but has very bad nights, though she does not keep her bed. I am indeed most heartily concerned for your amiable Princess; pray God preserve her from all pestilential disorders, and grant her health and years of peace and joy!

Your account of my dear mama has revived our spirits. My brother was here this morning before eight, to know if I had had any account of her? I hope all our entreaties will prevail on her to be very careful of herself—she cannot give us a stronger proof of her affection. I forgot whether asses' milk used to agree with my mother; if it does, and she has any remains of a cough, I wish she would take it, 'tis a sovereign remedy, and the greatest sweetner of the blood in the world. Mrs. Secker[1] and Mrs. Talbot[2] have been to see me; the reason that prevented their coming sooner was a melancholy at-

---
[1] Sister of Bishop Benson, and wife of the Archbishop of Canterbury.
[2] Mother of the well-known Catherine Talbot.

tendance they paid Mrs. Cocks,[1] my Lord Berkely's daughter, who died the 14th day after she was brought to bed.

Lord W.'s[2] house and furniture in the square are to be sold out of hand; it has been reported he is to have one of Mr. How's daughter's and 20,000*l.*, but I fear 'tis not true, as the only hope there is of a reformation is his marrying some discreet woman who may, by her good humour, *gain the ascendant* over him. My heart is grieved for his sisters: he *must* if he *goes on* in the train he is at present be ruined, and they inevitably crushed by it.

The Duchess of Portland's coach came for me just as I arrived at this period; I have been with her ever since eleven of the clock, found her very complaining with a pain in her head and a *very bad cough*: she is better this afternoon, and says a thousand kind things of her "*incomparable Pipkin*," and calls herself all to nought for having been so long in her debt. Dear little modest Dash is just come in, and blushes of the deepest dye adorn her cheeks for her omissions to you—they both swear their "*hands* are *guilty*," but their "*hearts* are *free*." I wish you could safely send me *the antique shell nosegay*; I am going to fill a glass case with shell-flowers, and they may give me, as you say, some useful hints.

As soon as I had dined I went to Masham Street to make a visit to Peg Isaacson and Miss Lawson—found them at home. I fancy by their manner of talking, Jack

---

[1] "Died, in February, in childbed, the Hon. Mrs. Cocks, wife to James Cocks, Esq., and daughter of the Rt. Hon. the Lord Berkeley, of Stratton."—*London Magazine.*

[2] "*Lord W.*"—Lord Weymouth, who did not marry again.

Lawson (*Wid'*) is going to tie *the noose again*, but as there was company I thought it not so well to ask questions. Adieu. Oh Lady Throck. is brought to bed of a daughter, and is very well and had a good time; Sir Robert confined to his bed with a bad cold; Miss Birch wrote the Duchess word of it.

Mrs. Pendarves to Mrs. Ann Granville.

Park Street, 17th Feb. 1738-9.

I have no more time to write than whilst my brother dresses and the cloth is laid for dinner. I got up early this morning with a full intention of writing you a long letter, but every moment produced some interruption; the last was Mrs. Lloyd's coming in to make me a visit, and Lady Dysart's calling me to go to the Painter's, from whence I am just returned. You are very good in giving me so constant an account of my mother; did I not know your truth is to be depended on, I should be excessively uneasy about her, but you seem to assure me so sincerely of her being better that I believe you. Can't she take *turnip broth?* if it is a little disagreeable at first a little use will make it tolerable; *I actually love it better* than any soup, it is very good for a cough, and cured mine. I go to-night to the oratorio—no I mean to Alexander's Feast [1]—with Mrs. Carey. The post before last I received a letter from Sally, with an account of the Bishop of Gloucester having said that *her husband was an immoral man*; at which *she fired*, writes a long letter to the Bishop, and

---

[1] Alexander's Feast was represented on the 17th and 24th of February, 1739. It was first performed on the 19th of February, 1736. Schlœcher says of this work, "Everything is superb in that work, in which Handel once more displayed the sovereign power of his genius for choral combinations."

begs to know the aspersors of her husband's chastity? The letter was *wrote so well*, that I sent it on to the Bishop, and last Thursday morning he came and made me a visit, and brought a letter in answer to Mrs. Chap., which he gave me to read: it was good-natured and civil, clearing himself of ever having said such a thing, or so much as ever having heard it mentioned. We had much discourse about them; I would not teaze him on the *old subject*, but I said, I hoped if they staid till Midsummer, it would be no offence; he said *not*, and that he " should be glad to serve them," when it lay in his power. I spoke about the Gwinnets, and find him much discontented about them. He says, they have a reasonable income, if they were tolerable managers; that Mr. G. has most shamefully neglected Hatherley, and he is glad the house is burnt down; I put in a word or two to mollify matters. Our dear good generous Duchess has given me five guineas for the poor Gwinnets, so I owe you ten on their account, which be pleased to draw on me for, when you think proper.

I asked the Bishop how young Newton behaved, and what he thought of him? He said, "if he had known as much of him when he first came to Gloucester he should not have left Oxford; and spoke very handsomely and kindly of him, but that he had been told he *maintained his friends* at the Priory, and that prevented his paying some money he *ought* to have done about Taunton. I answered for that being a mistake, and that he is so reasonable and so sensible as to listen to advice, and to reform anything in his behaviour the Bishop disapproved of: whatever he does, don't let him neglect obliging the Bishop, and to be cautious of the Dean and civil to him.

I dined yesterday at Whitehall, and so did my brother; and Pip's health was most affectionately drank. The Duchess has had a very bad cold; she has great remorse about not writing to you, but considering the number of affairs she has to manage I am amazed she does so much. I have not heard from Ireland these ten days or more; their silence frightens me, for I believe poor Donnellan is in a very dangerous way. Lady Carteret is something better. My Lady Sunderland will be very glad of your campanula and vetch seed; she and all hers are well. Dinner is now ready, and I must say adieu.

Mrs. Pendarves to the Lady Throckmorton, at Weston, near Olney, Bucks.
24 Feb. 1738-9.

I must congratulate my dear Lady Throckmorton on her having a daughter—if a son would have been more acceptable I wish you had not been disappointed; but my joy on this occasion is, that you are well and past the dreadful hour; I was concerned to hear of Sir Robert's being ill, but hope he is quite recovered. All the world in these parts have suffered from violent colds; our dear Duchess has had her share, but goes abroad again, and I hope will have no more confinement, for it does not sit very easy upon her active spirit. It is a great satisfaction to me that you have your agreeable friend Miss Birch with you, and though you have one friend that exceeds all others in your affection—a *female friend,* who is tender, ingenious and entertaining, must be a great comfort to you under your present situation; may I flatter myself you have *not thrown me by* amongst rubbish that is no more to be taken notice of? I made as many excuses for you before you was brought to bed as you could wish to have, considered it might be uneasy to you to write, and grieved most truly for you when I heard how ill you had been, but I won't promise to go on in this indulgent way; for I have considered you long enough, and now must take my own interest into consideration. A letter I insist upon having as soon as you can grant such a favour without hurting your head or eyes, though I would rather have you silent than that you should receive the least injury on my account; when you write pray tell me something about the little girl. I know how well you can talk as a friend, a daughter, and a wife; to *complete your character*, I wish to hear you as a mother! My particular compliments attend Sir Robert Throck. and Miss Birch (for I can't help thinking myself well enough acquainted with her to take that liberty). I am most sincerely,

Dear Lady Throck.'s most faithful and
Affectionate humble servant,
M. Pendarves.

My brother charges me with his most humble service and congratulations to your Ladyship and Sir Robert.

The above letter is addressed to Lady Throckmorton, at Weston, of which Lipscombe gives the following account:—"The manor house of Weston Underwood (two miles west of Olney, Bucks) was nearly rebuilt by Sir Robert Throckmorton, in or about 1578. The scenery of the park and gardens, with the course of the river, and the venerable groves which shelter the mansion, have been the theme of Cowper's muse. An extensive and valuable library and numerous family portraits were amongst the ornaments of Weston, but many of them, with divers coats of arms in painted glass, were removed to Coughton, in Warwickshire. Soon after the accession of Sir Charles Throckmorton to the estate at Coughton, the old mansion at Weston, being much dilapidated and decayed, was taken down, except the chapel-wing and a portion of the offices; and the proprietor removed to the more ancient abode of the Throckmortons at Coughton. When the mansion was demolished in 1827, hiding-places were discovered which had probably been unknown to the family during many years. In the floor of one of the garrets, near that which had been made into a chapel, was a trap-door, opening into a small room below, within which was a closet, containing an old bed, and a ladder long enough to reach the trap-door; in another place was a concealed door, which when bolted within-side, could not be distinguished from the wainscot." Miss Stapleton, the "*fair Catherina*" of Cowper, was the wife of a grandson of Sir Robert Throckmorton, so often mentioned in these letters, and the Bulfinch celebrated by Cowper belonged to *Mary Catherine*, wife of another grandson, who succeeded to the baronetcy on the death of the husband of the "*fair Kitty Collingwood.*"

Mrs. Pendarves to Mrs. Ann Granville.

Brook Strt., 3rd March, 1738-9.

Like a most noble patriot, I have given up all private advantages for the good of my country. I must tell my dearest sister that Tuesday and Thursday I embarked, with the Duchess of Queensbury and Lady Wallingford, I may say in a *sea of troubles*—a rough one I am sure it proved to us, though we came off without being wrecked. My brother wrote to you last Tuesday and promised to inform you of my undertaking, but that was a day of *calm delight* to Thursday. We got into the gallery; and by twelve o'clock, were tolerably well placed; heard the merchants[1] tell their grievances plainly and honestly. The examinations that followed were tedious, no debates that day; the Duke of Argyle spoke once, and very agreeably, the house was not up till eight. I went home with Lady Westmorland to dinner. Lord Cobham[2] talked over the business of the day, and gave me more entertainment than the whole House of Lords: that thin, decayed carcase of his contains a spirit that is surprizing.

When I came home at night, I found two letters from Miss Granville, to *acquaint me* with Lord W.'s[3] going to be married to Miss H., that they were all to be hurried forthwith to Longleat, to *settle for ever*, the house in town to be sold, and no hopes of their coming any more among their friends in this part of the world. You cannot imagine the distress, fright, and *disappointment* of poor Miss Gran. upon Grace's account; and she entreats me so pressingly to come to her, that I go next Monday, and stay till Wednesday. Old H. is a cunning man, and will keep the Viscount safe, if once he has caught him; his numerous family will thrust others out of doors, and I can't say the prospect promises well. I will advise them to the best of my power, but Providence will do better for them than all

---

[1] The oppressive conduct of the Spanish Government towards British merchants, was brought before the House of Commons by letters and memorials, and their grievances were formally stated by counsel at the bar of the House. The result was a declaration of war against Spain, in 1739.

[2] Lieut-General Sir Richard Temple, Bart., was raised to the peerage in 1714, as Baron Cobham, and in 1718 was created Viscount and Baron Cobham, in default of male issue, with special remainder to his sister Hester, the wife of Richard Grenville, Esq. Lord Cobham married Anne, daughter of Edmund Halsey, Esq. He died childless in 1749, and the Stow estate, with the title of Viscount and Baron, devolved upon his sister, who was in the same year created Countess Temple.

[3] Thomas Thynne, 2nd Viscount Weymouth, was only twice married.

our forecast, and as you say it is the only dependance that can be relied on : however human endeavours are allowed, and more—they are required. This took me up *all Wednesday*—I wrote her a volume of the best comfort and advice I could send her, dined with Sir John Stanley to consult about them, which took up so much of the day, I could not find time to write to you; and on Thursday morning I was to be with Lady Westmoreland by ten, which I punctually was.

Again she and the Duchess of Queensbury, Mrs. Fortescue, and myself set forward for Westminster, and got up to the gallery-door without any difficulty. There were thirteen ladies more that came with the same intention. To tell you all the particulars of *our provocations*, the insults of the door-keepers, and our *unshaken intrepidity*, would flourish out more paper than a single frank would contain, but we bore the buffets of a stinking crowd from half an hour after ten till five in the afternoon, without moving an inch from our places, only see-sawing about as the motion of the multitude forced us. At last our committee resolved to adjourn to the coffeehouse of the Court of Requests, where debates began, how we were to proceed? it was agreed amongst us to address Sir Charles Dalton[2] for admittance. The address was presented, and an answer returned, that " whilst *one lady* remained in the passage to the gallery, the door *should not* be opened for the members of the House of Commons;" so we generously gave them the liberty of taking their places. As soon as the door was opened

---

[1] Mary, daughter of Lord Henry Cavendish, and wife of John, 7th Earl of Westmoreland.
[2] Sir Charles Dalton, Gentleman Usher of the Black Rod.

they all rushed in, and we followed; some of them had the gallantry to *give us their places*, and with violent squeezing, and such a resolution as hardly was ever met with; we riggled ourselves into seats. I think that was the first time I wished to be a man—though nothing less than a peer. The Duke of Argyle spoke soon after we came in, but before that my Lord Cholmondely moved that an address of thanks should be sent to the King for the Convention; the minority opposed it gallantly. My Lord Chesterfield spoke most exquisitely well,—with *good sense, wit, and infinite spirit:* I never was so well entertained in my life as with his speaking! I wished you there for that hour, though I had suffered so much to gain the entertainment.

Everything *after him* was dull and heavy; much *circumfloribus* stuff was talked of on the Court side. They might have spared their breath; their convincing argument was *in their pockets*—not on their tongue: they had a majority of twenty-one, and though they seemingly conquered, they made a poor figure! Am I not a furious politician? But enough of these affairs, those of friendship suit my nature better, where the struggles that arise are from very different principles than what animate courtiers and politicians, whose selfish views, under the glare of the good of their country, so often fill their hearts with a train of evil thoughts. Oh! how happy are we, not only ourselves to be free from these engagements, but to have no friend entangled by them! This moment my brother has brought Mrs. Lloyd in; it is two o'clock. I walked to the Duchess of Portland's this morning, breakfasted with her—came back; twelve millions of impertinences. Oh for the banks of the

Dove! or any retreat where we could enjoy each
other's company. I shall be very glad to see Barrow,
and will serve him to the utmost of my power: I admire
his generosity to the Gwinnets. You *may* tell them Lady
Sun. was their benefactress. I will write to you from
Windsor. What a strange hasty scrawl is this, in answer
to your interesting letter! Poor Lady Throck. has been
in the utmost danger, and her child is dead! but Sir
Robert writes the Duchess of Portland word that he hopes
she is in a fair way of doing well. It is much joy and
comfort to Bunny and myself that mama is better. Our
best duty and wishes attend her.

Yours ever and ever.

Mrs. Pendarves to Mrs. Ann Granville.

Brook Street, 26th March, 1788-9.

I have wrote to my brother and enclosed your letter,
Sir John Stanley's groom met him five mile beyond
St. Alban's very well. Saturday, Sunday, and Monday
were tolerable days for travelling, though sharp and cold.
I hope he has, by this time, forgot his toils in the
enjoyment of his farms and meadows. I must have a
speaking-trumpet that will convey my voice very far, to
be heard by Will. Stanley if I should ask him about
Mrs. Cull, for he is not in London; if the weather
mends I think my mama will do very well in going to
Cranham; nothing can be more effectual than change of
air for such a cold—I hope in God it will have the
desired effect. The weather has been so excessively bad,
and is still so pinching cold, that no constitution is
sturdy enough not to feel bad effects from it. Sir John

Stanley is low, and complains of being grown weak and faint. He has had the toothache, which is a teazing pain and dejects the spirits extremely: when the wind changes, and the sun shines, I hope all these complaints will be removed; but till then I don't expect they should. I dined last Sunday with Sir John; yesterday morning he made me a long visit, and met Mrs. Kitty Lloyd here, who lives in the neighbourhood, a great friend of Lady Westmorland's—a smart sensible woman. I was engaged with my crayons, and painted whilst they talked the world over, and now and then put in a word to let them know I had my ears at liberty though my eyes were employed: that *double entertainment* is a high regale to me, but it comes seldom in my way.

How few are they that are qualified for conversation! for if it runs *too high* or *too low* it ceases to be a delight; the one puts the attention so much upon the stretch that it soon tires the spirits—the other is insupportable after half-an-hour. I staid at home the rest of the day, eat my morsel like a hermit, without any spectator save my faithful Dapper. After dinner Madam Dashwood made me a visit for an hour and George Jackson; in the evening came Lady Colladon, and we had an uninterrupted tête-à-tête of three hours.

Mr. Montagu mends very slowly, and 'tis much feared he never will recover the use of his leg—a melancholy prospect for a man in the prime of his life, but he bears it with great patience and cheerfulness. Lady Colladon has promised to speak to Princess Caroline about the Queen of Bohemia's picture; I have heard nothing from Lady Hertford, did Mrs. Duncombe write to her? I long to know how you determine to bestow your sweet person when my mother can spare you: whilst her complaint continues I know you can't be spared. Nothing could have hindered my coming to see my mother, (notwithstanding the badness of the ways and weather,) but knowing she had you with her whose tender affection would think of everything that was proper to done for her. My brother was quite uneasy at not being able to make her a visit, but ever since her being ill he has been engaged in settling, with my Lord Gower and Lord Carteret, that part of the Albemarle estate that was undivided, and has been obliged to meet lawyers at his own house or at Stanley's once or twice a-week : at last he has been forced to leave it undone till he returns, or he would have run the hazard of losing a <u>chap</u> for his lands, for he has now in his hands about two hundred pound a-year, which will turn to bad account if he does not settle it,—thus stands the state of his affairs.

I had a kind long letter from Mrs. F.[1]; but alas! 'twas to tell me she does not come to town this year : the young squire was expected last night at Whitehall at the old house, where he is to be one fortnight only. I have sent for the girls to town—they are to come on Thursday ; and they meet him at dinner on Friday. I must contrive to make up a set at whist, and I will take a box one day next week and ask him to be of the party. 'Tis unlucky my brother's being out of town at this time, but after all Providence will do better than we can—there rests the anchor of hope.

I find Barrow is an honourable man: I hope I shall see him again before he goes out of town. I believe he is now at Twickenham; I wish I could do him any real

---
[1] Mrs. Foley.

rvice; when I see Stanley I will ask him how such a
an *can be served?* I wrote you a long letter last post.
write to you by this because on Thursday mornings I
we not an hour to spare even to you, as it is appro-
iated to Kellaway and Goupy, and by Saturday I hope
may give you some account of our young people. "Now
upid be kind," &c.

I had a letter last post from Lady Sarah C.: she was
the height of felicity, her sister was with her, and
r eyes are almost well. I feel with her the joy of seeing
iose we love tenderly well and happy. Since I wrote this,
r. Atwell has been here: I have spoken about young
ewton's having St. Mary's; he says he has spoken to
e Bishop—it *cannot* be done for him for the Master
Pembroke has thoughts of taking it himself; but says
he does, he will make it so well worth Mr. Newton's
ficiating as curate for him there, that it will be *better*
him than the living, as he will be obliged to quit
unton for it. The Duke of Portland has just brought
e the Princess's letter for Lord Cornbury,[1] and a few
rds to myself which I shall soon acknowledge, and will
her faithfull post in delivering her precious letter to
r much honoured Lord Cornbury. Dr. Atwell says
rs. Pit told him you "would not thank him for a visit
er having been corrected for not waiting on you."

"*Lord Cornbury.*" Henry Hyde, only son of Henry the last Earl of
rendon, was called up to the House of Peers, by the style of Lord Hyde,
l died unmarried, before his father, at Paris, 1753. He was Pope's Lord
nbury, the same to whom Bolingbroke addressed his *Letters on the Study
History*, and to whose comedy of *The Mistakes* Walpole wrote the "Ad-
tisement," in the name of Mrs. Porter, the actress. Walpole calls him,
'his amiable and disinterested lord;" he died by a fall from his horse. He
s brother of the Duchess of Queensbury.

VOL. II. E

The Duchess of Portland to the Lady Throckmorton, at Weston, near Oulney, Bucks.

Whitehall, May 8th, 1739.

What shall I say to dear Lady Throckmorton for not complying with her obliging request in letting her know how the little boy did; he is now, thank God, perfectly well, and has had no more fits; I hope he will continue so. I flatter myself you recover apace, and fancy you will soon begin your rambles: I wish they were to end in coming to London, for I have a most prodigious desire to see you; and except I can be so happy in the winter at Bulstrode, I don't know when I shall, for I shall be kept in town for the old occasion all this summer. I am very much obliged to Sir Robert for admonishing you to write to me; indeed your epistles are great joys to me, and you are very sensible of the hurry I live in, that it is not always in my power to do what I like best, or you would have been epistolized much sooner, and I expressed my gratitude for your kind inquiry. I delivered your letters to Penny and Pipkin, which they were both very happy with, and design writing very soon. I see them as often as I possibly can, and you will believe I am very happy when I do.

I have just received the most obliging of letters from my dearest Colly, which makes my silence appear ingratitude of the blackest dye; but I hope you are convinced of my affection for you, and know me too well to imagine I change with every blast, for believe me sincerely attached to you, and I wish it were in my power to show my affection to you more than by words. I am surprized Penny and Pip have not wrote to you; I shall see them to-night and tell them your kind remembrance; indeed, my dear Colly, we often talk you over, and the many happy hours we often spent in your company, and heartily wish they were to come over again. I hear Madame Latouche has put out an apology for living with his Grace, and declares that "love was the predominant and hereditary passion of her family;" I wish much to see it. Lady Dorothy Boyle and Lord Euston[1] are to make a match. Miss Pit and Lord Barrington,[2] they say, are wedded, but I can hardly think it, for Lord Strange[3] is always buzzing in her ear and dancing with her.

I will tell you a piece of news you will be glad to hear, and that is, mama has made me a present of her fine emerald drops. Lady Margaret Bentinck[4] is come over with her spouse, so we have nothing going forward but feasting from morning to night, which I am quite sick off, and heartily wish it was over. I must now go and dress for a feast at his Grace of Kent's, for if I am not in time the little old man will have no mercy upon *those stilts* of his. Adieu, the girls are very well; my Lord's best complements attend you—we both join in the same to Sir Robert. Pray when you write to your mama assure her of my humble service and best wishes. Yours most faithfully and obediently.

---

[1] George Earl of Euston, eldest son of Charles, 2nd Duke of Grafton, married in 1741, Dorothy, eldest daughter of the Earl of Burlington. He died without issue, in July, 1747.

[2] William Wildman, 2nd Viscount Barrington, married in 1740, Mary, daughter of Henry Lovell, Esq., a relict of the Hon. Samuel Grimston.

[3] James Lord Strange, eldest son of Edward Stanley, 11th Earl of Derby. He married in 1747, Lucy, daughter of Hugh Smith, Esq., and died in June, 1771, before his father.

[4] Margaret, daughter of William Earl of Cadogan, married Charles John, Count Bentinck.

Mrs. Pendarves to the Lady Throckmorton, at Weston, near Oulney, Bucks.

Upper Brook Street, 15 May, 1739.

My dear Lady Throck. so kindly expresses a desire to hear from me, that I should be most ungrateful to omit any longer my acknowledgments for the welcome favour of your last letter. I have so sincere a pleasure in hearing from you that I can't help wishing it could be oftener repeated; but as that is more than I can be gratified in, I will accept of your favours just as you can conveniently bestow them, and be thankful to have any share in a friendship so much valued and desired by all who know you. My sister is with me, and I hope will stay a month longer; she then goes with my brother into Staffordshire. If you should then be at Weston, and there is a possibility of her making you a visit, she certainly will. My brother was hurried down in the country, in miserable weather through dismal roads, two months' ago, but returns in a fortnight to fetch my sister: he has so great a desire to pay his respects to your Ladyship and Sir Robert that I am sure he will lose no opportunity he can make use of of giving himself that pleasure. My sister and I, in our tête-à-têtes, often delight ourselves in talking of our amiable *Colly*, in recollecting the hours we have passed together, adding sincere wishes for their renewal!

Is London *so very* odious to Sir Robert and his fair lady as to destroy all hopes of ever seeing you here? You are both misers: you each lock up your treasure, and will not let the rest of the world partake of your happiness; but I am not surprized at either of you, much more at those that don't know how to value or enjoy the blessings they possess. Our well beloved Duchess is very well, though in a multiplying way; she looks extremely well, and is good and lively as ever, truly affectionate and constant to her old friends. She has fretted excessively at having occasioned you so much uneasiness about the little marquis by her being so long silent—the children are all well. I believe she will be in town the greatest part of the summer, which, was it not for the allay of what occasions it, would be great joy to me; as it will be some satisfaction to me to be near her when she is confined and wants company.

I propose retiring to my grotto at Northend as soon as my favourite companion leaves me, choosing solitude rather than society when I can't have those I like best with me. With infinite pleasure should I accept of your most agreeable invitation, if it were in my power to comply with it, but I am under an engagement to spend all the time I can spare this year at Northend, except a short excursion I am to make to Windsor. My sister begs to know where your warbler, Miss Birch, lives, that we may contrive to meet before our retirement into the country. I live in hopes you will mend your pace in writing, and by giving me proofs of your inclination to me, confirm me if possible more strictly,

My dear Lady Throck.
Your affectionate and faithful
M. Pen.

Mine and my sister's best compliments attend Sir Robert.

Mrs. Ann Granville to the Lady Throckmorton, at Weston, near Oulney, Bucks.

London, 25 May, 1739.

That person must ill deserve the name of friend who can forget a thousand acts of kindness and resent one seaming neglect! No, my dear Lady Throck. I suffered a great deal more from the apprehension of your being ill, than the imagination that you had forgot me, for I believe your honest heart incapable of change; therefore Sir Robert will find upon examination, that I have not so much merit as he fancies. However, if he pursues his kind intention I shall be much obliged to him, and desire no better situation than to be near the most agreeable couple in the world.

I have been in London just a month, found my sister, our Duchess, and all friends well. I only wait my brother's return out of Staffordshire, and when he has dispatched some business in town I return with him for the rest of the year to Calwich, and if we can wait upon our agreeable friends at Weston, it will be a great satisfaction to us. Indeed my dear Colly, I do most earnestly wish to see you, as does Pen; but alas! I am not to be happy in her company this year; she stays with Sir John Stanley, and as she does *what is right*, I ought to be contented; her best wishes attend you and Sir Robert, I join in all your *rural* entertainments, which are infinitely more to my taste than courtly pleasures.

I can't give you much account of what passes here, because I attend so little to the common conversations that the news makes no impression upon me; Miss Campbell is to be married to-morrow to my Lord Bruce.[1] Her father

---

[1] Married in June 1739, the Right Hon. Lord Bruce, to Miss Campbell.—*London Magazine.*

can give her no fortune; she is very pretty, modest,
well-behaved and just eighteen, has two thousand a-year
jointure, and four hundred pin-money: *they say* he is
cross, covetous, and threescore year old, and this unsuit-
able match is the *admiration of the old* and the *envy* of the
young! For my part *I pity her*, for if she has *any notion*
of social pleasures that arise from true esteem and sensible conversation, how miserable must she be! and
how little can the show of gold and equipages make up
for all the disagreeable hours she passes at home.

The Parliament is still very busy about the Spanish
affairs, and some people think they will sit *all the summer*.

I met Mrs. Birch in the Park; was rejoiced to see
her. She comes next Wednesday, and then I will indulge in talking of you; an ever pleasing theme to your
affectionate

PROSPECT.

Pray write to me sooner than usual, and assure Sir
Robert of my respects. Bindon is at Oxford; I had a
witty letter from her last post.

Mrs. Elstob to Miss Granville.

Evesham, Augt. 4th, 1739.

My dear friend's letter afforded me so many pleasures,
that I am at a loss where to begin to return my
thanks; the delightful account you gave me of your
sweet retirement, not only made me wish myself with
you, but even fancy myself to be there; my imagination in an instant conveyed me into Sir John's library,
where I found your most valuable sister and self

perusing a well chosen book, from whence I thought I waited on you both into the pleasant garden you describe, and had the advantage of receiving your ingenious sentiments on the subject you had been reading. These agreeable thoughts prevented for some time my reflecting as I ought on my vast obligation to you for so kindly communicating to me the acceptable news of the health of our most excellent Duke and Duchess, and their dear little family, and with their favourable thoughts concerning me—an honour far greater than I deserve, and must be acknowledged by me to be entirely owing to their great humanity, and to the good-offices of your worthy sister and self, to whom my most dutiful respects are due. You will no doubt know as soon as anybody when her Grace is brought to bed; I shall be much obliged to you if you will be so good as to let me know, that I may take the first opportunity to congratulate her on that happy occasion.

I have had the pleasure of seeing my dear and valuable friend, Mrs. Chapon, twice since I have been here, who, notwithstanding the great hurry she was in, was so good as to spend a night with me each time, and am not without hopes I shall be so happy as to see her again soon, though she is removed farther from me. The last time she was here, I had an exceeding pleasure, though not without some concern, at hearing a long and *warm* dispute between that charming woman, and Mr. Ben. Seward, on some methodistical notions, in which it was by better judges than myself agreed that the *female* antagonist had *much the advantage over him*; it is surprizing to see how indefatigable he is in endeavouring to gain proselytes, and likewise what success he meets with! Pray God if

it be his good pleasure to put a stop to these miserable delusions, for the consequence, in my opinion, seems to be very terrible. I am quite ashamed of this tedious epistle, and will therefore only assure you that I am, to dear Mrs. Pendarves and yourself, a
  Most grateful and affectionate servant,
        ELIZABETH ELSTOB.

I had just finished this, when I had the favour of yours, which transported me inexpressibly to hear that her Grace was safely brought to bed, that she had so good a time, and that she and the little lady[1] are both so well, for which I return my thanks to Almighty God, for this joyful news. I begin to be impatient to be doing my duty, and shall therefore heartily rejoice when that happy time comes. In the meantime, the best and sincerest wishes that can proceed from a most grateful heart, attend the two incomparable sisters from their
  Most affectionate and obedient servant,
        ELIZABETH ELSTOB.

Mrs. Ann Granville to the Lady Throckmorton, at Scarborough, in Yorkshire.
        Northend, 15 August, 1739.

For fear my dear Colly should see in the newspapers an account of the Duchess of Portland and be alarmed, I write to let you know really how she is, though I grieve to say not as well as we wish her to be. Doctor Sand's says there is no danger, but she has fever on still, is reduced, extremely low and weak, and had a blister put on

---

[1] Lady Margaret Cavendish Bentinck was born in July, 1739.

to-day. Sands desired yesterday that another physician might be called in, but she would not consent, and indeed I believe her very safe in his hands as far as human skill can reach. We go to town to-morrow to see her, and you shall not fail of a particular account from me every post till she mends. I know what your tender heart feels for so valuable and good a friend, and I feel for *you*, for *myself* and for *everybody* that is happy in her friendship; but imagine nothing worse than what I tell you, for I am quite just in my relation; it is what my brother brought us this morning, and he had it from Mrs. Farran. I long to hear that the waters agree with you and Sir Robert; pray let me have that pleasure soon. Did you receive my letter by Gleg?

Sir John Stanley is come home very well from Tunbridge; the world is so divided I can send you no news, and the weather is *so hot* it dissolves all one's senses. I hear Bindon is in town, but I can't tell where nor how to get at her. I must hear oftener from you than I have done of late, or I shall never attempt writing you a long letter again. Sir Robert Throckmorton's generosity to the Bath hospital makes a very fine figure in the newspapers. My brother and sister desire their particular compliments to your Ladyship and Sir Robert. We shall all be happy when it is in our power to wait upon you at Weston.

Miss Ann Granville to the Lady Throckmorton, at Scarborough in Yorkshire.

Northend, 18 August, 1739.

How hard it is to be obliged to give pain where one wishes only to communicate joy and happiness! But 'tis the will of heaven, my dearest Colly, that we *must resign* our most amiable Duchess! My sister and I were at Whitehall yesterday morning. The Duchess's fever was then *as high as ever*, nor has there been any intermission for thirty days. Doctor Sands then insisted upon a consultation; Brocksome was at Windsor; Mead came, and only confirmed Doctor Sands' prescription, which was a *blister upon each arm, and a vomit!* We were obliged to come back to Northend, which was a great grief to us. Last night we heard she was worse; this morning Sands *gives her quite over,* and poor Aschard sent us the mournful message that they "*only expected the great change.*" How many are involved in this misfortune! My poor Penny *is inconsolable.* I won't pretend to mention my own sufferings, my dear friend, for I should only increase yours, and your part of the affliction is a great aggravation to mine. The poor Duke is truly sensible of his irreparable loss; I *promised him* to write to you to-day. But can add no more, but that I am in every circumstance of mind or body,

Your faithful and affectionate
ANNA.

Penny's best wishes attend you and Sir Robert, to whom I beg mine. Pray write one line to me immediately, for I shall be very uneasy to know how you do; and if possible, keep up your spirits; you have a good comforter, that I am sure will do every thing in his power to alleviate your sorrow.

Saturday night,

I am *this moment* come from Whitehall. *The Duchess is better*, and they have great hopes of her being able to struggle through it, though her fever is not abated. I hope in God, I shall be able to send you better news next post!

Miss Ann Granville to the Lady Throckmorton, at Scarborough, Yorkshire.

Northend, 22d August, 1759.

With the greatest joy imaginable I can assure my dear Lady Throck. that our dear Duchess is out of all danger! She began to mend on Saturday night, her fever abated, Sunday she was much better, and yesterday morning my sister and I was at Whitehall, and had the agreeable account from both the doctors that there was "nothing more to fear;" present weakness must be expected after so dangerous a distemper. You may guess the happiness this recovery gives to poor Lord and Lady Oxford, who were in the deapest affliction; and the Duke has shewed himself very sensible of the blessing he enjoys in so excellent a creature; poor Achard has been almost distracted. But I will dwell no longer upon melancholy reflections, since the bad is past: we will only think of future happiness, and let me intreat you, my dear Colly, to come to town, that you may have Doctor Sands' advice in case you should want it, for he certainly has been the only human means of the Duchess's recovery. He has watched her constantly, and never went to bed for four nights; and has more skill, tenderness, and caution than I have ever seen in anybody. For his own justification he would have Doctor Mead, but he only confirmed what the other prescribed; so Sands ought to have the whole credit of a cure. And now be quite easy, and when you don't hear, depend upon the Duchess's continuing well; should any alteration happen I will certainly let you know: I now expect to hear from you; tell me what you do, and how *your fine Duchess* is liked. Is not Doctor Shaw your physician? he is esteemed a very good one, and I am sure was of great service to some friends of mine (the Foley's): I wish he could prevail upon them to go to Scarborough again. My brother and sister's compliments attend you, and all our good wishes to Sir Robert. Have you heard Mr. Kellaway upon the harpsichord? he is at Scarborough and a most delightful player, very little inferior to Handel. Adieu, my dearest Colly, believe me ever yours

Most faithfully,
A. G.

Mrs. Ann Granville to Lady Throckmorton.

26 Sept. 1739.

Though I have but a fortnight to stay in town, and every moment cut out, yet I must thank my dearest Lady Throck. for the vast pleasure of her letter; every favour of yours is dear to me, and though I obey your commands of silence, I shall place it in my heart, and think of what you will not allow me to speak. The description of your Sunday evening's entertainment diverted me excesively, and our Duchess, with whom I received your letter. We agreed that the Duke of Leeds[1] had great reason to be discontented that you should be so fond of your "own Sir Robert," a man so different from the generality of the world, who has been married almost two years, and can now find out more perfections in his fair Colly than when he was first in love, and she still thinks him the most amiable of mankind! these are *not sentiments* to carry to Scarborough and Bath! You will draw the ridicule of the whole world upon you for being so particular, for unless it is the Duke and Duchess of Portland, there is not a couple in London but grow happily indifferent in six months! and if they drag the chain as many years, *what joy it is to part!* A present instance is the Duchess of Manchester; her Duke is dying,[2] and do you think she'll spoil her eyes with crying? No, no; she has better employment for them!

People are marrying like mad: Sir Robert Clifton and Lady Loom;[3] Lord Harrington[4] and Lady Anne Montague;[5] Mr. Leveson, and Sir Richard Wrottesley,[6] a Staf-

---

[1] Thomas, 4th Duke of Leeds.

[2] William, 2nd Duke of Manchester, died 21st October, 1739. His wife was Isabella, daughter of John Duke of Montagu. She married, 2ndly, Edward Hussey, Esq., of Ireland, who assumed the name of Montagu, and was created Earl of Beaulieu.

[3] Sir Robert Clifton married twice; 1st to Lady Francis Coote, and 2ndly to Miss Lombe, eldest daughter and co-heir of Alderman Sir Thomas Lombe, Knt.

[4] William Stanhope, Lord Harrington, married Anne, daughter and heir of Colonel Edward Griffith, by whom he had two sons, (twins,) born December 18, 1719, when their mother died. Lord Harrington does not appear to have married a second time. In 1742 he was created Earl of Harrington, and died December 8, 1756, and was succeeded by his only surviving son, William, 2nd Earl of Harrington.

[5] Lady Anne Montague, daughter of the 1st Duke of Manchester, died unmarried.

[6] The Rev. Sir Richard Wrottesley married Lady Mary Gower, daughter of John, 1st Earl Gower.

fordshire knight of 18; a daughter of my Lord Dartmouth's[1] to I don't know who; and Lady Bell Bentinck[2] to Mr. Monck (an Irish gentleman), nephew to Sir John Stanley; but it is at present a secret; but I am sure you will be glad to hear our dear Duchess is likely to be eased of a troublesome companion; thank God she mends every day, and except a weakness in her knees, has not one symptom of illness left. We talk of our most amiable Colly and wish for her every day. I hope this will find you perfectly well, and arrived at Weston with your own Sir Robert, to whom I desire my best wishes; my sister's ever attend you both, and my brother's compliments. Bindon was in town; I saw her once, but she is not in spirits and looks old. Had I time I could say a thousand things to you, but they would not express how much I am

   My dear Lady Throck's
     Most faithful and obliged
         ANNA.

It grieves me not to see sweet singing Birch, but she is such a journey from me; I have no coach and nobody will give me one, so must be contented, but not pleased.

I brought my letter to our Duchess to know if she had any commands; her good wishes ever attend you, and she desires to hear from you very soon; she mends every day, and I hope will soon be able to visit Alexander.

---

[1] Lady Anne Legge, youngest daughter of William, 1st Earl of Dartmouth, married, in 1739, Sir Lister Holte, and died the following year.

[2] Lady Anne Isabella Bentinck, daughter of Henry, 1st Duke of Portland, married, November 8, 1739, Henry Monck, Esq.

The Duchess of Bedford[1] was brought to bed to-day of a son; how happy does it make her!

The Duchess of Portland to Lady Throckmorton, at Weston, near Oulney, Bucks.

Whitehall, Nov. 1, 1739.

Indeed, my dear Colly, I grew quite impatient for the pleasure of a letter from you, and begun to fear you was out of order, and was going to write to you when I was blessed with yours. I long more impatiently to see you than ever I did in my life; and yet your absense ever was most cruel to me, but I can never be thankful enough for your kind concern for me; believe me I am most grateful, and my heart will be ever the same. You say you have been out of order, but don't say what was the occasion, which I take a little amiss; but I had the pleasure of Lady Montagu's company, who informed me. I wish, my dearest friend, you would lye-in in London, and be under Doctor Sandys' care; I have more reason to speak well of him then ever I had in my life, for it is entirely to his great skill and care that I am recovered: and is it not the same, whether you come before you are brought to bed or after? I am sure Sir Robert and your dear mama would be of my mind if they knew his merit as well as I do. If you have any commissions in this part of the world, employ me, and I will perform them with pleasure and to the best of my capacity. I sincerely share in your joy of Mrs. Collingwood's being with you; I love

---

[1] Gertrude, eldest daughter of John, 1st Earl Gower, married, in April 1737, John, 4th Duke of Bedford, and had a son, Francis Marquis of Tavistock, who died before his father in 1767, and a daughter, Caroline, married to George, 3rd Duke of Marlborough.

her much, and beg my very best compliments to her and Sir Robert. Do consider of what I have said to you, and come to town; I must not write more for fear of my eyes; but I am very well, *only weak*, and whilst I have any being,

Your most faithful, affectionate friend and servant.

My Lord is your slave, and likewise Frere Bonaventure. All the Twopennys[1] are very well. Write to me soon, my dear. Once more adieu. Heaven guard you!

Mrs. Pendarves to the Lady Throckmorton, at Weston, near Oulney, Bucks.

Brook Street, 28 Novr, 1739.

It is an easy matter to resolve on doing what is right, but to perform it is a difficulty not easily overcome. This has been my case in regard to my dear Lady Throck., who has shared much more of my thoughts than perhaps she will do me the justice to believe. I don't know if any of my friends that have the honour of corresponding with your Ladyship, have told you of the bad state of my eyes. They were for above a month excessively bad,—so violently inflamed, that I have been obliged to go through abundance of physical discipline. It punished me extremely for the time, but it allows me now the pleasure of addressing myself to my much esteemed Colly. Though I am a guilty wretch and cannot entirely justify myself having been so long unthankful for your very obliging and welcome letter, I must put you in mind of your own dilatory proceedings, and must add, had I hopes of a quick return to my letters, nothing could so effectually

---

[1] "The Twopennys," the children.

spur me on. Our dear charming Duchess, (for whom I know by my own heart you have suffered infinite anxiety,) is now as well as you can wish to have her—good looks, good spirits, and every good belonging to her that mortal woman can be possessed of. We talk of you very often, and lament our being so entirely deprived of your company. Though we are sensible of your happiness at home, we cannot help envying Sir Robert for being the sole possessor of our agreeable friend, and though you are so good as to say you have still the same love for your friends as you had when your heart was at liberty, how is it possible not to wish to see and converse with you? are there no hopes of our being so happy, or is the *wicked town of London* so *hateful to you both*, that we must despair of seeing you in it?

As to my having the happiness of waiting on you at Weston, it is a beautiful prospect at a vast distance, mountains and rivers interpose, and I can only see it in perspective. In the spring I shall go to Gloucester, from thence into Herefordshire, and so on to Staffordshire. To have known and liked you so well, and to be denied the pleasure of meeting, is what I must sincerely regret. I am told you are not very well—I hope it is only an illness that a few months will cure; I can't but wish you in the best hands at that time. As for news I know of none: war is talked of in all companies, and the *ladies* and *toupées* talk as smartly about it as any blustering captain of them all, but my disposition always inclines me to wish for peace. I tremble at the thoughts of a battle, and of the many lives hazarded for our ill conduct and ambition,—but this is being a *mere stupid woman!* The concerts begin next

Saturday at the Haymarket.¹ Caristini sings, Peschetti composes; the house is made up into little boxes, like the playhouses abroad; Lord Middlesex is the chief undertaker, and I believe it will prove to his cost, for *concerts will not do.* I hear no news; if I did I should most willingly prolong my visit. My sister is at Gloucester, and my spirits consequently not very flowing. I congratulate you on the joy of seeing Mrs. Collingwood, and beg my compliments to her and to Sir Robert Throckmorton.

I am dear Lady Throck.'s
most affectionate & faithful,
M. Pendarves.

Postscript in Duchess of Portland's handwriting.

I hope my dear Colly has received my epistle, which was full of good wishes for you. I hope you will take my advice and *come to town.* My best compliments to your good mama and Sir Robert. Write to me soon. Ever yours.

Aug 7-2

Mrs. Elstob² to Miss Granville.
Whitehall, Xtmas Day, 1739.

I am certain my dear Miss Granville will not be displeased to be made acquainted from my own hand, though imperfectly, with the inexpressible pleasure and satisfaction I at present enjoy. Should I presume or pretend

---

¹ December 1st, 1739, an Italian serenata, called Diana and Endymion, was performed at the little theatre in the Haymarket. The composer was not named, but it appears from four of the airs which were printed by Walsh that it was composed by Pescetti, and that Carestini and Muscovita performed the principal parts.—*Burney's History of Music.*

² Mrs. Elstob went to the Duchess of Portland in 1739, between the months of September and December.

to enumerate all her Grace the Duchess of Portland's perfections, you who are so good a judge and are so well acquainted with them, might with good reason think me extremely impertinent. I will therefore only tell you, that I am every day more and more charmed with her, and notwithstanding your excellent sister and self had, before I saw her, given me a most glorious character of her, I find every time I have the honour to wait on her, which is pretty often, though to me not often enough, there is something in her still more charming which increases my admiration and improves myself. The children by their sweet endearing temper plainly discover whose offspring they are; they are very fond of me, and even the little Marquis desires his nurse to bring him to " *Tob*," as he calls me. I am highly satisfied with their capacities, and don't doubt but in a little time there will be many testimonies given by their visible improvement that they are very good; the whole family is very civil to me, so that in all respects you will believe that I am very happy.

After having given you an account of my happiness in this noble family, I must beg leave to say something of the incomparable author of it, the not to be parallell'd Mrs. Pendarves; of whose merits before I had the honour personally to know her I had entertained very exalted ideas, which to my great surprize upon a nearer acquaintance fell very short of what she deserves. In few words, I think her one of the *finest women in the world in every respect*, (without doing any injustice to the most accomplished of her sex,) and I not only love her, but admire her. I beg you will be so good as to make the proper compliments for the season acceptable to Mrs. Granville, dear Mrs. Chapon, and yourself from

Your most grateful and affectionate servant,
ELIZABETH ELSTOB.

I told her Grace one day last week I designed to write to you, when she bid me tell you she would do the same very soon; and about the same time Lady Wallingford desired me to tell you she had "*great fault to find with you.*"

The little charmers send you their service.

The Honble Grace Granville, (afterwards Mrs. Foley,) to Mrs. Ann Granville,

Windsor, January y. 1st.

[Before or in the year 1740.]

Your letter, dear cousin, gave me great pleasure, and I was rejoiced at its being dated from Bath, where I have wished you extremely ever since I heard of your being out of order. I am glad Mrs. Foley[1] prevailed with you to make her a visit, which gives you an opportunity of establishing your health, and of obliging a friend which I know is great delight to you. We are at present very happy in Mrs. Pendarves' company; we talk of you, and wish it were possible you could be with us, it would add much to our satisfaction. I believe it will be a great while before we go to town; it's no sort of grievance to me, for I think the country has charms all the year round, and when one is with people one likes all places are agreeable.

---

[1] Mrs. Foley (born Unitt).

My sisters desire their best compliments to you; my sister Granville[1] joins with me in the same to Mrs. Foley: her acquaintance will make us very happy, and we are much obliged to her for being desirous of ours. My brother[2] was here about a fortnight ago, but is again returned to Long Leat; he rambles so much about, that I must beg you'll not enclose your letters to him, for I am always too impatient for them, to be delayed that pleasure longer than I ought. I entreat you, dear cousin, not to be so ceremonious as to write to me oftener than is convenient to you, for I had rather be deprived of a very sincere satisfaction than that you should do anything that might be the least prejudical to your health, which is most truly wished you by, dear Miss Granville,

Your most affectionate and faithful,
G. GRANVILLE.[3]

Mrs. Pendarves to Mrs. Ann Granville.

22nd Jan., 1739-40.

After such a day of confusion and fatigue as yesterday, my dearest sister I am sure is too reasonable to expect my head should be composed enough to write a folio, so I very prudently, knowing my own strength, undertake but a quarto.

Lady Dysart, Miss Dashwood, and I went together. My clothes you know. I was curled, powdered, and

---

[1] "*My sister Granville.*" The Honourable Ann Granville, eldest daughter of George Lord Lansdown.
[2] "*My brother.*" Lord Weymouth.
[3] The Honourable Grace Granville, daughter of Lord Lansdowne, married Thomas Foley, Esq., (afterwards created Baron Foley,) on the 28th of March, 1740.

decked with silver ribbon, and was told by critics in the
art of dress that I was well dressed. Lady Dysart was
in scarlet damask gown, facings and robings embroidered
with gold and colours, her petticoat white satin, all
covered with embroidery of the same sort, very fine and
handsome, but her gaiety was all external, for at her heart
she is the *most wretched virtuous woman* that I know!
The gentle Dash[1] was in blue damask, the picture of
modesty, and looked excessively pretty. She danced, and
was only just so much out of countenance as to show *she
had no opinion* of her own performance, but courage
enough to *dance very well*. The Princess's clothes were
white satin the petticoat, robings, and facings covered
with a rich gold net, and upon that flowers in their
natural colours embroidered, her head crowned with
jewels; and her behaviour, (as it always is,) affable and
obliging to everybody. The Prince was in old clothes
and not well; he was obliged to go away very early.
The Duchess of Bedford's clothes were the most remarkably fine, though finery was so common it was hardly
distinguished, and my little pretension to it, you may
imagine, was easily eclipsed by such superior brightness. The Duchess of Bedford's petticoat was green
paduasoy, embroidered very richly with gold and silver
and a few colours; the pattern was festoons of shells,
coral, corn, corn-flowers, and sea-weeds; everything in
different works of gold and silver except the flowers and
coral, the body of the gown white satin, with a mosaic
pattern of gold facings, robings and train the same of
the petticoat; there was abundance of embroidery, and

---

[1] "*The gentle Dash.*" Mrs. Dashwood.

many people in gowns and petticoats of different colours. The men were as fine as the ladies, but we had no Lord Clanricard.[1] My Lord Baltimore was in light brown and silver, his coat lined *quite throughout* with ermine. His lady looked like a *frightened owl*, her locks strutted out and most furiously greased, or rather gummed and powdered;[2] Lady Percival very fine in white satin, embroidered with gold and silver; Lady Carteret in a feuille mort uncut velvet, trimmed with silver flounces— grave and handsome; Miss Carteret a flowered silk with coloured flowers, and glittering with all her mama's jewels; she danced with a very good air, her person is really fine; but my Lady Carteret's agreeable countenance and easy air pleased me more than younger beauties. Miss Fortescue looked like Cleopatra in her bloom; I thought her *the handsomest woman* at the ball; she was in pink and silver, and very well drest. The Duchess of Queensbury was remarkably fine *for her*, had powder, and was tolerably dressed; she had put on all her best airs, and certainly shewed she had *still a right* to be called "*beautiful*." My Lord Carlisle, his lady, son, and two daughters,[3] were all excessively fine. But I grow sick of the word "*fine*" and all its appurtenances, and I am sure

---

[1] John Smith, 11th Earl of Clanricarde, succeeded his father in 1726. He married Hester, youngest daughter of Sir Henry Vincent, Bart., and died April 21, 1782, when he was succeeded by his eldest son, Henry, who in 1785 was created Marquess of Clanricarde.

[2] This is the first allusion made to the wife of Lord Baltimore, and one of the *very few* instances when Mrs. Pendarves permitted herself to joke on the absence of personal charms.

[3] Henry, 4th Earl of Carlisle, married in 1717, Lady Frances Spencer, daughter of Charles, 3rd Earl of Sunderland. Their two daughters were—Arabella, married to Jonathan Cope, Esq.; Diana, married to Thomas Duncombe, Esq. The sons died in their father's lifetime.

you have enough of it. The ball began at nine, and I left them smartly engaged at the hour of twelve; Lady Dysart was obliged to go between ten and eleven to her surly ill-bred Lord, and Dash and I were glad to walk off before the company broke up, by which means we got easily to our chairs.

Extracts from two Letters of Miss Robinson (afterwards Mrs. Montagu) to her Sister.

Whitehall.

On Tuesday I was at Lady North's, to see all the fine clothes that were made for the Birthday. Lady Scarborough was richly dressed, the Duchess of Bedford very fine, Mrs. Spencer had a white velvet, but the Duchess of Queensbury was such as should be seen at "*courts, and feasts, and high solemnities, where most may wonder at the workmanship;*" her clothes were embroidered upon white satin, with vine leaves and convolvolus's, and rose-buds, shaded after nature; but she, *in herself*, was *so far beyond the master-piece of art* that one could hardly look at her clothes—allowing for her age *I never saw so beautiful a creature.*

Miss Robinson again writes:—

Whitehall, 1740.

We had company at dinner on Monday, and in the afternoon I went to Lord Oxford's ball, at Mary-le-bone. It was *very agreeable*; I will give you the list of company as they danced. The Duchess and Lord Foley, the Duke and Mrs. Pendarves, Lord Dupplin and Dash, Lord George and Fidget,[1] Lord Howard and Miss Cæsar, Mr. Granville and Miss Tatton, Mr. Hay and another Miss Cæsar. The partners were chosen by their fans, but with a little supercherie in the case. I believe one of our dancers failed, so our worthy cousin, Sir T—— was invited and came; but when he had drawn Miss ——'s fan, he would not dance with her; but Mr. Hay, who (as the *more canonical* diversion) had chosen cards, danced with the poor forsaken lady. The knight bore the roast with great fortitude, and, to make amends, promises his neglected fair *a ball at his house.*

Mrs. Ann Granville to the Lady Throckmorton, at Weston, near Oulney, Bucks.

Gloucester, 7th Febry., 1739-40.

A very disagreable succession of colds upon myself and friends has prevented my returning dearest Lady Throck. thanks for her last favour. I always rejoice to hear from you, as I should much more to see you, and grieve to think how long it is since I was so happy, and hope this *new year* will be more fortunate to me than the last; though I am sure if I were never to see you again I should always love you, because I think you faithful and sincere. I should have began my letter with the wishes usual upon the season, but I feel my heart as zealous for the good of my friends in every month of the year as January, and beg you will believe my wishes ceaseless for your happiness and your "*own Sir Robert's,*" and that you may continue each others as long as you have the capacity of loving, and that I believe will be the last sense that leaves you.

---

[1] "Fidget," herself.

I have a question to ask you, my dearest Kitty, that requires all your secrecy and prudence, (which I depend upon,) and for your truth I cannot doubt it; therefore without any preamble I desire you will inform me what Sir Robert's *real opinion* is of Mr. Dewes and your's, if you know him. There is a person he is recommended to, but she is quite a stranger to him and is my friend, and therefore I make an inquiry about him, but I must entreat that not a word of it be mentioned to anybody, because the thing is an entire secret. The person I speak of has no notion of happiness in a married life, but what must proceed from *an equality of sentiments* and *mutual good opinion;* and therefore she would be glad to know if Mr. D— has agreeable conversation, generous principles, and is not a lawyer in his manners. I remember Sir Robert told me something about him at the Bath, but I have forgot what? Once more, my dear friend, be secret and never by word, look, or gesture discover what I have said to you: when I am allowed to say more I will; and answer my letter as soon as you can. Don't enclose your letter to the Duke, but send it directly to me at Gloucester by way of London, and let me know your direction. I rejoice Mrs. Collingwood is well, and beg my compliments to her. Are you not all froze to icicles? There never was known such weather, but I hope you preserve a warm corner in your heart for her who is ever,

My dear Lady Throck.'s
Most faithful affectionate,
NANCY.

P.S.—Our dear Duchess is so well that she frolics at Frost fair, and does all sorts of merry pranks. How does music flourish in your household? with me, alas! it dies. What is become of the merry skeleton Mr. Watkins?

I mourn the loss of your old servant; if you hear of a proper place for the young woman I mentioned to you, I am sure you will not forget her.

The above letter of Ann Granville to Lady Throckmorton is another curious instance of the way matches were arranged a hundred and twenty years ago, and how gentlemen were *assisted* by being "*recommended*" to the lady of their fancy by a mutual friend, before they were personally made known to her. It appears that such a friend had *recommended* Mr. Dewes to the favourable consideration of Mrs. Ann Granville, upon which she wrote to her confidant and correspondent, Lady Throckmorton, to know her opinion, and that of Sir Robert, of the individual named; very discreetly speaking of herself as her *own* "friend."

Mrs. Ann Granville to the Lady Throckmorton, at Weston Underwood, near Oulney, Bucks.

Gloucester, 20 Feb. 1739-40.

I rejoice to hear by your letter, my dearest Lady Throck., that you are well again, though you don't tell me of what you have lain in, whether poetical fancy's lively imaginations, or a little infant full of blooming graces—I hope the last, but as children are precarious blessings I am afraid to be too particular in my inquiries. In hopes of your gratifying my curiosity I will satisfy yours, by telling you the *guess was right*. I am sure my friend thinks herself excessively obliged for the warmth and goodness you express for her happiness; in every condition of life your friendship must be a vast increase of it, or alleviate any misery Providence shall please to inflict upon her. The inquiries Sir Robert would be so good to make will not now signify, because the parties *are to meet* in about a fortnight to see if they like well enough on each side (for at present they are strangers) to permit any procedure in the affair, and *then* friends will be consulted, and they will consider all particulars. But my friend was *in hopes* that he lived near you in Buckinghamshire, and indeed that would be a great inducement to her to listen to it, for she would be most happy to settle in your neighbourhood, for she loves the charming Kitty, and admires "your own Sir Robert" more than she can express. I shew the confidence I have in your secrecy and truth by speaking so freely of what is at present unknown to all the world but two people: how it proceeds you shall hear. *My friend* thinks a *chez nous* with a man of sense and worth is preferable to the unsettled life she now leads, and being continually divided in her heart what friend to remain with; for while she is with one the other wants her, and makes a perpetual uneasiness in her mind. Your advice will always be of service and pleasure to her; but she can never expect so much happiness as you wish her, because she is *not qualified* to *give so much*. I hope Sir Robert is quite well again. I beg my compliments to him and Mrs. Collingwood. I am ashamed to send you a letter of so little entertainment, but I have really a bad cold; *an hour's conversation* with you would be infinite delight to, my dearest Lady Throckmorton, Your most obliged and affectionate,

NANCY.

Let me hear from you soon, and don't mention to Pen when you write the subject of our present corresspondence. Don't you think their balls at Whitehall are pretty things? Our dear Duchess continues very well. If Sir Robert is not well you must come to Bath this spring. By these blots you will certainly believe me entêté, but indeed I am not.

From the injunction not to mention to Mrs. Pendarves the meeting arranged for Mr. Dewes to be presented to Ann Granville, it is evident that Mrs. Pendarves was NOT the "mutual friend", who recommended Mr. Dewes, but it might possibly have been Mr. Granville, as it is hardly to be supposed that any one less nearly related and of less influence would have induced Ann Granville to keep this secret from her sister, and *he* would naturally expect Mrs. Pendarves's advice must be *anti*-matrimonial.

Mrs. Pendarves to Mrs. Ann Granville, at Gloucester.

25th February, 1789-40.

After my desponding letter, I ought to write to you in my joy, and I have much more to tell you about our lovers than either time or eyes will allow me to write. But first, in my brother's name and my own, I must thank our dear good mama for her kind present of good things, and you for yours. Your account of her is not right, but we hope in God that as soon as the sharp winds and ice soften, her complaints will melt away. There is no such thing in London as fish, or she had had some long ago, in hopes that a new dish might tempt her to eat. I was very much pleased at your submitting to be let blood; I should have done the same *had I time*, but now I am so much better I don't want it.

Yesterday *the lover*[1] dined here, and went through the travels of Hercules before he could come to his Omphale, for he was obliged to pay away above £20,000 in the morning, and was in every corner of the town; but he came to us at four; I don't know which looked most modest of the two, and both behaved very properly. After dinner and coffee we left them alone, and he made a declaration of his passion, and said everything that was proper; Miss Grace[2] is perfectly well pleased with his behaviour. Mrs. F.[3] made the sisters a visit in the morning, in the afternoon I sent Miss Granville[4] to Lady Wa^r. ball as *my deputy*, and went with the bride elect to Mr. Foley's. She played at whisk with father, lover, and sister, whilst Madam and I had a tête-à-tête to our mutual satisfaction; we all wish for you every moment. To-day we dine at Mr. Foley's—to morrow all dine with me; the young man goes out of town on Monday, and stays three weeks, but 'tis unavoidable.

I am now at our new ally's; everything goes as our hearts can wish, and truly for so fair a prospect, Cupid and his hearts may well be accepted without fearing the lurking chain. The *devise*, the *verses*, and the *letter* are excessively pretty.

---

[1] Mr. Foley.
[2] "Miss Grace."—Grace Granville, daughter of George Lord Lansdown.
[3] "Mrs. Foley," born Unitt, step-mother to Mr. Foley, "*the lover*" of Grace Granville.
[4] "*Miss Granville*." The Honourable Anne Granville.

Mrs. Pendarves to Mrs. Ann Granville.

Brook Street, 29 March, 1739-40.

This moment we are returned from Audley Chapel, where we have been witness of the union of two people[1] that seem made for the happiness of each other. It has at last been concluded in so great a hurry[2] that I hardly think I am awake, but fear I shall start and rub my eyes, as out of a dream, before I can finish my letter. The writings were signed this morning, and at twelve all the company assembled in the vestry. Lord Foley and my brother were the bridemen; Miss Granville and our Miss Foley the bridemaids. My Lord's sister is not well, and can't come amongst us; the bride and bridegroom look modest but well pleased. Lord Weymouth gave her away; at eight all the company meet at the Bedford Head Tavern, where my Lord Weymouth gives a very fine *supper,* there is to be the harper, and we are to play at cards. Lord Wey. Sir John Stanley, the bride and bridegroom, Miss Granville and my brother dine with me, that is with my brother, for *he* gives the dinner, which is a very handsome one. I think I have told you abundance, considering the engagements of the day. At night Gran and I put the bride to bed at her father's house,[3] she has behaved herself excessively well, and so has he in every particular. They go out of town to-morrow morning, and propose being at

---

[1] The Honourable Grace Granville, daughter of George Lord Lansdown, married Tho. Foley, of Stoke Edith, Esq., in the county of Hereford; and on the death of Lord Foley, 1766, his estates were inherited by his cousin above mentioned, and the title, by a new creation, continued to him.

[2] "*In so great a hurry.*" Mr. Foley proposed on 24th February, and was married 29th March, but the match was evidently arranged by friends before they met, only leaving them freedom of decision afterwards.

[3] "*Her father's house.*" George Lord Lansdowne.

Gloucester on Tuesday night or Wednesday noon. I shall envy them the pleasure of seeing you and my dear mama. Your new cousin[1] very readily and thankfully accepts of her kind invitation; I hope next Tuesday to be able to send you a composed letter. Now, I can only tell you I *saw* our dear Duchess yesterday, which was a great satisfaction, as I have of late had but few opportunities. My company call me.

Adieu, yours ever.

Mrs. Pendarves to Mrs. Ann Granville.

22 April, 1740.

Your letter to my brother has *cheered my spirits* a good deal; I think Mr. Dewes behaves himself like a man of sense, and with a regard for you that must recommend him to the favour of all your friends. My brother and myself will receive him with a great deal of pleasure as soon as his business permits him to come to us, which I find will not be this week, and I can't see any obstacle to prevent the proceeding of this affair. As soon as we have met, and that he has settled with my brother, then we may proceed to particulars, buying wedding clothes, and determining where the ceremony is to be. Miss Sutton has got the small-pox, but, thank God! in all appearance she will have it favourably; I should not have told you now, but suppose Mrs. Gibbs may have an account, and as you love the dear little girl, I was afraid you might be frightened to have the account from other hands; yesterday was the second day, Dr. Shaw is her physician, and she has no one bad symptom. It will be a great blessing if she recovers to have it over.

---

[1] "Your new cousin." Mr. Foley.

Sir Robert and my Lady Sunderland are gone to Mr. Sutton's house in Audley Street, and keep up their spirits very well, Mrs. Tichborne is chief nurse. I own I am surprized Mrs. Pulteney does not undertake the charge, who nursed three of her own daughters so successfully, and is *more* to be depended upon than Bess, who is ignorant and conceited. The newspapers say Sir Francis Child[1] is dead—I fear it is true; Mrs. Carey told me one day last week that he lay dangerously ill. *What riches* flow in on Sam Child, who has not a heart to enjoy it! and how many fine things that he does not understand the worth of!

Last Saturday I went a most notable expedition. I told you it was to be, and designed you an elaborate description of our performance; but my head is not clear enough for such a task. Our company you know: we sat out, two hackney-coaches full, from Whitehall at ten. Our first show was the *wild beasts* in Covent Garden; from thence to St. Bartholomew's Hospital—the staircase painted by Hogarth, the two subjects the Good Samaritan and the Impotent Man; from thence to Faulkner's, the famous lapidary, where we saw abundance of fine things, and the manner of cutting and polishing pebbles, &c.; then to Surgeons' Hall to see the famous picture of Holbein's of Harry the Eighth, with above a dozen figures in it all portraits; then to the Tower and Mint—the assaying of the gold and silver is very curious; saw *lions, porcupines,* &c., armour and arms in abundance; from thence to Pontack's to a very good dinner;

---

[1] April, 1740, died, Sir Francis Child, Knight, President of Christ's Hospital, and Knight of the Shire for Middlesex. He was Lord Mayor in the year 1732.

and then proceeded to the round church in Stocks Market—a most beautiful building.

This is the first letter preserved from Mrs. Pendarves in which there is any allusion to Mr. Dewes. Her previous letter, on the 29th of March, did not mention him in any way, and it must have been within the twenty-one subsequent days that she was informed of his proposal to Ann Granville, and of her intention of accepting him. The letters of Mrs. Pendarves not having been preserved on this occasion, leads to the inference that (if not hostile) she was not very favourable to his suit; and in the present letter the sentences in regard to him are so few and measured, that it affords a confirmation of the probable fact that she did not think of her sister's marrying him with satisfaction; and although too honest not to give Mr. Dewes the commendation which she believed he deserved, yet that she could not bring herself to enlarge upon the subject, but was glad to make it as short as possible, and to fill her letter with other indifferent subjects. It must also be remarked that Mr. Dewes was apparently only known to Mrs. Pendarves by report. It is moreover evident that Mr. Granville *was* the person to whom the principal communications were made in relation to this marriage.

Smith says, in his "Antiquarian Ramble," that "in Christ Church Passage, leading from Newgate Street to Christ Church, nearest to Bagnio Court, stood the ordinary of the once famous *Pontack*, probably the first house for genteel accommodation in eating known in the metropolis. It was opened by a person of this name, soon after the great Revolution in 1688, and remained till about the year 1780, since which the site has been occupied by the new vestry. This house was called Pontack's, from its being the sign of Mr. Pontack, who was a president of the Parliament of Bordeaux, and from whom also the best French clarets derived their name. This was the first public place where persons could bespeak a dinner from four or five shillings a head to a guinea." The Stocks Market was a fine market for fruits, roots, and herbs.

Stow states, that Henry Wallis, Lord Mayor in 1282, caused

divers houses to be built towards the maintenance of the bridge in a void place, almost in the middle of the city, where had formerly stood a pair of stocks for the punishment of offenders, and appointed near them a market-place for fish and flesh, which took its name from the stocks once placed there and was called *Stocks'-market*. In 1322, 17 Edw. II., a decree was made that none should sell fish or flesh but in the public markets of the city, which were then but four besides this, and then this market was farmed at 46*l*. 13*s*. 4*d*. *per ann*. From this time the market grew bigger, and other houses were built about it, insomuch that in the year 1543, there were so many stalls and chambers in and about it as were let at 82*l*. 3*s*. *per ann*. At the conduit in this market was erected a statue of King Charles II. in armour, with his head uncovered, all carved in marble upon a large and lofty pedestal, eighteen foot high, represented trampling on an enemy with his horse's feet; the conduit is enriched with his arms within a compartment of *fishes*, and finely cut in stone. "Here," says Pennant, "stood the famous equestrian statue erected in honour of Charles II. by his most loyal subject, Sir Robert Viner, Lord Mayor." The statue was removed in 1738, when the present Mansion-House was built on what was formerly the Stocks' Market. Behind the Mansion-House is the church of St. Stephen's Walbrook, the chef-d'œuvre of Sir Christopher Wren.

In allusion to the Duchess of Portland's expedition with Mrs. Pendarves to see the City sights, Mrs. Donellan writes to Miss Robinson as follows—

London, April, 1740.

"Since my last I passed a most agreeable day with your friend and mine. The Duke and Duchess of Portland proposed a jaunt into the City, to see City shows, and were so obliging as to ask me (with Mrs. Pendarves) to be of the party. We were four men, four women; our fourth woman was Lady Wallingford, whom I never saw before, but she seems good-humoured and civil; our four men, the Duke, Lord Dupplin, Mr. Achard, and

Doctor Shaw,[1] all new to me. We set out at ten in two hackney coaches, and stopped at *everything that had a name*, between us and the Tower, going and coming, and dined at a City tavern. I am not apt to fall in easily with strangers; but there was such an agreeable freedom in the whole company, and especially in the amiable Duchess, that I never spent a more agreeable day. For our dessert the Duchess and I had a conversation concerning you, of more flavour than the finest fruit; I won't tell you what we said, but that we agreed in our opinions."

Mrs. Elstob to Mrs. Ann Granville.

Whitehall, May 6th, 1740.

I have nothing to say for myself, my dear Miss Granville on account of long silence, but a repetition of what I told you in my last, that my dear little charmers allow me but very little leisure. You desired me in yours, not to let them forget you, and I can assure you, they do not. As a proof of it I must let you know, how much you are in Lady Harriett's[2] favour. It is not long since she was to go to her Grace, as usual after dinner; but suspecting there was company, and being in one of her little shy humours, she could not be prevailed upon to go in till she was told there was "nobody but Mrs. Pendarves and Miss Granville;" upon which she ventured in; but when she found it was *not you*, she ran out and burst out a crying, and said it "was not her Miss Granville." However she is now become very fond of Miss Granville, and

---

[1] The traveller.
[2] Lady Harriet Bentinck, who afterwards married George Harry, 5th Earl of Stamford and Warrington.

says she loves her for your sake, as she says she does also Mr. Granville, " because he is your brother." I need say nothing to you of Lady Betty; you are well acquainted with her admirable temper. I dare say she has as great an affection for you as her sister has, though she does not express so much : she learns exceedingly well, and loves her book and me entirely; nor is she ever more happy than when she is with me, and we study together, even by candle-light, like two old folks.

I want nothing here to make my happiness complete as this world can make it, but the pleasure of seeing Mrs. Pendarves oftener, who is entirely engrossed by her Grace. I can send you nothing new from hence; Mrs. Pendarves can do it better, who hears and sees more than I do, who I know so frequently entertains you agreeably in that way. We begin to talk of going to Bulstrode, where I long to be, because I shall I hope to have the honour of more of her Grace's company—for it is impossible to have any of it here; and I am not without hopes I shall be made happy by seeing dear Miss Granville there before we return, which will add greater delight to the place. In the meantime I shall please myself with those hopes, and continue for ever to be your

Most grateful and most affectionate servant,

ELIZABETH ELSTOB.

The following pages are part of a letter of Mrs. Pendarves. It appears to be an account given her by an eye-witness of the reception of Princess Mary of Hesse on her marriage.

Her Royal Highness the Princess Mary of Hesse set out from London June the 6th, and arrived at Millenshall the 15th—a hunting seat of the Prince Stadtholder of Hesse (which they say is the proper appellation of the bridegroom's father), and about three German miles from Cassel; from whence a message was sent to notify her being come thither. The next day the Prince and Princess of Orange, the Prince Stadholder and the Bridegroom, the Prince and Princess Maximilian, with the three Princesses their daughters, Princess Mary of Hesse, and Prince George, came to Millenshall to dine with her Royal Highness, who was almost drowned in tears for whom so much magnificence was prepared. When they alighted from their coaches, the Prince Stadholder went first to make his compliments to the Princess, with whom he stayed a very little while; then he introduced Prince Frederick, and after about a quarter of an hour's conversation, the Princess Royal[1] was admitted for a *few minutes*; then Prince Frederick conducted his Bride into the apartment where the rest of the company were assembled, and soon after they went to dinner. About seven in the evening they returned to Cassel, leaving the Bride to enjoy her solitude at Millenshall till the next day, when all the company who dined with her met her about half a German mile out of town, where there were tents pitched—the Prince and Princess of Orange could not be there on account of precedency. From thence began the cavalcade for the entry, which was exceedingly grand,—a description of which is published by authority in the Cassel Gazette. In the evening, the nuptials were performed in one of the great rooms of the castle; the Bride was in the same dress

---

[1] Anne, Princess Royal of England, and sister of the Princess Mary, was married to William Prince of Orange, in 1734.

in which she was married by proxy. They afterwards supped in public. When the dessert was taken off, they stood up to drink the King of Great Britain's health, at which the cannon from the ramparts were fired. The King of Sweden's and the Bride and the Bridegroom's healths were drank in the same manner. Then the Prince and Princess and the great officers of the court danced the mystical dance, or Hymeneal dance, the manner of which is this: all the nobility, and great officers of the court and army, with white flambeaux lighted in their hands, begin a dance to a very solemn tune, and the Princess and Bridegroom bring up the rear; after which the rest of dancers dance themselves into a circle, the Bride and Bridegroom being in the middle; then they divide into two lines, the Bridegroom leads his Bride to her apartment, the dancers following two and two with their torches to the door of the bedchamber, where they all stopped and put out their flambeaux with great silver extinguishers.

The next day all the officers both civil and military, and the clergy, were presented to her Royal Highness. At night there was a public supper and a ball; after the minuets were ended they danced a few English country dances. The 19th, they dined in public, and went to the Orangerie, in the afternoon where they played at cards and supped. After supper they formed a grand cavalcade, from whence they proceeded through the old and new towns of Cassel, both which were finely illuminated; especially the triumphal arches which were erected at the several gates. They then returned to the Orangerie, and the evening was concluded with a ball. The next day after dinner the Court went again to the Orangerie, played at cards and supped as before, and then walked in the gardens, which were finely illuminated; particularly an eminence at the end of a great walk was contrived to cast out fire in imitation of Mount Vesuvius. The next day, which was Saturday, was a review of horse and foot guards; and at night a ball at Court which concluded the week's festival.

There was at the public dinners and suppers 180 covers, and the form of the tables represented an F and M; the whole was conducted with surprizing magnificence, and the English, who were present treated with all marks of distinction and politeness.

The *London Magazine* states: "On Thursday the 8th of May, 1740, the Princess Mary, daughter of King George II. and Queen Caroline, was married to the Prince Frederic of Hesse Cassel, her brother the Duke of Cumberland acting as procurator." On Friday the 6th of June following, the Princess embarked at Greenwich on board the "Mary" yacht, and procceded to Hesse Cassel. On Thursday the 17th of July, the same Magazine announces that the Czarina has conferred the Order of St. Catherine on H.R.H. the Princess of Hesse. On the last Sunday of the same month the Prince Frederic and his bride waited upon King George II. at Herenhausen.

CHAPTER VI.

FROM THE MARRIAGE OF MRS. DEWES TO MRS. PENDARVES'S
MARRIAGE WITH DR. DELANY.

1740—1743.

The Honble. Mrs. Foley to Mrs. Dewes.[1]

Stoke, August 24th, 1740.

If the warmest wishes of a most sincere friend can add to your happiness you'll be the happiest woman in

---

[1] *Des Ewes, d'Ewes, Dews, Dewes.* This family descended from Otho des Ewes, of the duchy of Guelderland, who was ancestor of Gerard des Ewes, Dynaste, or lord of the territory of Kessel, who married Anne, daughter of the Prince de Horne, and whose descendant Adrian, younger brother of the Lord of Kessel, came into England when that duchy had been depopulated in the wars by intestine discord. Adrian des Ewes came to England in the reign of Henry VIII., and died of the sweating sickness 5th Edward VI. His grandson Sir Paul, was the father of the famous Sir Symond d'Ewes. The last baronet was Sir Jermyn d'Ewes, of Stow Hall, Suffolk, who died at Thetford, in Norfolk, April, 1731. He was named after his maternal grandfather, Thomas Lord Jermyn, whose title became extinct 1708. John d'Ewes, the husband of Ann Granville, was descended from the third son of Gerard (or Geerardt) son of Adrian, who with Alice Ravenscroft his wife, was buried under the fine monument in the church of St. Michael Bassishaw, London, mentioned in Weever's Antiquities. John d'Ewes was son of Court D'Ewes of Maplebury and grandson of Richard d'Ewes of Coughton, who married Mary daughter and co-heir of Edmund Court of Maplebury. Curious accounts may be found of the Des Ewes family, Elia Rensweri, Basil. Geneol. Acutusrum—Edit. Francfort, 1592, p. 102.—*Genealogical History of the Netherlands*, Book 5, p. 2 to 7. Printed 1609. *Escheats 34th Elizabeth, Part 1st, No. 11. Essex,* in the Archives.

the world, my dearest cousin Dewes, and I most heartily wish you every blessing which can be possibly possest in this world. The character I hear of Mr. Dewes gives me the greater satisfaction imaginable, for with such a partner your friends, I thank God, have no doubt to make of your happiness, which will be, I hope, of long continuance. I much wish to be acquainted with my new cousin, to whom, though at present unknown, coming from you, I hope will accept my compliments and sincere congratulations on this occasion. Of his happiness I am *certain*, as everybody must be who knows your merit. I hope you got safely to your own house, where I heartily wish you to live to enjoy many happy happy years. I was forced to beg the favour of dear Penny to convey this epistle to you, not knowing how to direct, and I could not defer letting you know how filled my heart is with affection to you. Mr. Foley's compliments wait on the Bride and Bridegroom; there is no one, I am sure, who is more sincere than he is in his congratulations, nor wishes you more truly happy. I am desired to make the compliments of this family to you both, and likewise to return my cousin Dewes thanks for the interest he gives Mr. Leckmere and Pit. Mrs. Leckmere is at present at Stoke, but leaves us to-morrow; she is an extremely agreeable woman. I have eloped this evening from all the company, being resolved nothing should hinder me following my inclination in assuring you how well and how sincerely you are well-wished by,

  Dear cousin,
    Your faithful and affectionate G. FOLEY.

P.S. Mrs. Foley hopes you received her letter. We had an infinite deal of company here on Saturday (the fashionable day amongst the Granvilles), but I was absent in thought from them the whole day, and I wished I could have conveyed my person to Gloster where my heart and good wishes were all the day.

Poor Mrs. Griffiths has been such a *comedy* and *tragedy* as I never saw; she says, "Poor soul, I wish her all the happiness this world can afford her." Bloxum[1] hopes you won't think her pert in bearing "*duty*" and "*wishing joy*."

As Mrs. Pendarves' correspondence with her sister appears to have ceased during the latter end of May, June, and July, it is to be supposed that Ann Granville came to London to make preparations for her marriage, which appears to have taken place in August of the same year (1740), after which Mrs. Pendarves remained with her mother at Gloucester. From the time of that marriage there is not a word which does not indicate that Mrs. Pendarves not only had reconciled herself to a third person sharing her sister's regard, but that she had, with that disinterested affection which formed so prominent a part of her character, satisfied her mind by discovering the solid merits of Mr. Dewes, whose character evidently rose upon her year by year. It may be a matter of surprise at first sight, that Ann Granville should have been disposed to listen to the suit of any one not absolutely recommended by her sister, but many circumstances contributed to induce her silence until she had decided for herself. Mr. Dewes was personally unknown to Mrs. Pendarves, and therefore she could not give any individual opinion; she had so high an opinion of Ann Granville's deserts, that she would have been certain to consider any younger brother a very bad match for her, and would have had a natural desire to defer a separation of interests, or any change in the confidential communications which had hitherto been the solace and comfort of their lives for any uncertain or remote advantage. It is needless here to explain again that the manner in which Ann Granville became acquainted with Mr. Dewes was in accordance with the custom of the day, and considered at that time as the height of propriety and discretion. That Ann Granville should

---

[1] "*Bloxum*." Mrs. Foley's waiting-woman.

have determined to marry if she met with a person she liked whose principles she could trust, and whose position entitled him to a fair hearing, is not surprising. She had relinquished the offer of a place at Court, which would have separated her entirely from her mother, and for which she evidently had had a great inclination; she was not, like her sister, living in the world and able to choose her own society. She languished in the old town of Gloucester, from whence her occasional escapes to a more congenial atmosphere enabled her to strike the balance and decide in favour of a country home of her own, with a companion she could esteem and love, and where she would still be within reach of that mother to whom both daughters were devoted. Thus it was that the beautiful and gentle Ann Granville married Mr. Dewes, whose descent was as ancient, though not quite so illustrious as her own, and whom she preferred, with a moderate fortune, to the numerous admirers who had previously been rejected because their principles did not keep pace with their estates.

Miss Robinson writes from Bulstrode, August 21st, to Mrs. Donellan as follows:—

"Our friend Penny is under great anxiety for the change her sister is going to make. I do not wonder at her fears. I believe both experience and observation have taught her the state she is going into is in general less happy than that she has left. However, Pip has a *good prospect*,[1] for they say the gentleman has good sense, good nature, and *great sobriety*: these are very good things; and indeed what a stock of virtues and qualifications ought to be laid in to last out the journey of life! Where so much lies through the rugged ways of adversity, all will hardly serve to lengthen love and patience to the end."

---

[1] "A good prospect." From Mrs. Dewes's having called herself *Prospect*, it is probable the name arose from her friends justifying her marriage on the ground of expectations.

The Duchess of Portland to Lady Throckmorton.

Bulstrode, Augst. 25th, 1740.

My dear Lady Throck's letter gave me pleasure, but not so much as I could have wished if it had brought me the news of your perfect recovery, which would be one of the greatest joys I can receive. I fancy it has been a good deal owing to the badness of the weather, that you did not receive the benefit one could have hoped for, but I don't doubt but that you will be the better for it, before you leave Tunbridge. I had a letter last week from Doctor Young; I am extremely sorry he has been so ill, but hope he will still favour us with his company, I design troubling of him soon. At present we lead a most stupid life. The S—— is here, and then, you know, all must pass *in ceremonials*; Mr. Ford left us yesterday morning in order to set out for Cambridge, where his nephew is to stand in the room of the *Gog* or *Magog*; in my humble opinion a bad project that will cost a great deal of money, and I don't know that either of them has it to spare. And then besides I could not bear to go and live in a stinking inn, six miles from a fine seat which I just now sold. That may be *pride* in *me* and a wrong way of thinking, but I must own to you, it is such a pride as I would not conquer; don't mention this to a mortal I beg, for it is not proper it should, but I know you are so indulgent to interest yourself in what concerns me that I can't help opening my heart to you.

Thank God, the children are perfectly well; poor Bill has been stung by a wasp upon both his hands to-day, but he plays about, and does not mind it. I expect my company will stay a month with me; must I not hope for the pleasure of seeing you any part of this year? it would make me extremely happy. I hope Sir Robert is perfectly well and returned some time to you; my best compliments attend him and Mrs. Collingwood who I hope continues well. The wind whistles most melancholy; I should not rejoice at the near approach of winter, but as I have so agreeable a companion with me, I can't wish to leave the country. I hope my next may be longer, but at present time is very scarce, and I have many epistles upon my hands. I heard of two weddings to-day—Lord Brooke to Lady Bell Fitzroy [1] and Lord John Sackville to Miss Leveson. [2]

I hear Pip [3] *is married.* Adieu,
   Ever yours with the most unfeigned affection.

Fidget,[4] my Lord, Mr. *Pots*, and *Frère Bonavanture* are yours and Sir Robert's devoted.

The Honble *Dame A. Granville*[5] *to Mrs. Dewes.*

Windsor, ye 26, 1740.

Accept, fair cousin, my sincere congratulation on this solemn occasion. May all the happiness belonging to a matrimonial state attend on you! and though I have not the pleasure of knowing Mr. Dewes, I am sure he knows how to distinguish sense, virtue, religion, and merit, by

---

[1] Lady Arabella Fitzroy, daughter of Charles, 2nd Duke of Grafton, married May 29, 1741, to Francis Seymour Conway, Lord Conway, afterwards Earl of Hertford.

[2] Lord John Philip Sackville, son of Lionel Duke of Dorset, married Lady Francis, daughter of John Earl Gower.

[3] "*Pip.*" Ann Granville, Mrs. Dewes.

[4] "*Fidget.*" The name given to Mrs. Montagu on account of her great activity of mind and body. Mrs. Montagu says in one of her letters in speaking of an old-fashioned table, " *Why so many legs should be required to stand still, whilst I can* FIDGET *on two, I own surprises me.*"

[5] Eldest daughter of George Lord Lansdown.

his choice of you. Pray write to me soon, that I may have under your own hand that you are as happy as I can wish you; oh, that I could hear you say so by word of mouth! Dear Ann, tell me in your next that I shall have the pleasure soon, and you will please me much. How happy all our kindred will be when they meet at Stoke and at Newport;[1] for there I suppose Pen and Mr. Granville will go. I believe I need not tell you I wish myself with them—you will easily believe I do, but since that can't be at present I must be contented with thinking over their happiness at a distance, but hope next year to be an eye-witness of it. I have heard no more particulars in regard to my brother's affairs but what I wrote you word of, but flatter myself they are going on in the same train I mention. Betty[2] desires her compliments and best wishes to you, and both desire our humble service to Mr. Dewes, who I hope to be acquainted with. I have not seen the sweet Duchess of Portland some time, for Lady Oxford is with her. Mrs. Pringdon is well. Madame Jane was here on Sunday, and always inquires kindly after you; I send this letter to dear Pen, not knowing how to direct to you—let me know in your next letter: but wherever you are may heaven protect you with his choicest blessings, are, dear Mrs. Dewes, the wishes of your ever

Faithful and affectionate,
A. GRANVILLE.

---

[1] At "*Stoke and at Newport.*" Stoke Edith Park, and Newport in Herefordshire, belonged to Thomas Foley, Esq., who married Grace, youngest daughter of George Lord Lansdown, and sister to the writer of this letter. He was afterwards created Lord Foley, having inherited the property of his cousin, the 3rd Lord Foley, on the decease of that nobleman.

[2] The Honourable Elizabeth Granville, afterwards Maid of Honour to the Princess of Wales.

Mrs. Pendarves to her sister Mrs. Dewes.

29 Aug. 1740.

I shall not be able to write to you a comfortable long letter till I get to Stoke, for I have my head and hands full of affairs. I have had an account from Mr. Harbin that my Lord Weymouth is settling his affairs, but designs to allow his sisters only £200 a year for the entire maintenance of both, and that to depend on his will: what a prospect is this for them after the expectations he has given them! I have this day wrote four letters in their behalf, which have cost me much thought, and I wish they may prove of any service. I have wrote to Sir Robert Worsley,[1] Sir John Stanley, Lord Weymouth, and Mr. Harbin. I was in hopes to have had this afternoon to myself to write you a more intelligible letter than this scrawl will prove, but Dicky Bateman and his sister are just—— Here I was called away last night to entertain them, they supped with us and have set out this morning in most dismal weather for Shobden in Herefordshire, which it seems is but four miles from Newport. This morning I have been at church. You are called to mind in all my moments, whether serious or gay, and if I had an inclination to forget you, that could not happen here, where everybody enquires after you, and send you wishes without end, even Bem honoured us this morning with a compliment on your account.

The Bishop is not yet returned; I believe he comes to-morrow. I have got a very neat tea-chest for Mrs.

---

[1] Sir Robert Worsley, of Appuldercombe, married in 1690, Frances, only daughter of Thomas, 1st Viscount Weymouth. His daughter Frances, married John Lord Carteret.

Yate, which shall be filled with tea and delivered to her as your act and deed; I saw Mr. Yate at church this morning, and he wishes you much joy and happiness; he says very handsome things of my brother Dews, and desired his compliments to both. To-morrow, madam, the city of Gloucester is to be entertained at Mr. Whitfield's great room with the Miser,[1] performed by the celebrated Cheltenham strollers, and an assembly and ball; the whole to conclude with a supper. The particulars of all these extraordinary affairs I will communicate by word of mouth, for I despair of finding time for writing. I went to the top of the Tower with my brother, and Mr. Newton, and the telescope—it was very fine. I wished I could have seen *Bradley* :[2] if I had it would have been no easy matter to have removed me from a spot that showed me such a prospect.

P.S. Mr. Edward Stanley dined with us on Friday, and is much yours and your husband's humble servant. He went away yesterday morning towards Cheshire.

From this letter it appears that Mrs. Pendarves must have gone to Gloucester with her brother for her sister's marriage, and remained there till she went to visit her cousin, the bride Mrs. Foley, at Stoke.

---

[1] *The Miser*, composed by Henry Fielding, 1733-1744. This play was acted with great applause at the Theatre Royal, Drury Lane. In the *Daily Journal* for January 11, 1734, is the following advertisement: "At the Theatre Royal, Drury Lane, on Monday next, the 14th of January, will be presented a comedy, called *The Miser*. The part of Lovegold, the Miser, by Mr. Norris; Lappet, by Mrs. Clive."

[2] "*Bradley*," Mrs. Dewes's residence.

Mrs. Elstob to Mrs. Dewes.
1740.

Were I not very well acquainted with my valuable friend's great clemency and goodness, I could not have the assurance to write to her after so long a silence. I must confess I am extremely ashamed that I have not sooner made my acknowledgments for your most obliging letter, but am much more out of countenance, that I have not acquainted you with the inexpressible satisfaction I received when I heard you were so happily married, and that I have not presented you and the very worthy gentleman you have made happy with my more early congratulations, nor assured you of my sincere prayers and wishes for your long enjoyment of all the blessings heaven can give; in this my dear little charmers join with me, and would I am sure tell you so themselves could they make use of pens and paper; Lady Betty often talks with pleasure of writing to you, and Lady Harriett is *Miss Pip* almost every day, and pays me visits under that name; the sweet little Marquis, who is certainly the finest child that ever was, takes horse to carry you my compliments. I heartily wish you could see them, and partake of the pleasure I enjoy in them, for I am sure they would highly delight you. Dear Mrs. Pendarves makes me doubtful whether we shall be so happy as to see you here or no: it will be a *great disappointment* to our great people if you don't come, but will be to no one a greater concern than to

Your most grateful and most
affectionate servant,
ELIZABETH ELSTOB.

I hear you have lately had a visit from one of my favourites, and hope you like her as well as I do—I mean Miss Hopkins.

Lady Throckmorton to Mrs. Dewes.

September 4th, 1740.

Hearing my dear Nancy is become a wife, I must assure her of my congratulations and sincere wishes for all possible happiness, which I know none more deserving of than herself, and the *extremely good character* of Mr. Dewes makes me hope she'll enjoy entire felicity. Now I shall be even with you for all your banters upon me, and assure yourself, my dear Nancy, if I find (what I hope I shall not) the least abatement of your friendship for me, you shall never hear the last of it. I long to see you, and hope we shall meet in London next winter; you can't imagine what joy I shall have to see you and your love together. I beg if you think proper you'll make my compliments to him, for though I have not the honour of personally knowing him, I must love him now he belongs to you. You see I write in the old free style, depending on your *not* shewing my letters to your husband, as I *never* shew yours to mine. Pray write to me as soon as you have a leisure minute, for I am impatient to have a letter from *Mrs. Dewes* and to know from her own pen that she is as much my friend as dear Miss Granville was.

I was almost angry with you for not answering the letter I wrote you from London, but then I considered you must be in a hurry, which might occasion strange things to ensue, such as your silence, &c. Pray give my kind love to *the widow*, and tell her I have some crayons for her, which I shall leave at her house in London.

I hope to go from this place in a few days, so you must direct at Weston, and pray tell me if Newport Pagnell will be your way to London from Warwickshire. Sir Robert desires his respects to you, and begs you will receive *here* his compliments of congratulation; mama joins with me in the same, and

I am, my dear Nancy,
Your faithful humble
C. THROCKMORTON.

Mrs. Pendarves to Mrs. Dewes.

Stoke, 5 Sept. 1740.

I came to this place last Wednesday, well conducted by our good friend's equipage; found the roads tolerably good and am charmed with the infinite beauties of the place. The house, its situation, the park, and woods, are all delightful; and the happiness that seems to reign amongst the inhabitants of this sweet place greatly contributes to make everything about them agreeable. How much you are talked of, how often wished for, and what blessings are called for to attend you on all occasions, are subjects that would take up more time and paper than I have to spare; but in the midst of my pleasures here my thoughts are working how to enjoy my chief earthly happiness, and not hearing from you as regularly as I could wish to do is an alloy to all my pleasures, and makes me still more impatient to come to you, where nothing will interrupt our conversation. My cousins have begged so hard to have me see Newport, that I don't know how to refuse, so next Monday we all go in a body and return on Thursday; and the Monday after that, which will be the 15th of Sept., I propose setting out for Bradley. I shall have Mr. Foley's coach, and will be at Windsor by one o'clock if possible, and beg Mr. Dewes will send a servant there to direct which will be the best road from thence. This morning I have been in the chaise with Mr. Foley all over the park, and am charmed with every part; to-morrow we go to Hampton Court, and the rest of my time I have already told you how we are to spend it. I have chosen the chintz-room, because it was yours, but what consolation is that to me? Do I not think of you wherever I am? Most certainly I do. I caught a little cold a day or two ago, and have had a touch of the disorder my eye is subject to; it is better to-day, but I dare not use it much. I was hurried out this morning, and had scarce time to dress me, (it being *show day*), and the light is now so much declined that I can but just see to add my brother's kind compliments, and my own, to Mr. Dewes and yourself. I shall hardly be able to write above once more before we meet. My dearest love, I am for ever yours,

M. P.

Is not Dapper excessively impertinent? I hope you have had all my letters? Since we parted I have had, alas! but one.

---

[1] Hampton Court was at this time in possession of Margaret, Countess of Coningsby; whose sister, Lady Frances, married Sir Charles Hanbury Williams, one of whose daughters and co-heirs married William Anne, 4th Earl of Essex, who at the death of the Countess of Coningsby became the possessor of Hampton Court. It was sold by the 5th Earl of Essex, to Richard Arkwright, Esq.

Mrs. Foley to Mrs. Dewes.

Stoke, Sept. 5, 1740.

I have with utmost impatience waited for a letter from dear Mrs. Dewes, to inform me not only how she got home, but how to direct to her; but vain were my hopes, and I positively shall be almost angry if I have not a line to-morrow night, though my dear Pen, amongst ten thousand other pleasures, has given me that of knowing you are well, which next to seeing you is the greatest happiness I can have. How much I long to do that is not in my power to tell you, but you may guess when I tell you I am fully as impatient as ever Mr. Dewes was; but, alas! I have at present no prospect of that satisfaction, therefore make it up to me by giving me a full and true account of yourself, your habitation, and all that belongs to you. Matrimony is apt to make people lazy,—don't indulge at first, once a week I shall expect to hear from you, and I am sure if Mr. Dewes knew how well I loved you, he would not grudge me one hour in a week. My particular compliments attend him. This *whole family* (as well as Lord Foley) are obliged to him, and return *thanks for his interest*. Don't I, my dear Mrs. Dewes, give you a strong proof of my attachment to you by giving up one moment of my dear Pen, especially as she has allotted me so few. She is very well, and speaks for herself, so that 'tis needless for me to do what she can do so much better. Mr. Granville is very well also, and is so good as to seem to like being here; to-morrow, if dry, we go to Hampton Court, which will bring the agreeable moments I spent there with one Miss Granville fresh in my mind, and many wishes will there be made that you were of the party. Monday we go to Newport, and return on Thursday; you'll perhaps guess by my going out to stay, that the cold bath has done miracles and cured me already, but indeed I am far from being well, and were it not that I can't bear the thoughts of losing Penny's company, and I find the Lord of the Manor will never forgive it, I would upon no account stir. I had a letter from Bath last post; my sister[1] and the Captain desire their compliments, and good wishes; she will write as soon as she knows how to direct, which I shall send her word to-night. Your god-daughter, Pat Griffiths, has the small-pox, but is in a fair way; her mother knows nothing of it, nor do I design she shall, till she's recovered; she desires her duty to you and Mr. Dewes, and wishes you all the happiness in the world; but *"Lord have mercy upon me, she was very sly to carry it off so!"* The Rector lays it to heart, and never comes near the house. I have also speeches from them and Mrs. Wolstenholme. Our sweet Primrose[2] is very well, but poor thing, in great concern about her brother's affairs,[3] though she does not yet know half: between friends, he's a monster, and I am heartily grieved for the young ladies, and the more so as the old Countess has the pleasure of triumphing over them.

---

[1] Mrs. Richard Foley.
[2] The Honourable Mrs. Foley.
[3] "Her brother's affairs." Lord Weymouth.

The Honble. A. Granville to Mrs. Dewes.

Old Windsor, y⁰ 6—1740.

I began to think dear Mrs. Dewes had determined not to write any more to me, by her long silence, but was agreeably undeceived by a very kind letter last post, for which pray accept my most grateful acknowledgments; you say so many obliging things to me that I so little deserve, but impute all your goodness to your usual partiality to your friends. You bid me write when it's convenient, and at all times I think it so, to assure dear Mrs. Dewes of my constant friendship, as likewise how sincerely I rejoice at your thinking yourself happy, and *that's the point* to make us so—being content with what Providence has allotted, and that my dear namesake's sense and religion will always make her.[1]

The morning I received your letter the Duchess of Portland was with us. I have received more friendship from her than was possible for me to expect, as likewise from the Duke. She told me that he and Lord Jersey[2] would come to some determination in regard to what could be done for a pension, but with all that she thought it necessary my brother should be acquainted with it, for was he not, might say it was without his consent *to the people* that *must* be applied to, and that would spoil all. The Duchess of Portland said that the Duke and Lord Jersey must write to him to let him know their intentions, and say that as *we are their relation* they hope he would not take it amiss if they endeavour to get something for us,

---

[1] At this time Mr. Dewes's income was very moderate.
[2] William, 3rd Earl of Jersey, was nephew of Mary Lady Lansdowne, and first cousin to Lord Weymouth.

as it was impossible to live on what he allows us. I am not quite of their opinion, but submitted to better judges, and therefore Providence will direct those that have such humanity and good nature I hope for the best. If my dear Pen and you do not approve of this, I wish you would write your sentiments to the Duchess of Portland. Say only that I had wrote you word of her goodness to us, and what else you think proper (yourself) to be done as coming from yourselves.

We have this morning received orders to leave this place, and we shall go to town on Wednesday till Saturday, for I intend to speak to Sir Robert W. myself, and then come to Windsor Castle, for it would be infinitely more expensive to stay in London; therefore what time I can spend there, I would choose to have it at the time the friends are there I like to see. These reasons considered, I believe Pen will think I am in the right to accept of Lady B's[1] house at present. I have a thousand things more to say, but have at this juncture not time, for I am, as you may imagine, in some hurry, and indeed am ashamed to think I have already been so long talking of myself; but will not have done till I have assured dear Mrs. Dewes that I am ever your faithful and

Obliged humble servant, A. G.

Mrs. Dewes to Lady Throckmorton.
Bradley, 10 Sept. 1740.

My dearest Lady Throck.'s first letter to Bradley was a great joy to me, but her second quite delighted me, to find that nothing excludes me from the friendship of my dear amiable Kitty, and I thank you for allowing

---

[1] Probably Lady Bateman.

me still to call you by a name that has ever been attended with pleasure; the continuance of your love will make a great deal of that happiness you so kindly wish me. I have yet met with nothing in that state (you seem so glad I am come into) but what gives me a fair prospect of happiness, and though *our cot* between two aged oaks yields nothing fine, it affords *content*, and will always do so as long as affection remains in the inhabitants, and supplies the place of great apartments, equipages, and state, though when *they are* joined all together, as at Weston, it is very charming indeed. But, alas, how rare! and I can't help thinking that there is for the generality more happiness in a middling than in a great fortune, and it is very proper for me to be of that opinion now, as Mr. Dewes's fortune is moderate, but his qualities are extremely good, which are to be preferred to riches, and I had no pretence to expect both. The country about us is so very dirty, that had we a good neighbourhood I should not be much the better for it; though were my dear Lady Throck. and her "*own Sir Robert*" at Coughton I should make a hard shift but I would often visit them, and hope, some time or other, to be so happy; though Mr. Dewes is not resolved upon fixing me here if he finds it inconvenient, and should we remove, how happy should I be to be near Weston.

We have had company every day almost since we came, and my dear Penny is with us now; but alas! she goes the beginning of November to Bulstrode: whether I go with her or no I have not yet quite determined. Three dreadful days' journey in the middle of winter to come back, frights me, for I shall not go to London this year, where Mr. Dewes stays but six weeks,

and if I went I fear Weston is not in my way; I shall rejoice if it is. Since I began this I have had a hundred interruptions, and I am ashamed to send such an incoherent dab, but hope it will just serve to show that I am, at all times, my dearest Lady Throckmorton's
Most faithful and affectionate
NANCY.

Mr. Dewes desires his best respects to your ladyship, and Sir Robert Throckmorton and Penny a thousand wishes. I beg to hear soon a particular account of your health, and hope my next letter will not be such a medley.

My brother spent a week here in his way from Gloucester to Calwich, and charged me with his compliments to you and Sir Robert; Mrs. Chapon has also been with us, and we have been happy in seeing a great many of our friends. Yesterday a plump red-faced gentleman dined with us, whose name is Petres, and as belonging to Sir Robert, I was glad to see him, and talked a great deal of Coughton with him. He gives the same character of your own Sir Robert that all the world does. I hope Mrs. Collingwood is very well, and beg my compliments to her. I could write to you many sheets, but have a dozen letters to answer, besides family affairs to mind that do not come within the inspection of *you fine ladies.*

Lady Throckmorton to Mrs. Dewes.

London, September 16th, 1740.

I did not know my dear Anna was become a wife, till the week before I left Tunbridge; and I wrote to her the very next post my joyful wishes on the occasion, and enclosed it to the Duchess of Portland; but I find you never received my letter, or at least had not before you wrote to me; therefore have ten thousand obligations to you for giving me the pleasure of hearing from you, when you had great reason to think I was undeserving that favour: but you may believe nothing except being deprived of the use of my right hand, could make me silent on a subject I have long wished to write upon, viz., your entering into the matrimonial society. I told you in my former letter that I wished you all joy and felicity (which I do with the greatest sincerity), and that I longed very much to see you, which is also very true; when shall I have that pleasure? Not this many months I doubt. This year I believe we shall not see *old Coughton*; but the next I hope will be more lucky. I think it barbarous to teaze brides; but yet I have an notion if we were to meet I should be very merry, and pay some old scores I owe you on the head of banters; but seriously I am quite glad to hear you confirm, what I have heard from many hands before—that Mr. Dewes *has all qualifications to make you happy,* which I am sure no one is more deserving of than yourself, nor any one more sincerely wishes than I do. Pray write to me soon at Weston, for I shall be there next week, and hope you'll give me the good news that you design to call on me in your way to London, which my own husband says is your direct road. He desires his compliments to you; I beg mine to Mr. Dewes, and that my dear Anna will still believe me,

Her faithful
KITTY.

The Honble. A. Granville to Mrs. Pendarves, at Mr. Dewes's, near Alcester, Warwickshire.

Old Windsor y⁺ 8 ———, 1740.

I received yours, my fair and amiable cousin, full of sweets to me, for every fresh mark of your friendship adds to my happiness; though I could almost find in my heart to huff you for flattering me. Your goodness of heart makes you glad to hear from your friends: but when my dear Pen talks of *my instructing her*, I could almost think you laughed at me. I look on my keeping up my spirits in our present situation as no merit of my own, but a gift and blessing from the hand of Providence, which *never* sends us more distress than what at the *same time* his Divine power enables us to bear. I speak by experience, who receive daily marks of his blessing by bestowing on us, unworthy mortals, a fortitude of mind to support our worldly disappointments, which did we make a proper use of, ought to instruct us not to set our hearts "on any child of man:" but build our hope on a much surer foundation. Although my thoughts since I began writing to my dear Pen have been more celestial than terrestial, still I think whilst we are in this world (though not with too much anxiety), that it is a duty incumbent on us to endeavour to be as happy as we can; and if our affairs succeed let us thank our great Benefactor,—if not, "his will be done," whose wisdom directs everything for our good. Could we bring ourselves to acquiesce without grumbling, we should contribute much to our present happiness.

By this time I hope you have received my letter with

Lady Jersey's[1] answer. I wrote last post Mrs. Dewes word my conversation with the Duchess of Portland and should be obliged to you if you would write your opinion on the subject to her, which must have weight on every one that you will speak your mind to, for as you were the person that was so good to apply to my brother about a pension, you are better able to judge what method will be most likely to succeed. Now as to Lady B.'s, you know whatever offer is made one in distress, let it be ever so small, is still an obligation, and I believe I shall convince you at present it is *better* being *there* for a little time than at your house in town, and less expensive, and I do not know in what situation your house stands, though I am told it is *not made over* to the trustees.[2] But my brother *may imagine* we want to intrude on him, and a thousand things that may be put in his head: for *I can't give him up*, but really believe he has been ill-advised, and being so much reduced himself has made him more easily comply with his later behaviour to us. But, my sweet Pen, I know your heart: *you think* that if Weymouth had your house still in his hands, he might be persuaded to let us have it; but *if it is* still *his*, I hope those will remain in it that make the ornament of the place, and never take in your head, that I could bear to be the occasion of your leaving

---

[1] Anne, daughter of Scroop, 1st Duke of Bridgewater, and relict of Wriothesley, Duke of Bedford, married 23d June, 1733, to William, 3rd Earl of Jersey.

[2] It appears from this sentence, and others in this correspondence, that Mrs. Pendarves rented a house of Lord Weymouth, and that she was anxious his sister should make use of it in her absence, not only as a temporary convenience, but in the hope Lord Weymouth might be induced to let them have it.

a place that I know is convenient to you: which would vex me much more than having a house rent free would do me good.

I have wrote two letters to my brother; in my last I mentioned everything in as civil a manner as I was capable of, and put him in mind of our arrears; but when we go to London, which please God will be one day this week, I shall see Sir Robert Worsley, and then shall tell him the situation of everything. He has shown more feeling for us than any of the rest—I *mean* of *the trustees.* As to Mrs. Petite,[1] she will live with her friend Mrs. Favor;[2] as for poor Mrs. Bourgois,[3] she says she can't bear the thoughts of leaving us: she *will have no wages*, but says she shall be happy in doing anything, let it be *what it will,* to serve us. I know the tenderness of your heart, that you would not know what to say to anybody you find so affectionate; I am sure I do not, for I am surrounded with many difficulties. God guide me in whatever I do for the best! I always think of Mr. Pope's prayer ("*Teach me to feel another's woe.*") I sincerely do for those that suffer at present with my fall of fortune; and wish *I alone* was the only sufferer; but let my pocket be ever so low, my heart will always be great in affection to my dearest cousin: this I beg of you to believe, as likewise that I am

Ever your obliged humble servant,
A. GRANVILLE.

Betty is your humble servant, and desires hers, and your humble servant's compliments to Mr. and Mrs.

---

[1] An old retainer from Long Leat.
[2] An old servant.
[3] An old waiting-woman.

Dewes. I have wrote to my sister Foley already about lacing strait; she assured me she *does not*. Her *jumps*¹ will go next Sunday, and I dare say she'll put them on. Mr. and Mrs. Foley come to London when the Parliament meets, which is the 18th of November.

The affection which Mrs. Pendarves and her sister entertained for the three daughters of Lord Lansdown, is accounted for by the excellent tone of mind, and the complete resignation under their trials, which is evident in the course of their correspondence, as well as the kind and forgiving feelings evinced about their brother, Lord Weymouth, even *after* his extravagance had produced its usual results of selfishness and injustice towards those whom he had promised to support and protect.

The Honble. Mrs. Foley to Mrs. Dewes.

Newport, Oct. 23d, 1740.

Though we have not yet, thank God, had any very severe frost, I really till last post began to fear the weather had been more violent in Worcestershire, and had froze my dear Bradley cousin's fingers up, which prevented me having the satisfaction of either hearing from you or your fair sister. I was just going to inquire what was the reason of so profound a silence, when I received a most sprightly letter from you, which convinced me you were not quite fallen asleep, and gave me so great pleasure, that it demands my most best acknowledgments, which I desire you to accept. Miss Foley and I have been at Newport this fortnight; we intended returning this morning to Stoke, but a deep snow falling last night, and a

---

¹ "*Jumps*," stays.

prudent coachman not caring to venture to drive, makes us remain here till we can go without any danger. I am obliged to you for your kind advice to me to behave prudently and to be warned by other's ill, and I have so great an opinion of all you say, that certainly I should be very cautious of running into danger. Not that I can possibly think myself of so much consequence as you are pleased to tell me I am, and I hope the advice you give to others you will for the sake of your friends follow yourself, and not venture in bad roads, for fear—to make use of your own words—"The child unborn may rue the day." I hope you'll not determine too quickly on going to Bulstrode, though if you think you may venture to go without doing yourself any harm, I should grieve that the good Duchess of Portland should be deprived of the great satisfaction it would give her of seeing so valuable a friend; and as then you'll be amongst so many experienced people, that you can't fail having a proper care taken of you in any condition. Therefore, all things considered, I hope the fair sisters will undertake their journey *together*, and think then what pain you'll save yourself by not parting with sweet Penny, for I know by experience what trouble that gives, and hope in your next I shall hear you are fixed to leave Bradley for some time; 'tis thousand pities your *oak* is so ill situated; not but what if you have as much cold and snow as we have here, were it placed in your garden it would be of no service to you.

I had last post a letter from my dear Violet; they are now at Windsor-Castle. It is very obliging in the Duke and Duchess of Portland to interest themselves in my sister's affairs; they can have no other motive but what flows from their generous hearts. Lord Jersey I know always said he had great affection for my sisters, and I am glad he now shows his friendship by his actions. I must look on whatever befals so near relations almost in the same light as if it happened to myself. I am sure that is the way of thinking my dear Penny and Mrs. Dewes have, by the *very great share* they have always taken in whatever accident in life has happened to us. With *so many good friends* and an entire trust in Providence, I hope they may still meet with a great deal of comfort in this world; but it has been a most sensible affliction to me, to find those who I know to have so much merit meet with such variety of Fortune's frowns.

I am glad you are so well pleased with Ponto,[1] and that you find him a philosopher amongst many more perfections; not but, could he have as great a notion of philosophy as you imagine, I fancy he would make use of it in reflecting of *his happy change*; for I must confess Bradley is a much *happier castle* than *Stoke* to Ponto, and he finds himself now a king when behold a little while ago he was looked on like a dog. Our friends at Stoke are all well; Mr. Jackson came hither yesterday, he tells me he has not known Mrs. Foley so well in health a great while, which account gives me infinite satisfaction. Mr. Foley and his sister desire me to make you and Mrs. Pendarves their compliments. Pray assure her of my warmest wishes and sincere affection. Dinner-bell is just going to ring, and I not one bit dressed, so must conclude in begging your belief

Que je suis toujours votre très affectionnée G. FOLEY.

Mr. Foley and my best compliment wait on Mr. Dewes.

---

[1] "Ponto," a dog.

Mrs. Dewes to Mrs. Pendarves.

Melancholy forsaken Bradley,
Thursday evening, 5 o'clock.

There is a kind of sorrow that enlarges the mind and dissipates all trifling occurrences beyond anything that we call mirth and merriment can do; such is the present sorrow that fills my heart at parting with the best of sisters and most amiable friend. I feel the sharpest pangs for the loss of her company, recollect every tender expression, endearing look and action, that by so many pleasing ways engaged my affection, but at the same time I consider I should be unworthy that inestimable love of hers if I did not root out as much weakness from my heart as I can, therefore I have not indulged myself in lamentations to-day, but roused up my most laudable resolutions, and *done everything* to *divert* and *amuse* myself. You was so cruel, my dear Penny, as not to let me hear one of your dear steps this morning, for which I listened most attentively, but since you denied me that pleasing pain I composed my spirits, went to sleep and took a nap, rose with heavy steps, and came to the deserted parlour and solitary breakfast, which I swallowed like a pill, as fast as I could, then took up a Guardian, then the Bible, then rummaged upstairs, opened and shut your drawers a hundred times, because they *had been yours*; could bear the room no longer, called for Jenny Mare, went through many a slough without knowing where I was till I arrived at Mrs. Harford's, and her *bawling* and the others *hemming* were insupportable; came home in a violent hurry, found a man begging for a fire, considered the deplorableness of his case without fortune and seeking the world over for friends, set down to dull mutton (riding had made me hungry); Jenny Tic purred out what consolation she could, made Sally talk to me all dinner-time, and after grace went to the harpsichord, but could play nothing but anthems, and those horridly, till I was happily interrupted by Charles, who delighted me with the good account of your safe arrival at Evesham. I hope in God the rest of your journey will be as prosperous!

And now I have told you all this day's transactions, to tell you what my heart feels of love and gratitude no day or night can suffice! I am going to drink your health in chocolate—your own dear chocolate, shall eat my egg and go to sleep because it is the only way I can see you now, and my imagination I am sure will not deceive me there. I hope you will as punctually relate every thought and action as I have done since we parted, which already seems an age. Miss Hopkins sent me a very genteel letter, and I have pleasure at the thought of her coming, for I shall soon want a rational companion. Ponto and Puss do very well to-day, but they will not serve long, not but I think them *more dull* than usual, all my family are sensible of your loss, and say "*that Mrs. Pendarves' looks enlivened them*," which recommends them to my favour.

Since you are passed with safety through our wretched green and vale, I don't apprehend any future danger in your journey; but I think of the pleasure you will have at Bulstrode, the consolation and advantage you will be to poor Violet.[1]

But as if all melancholy things conspired together this

---

[1] The Honourable A. Granville.

day, I have just received a sad account of a poor man (son-in-law to our farrier) who was found dead this morning under a hedge, by Fishers—a house at the end of our green that you went by to Hanbury. There was a man with him just alive enough to give this account, that they were going by that place last night when a woman on horseback was stuck in a slough. They helped her out, she rewarded them with a bottle of what she called *brandy*. They drank it all up immediately, and one *never waked again*, the other is very ill! all the art of our wise legislators cannot prevent the mischief of those *direful drams* that in some shape or other walk round the world; but they will never do you any harm.[1]

I hate to leave you, though you know how many letters I have upon my hands, and particularly our lovely *Queen*,[2] to whom I will do myself the honour of writing next post, and then I shall not write to you because you will hear of me; I hope change of air will cure George's cold, my kind wishes attend her. I rejoice to think you have got Dapper in a whole skin with all his own understanding again, and I am quite concerned that I took no leave of Joe.

Mrs. Dewes was at this time alone at Bradley, while Mr. Dewes was spending the six weeks in London to which she had before alluded, and which was entailed by his profession of the law, his elder brother being then alive.

---

[1] Mrs. Delany used to say she never habituated herself to wine in her youth; that such stimulants were not required.

[2] "*Queen*," a nickname for the Duchess of Portland.

Lady Throckmorton to Mrs. Dewes.

Weston, November 6th, 1740.

I was quite charmed to find by my dearest Nancy's kind letter that she is desirous our friendship may still continue; for I think I can answer that it will never fail on my side, but I'll leave this point to be more fully discussed when we meet, which I wish heartily may be very soon. I am persuaded Newport Pagnell *is* the road from Bradley to London, and I fancy Mr. Dewes might easily contrive to leave you here in his way thither, which I am sure would make me very happy, and not less so my own Sir Robert, who always maintains a most sincere respect for a person he calls "*Prospect*," whom he often talks of with great pleasure: he is at present at London, and left me a melancholy widow. I wish you were here to comfort me, for by this time I guess you'll have learnt to pity these kind of afflictions, which you had not much notion of before: but strange things do ensue upon the change of a state. I am quite glad to hear from all hands you have so fair a prospect of happiness, and long to see you in your "*cot*" (as you call it), between the *two aged oaks*, the description of which delights me. You are quite in the right to prefer it to equipages and state, for those kind of things, according to my way of thinking, were only made to hinder the enjoyment of life.

I have a distant view of seeing you at your own house next summer, for we talk of spending part of it at Coughton,[1] which will make me infinitely happy if you are at Bradley; though I hope to see you here first,

---

[1] Coughton, in Warwickshire, the old family place of the Throckmortons.

and beg you'll have some serious thoughts of it. But I am almost affronted at you for taking me to be *so fine a lady* as not to mind *family affairs*, which I take to be the only sphere a woman can possibly shine in, therefore *come here, and I'll show you your mistake*, for you'll find me as errant a country Joan as ever frequented a hen-house or dairy.

I imagine by this, Penny is at Bulstrode; and hope she had a good journey. I pity you for losing her, but not so much as usual now you have got a comforter. You are very good to enquire after my health, of which I cannot brag much though I don't want for *spirits*, particularly when I am writing to you. But I must now bid you adieu, and go see what's doing in the *cheese-chamber* and the *apple-loft*. Pay my compliments to Mr. Dewes, and believe me, my dear Anna,

Your faithful
KITTY.

Pray write soon a long letter.

Mrs. Foley to Mrs. Dewes, at Bradley, near Droitwich, in Worcestershire.

Stoke, Nov. 11th, 1740.

I am, my dearest Mrs. Dewes, quite out of patience with your post, for your letter dated the 4th I did not receive till last night, and one you mention to have wrote in answer to mine never came to my hands: can you blame me for being anxious, and indeed a little uneasy, to be six whole weeks and never hear one word from a person so dear to me as you are. I should be very sorry to add to your grief, but my friendship for you is so tender that if I in the least suspect a diminution of it, I am more desperate than it is possible for a lover to be in that case, and in my hurry of spirits say things that *afterwards* give me concern—as giving you the least pain always does. Human nature is so perverse it often makes our greatest happiness the cause of trouble, and instead of presenting to our minds thoughts that are agreeable, is ever raising phantoms that teaze and alarm; and maugre all our care; 'tis not always in one's power to be proof against them, especially in regard to those we love. Friendship, though the greatest of all earthly blessings, is not without alloy, which shows there's no such thing as happiness on this side of the grave. You will perhaps say " *these are troubles of your own making, and they may be avoided,*" but though one may endeavour at it, yet it is wholly impossible to be a stoic in friendship, and ten thousand different cares and fears will arise even whilst with one's friends—how much more at a distance, when one *raises* a devil without thinking how *impossible* it is to *lay him* ?

I confess ingenuously to you, there is but one person in the world for whom I have a greater regard than yourself; judge then by your own heart if a short formal letter now and then (after so many years corresponding in quite a different manner) was not sufficient ground for jealousy; and to deal plainly with you, I cannot with common patience think of giving the least bit of your heart that ever I was possessed of even to Mr. Dewes himself. If you give me but the shadow of a reason to think I am in danger of it, you must expect to be reproached, for when the cup is full it *will run over;* and though I thank God I can give up most things else without repining, it is impossible for me upon any consideration to part with your friendship—so don't be so barbarous to rob me of the least bit of almost the one thing necessary to my wellbeing here. As I know how much you suffer at parting with those you love, I'll not renew or aggravate your grief by condoling, but must tell you I am quite miserable at your being so much alone. Have you not *one* agreeable neighbour to be with you? I should have thought *even at Christmas* you might have come from Bulstrode, and suppose your roads are passable for a *horse* at any time; but I forget myself, and it may be improper for you to venture: but I desire you'll be pleased to contrive your call to London when all your friends are there, and not be so awkward as to be there when you can see nobody but your nurses. Our sweet Primrose[1] is quite angry with you for burying yourself, and wishes you would come to town, if it is merely to see her.

I am in great hopes we shall contrive to go to town together. The Parliament meets the eighteenth, but I don't suppose any business will be done till the holydays are over, and London agrees so little either with our pockets or inclinations, that we shall not be there longer than needs must. I believe this is the last visit we shall make it for some time, for Mr. Foley seems resolved not to be in the House again. By the time we go up I suppose Mr. Dewes will be coming down, and am afraid we shall be as like buckets as your brother and I were for many years. We have not settled where we shall be, but have wrote about a house in Suffolk Street that has been inhabited all the year, for I don't suppose I shall have two days' notice of going, and we are, I think too much invalids to go into an unaired house. I find Miss Granvilles are gone to

---

[1] Grace Foley, born Granville.

Windsor Castle; I am charmed with their behaviour on this melancholy ocasion, and do sincerely think that even a primitive Christian could not have shown more resignation, and in short every other virtue that the circumstance requires, in greater perfection than Miss Granville has, and if I only wished to serve her before, I am quite miserable not to be able to do it now: however, I'm determined no endeavours of mine shall be wanting, though alas! the power I am afraid will. My regard for my dearest Anna made me a well-wisher to every branch of her family, but the behaviour of our dear Primrose,[1] her sweetness of temper, goodness of heart, and in short every other amiable quality, joined to the desire she seems to have (and which I dare answer for her being sincere in, as I think she has not the least guile) of *promoting the harmony* I ever wished to see subsist in *this family*, will entirely attach me to them, and make it impossible for me not to bear a share in whatever relates to those who are so *nearly* allied *to her*.

I have been so often interrupted since I began this, that I don't believe it is possible for you to even guess at my meaning; but as you are quite alone it will serve to amuse you for want of better entertainment. I have a notion your house affairs, when you have modelled them, will be an epitome of goodness, but it must be provided you take none of your maxims from me. Your partiality to me makes you imagine that many rules of my laying down, which are merely the effect of stupidity, are right in fact, but if you put them in practice you'll find them only calculated

---

[1] "*Primrose*," "*Violet*," and "*Daisy*, were the names by which Mary and Ann Granville designated their three cousins—Grace, Ann, and Elizabeth, the daughters of George Lord Lansdowne.

for my own indolent way of thinking, for they cannot make anybody happy that has good sense and vivacity. I assure you the indifference I show in the management of my house, and in all my other affairs, is more owing to a want of application, joined to the two other qualities just now mentioned, than to any merit of mine; and that which passes with you for good conduct is nothing but an insensibility, which I acknowledge as a fault, though I fear I shall not be able to mend. If Griffiths hears of a servant that she thinks will do, she'll let you know. She is now settled in her house at Hereford, my father has behaved extremely well to her, and received her with as much kindness as if she had never offended, and they have seen one another most days. But I'm afraid they will not continue to do so long, for the Captain is coming home, and I reckon his pride and ill-temper will soon knock all harmony on the head. Your little sweetheart is still with me, but I am to deliver up my charge this week, which I shall be sorry for.

Our church is at last covered in, and the outside workmen, after much plague, discharged; they are proceeding within as fast as possible. We have the pleasure of thinking it will be very handsome and warm too, which to us invalids is no small recommendation. It will be great joy to see it finished, for it is a very disagreeable thing to go so far to church, and this winter-time it is impossible for the maid-servants to go constantly. I think that's an inconvenience you have at Bradley. It will be great pleasure to me to hear Penny is got safe to Bulstrode, though I don't expect a letter from her now she's at a distance from you, for if the Duchess gives her up at all, it will only be whilst she can write to *you*, but

I hope to have the pleasure of snatching her for a few moments when we get to town, though that is a difficulty; but I can't blame people for doing what I most certainly should, had I as much rhetorick and entertainment as they have. I think I have heard you say you had patience to read the Fairy Tales, so have some hopes you'll not commit this to the flames till I have assured you how angry soever I was when I wrote last I am now as pacific as *the Cardinal,* and 'tis impossible for me to cease to be

    Dear Mrs. Dewes,
      Most sincerely affectionate
          E. FOLEY.[1]

P.S. Please to put "*post town at Gloster*" upon your letters; if they don't come safe then, we *will try* by way of London. I am charged with particular compliments from all here, but as they are too numerous to particularize, you must be content with being assured they are all your humble servants. Your Cousin Foley went to Newport to-day, but as he left *his Grace* behind him, I hope to see him again soon; poor Mrs. Bloxham has been almost wild with her teeth, has had three drawn, and I am afraid must part with a fourth, which she talks very calmly of, she is really very ill.

---

[1] Elizabeth, fourth wife of Thomas Foley, Esq., of Stoke Edith, Herefordshire, was the daughter of Robert Unett, Esq., of Birchwood, and sister of Mary Unett, alluded to in this letter as being "settled in her house in Hereford," who married Captain Richard Foley.

The Hon.`ble` Mrs. Foley to Mrs. Dewes.

Stoke, Nov. 18th, 1740.

Had not last night's post brought me a very obliging epistle from my dear Mrs. Dewes I should have followed my inclination, and not so far have stood on ceremony as to punish myself so much as not to have this post enquired after you in your solitude, but must now add my thanks for the favour of yours. Though a mind like yours, with all the ingenious employments you are mistress of, can *never be as miserable without company* as the generality of people are, I must own your present solitary situation, and your description of it, is enough to give your friends the spleen to hear of it, let them be ever so gaily inclined. It was great grief to both Mrs. Foley and me at reading your dismal account of the badness of your roads, that it is impossible for us now to meet, and have it only left us in our power to repine at being so far apart from one whose company would make us all happy. What an uncomfortable situation is this! Do endeavour, my dear cousin, to make it quite pleasant to us all, and remove your quarters to this side of the world.

Mr. and Mrs. Foley desires me to tell you of a place which is now to be sold, between Newport and Stoke, an extremely pretty house and gardens, much about the size you'd choose. It is three mile from Hereford, and surrounded with good roads you may now walk there in your slippers, it being on a gravel. The estate about it is two hundred pounds a year, which is, I fancy, near the purchase you would choose to have; the name of the place is *Burfield*. Perhaps Mr. Dewes may think it too far from London, but it will never be a day's difference more than he is obliged to be now, and the situation must be much more agreeable to you than Bradley. indeed I shall fear that Bradley will not be healthy in the winter, for in *so dirty* a country it must be intolerably damp, and you not able to use any exercise, though perhaps it won't be proper for you to use much, as you are always very prudent. I did believe, besides other *particular* reasons, that it was your prudence which hindered your going this winter to London, but as Mr. Dewes is to be there, I can't imagine anybody could have found fault with it. By your complaisant obliging behaviour I am sure you won't fail of gaining the hearts and affection of all your new relations; in your case I am sure it is your own merit which will make you esteemed, where, as *in my own case*, I am sensible it is Mr. Foley's partiality which makes him behave in the obliging manner he does to me, for were he to see impartially, alas! I fear I could expect but a small share of the good opinion I have now great reason to think he has of me. His own temper is *so good*, and that, joined to a great share of good sense, which makes it entirely my own fault were I not happy, and indeed you was not at all mistaken in the opinion you had of his worthiness; and to give my dear *Mrs. Dewes* her due, she seldom fails in her judgment of anything she thinks worth her while to consider.

I rejoiced to hear our dear Penny got safe to Bulstrode. Mrs. Foley has had a letter from her, wherein she says she has seen my sisters, and that they are very well; God grant success to whatever their friends undertake for them! My heart has equally shared with them the frowns of fortune they have met with, for one's own prosperity can never make one suffer with less pain the adversity of our friends; but as to my sister Granville,[1] I love her *so very sincerely* that I look on all events of fortune which happen to her, as the same as if I personally felt the same inconveniencies from them. I shall be very happy to see them and dear Penny, which will be the second week of January. When Mr. Foley goes to town we shall remove to Newport; Miss Foley insists on staying with me, and I shall be very much pleased with her company, but at the same time shall be sorry she deprives herself in being from Mrs. Foley, which must naturally be more to her advantage and more agreeable, being in London. All here make you their compliments.

Thank God the cold bath does, I think, agree with our good friend Mrs. Foley, which is a great blessing, and no one has greater reason to rejoice at it than myself: I really look on her quite as *a treasure to this family*. She favours me with a particular friendship, which I most sincerely esteem, and shall ever make it my study never to forfeit what I really so much value. She has so great a sincerity of heart and tenderness for those she professes a friendship for, that it is impossible the more one knows her not to have one's kindness increase for her. She lives with me really more like a sister than as one who has but newly come into the family, and I can boast of no merit to deserve the indulgence shown me by so worthy a person.

Your good mama has been so obliging to get me a bit of the Bishop of Gloucester's *purple bed*; I think, of the sort, it is the *most handsome stuff* I ever saw, and intend furnishing our apartment in town with it in yellow. You are, my dear cousin, quite in the right in saying "Mr. Dewes knows how to distinguish things excellent," that I can easily judge by his choosing

---

[1] The Honourable Ann Granville.

you. My paper puts me in mind that it is time to conclude; my inclination would be to say a great deal more, but only now have time to assure you, ma très chere, that I am

Yours most affectionately,
G. FOLEY.

Mrs. Dewes to Lady Throckmorton.

Bradley, 28 Nov. 1740.

I received my dearest Lady Throck's last favour at Mapleborough,[1] where I love to go because it is nearer Coughton than this place. How happy shall I be to see you there this summer! And when you condescend to bless our humble *Oak*, I shall envy none who are possessed of a palace without such delightful company. How good you are to wish me at Weston! where I certainly would be, had I wings; but without an aerial conveyance it is impossible to pass the sloughs and dirt of this country, which in that particular is *quite abominable*. I hope by this time your own Sir Robert is returned, for I find you can but ill support his absence. 'Till I have been married as long as you have, I must not yet pretend to complain of separation; but as I like Mr. Dewes's company, I had rather he was at home than abroad, which he has been these three weeks. He and Penny left me together; she stopped at Bulstrode, where I should have gone, but the badness of the roads to come back frighted me. Mr. Dewes will return before Xmas; and did he know where Sir Robert was in London he would wait

---

[1] Maplebury, in Warwickshire, the residence of Mr. Dewes's father and mother.

upon him. I spent a whole week at Mapleborough, and am very kindly treated by my new friends, who are plain but good sort of people: *politesse*, to be sure, is much *more engaging*, but one can't have everything to one's wish, and in general I have great reason, and am quite satisfied with my new state of life. I am much diverted with the description of your employments, and should be excessively glad to see you routing about your mansion. Is Mrs. Collingwood with you? and how does Miss Throckmorton like England? You must excuse questions, but where one loves it is natural to be inquisitive, and that I love the ever-dear and charming Kitty, I hope I need make no profession now, but yet I like to repeat it.

I rejoice to hear by Penny, that our dear Duchess is well. I wonder all the Garters are disposed of and the Duke of Portland left out.

Do you not mourn for the Czarina?[1] I do: though many women deserve to be great, there are so few raised according to their merit, that when a woman shines as she did, I wish her to maintain the post a great while. But all human things are transitory, and must change; empires fall, and birth nor beauty cannot turn aside the shafts of death; but love and friendship are immortal, and the union of souls founded upon virtue will last for ever, and shine in future glory; even when the sun and stars shall fail, those bright sparks remain. Continue, there-

---

[1] The following notice appeared, under "Foreign Affairs," in a paper of November, 1740:—"The late Empress having conversed much with foreigners, and understanding their languages, she protected the strangers that were invited to Russia by Peter I., favoured the arts and sciences that then began to flourish there, and governed according to the maxims of that truly great monarch."

fore, to love me, my dearest Lady Throck, for I shall ever be,

Your constant and affectionate, NANCY.

Prospect will always be glad to be remembered kindly by Sir Robert, for whom she has a real value and esteem, upon a double account,—his own merit, and belonging to you. Where is Mr. Morrell? and have you taken any pains about music? Did I tell you that Mr. Dewes has presented me with a very fine harpsichord, which tempts me to play more than ever; but it gave me more delight from my sister's fingers than my own. I could be quite angry with you for supposing anything can lessen my grief at parting with her.

Do you ever hear from sweet-singing Birch?

Lady Elizabeth Cavendish Bentinck[1] *to Mrs. Dewes.*

Bulstrode, 23 Nov., 1740.

DEAR PIP,

I love you with all my heart. Mrs. Elstob gives her service to you. I thank you for the pretty letter you sent me by Penny. I learn very well the Common Prayer-book and Bible, and have almost got by heart the Turtle and Sparrow. Papa and mama's best compliments to you. I have learnt Molly Mog of the Rose, and am learning now the English grammar. I should be very glad to see you, and am

My dear Pip, your affectionate friend
ELIZABETH CAVENDISH BENTINCK.

---

[1] "*Lady Elizabeth Cavendish Bentinck.*" Eldest daughter of the Duchess of Portland, afterwards Lady Weymouth.

The Marquis of Titchfield to Mrs. Dewes.

Bulstrode, 30 Nov., 1740.

Dear Pip,
Dear Pip,

I wish you was here to play at hoop with me, and sisters and sister Peggy. I have got a gold coach-and-six papa gave me, and the horses are two dragons, two sober-sides, and two snips; but you are too big to ride in my coach. "*Tantive*" that's the hunting song,—I can sing it all. My love and kiss to you. That's all from your
Affectionate servant,
Tichfield.[1]

Miss Robinson writes December 2nd to Mrs. Donellan from Bulstrode.

"Madame Pen is copying Sacharissa's[2] picture from Vandyck, and does it with that felicity of genius that attends her in all her performances. I believe, could Waller see it, he would begin to make *new verses on her*, and ask of the picture, as he does of the image of his dream—

'Where could'st thou find
Shades to counterfeit that face?'

If Sacharissa could have known '*the Stella*' *of a future age* would have copied her picture, I should not have blamed her for sitting for it; but for her, who *knew not* such future honours would attend her, to sit to a *mer-*

---

[1] The Marquis of Titchfield, brother of Lady Elizabeth Cavendish Bentinck, and grandfather to the present Duke of Portland, (1860.)

[2] "*Sacharissa's picture.*" This picture is in the possession of the Editor, and was copied from Vandyck's original, which was lent to Mrs. Pendarves by a relation of Waller's, then residing at Beaconsfield.

cenary artist, after she had been so pourtrayed in never-dying verse, and to wish to give any other impression of her face, was ill-judged; *the lover* and *the poet* make the fairest and most beautiful representations. From Vandyck you judge she was a pretty woman, but from Waller you imagine she was a charming goddess; and surely immortal verse is the Elysium of vanity!"

Mrs. Pendarves to the Lady Throckmorton, at Weston, near Oulney, Bucks.

Bulstrode, 5 Dec, 1740.

I am sure you must have thought me a most unmannerly as well as ungrateful creature, to have been so long without making my best acknowledgments to you my dear Lady Throck. and to Sir Robert, for the crayons; it was excessively good and obliging in you both to remember me. I was told you had such a favour for me, and I waited till I could give your Ladyship an account of my having received them: they are not yet come to my house; it is very likely they may have been brought, and my servant not in the way to take them. I was much rejoiced at the sight of your dear hand again, being conscious how little I deserved such a mark of your remembrance; but this has been an extraordinary year of hurry with me, and my mind has had as little rest as my body.

Were I to describe the variety of scenes and countries I have passed through I should swell my letter to an unreasonable size, and fatigue you as much as if you had been my fellow-traveller, but not entertain you so well. But to crown all my toils, *I hope I may venture to say* I do think my sister happily settled. You that have a tender heart, my dear Colly, (I can't give up the much loved

name), can easily guess what agitation of spirits I have
been under, for marriage *is serious and hazardous*, and
you know what my fondness is for my sister. You
say very right, I am extremely happy at Bulstrode, and
'tis Bulstrode alone that could make me cheerful and
easy when parted from my sister. But as our joys circu-
late very fast, mine will ebb as well as flow, and London—
odious London will rob me of the delight I now enjoy.
That little exclamation against the renowned metropolis
is *entre nous*, for I would not openly declare my thoughts
on that subject for fear of being hissed off of the stage as
soon as I made my appearance again. I hear what would
be whispered about me with a shrug of the shoulders,
" *ten years ago she was of another mind—you may see the
reason plainly in her face.*" Let them talk as they please, I
shall silently keep to my own opinion, and cannot see
and hear everybody admire our dear Duchess without
sighing, that she should be everybody's more than mine,
for her conversation is really so great a pleasure and
advantage, that I must regret the days and hours that
destine it to a crowd. She is very well and most sincerely and affectionatly her dear Colly's. Fidget is a
most entertaining creature, but as I believe you are
better acquainted with her than I am I shall not attempt
to draw a likeness: she would prove too difficult a task
for my pen as well as pencil; for there are some delicate
touches that would foil the skill of a much abler artist
than I pretend to be. I am called away and can only
add the compliments of this house, and my own in particular to Sir Robert and Mrs. Collingwood.

I am ever dearest Lady Throck.'s

Most affectionate and faithful, M. PENDARVES.

Miss Robinson, writing to her sister from Bulstrode, says:—

"I cannot add much to the length of this, for I am to preach elsewhere. The Duchess and Mrs. Pendarves are expecting me above to *read a sermon*, which, as unfashionable as it is, I have the *courage to own* amongst friends."

In another letter she says to Mrs. Donellan.

"If the world be made for Cæsar let him have it, but I will have *my castle in the air*, where my imagination shall entertain itself. You have one of the best apartments in it, and I sometimes make bold to snatch the Duchess of Portland from her great possessions on earth, to refresh herself in my airy mansion; and I take Penny too from *her business* of *doing good in this world* to her *speculative* employment of despising its vanities! I think, too, I would have Sir John Stanley, for we see age does *not* spoil his understanding, and I think *Cupid will not*, so let him be one."

Mrs. Pendarves to Mrs. Dewes, at Bradley.

Bulstrode, 12th Dec., 1740.

I am just come from the tea-table, where we have had a warm dispute occasioned by Madame de Sevigné's letters, which one of the company said, were very fulsome and wanted variety of expression to make them agreeable, and that a very sincere affectionate person could never be at a loss for a new thought on such a subject as friendship. If they were, it was a mark that their affection was not very warm. The lady that started the dispute would not yield that point, but maintained the heart might be very warm though the imagination was not very bright. Another lady in the company said *that* was her opinion too, and that *words may be wanting where love is not*; upon which says a wise philosopher in company, " What need have you to be in a fuss about sweet words, cannot you say *My Syrup of Violets*, or *My Syrup of Cowslips?*" This turned the disputant spirit into a loud laugh, dispersd the company, and gives me an opportunity of flying to her for whom no expressions can be too kind to do justice to her merit and my love.

We have been this morning to see Mrs. Tatton and her daughter, but found only the mother; Tatty was gone to make a visit: they live near Uxbridge. When I came home I found a letter from Miss Granville, with one enclosed from Lord Jersey, where he insists on her going to town, for he can do nothing for her unless she does. I don't understand of what use such an expense will be to her, but she must humour him or he may make it a pretence of flying from what he first promised. I go to her to-morrow morning to tell her my mind at large upon it; but I wish it could be deferred till her sister was in town. But when I *am there* I can't offer her my house, as it can only contain myself and my other self, and like Sir Paul Methuen's ring that was refused by his mistress, upon which he flung it into the sea, since it can't be possessed by my first friend, it shall be offered to no one besides. Lord George Bentinck, the Colonel, and Mr. Harley are expected here soon. I have had a letter from Lady Sarah Cowper. Mrs. Pointz is very well and brought to bed of a son. Lady Cowper is much worse than she was, and the Duchess of Newcastle in the same way and very bad. The Duchess of Leeds[1] is very much commended; she has behaved herself with great civility and complaisance in the country amongst the Duke's friends and neighbours, and I hope she will appear as well in a crowd as she has done in the shade. Such examples are wanting, and if the Duchesses of Portland and Leeds with the charms of youth and every other attraction *cannot* bring *virtue into fashion*, I am afraid we must not expect to see her tread the stage in our days. I heartily wish she may have as much merit as our Duchess has, but I cannot think she will come up to that.

I had a letter last post from Sally, the only one I have had since I saw her at Bradley; it was quite a domestic one, with an account of Jacky and Sally, Hally and Kitty. I own such a downright fire-side epistle from her disappoints me, though I wish all her family well, and am glad to hear they are so. I find she carries her daughter Sally with her, and her son Jack is to be at Mr. Viney's. I could have wished it had been convenient to have gone there alone. Fare well. The Duchess of Portland has been two days without receiving one letter, at which she sighs and laments most heavily; I hope you will write to her soon, for she loves "her Pip." Her Grace, the Duke, *Miss Fidget*, *Mrs. Pots*, and the *Philosopher* all send their kind compliments; mine to Miss Hopkins. Mrs. Elstob is pretty well; the children very well and *most delightful*. This is the third letter I have directed to you at Droitwych.

---

[1] Mary, daughter and heiress of Francis Lord Godolphin, married, 1740, Thomas, 4th Duke of Leeds.

Mrs. Pendarves to Mrs. Dewes, at Bradley.

Bullstrode, 21 Dec. 1740.

If the weather is as cold at Bradley (as I much fear it is) as with us, should I be silent a post, you may perhaps imagine I am no better than Lot's wife. As yet, I am flesh and blood, but if the frost and extremely sharp winds continue much longer, the Lord knows what I shall be! so I will make use of my time whilst I have strength and motion; my best faculties must be devoted to my most dear sister, whose tender affection warms me in the midst of the severest cold. The wonder that used to arise on *our* constant correspondence by the idle men of the house is transferred from me to Miss Robinson, who writes to *two* of her family constantly *every post*, and is *as regularly answered*, and one of them is her sister. This gives me an opportunity of stealing to you unobserved.

Yesterday morning the Duchess received your charming packet; she gave me leave to partake of the feast, for her disposition makes her always ready to communicate whatever gives her pleasure; your letters always do, and she bids me give her kind love and thanks. The Duchess will hardly be able to turn[1] anything for you before she goes to town, and I had given orders for the books, &c., to be sent you by the coach before I knew you had a box to come out of town. We have begun Pamela, but I will not say anything of it till you give me your opinion. By the time it comes to you I suppose you and my good brother may have chattered over all the transactions that have passed dur-

---

[1] The Duchess of Portland was celebrated *for turning*. She turned in wool, jet, ivory, and amber.

ing your separation, and may be glad to read a new book for variety. If it affords you any amusement, my design is answered; you enclose me a letter for Mrs. Duncomb, but I don't know where our rambling Princess[1] is: she has not given me notice of her abode in town; but I will enclose it to Donellan, who will know where to find her as soon as anybody. I hope you are as wise as I am, and set with *hood and cloak on* by the fire-side. The Duchess of Portland *dines and sups in hers*,[2] and it would divert you to see the wrapping up there is amongst us.

As for all the remarkable news of London, if there is any, I presume Mr. Dewes has told it you. I hear a monument is now putting up for Shakspeare[3] in Westminster Abbey. Many Latin inscriptions have been offered to adorn the same and set forth his worth, and one was sent to Pope for his approbation; the sense of it meant that after many years neglect Shakespeare appeared with general acclamation. Mr. Pope could not very well make out the author's meaning, and enclosed it to Dr. Mead with the following translation:—

"*After an hundred and thirty years' nap,
Enter Shakespear, with a loud clap.*"

I will, if I have time to copy it out, enclose you a copy of verses of his that I believe have *not* come in your hands, but there is a line or two I think had better have been omitted. I wish poets would be more delicate, or, at least, have some respect for those that are so. Our day is positively fixed for leaving Bulstrode—this day fort-

---

[1] Mrs. Duncombe.

[2] The Duchess of Portland's partiality for soft warm hoods and cloaks increased with age. The Editor's mother had often seen her take off *five*, of various textures of silk, when she came out in an evening.

[3] In 1741 a monument was erected to Shakspeare in Westminster Abbey, and paid for by the proceeds of benefits at the two great theatres.

night; my great consolation is that my letters will have less way to go. I told you I was engaged with Lord Bacon: I shall go on with that study this winter, when I can find time for reading. I like him excessively. I am now reading his book of the Proficiency and Advancement of Learning, in which there are abundance of fine things, though some a little too dry and learned for me. I take reading of abstruse and difficult books to be something like children's spelling hard words, which at first they don't understand, but upon hearing them talked over and diligently using and attending to them, they come to know their use: his language is strong, and noble, and lively, and I am impatient to go on, for his Essays, they say, are very entertaining.

Mr. Handel has got a new singer from Italy. Her voice is between Cuzzoni's and Strada's—strong, but not harsh, her person *miserably bad*, being very low, and *excessively crooked*. Donellan approves of her: she is not to sing on the stage till after Xmas, so I shall not lose her first performance. Everything harmonious and delightful will bring you more strongly to my mind, a seat that you possess *without a rival*. My kind service to Mr. Dewes; all here send compliments. I have heard nothing from Miss Granville since she first went to town; I fear she has not met with success, for if she had she would have wrote me word. I had a letter from Mrs. Foley last week, but Mr. Dewes has seen her since that.

From the Honble Mrs. Foley to Mrs. Dewes.
Newport, Dec. 30, 1740.

A fault confessed with hearty repentance I am sure will meet with forgiveness from one so righteous and good as my dear Mrs. Dewes, though I own I am almost unworthy of being ever again received into your gracious favour after having been so long in my acknowledgments for your last extremely obliging epistle. Though in some measure I am not as guilty as I must appear tó you to be, for I have this to say in my defence, that by our being removed from Stoke before your letter came thither, and being under cover to Mr. Foley, it rambled some time before it came to my hands, which deprived me of a sincere satisfaction. But, however, I'll pretend to make no excuse for myself, for undoubtedly my thanks ought to have attended you long before now; therefore I lay myself at your feet and implore your royal mercy, my *most gracious Queen Anne!* I am obliged almost every week to *write volumes* to our good Mrs. Foley, who has been so good to undertake the trouble of furnishing our house in town for us, so that we have many matters of business to settle between us which require a constant and long correspondence to pass, and this has indeed employed great part of my time. But my thoughts and good wishes have often and will always attend Bradley, but I can most sincerely say my heart is always full of tender affection for you, and wish you at all times, and more particularly at this season, all health and happiness, and a long continuance of it for many years. May the same good wish attend you that I had made me t'other day by a particular friend,—"*that you may see many happy years, your children's children, and peace upon Israel.*"

I must always obey your commands, or else I should never think of troubling you with particular accounts of so trifling a subject as that relation of yours, Mrs. Foley; but since it is your desire to know how she fares in this world, I must tell you she is perfectly well, and very much your friend and humble servant. How happy would your presence have made us here, my dear Mrs. *Dewes*, and how do I abominate those nasty sloughs which prevented your coming, since you really are so good as to say your inclination would have made you venture to pass some time with us. The weather has been so bad that it has not permitted us to have much company, but we have been so good-humoured and *happy amongst ourselves* that it has made the time pass very agreeably.

You was a very true prophet about my being "fond of Newport," for I really find new beauties in it every day, even notwithstanding the weather has confined us much to the house. I have a pleasure in viewing out of my window the improvements which are making against another year, for Mr. Foley is very busy with his hedges, which will add much to the beauty of the fields, and cleanliness and little niceties of that kind, you know, I always humbly preferred before troublesome magnificence. Mr. Foley thought of you when he ordered this, and with pleasure—for he knew he should have your approbation: it has procured us the sight of several fine oaks, which before were hid from the house. Were it not for the thought of seeing my dearest Violet, Daisy, and Penny, I should leave this place with *great regret*, but the hopes of seeing them, you may believe, give me great pleasure. We propose going from hence to Stoke on Friday next, where we shall stay a few days and from thence proceed to Gloucester, where I had an invitation from Mrs. Granville's *own hand* to be at her house, which kind offer we shall do ourselves the pleasure to accept, and propose great satisfaction in having an opportunity of enjoying the happiness of her company. By this time I hope Mr. Dewes is returned from London to you; I rejoice you had the good luck to meet with Miss Hopkins as an entertaining companion in your solitude. I am not at all surprised at your being apprehensive of rogues': you used to laugh at me for being a coward when guarded, as you have often told me, by thousands, and that you were never under the least fear, but now you see your noble courage may be cast down. We laughed most heartily at your adventure. Mr. Foley and his sister make you their compliments; we all join in the same to Mr. Dewes. I can't find in my conscience to make you pay postage for this heap of nonsense, therefore shall send it to Mr. Foley to be franked, and by that means must still appear longer unthankful to you. But pardon and love me still, my dear Mrs. Dewes, and you'll add much to the happiness of,

Your affectionate and faithful humble servant,
G. Foley.

The following singular narrative was amongst the letters of Mary Granville. It bears date 1740, and is sufficiently curious to deserve insertion had it not been particularly preserved by her.

"Mrs. Vigor, among many curious occurrences in her travels, had an extraordinary interview with some persons, whom at that time she did not know. This was attended with a wonderful coincidence of circumstances, which happened in the following manner: "Mrs. Vigor, after having resided some years in Russia, was, upon the death of her husband, obliged to return to England. As she was with child, it was thought improper for her to proceed by sea; she therefore set out with her servants by land,

and the journey was performed in sledges, on account of the snow. They left Petersburgh, and passing through Livonia and Courland, arrived at Memel in Polish Prussia. She was here obliged to take up her quarters in an inn, which to her mortification she found full of Prussian officers and soldiers. This was an unfortunate circumstance, to Mrs. Vigor, whose situation at that time was critical, as she expected soon to be in a state of confinement. A gentleman who had attended her in her journey happened in the afternoon to go out, in order to make a visit to some merchants and other principal persons of the place, to whom he had letters; and in conversation he took the liberty to ask if it were not possible to obtain a private lodging for a lady, whose present place of residence was very inconvenient. A person quite unknown said, that he believed apartments were to be had, and those very commodious and retired, and as he was going home he would very soon send a particular account. This news was carried to Mrs. Vigor, and in about an hour a very polite letter came, subscribed 'Meyer,' (the name of the person spoken of above); and in this letter the apartments were pointed out, in which it was hoped that Mrs. Vigor would find every accommodation that she could desire; and added, that the "*sooner Mrs. Vigor came the better.*" The servants were accordingly ordered to get everything in readiness; and a coach being procured, they set out for the house to which they had been directed.

"Mrs. Vigor found it spacious and stately, and was carried up to a drawing-room, where they were treated with everything requisite, and there was afterwards a supper served up. They were in a state of wonder at these occurrences, but at last got intelligence from their servants, that the house in which they were, belonged to the very person who first gave intimation about apartments to be obtained, and afterwards wrote the letter. This raised their wonder still more. However, nothing transpired that night, but in the morning, at breakfast, the gentleman of the house made his appearance, and with him a young person who seemed to be his son. Mrs. Vigor got up, and mentioned how greatly she was obliged to him for his goodness, but at the same time told him how much she was embarrassed, as it was out of her power to make any return for these civilities. Mr. Meyer begged of Mrs.

Vigor and her friends to be easy on that head; for says he, "All I do is *a return:* it is in consequence of favours received—so that your debt is cancelled before it is incurred." As they did not seem to understand him, he proceeded to explain his meaning: "You must know," says he, "that I have a great esteem for the English nation *in general*, but I have obligations *to particulars* which enhances my regard. You see here this young man, who is my son; he was last year upon his travels in England, and passing down from the north towards the capital, he was taken very ill. His disorder was so violent, that he was forced to take refuge wherever he could find shelter, which was not easily to be procured. His distemper was the small-pox, and he was housed in a small dirty ale-house, where he must have died for want of care and accommodation. A gentleman of the place heard that a stranger was ill, and was so humane as to make him a visit. When he found the nature of his disorder, he ordered him to be wrapped up securely, and conveyed him in his coach to his own house. To this gentleman's goodness, and to the assiduity and attention of those about him, *my son owes his life,* and I am indebted for my son. Hence I make it a rule that *no person from England* shall come to this place without meeting from me every mark of regard that I can possibly show."—"Pray, sir," says Mrs. Vigor, to the son, "whereabouts was it in the north of England, that you met with this civility?"—"It was," says he, "at a place called *Methley*, near Leeds, in Yorkshire."—Mrs. Vigor was struck with this; "And pray, sir, may I ask what was the gentleman's name?"—"His name, madam," said the other, "was Goodwin."—"Sir," says Mrs. Vigor, "*it was my own father!*"

We may well imagine how Mr. Meyer's face glowed at this. What was before general civility was now hightened into the warmest gratitude: he testified the greatest satisfaction in having before his eyes the daughter of the person to whom he esteemed himself so much obliged. The son came up with great politeness to Mrs. Vigor, and told her he ought not to have waited for any previous *éclaircissement*, he ought to have known her at once; "for," (said he,) "no daughter can be more like to a father than you are to Mr. Goodwin." Mr.

Meyer begged of them now to be no longer under any difficulties on account of the little civilities which he might offer them. Mrs. Vigor had *a claim to everything*, for he was greatly in her debt. He sent the next day to his daughter, who was married to a person of consequence at the distance of a few leagues, and desired that she would come and keep Mrs. Vigor company; she accordingly came with her husband, and there was a renewal of civilities. It was particularly requested of Mrs. Vigor that she should take up her residence with them till she had passed the time of her confinement, but this could not be. Mrs. Vigor had received repeated solicitations from her friends to make her appearance as soon as possible in England, her affairs required it, and she was obliged to leave this grateful and hospitable family, after a residence of a few days, which she could have wished to have been as many years. Mrs. Vigor left Memel, and passing through Koningsburgh and Dantzick, arrived at Hanover; after a short stay here she set out for Holland and Helvoet, and from thence took shipping for England. This happened in the year 1740."

Mrs. Pendarves to Mrs. Dewes.

February.

I will proceed to give you an account of our doings at Norfolk House.[1] I told you what my clothes were. Dash went with me, she was in pale pink and silver very well drest, and looked like the picture of Modesty; we went at half an hour after one. I never saw so full a Court, the Prince was in black velvet, the Princess in white and gold and colours, a very fine rich stuff. She looked very majestic and well, and acquitted her-

---

[1] "*Norfolk House.*" Frederick Prince of Wales rented this mansion from the Duke of Norfolk, and inhabited it while Carlton House, which he had purchased from the Dowager Countess of Burlington, was being prepared for his reception. King George the Third was born at Norfolk House, June 4, 1738.

self, as she always does, with great propriety. My Lady Scarborough[1] was in violet-coloured satin, the petticoat embroidered with clumsy festoons of *nothing at all's supported by pillars* no better than posts, the gown covered with embroidery, a very unmeaning pattern, but altogether very fine. Lady Cobham and the Duchess of Bedford in rich gold stuff. Lady Bruce[2] in lemon-colour richly embroidered with silver and colours, a small pattern; Lady M. Tufton[3] white embroidered with garlands and *flower-pots* of flowers mixt with a great deal of silver, it cannot be described so well as it looked, for it *was handsome*; Lady Godschall had on a suit of clothes that were designed for her *in case she had been Lady Mayoress*, white satin embroidered with gold and browns, very fine.

The Duchess of Queensbury's clothes pleased me best; they were white satin embroidered, the bottom of the petticoat *brown hills* covered with all sorts of weeds, and *every breadth* had *an old stump of a tree* that run up almost to the top of the petticoat, broken and ragged and worked with brown chenille, round which twined nastersians, ivy, honeysuckles, periwinkles, convolvuluses and all sorts of twining flowers which spread and covered the petticoat, vines with the leaves variegated as you have seen them by the sun, all rather smaller than nature, which made them look very light: the robings and facings were little green banks with all sorts of weeds, and the sleeves and the rest of the gown loose

---

[1] Frances, daughter of George, 1st Earl of Orkney, married Thomas, 3rd Earl of Scarborough.

[2] Caroline, only daughter of General John Campbell, afterwards Duke of Argyll, and third wife of Charles Lord Bruce.

[3] Lady Mary Tufton, eldest daughter of Sackville Earl of Thanet, born in 1723.

twining branches of the same sort as those on the petticoat: many of the leaves were finished with gold, and part of the stumps of the trees looked like the gilding of the sun. I never saw a piece of work so prettily fancied, and am quite angry with myself for not having the same thought, for it is infinitely handsomer than mine, and could *not* cost *much more;* these were the finest ladies. Lady Carteret was in an ugly flowered silk on a dirty yellow ground, Miss Carteret in pale pink satin and *very gloroius with jewels;* Mrs. Spencer in a white flowered velvet very dull, but *all* the Duchess of Marlborough's jewels; Lady Dysart did not go, nor Lady Catherine Hanmer,[1] though she had bought clothes; my Lady Egmont's[2] brother died three weeks ago, and my lady out of perverseness would not let her go, for nobody observes forms for an uncle after they are buried. The ball was begun at nine, by the Prince and Princess, and lasted till I was tired of the number that sailed about. The finest man was Lord Annandale,[3] who is just come home: he is very tall, and what is called handsome, and much commended for his dancing. The men in general were not remarkably fine. Dash, by a mistake of her mantua-maker's was *spoiled for a dancer;* but she danced country dances with Sir Francis Dashwood,[4] who stuck by us all night, and is a very

---

[1] Lady Catherine Hanmer was the eldest daughter of John, Earl of Egmont. She married, 14 April, 1733, Thomas Hanmer, Esq.

[2] The Countess of Egmont was Catherine, eldest daughter of Sir Philip Parker A'Morley, Bart.

[3] George Johnstone, 3rd Marquis of Annandale, died 29th April, 1792.

[4] Sir Francis Dashwood married Sarah, daughter and heiress of Thomas Gould, Esq., and relict of Sir Richard Ellys. Sir Francis succeeded, in 1762, to the Barony of Le Despencer in right of his mother. He was at one time head of the War Office and Chancellor of the Exchequer, from May, 1762 to April 1763, and died without issue, 11 Dec., 1781.

entertaining man. We left the great crowd at one, and when I came home I found your letter.

Yours,
M. P.

I have some thoughts of going with my brother into Staffordshire early in the spring and meeting you at Gloucester, where I find you think of going towards July, for I don't know how to bear the thought of being from you at that time. Thus runs my scheme for you and me: my mother comes to you as soon as the roads will permit, and stays with you till June, at which time (if you are resolved against lying-in in London) I suppose you will return with my mother to Gloucester, and I shall have taken my tour to Calwich, and will come to Gloucester the beginning of July, and return with you to Bradley. By that time the summer will be too far advanced for you or my mother to go to Calwich, and he says now it would not be reasonable to desire she should leave you.

This letter was not dated, but the date is determined by the death of Lady Egmont's brother, Sir Philip Parker A'Morley Long, who died in 1741.

Mrs. Pendarves to Mrs. Dewes.

Jermyn Street, 23rd April, 1741.

This will be the last letter I shall date *from hence;* for next Saturday I remove from dust, noise, and hurry, to sweet air, tranquillity, and leisure; all *these delights* Northend *can give, and with them I choose to live!* where the Penseroso and Allegro will be blended, and set off each other so as to make it a life of perfect harmony—as much so as it is possible for me to find, without the addition of my dearest sister's company; but having *that* to *terminate* my view, I own I feel a very sincere pleasure in going to my much favoured bower, and notwithstanding the sharp winds that make a fireside no despicable place, I hope to warm myself with exercise, and defy sea-coal.

The Duchess of Portland is just as well as I hope you will be the latter end of July. I was her constant attendant Monday, Tuesday, and Wednesday, the three days the Duke spent at Windsor—such *tête-à-têtes* you know are rarities. On Monday I received both your letters; one of them I should have had the post before, but it came in company with yours from Mapleborough. I rejoice at your having performed that bold undertaking so well, and am sure it must please Mrs. Dewes to see you. I will cut out the arms for you as soon as I get to Northend, but you must send me a good impression. are yours to be with them? I have not time at present to thank Mr. Dewes for his kind lines in your letter; but at *my grot* I purpose doing handsome things by all my friends.

I have had no trouble, my dearest sister, about any of your affairs, but much pleasure; I shall send the box this week by the carrier, but cannot get Cicero for you. The bandbox, basket, and pincushion you must be so good as to accept of from me; I took them all of Mrs. Bowker, and hope you will approve of my performance. I will get myself *perfectly informed* of the new dress for the bantling, that I may instruct you when I come to Glocester. I have sent you four yards of coarse long lawn, and two yards finer for the little night-caps, etc.;

I suppose you will line the cradle with dimity or white calico, *quilted*. Let me know if you want anything of the kind or any other, and I will bring it with me; as for *pins*, I think you *must pay the compliment* to Glocester of buying pins there. I am sorry George had not time to make those things that are made, but had I sent them to you only cut out, I thought that would not be so good a direction, but some of the little niceties *were* George's work. The clock has struck three, and *I must* finish a picture before I dine; I have ordered my dinner at four, and at eight go to Dover Street, where Mrs. Foley holds a grand assembly; oh bear me to the plains of fair Northend, that I may no more be encumbered with these innumerable interruptions. The Duchess of Leeds, came to me at twelve, and staid till past two. For ever yours,

M. P.

Short stays and long stays are forgot, but make them of *long lawn*.

Mrs. Dewes to Mrs. Pendarves.
May 1741.

I congratulate my dearest Penny's arrival to the seat of delights, but you carry delight with you, and then *fancy* you *find it there*.

"Dame of the ruddy cheek and laughing eye,
From whose bright presence crowds of sorrows fly."

Health, content, and every blessing attend your steps, for you were certainly born to cheer as well as charm all your friends. How enlivening is the account of Northend in your last letter! And how delightful the good news of my Lord Duplin's advancement, and the kind

promise he has made for our friend's son! I hope
Providence will make him the instrument of putting
that boy in a happy station; and I believe he has a
heart capable of feeling how much good he can dispense
to others. I rejoice for my Lady Kinnoul; but I must
contract my rhapsodies, because franks are out of
fashion, but I beg that may not prevent your sending
one thought, for every word of yours is worth double
postage. I should have begun by answering your kind
packet of the 23^d, where you give so exact an account of
all the trouble you have had about my affairs, which I
am sure are all done to perfection; there is but one
thing I can complain of, and that is the bandbox and
basket. How, my dear sister, can I want any new proofs
of your love, when I have so many already grafted on
my heart? And why should you add to numberless
obligations, at a time when the hurry and bustle of a
remove[1] may make all unnecessary expenses inconvenient?
I could almost chide you, were it not ungrateful and you
won't be thanked; so I must end this subject with my
pen, but not in my mind. I suppose the box will arrive
to-morrow, and I will then give you an account of it.

I know full well how impossible it is for George to
do more work than she daily performs, and that is as
much as if she had *twenty* instead of *ten* fingers; but I
am sure I shall find some employment where her handi-
ness will be very serviceable. I am really concerned for
Dapper more than, as you say, *one should be for a dog*;
and as he got his bane at Bradley, it is a double grief to
me, but I will endeavour to forget him as I hope you will.
We have had a loss of that kind—Hector, the stately

---

[1] Mrs. Pendarves was about to change her house in London.

greyhound; he lay violently ill three days, and then expired. Charles thought him mad, but it has affected none of the other dogs, and they could give no account of his having been bit.

I am glad the Duchess of Leeds visits you so often, for it will be of service to her. I could easily have found a resemblance to *your nightingale* (which far exceeds Strada's description in fancy), but that the person I mean, neither knows nor will paint her own perfections, while she magnifies the smallest good qualities in others. No mortal could so sensibly describe the pleasures of the country as you do, did they not feel them exquisitely; but in *your bower* you have *art* joined to *nature* to make it beyond compare. Here we are all wildness, though not without our beauties, and though *no nightingales* reach our peaceful groves, they want not harmony, such as larks, blackbirds, and goldfinches. Our hedges and fields are verdant, and the apple and pear trees make a very gaudy appearance.

"They speak their Maker as they can,
But want and ask the tongue of man."

We can never talk too much of these rural delights; they soften and compose the mind, and *raise our thoughts* to the bountiful Author of all these beauties, who dispenses blessings and wonders in every plant and animal. I want to *send you* some of our *jocund lambs*—they raise our spirits by their innocence and liveliness, the cow is grown an absolute beauty, and is more worthy now of the honour of your pencil than when you drew her picture. Our grounds are covered with cowslips, and in short we have more spring and freshness than could be expected from so dry a season. But I cannot enjoy our solitude so much as if I were as nimble as usual, and when Mr.

Dewes leaves me, who is so kind to lead me through all the pleasant easy walks, and who enjoys *every field* and *every tree* as much as I do, I shall be forced to sit still. I was not the worse for going to Mapleborough, and received very obliging proofs of kindness and good will; Mr. Dewes is gone there to-day, and I had a great mind to have accompanied him, but mama thought it better not.

I am obliged to our dear Princess for a letter last post, which I will answer as soon as I can; my mother's kindest blessing attends you, and Mr. Dewes best wishes, with all our services to my dear brother, and respects to the beneficent Lord of "Beauty Spot;" and as long as you can enjoy Northend, I shall be in no concern about your not finding a house in town,—there's time enough for that between this and winter. This was wrote yesterday, and this afternoon I proposed adding to it, when Mr. Hunt came in and prevented me, at the same time Mr. Dewes was gone to Beckenham. I must leave room to give you an account of the box, which Charles is gone to Alcester for.

Welcome to May, my dearest sister—May the most pleasing month of all the year, and to me the happiest, for it produced every thing good in my much loved Penny.

Friday night.

The box is arrived safely, but it is too late to open it, so must defer a more particular account of it till next post; besides we have just heard of a very melancholy accident that has put us all to concern. Poor *Mrs. Dewes*[1] fell down to-day and has hurt herself very badly; they fear she has broke her leg or thigh. They sent to

---

[1] Mr. Dewes's mother.

two places for a surgeon, and could not get one. You know how good a son Mr. Dewes is, and how tender hearted to everybody,—and therefore imagine how much he is affected; he has sent to-night, and goes to-morrow morning. "He left Mrs. Dewes last night very well," which makes it doubly shocking to have an accident happen so suddenly.

The Honble *Mrs. Foley to Mrs. Dewes.*
Newport, June 12, 1741.

Though I so lately troubled dear Mrs. Dewes with a long epistle, I can't omit enquiring the first opportunity after your health on performing your journey to Gloster, where I heard you was expected on Wednesday, and hope you got there safe and well. I shall be very impatient to hear of you—not from you at present, therefore beg you to employ some charitable scribe to give me that great satisfaction. I suppose Madam Pen will now soon attend your fair ladyship: she had a scheme of bringing my sisters so far with her in their way to Herefordshire, but my sister Anne objects; so her reasons I suppose are good for so doing, but I know them not. They do not come hither till August; I shall envy them the pleasure of seeing you and yours *en chemin*. Mr. Foley and I have been quite by ourselves ever since we came hither. Mr. and Mrs. Foley come to us next week.

I beg you will make my best compliments acceptable to Mrs. Granville and Mrs. Dewes. Mr. Foley joins with me in the same, and desires me to add his humble service to you.

I am, dear cousin,
Your affectionate faithful humble servant,
G. FOLEY.

Mrs. Pendarves to Mrs. Dewes.

Undated.

I was transported with pleasure at receiving so lively and so particular an account of you as your last letter gave me. Nothing delights me so much as to know how you do, what you do, and every little circumstance belonging to you; I wanted such a cordial last night, for I had spent four hours in a melancholy way with our amiable Duchess, who is under great affliction for my Lord Oxford. He was taken ill on Saturday night; it is hard to say what his distemper is, but his whole mass of blood is corrupted, and one of his legs mortified; he is in no pain at present, and will soon be quite at rest. His daughter, who has, joined to the most lively sensibility, great gratitude and affection for him and my Lady Oxford, suffers a great deal now, and you may think I shall not leave her till her spirits are composed. I staid with her till 12 o'clock last night, and saw her with pain and pleasure; nothing can be said to her that her own piety and goodness does not suggest, and I hope she will bear this unfortunate stroke with a proper fortitude, for she is surrounded with many blessings.

My Lord Oxford has of late been so entirely given up to drinking, that his life has been no pleasure to him or satisfaction to his friends; my Lady Oxford never leaves his bedside, and is in great trouble; the scene is painful to all his friends, but he has sense and goodness of heart, and I hope proper reflections on this great occasion, and when the first shock is over there are circumstances that must be an alleviation to his loss. He has had no enjoyment of the world since his mismanagement of his affairs; it has hurt his body and mind, and *hastened his death;* pray God preserve us all from too great anxiety for worldly affairs!

Since I wrote this, Bet Castleman has made me a visit. She says she is the happiest of her family, but grunts and groans as usual, and sighs for a letter from you; but let her sigh on and write to *nobody* but Mr. Dewes and myself. When she left me I went to see Donnellan, who has missed her fit and is better—I hope in a fair way of doing well; from thence I came to Whitehall to dine with our dear afflicted Duchess; before I came I received a note from Lady Carteret, to desire me to come to her between six and seven to meet the Prince and Princess of Wales, who were to drink tea at her house. I sent my excuse, but as the Duchess was obliged to go to Lady Oxford's at six, I went to Arlington street. The Prince and Princess were very gracious and good-humoured, but my *heart* and *thoughts* were with the Duchess. I am just returned to her dressing-room. Lord Oxford, poor man, *is released!* She and the Duke are not yet come home. Thank God she is in good health, and I hope this unhappy stroke will have no other effect than what must naturally attend it. I will write to you next post, and let you know how she does; don't make yourself uneasy, for she bears up as well as can be expected; I shall stay in town two or three days longer than I designed, for I can't leave the Duchess till she is a little recovered; I hope to see Mr. Dewes to-morrow morning. I have not absolutely fixed my day, because it may be a day or two later than I designed, for if the Duke of Portland can go out of town about that time, it will be both convenient and pleasant to me to take the opportunity of travelling with them to Oxford.

Now good night, it is as impossible for me to express the impatience I have to be with you and my dear mama, as it is to say how much I am yours. Mr. Achard's particular compliments. The dear Duchess in the midst of her trouble remembers her "*dear Pip*."

The above letter is undated, but the death of Lord Oxford gives the period at which it was written. The following account appeared in the *London Daily Post*, June 18, 1741 :—" On Tuesday night last, died at his house in Dover Street, the Right Honourable the Earl of Oxford and Mortimer. His Lordship married Lady Henrietta Cavendish Hollis, only daughter and heir of John Duke of Newcastle, by whom he left only one daughter, the Lady Margaret, married to his Grace the Duke of Portland." It is further recorded on 23rd of June :—" About twelve o'clock this night, the corpse of the late Earl of Oxford (having been put in a leaden coffin, and inclosed in another covered with crimson velvet) will be removed from his Lordship's house in Dover Street to the Jerusalem Chamber, from whence it is to be interred in a pompous manner in Westminster Abbey. A guilt plate of curious workmanship, with the following inscription, is fixed thereon :—

The Most Noble Lord,
EDWARD HARLEY,
Earl of Oxford and Earl Mortimer,
And Baron Harley of Wigmore,
In the county of Hereford.
Born the 11th of June, 1688.
Died the 16th of June, 1741."

Lord Ossory writes to Dr. Swift on this occasion, 4th July, 1741 :—" Poor Lord Oxford is gone to those regions from whence travellers never return, unless in an airy visit to faithless lovers, as Margaret to William ; or to cities devoted to destruction, as Hector amidst the flames of Troy.

From Dr. Young[1] to the Duchess of Portland, on the death of her father the Earl of Oxford.[2]

Madam,
July 12th, 1741.

Could I have administered any consolation to your Grace, and had forborne to do it, I then should have been quite inexcusable; but I too well know that the first agonies of real sorrow have no ear, and that a man might as wisely talk to his friend in a fever, and desire his pulse to lie still, as to philosophize with a wounded heart. These, madam, are the strokes of Heaven, nor will they be defeated in their effect; nor, indeed, is it for our interest that they should. Of God Almighty's manifold blessings to mankind, his afflictions are the greatest—they will make us wise, or nothing will. We cannot bear an uninterrupted prosperity prosperously,— we cannot bear it without being a little intoxicated with the delicious cup, which will make our virtue reel if not fall. Hence an antient said, as wisely as wittily, that no man is so unhappy as he who never knew affliction; I therefore congratulate your Grace on what you suffer, nor let it sound cruel or harsh in your ear, for in this I am but a little beforehand with your own self; for shortly you will bless God for this great calamity, and find that the best may be bettered by the kind discipline of Heaven. Heaven suffers nothing to happen to man but what is for his temporal or eternal welfare; and our tears have as much reason to praise God as our triumphs. In what a blessed situation are we, then, madam, under such a Being, who does, who will do, who can do nothing but

---

[1] The Author of "Night Thoughts."
[2] This letter must have been given by the Duchess of Portland to Mrs. Pendarves.

favour good? What passion in the heart of man is half so natural, as the love of God while man is in his right senses? We have no motives of love, but either the excellence of the thing itself or its benefit to us; and in neither view has God any rival, or shadow of it. Now, why is divine love so natural to us? and why is it enjoined as the first and great command? Because, if this is complied with, a course of duty will be a course of delight; we shall have the same pleasure in it as a fine gentleman has in obeying his favourite mistress. Love carries the whole heart with it, and when our heart is engaged among toils and difficulties we find ease and pleasure, and nothing is too hard for the great alacrity of our attempts.

But is not love too familiar a passion for such insects towards the King and Father of all beings? It seems to be so. But I beg your Grace (for the Bible is a pretty book) to review the Gospel for Whitsunday, and to see what a familiar intimacy by that tremendous power is indulged to men; I never read it but with astonishment; nor is it possible for any one who reads it to suspect that any of His dispensations are really severe, who spoke to us in such language as the fondest father might make use of, and who will encourage no expectations in us that shall not be far surpassed by the event.

In a word, madam, Heaven is as solicitous for our happiness here as is consistent with its far kinder concern for our happiness hereafter; and our afflictions (which is saying much in their favour) plainly tell us we are immortal; *were we not* we should be as *free from cares*, but then we should be as *destitute of hope*, as the beasts that perish. May that Power who "bindeth up the broken heart," and giveth medicine to heal its sickness, be for ever your Grace's comfort and defence. Please to accept the most cordial good wishes for the re-establishment of your peace, and the most sincere respects for the sole foundation of it—your virtues, from

Madam,
Your Grace's servant,
EDWARD YOUNG.

What I write is not to inform but confirm your Grace, or rather to shew my court by shewing that in points of consequence I have the honour to be of your opinion.

Wellwyn, July 12th, 1741.

Mrs. Foley to Mrs. Dewes, at Mrs. Granville's, in Gloster.

Stoke, July 14, 1741.

Among many reasons that make Mr. Foley's being a candidate disagreeable to me, one of the greatest is its preventing my seeing my dear Mrs. Dewes this week, which I fully intended; but Mr. Cornwall, on whom Mr. Foley has laid many obligations, has no other way of returning them but by doing him all the mischief in his power, and has accordingly declared he shall have an opposition. Though this declaration will do no more than expose himself, yet it makes an early and more particular application to the freeholders necessary, and all our servants and horses are employed in carrying out circular letters, so that I must defer seeing you till you set up, which is really the most sensible disapointment I have met with a great while; for my affection for you is not of the common sort, and consequently not to be satisfied with making professions only; besides, I have many things to say to you improper to trust in black and white, would time give me leave to send them to you that way, but that alas! will not do. I wish I could spend it as much to my satisfaction as in writing to you, but there's no remedy but patience for this; so now I shall long to hear you are in a condition to hear me prattle to you, and at the same time dandle your babe, which I am very dextrous at. I needn't say how anxious I am about you, and how much obliged I shall be to anybody that has time to write, if it be but a line every post to let me know how you do. I think I must wish it may be a son, because that sex is generally most acceptable to the gentlemen, but for *yours* and *my own sake* I shall be *glad if it is a daughter.* It is a great pleasure to me to hear my dear Penny is so well, the secretary she employ'd writes so well that her apology was needless; I reckon the diversions of the assize will take her up a day or two. When does Mrs. Eastcourt lye-in?—I hope she will not interfere with your ladyship.

My brains are so full of nonsensical election affairs, having heard of nothing else this week, that you must expect nothing entertaining from me. On Saturday our sweet Primrose comes, and she will, if 'tis possible to be done, inspire me with a little life and spirit; which the being drawn out into the world, and the breaking all our schemes of improving this place, and living quietly in this sweet retreat, have quite damped, for I grudge every penny spent in London, and look upon it as robbing the tenants and poor of what ought to be spent amongst them. I wish everybody that has property in this county were of the same opinion, Herefordshire would not be so desolate as it is, for the largest fortunes are *entirely returned out of it*. Our church is almost finished, but by the blunders of the workmen, and obstinacy of Mr. Wickins, it will not be so handsome as the draught, which vexes me extremely; I wish Mr. Foley had not had so much complaisance in the affair. He is gone to day to Hereford, it being sessions; he has not been at home a week together since we came from London, nor is likely to be till he goes thither again. Pray is not there in Gloucester a person that draws very neatly for eighteen pence a yard square?

You mention not a word of Mr. Dewes, I hope he is well wherever he is, and that his mother has recovered from her fall? My letter will consist of questions, but I must ask after Mr. Granville, and what part of the world he is in?

And now, my dear Mrs. Dewes, it is high time to release you, but I cannot do it till have assured you of the particular good wishes (proper at this time) of your friends here. Griffiths desires duty and wishes herself with you by way of *good woman*; my most humble service waits on your good mama, who I hope soon to congratulate on her new title, as also Madam Pen.

I am, your ever faithful and affectionate

E. FOLEY.

---

*The Hon*ble *Mrs. Foley to Mrs. Dewes.*

Newport, Sept. 4th, 1741.

I hope my dear Mrs. Dewes does not impute my being so long a time without my assuring her the sincere joy I have at her happy recovery to be owing to the least want of regard to her, but really I thought my stupid epistle would sooner lower your spirits than raise them, and therefore depended on the goodness and eloquence of my dear Penny to make you sensible how great a satisfaction it is to me the hearing of your being restored to us again in good health; and I hope she has done me justice to you. I never felt greater joy than at seeing a letter to Mrs. Foley, directed by your own hand. It gave me as much pleasure as I had pain when I knew you was in misery, but there are no roses without thorns. Were it possible for me to envy my sisters any pleasure in the world, I should their having the happiness of seeing my friends at Gloucester: and, how do I wish to see your little boy! His merit to me *now* is being *your son*, but I hope to live to see him have so much of his own, that I shall love him on his own account. I rejoice to hear by everybody who has seen him that he is so charming a child. Mr. Snell, who is now with us, tells me he has not yet seen him, but he tells me my dear cousin is but yet very weak.

I shall be very anxious till I hear of your gathering more strength, which I dare say you'll do daily when you come about in the air; for I know that till I went abroad and drank asses milk, I could not walk a quarter of a mile without tumbling two or three times, as Mrs. Pendarves may tell you—*witness, the kennel in Jermyn Street.* I fancy my sisters will be with you Wednesday or Thursday next; they are to set out the eighth. I go to-morrow to Stoke to meet them. I wait the post now every minute with great impatience, and shall be much baulked if your fair sister don't epistle me this post. I fear I shall be tempted to call her not a lady of her word, which I must do this instant, for the letters are come, and not one for me. Oh! fye for shame! Pray present my most humble service to Mrs. Granville and Mr. Dewes. Tell your sister I hear of her *flirting at balls*, which I suppose take up her time so much she can't spare a few minutes upon me; but I am much huffed at her tantalising me by promising a long letter. But wicked as she is, I am her sincere, humble servant, and yours, my dear Mrs. Dewes,

With the utmost affection,

G. FOLEY.

Pray what letters you favour me with next, direct to Stoke: I shall be there a fortnight. Both Mr. and Mrs. Foley are better than ever I saw them. Adieu.

Mrs. Pendarves to Mrs. Dewes.

19th January.

Not all the riches of "*the Nabob's wife*," could give me half the pleasure that my dearest sister's letters do. I have copied out (as I know you to be a curious lady,) a most extraordinary description of a fine lady, '*tis genuine*. This letter came about five months ago to a particular friend of Lady North's, who gave me leave to copy it for you.

Last Monday Mr. and Mrs. Percival, and Donnellan, and the two Granvilles, dined with me. We were all engaged to Lady Catherine Hanmer's. Just as I got into their coach to go there with them, the post brought me your letter, which burnt in my pocket; I set down the Percivals at Lady Cath., took the coach to Mrs. Hannah

Lowther's,[1] whom I luckily found at home and alone, and begged leave to read your letter, which was granted, and I enjoyed the rest of the evening with good spirits.

I rejoice and bear my part in the comfort and entertainment you have had from Sally, and wish it were convenient to her to continue with you, but I fear she is now gone, and Mr. Dewes upon the wing to leave you, and you an hundred miles from me, and no possibility of making you a winter's visit, or to be able to fly to you for a fortnight or so now and then! What a delight! a delight out of my reach, since you are and must be at such a distance. I think it not necessary for Mr. Dewes to hasten to town upon what I have said; if he comes to term that will be time enough. Old G. snapped my nose off for saying I had sent for him, she said "she would give it under her hand and seal that she would lose no opportunity of serving you and him, but all preferments were uncertainties, and she would not give too much encouragement for fear of not succeeding." My brother thinks it probable she may do something, but she is mother to ——, and he is a broken reed! I am glad you have got our little god-daughter[2] Sally; I hope she will improve from your advice, and *by all means curb her* if she is *too forward in giving her opinions*; a conceited man or woman is *abominable*, but a conceited girl is *insupportable*. Conceit or opinionativeness becomes no sex or age: those that know the world *most* make a *bad figure* with it, those that have *not* had

---

[1] Hannah, youngest daughter of Alderman Lowther. She was Maid of Honour to Queens Mary and Anne, and died in 1757, at the age of a hundred and three.

[2] Sarah, daughter to Mrs. Chapon, to whom both Mary and Ann Granville were godmothers.

an opportunity of seeing the world *are ridiculous with it.* It ought to be *rooted out betimes;* it is a weed that otherwise will choke the most delicate qualities of the mind. I should be most heartily rejoiced if Sally's observations on the poor sick child might be depended on, and in truth young children will get the better of very long illnesses. If he holds out till spring, Cheltenham waters will certainly do well for him; I have not much to say of Smart's skill, I fear his medicine hastened my poor George,[1] to her end.

Fine ladies will be fine ladies everywhere; when it is amongst their like it is very well, and is not distinguished so as to give great offence; but at Cheltenham and such places, (where the sober and sedate are terrified at any extraordinary word or action,) it shews extravagance, and tis only seeing the great variety of the world that can make one patiently bear the violent affectations of great part of it. I own I am not offended at those things—they would hurt me if those I love were guilty of them, but in others it diverts me like an odd character in a play. Our friend Dr. Young, as you have lately observed, has helped us much on these occasions; but if all the world were prudent and regular in their behaviour, it would not be half so diverting as it is now.

To-day I dine with Lady Sunderland, in the afternoon go to Fidget Montagu[2] and Lady North. To-morrow at ten to dress the Duchess of Portland, and in the evening, if I can get into the Duke of Grafton's gallery, Donnellan, my brother, and myself design to go to the

---

[1] From this sentence it appears that the *faithful George* had died between Mrs. Pendarves' visit to Gloucester, to nurse Mrs. Dewes, in the summer and autumn, and the following January.

[2] "*Fidget Montagu.*" Miss Robinson.

ball at St. James's. If I have time to finish the other page I will not send it unsullied, *if you will accept of* the nabob's lady, who I hope will entertain you.

I saw Mrs. Montagu yesterday; she looks handsome, fat, and merry; she is in excellent spirits and very happy, and talks of "*her young family*" as cordially as if she had been married five years; I hope her good spirits will hold out, for she will want them before all is over. I supped at Lady Sunderland's, after making my visit to Lady North, who always enquires after you; I think Miss Sutton grows every day more agreeable in her conversation, but she has a *melancholy turn*, and tenderness of heart, that give me some anxiety about her: two nights ago as she passed through Grosvenor Square, she saw a hearse and funeral attendants, which affected her so much, when she considered the distress there might be in the house where it was, that she came home to my lady Sunderland all in tears. She loves very few, but has a general compassion in her nature, and those she does love she doats on; you are one of her favourites. The coach is come, now for curling, tiffing, &c., &c., &c., &c. Our Duchess will be almost as fine as the nabob's lady, and infinitely more valuable.

The following MS. was sent by Mrs. Pendarves to her sister, with an account of the marvellous jewels which adorned the wife of a certain nabob, the account of which had been transmitted by a friend from Madras. "The Moorish lady" herein described is alluded to in the preceding letter, in a manner which would indicate that she was a personage who had been publicly mentioned. Neither the letter nor the narrative have any date beyond the 19th of January, but it seems probable that it belonged to the year 1742.

"We have had a great man called the *Nabob*, (who is the next person in dignity to the Great Mogul) to visit the Governor, who, with the councillors and all the chief gentlemen of Madras, went in great state to meet him. His lady, with all her women attendance, came the night before him. All the guns fired round the fort upon her arrival as well as on his; *he* and *she* are Moors, whose women are never seen by any man upon earth excepting their husbands. He staid there about a fortnight, but his lady remains here in the Black Town still. His attendants consisted of many thousands of people. The Governor waited on him at his house in the Black Town, and he returned the visit to the Governor. All the ladies in the town went to see him go; it was a fine procession of palankeens, and he is a fine man in person. The riches of his dress with pearls and diamonds is beyond description. He sent the Governor a fine present in a large filligrane silver box placed on the back of a fine Moorish horse adorned with all manner of fine gold and velvet trappings, and I believe nearly a thousand horse and foot people to attend it. After he left Madras Mrs. Binyon (the Governor's lady) went to visit his lady. The Governor was so obliging to write to me over night to invite me and your sisters to go with Mrs. Binyon the next morning to visit this great lady. We drest ourselves in the very best of everything we had, and went to the Governor's, where we breakfasted, and found Mrs. Binyon *as fine as a queen*. The Governor made tea for us, that we might not put ourselves out of form. Mrs. Beard (who is sister-in-law to the Governor) and her daughters made up the rest of the company.

We had all the Governor's attendants as well as his lady's, and his music playing before us all the way, and thousands of people looking at us as we passed; we had about a mile to go. When we arrived, Mrs. Binyon was handed by a lady who was to introduce her through two halls, which brought us into a large garden, and presented her to the *Nabob's* lady, who was seated in the middle of a pavilion at the end of the garden upon a settee covered with rich embroidery upon crimson velvet; embroidered carpets hung all over it and went under their feet. She received us with the utmost gentility, and paid her proper compliments to us all.

"I must now give you a description of her person and dress, as well as I can. Her person slim, genteel, and middle-sized; her complexion tawny, as all the Moors are; her eyes as black as possible, large and fine, and painted at the edges, which is what most of the Moors do; her lips painted red, and between every tooth, which were fine and regular, she was painted black, to look like ebony. All her attendants, which were about thirty ladies, were the same; her face was done over like frosted work with leaf gold; the nails of her fingers and feet (for she was bare-footed) were painted red, and likewise the inside of her hands. You will perhaps think this a strange description, but I assure you it is literally true. And now for her dress; her hair was as black as jet, very long and thick, which was combed neatly back, and then braided till it hung a great deal below her waist; she had a fillet of diamonds round her head, edged with pearls of a large size; her earrings were as broad as my hand, made of diamonds and pearls, so that they almost covered each side of her face; she had a nose jewel that went through her left nostril; round her neck she had *twenty rows* of pearl, none less than a pea, but some *as large as* the *end of my little finger*, from her necklace there hung a great number of rows of large pearl, which came down below her waist; at the end of which hung an emerald *as large as my hand and as thick*; her coat was made of fine gold muslin, made close to her, and a short sleeve; a gold vail hung loosely over her head, and the rest went over her body,— all the front of it was trimmed with a row of *large pearls*. She had a girdle, or rather a large hoop, made of diamonds, which went round her waist; it was above an inch broad; several strings of large pearls were tyed round her waist, and hung down almost to her knees, and great knots of pearls at ye end of them; ten rows of pearls round her wrists, and ten round her arms, a little above her elbows, and her fingers every one adorned with rings of all sorts and sizes; her feet and ancles were adorned much finer, *if possible,* than her hands and arms. In short, Mrs. Beard and myself concluded she had many *more* pearls and diamonds than would fill a *peck measure!* Some of the ladies who attended her were as fine as herself; she had her little son brought in to see us; the riches of his dress were I to describe, you would imagine it some fairy story. He was adorned and loaded with pearls and diamonds; the very fan that was carried to keep off the sun from him (and in make like a round fire-screen, only four times as large) was crimson velvet set in figures with *diamonds and pearls.* I own I thought myself in a dream all the time I was there.

"I must now give you a description of the pavilion, which was very large, and all the bottom covered with

fine carpets, and entirely hung round with muslin, and
the same all over the inside of the roof, with a deep
valance in the middle. In one corner there stood her
bed (or cot, as we call it); the frame-work and pillars
of it were *solid gold*, and gold gauze curtains, and a rich
counterpane, several fine dressing-tables with large filligrane candlesticks upon them. At the entrance of the
pavilion there was a long embroidered velvet cushion,
with a pillow of the same at each end; this was opposite
to the settee the lady sat upon. For us to walk under there
was something like an awning made of crimson silk,
which went all on the outside of the pavilion, and was
supported with pillars of gold. We had two golden
censers of incense and sandal-wood which almost suffo-
cated us with the perfume. Our entertainment was tea,
that seemed to be made with rose-water and cinnamon—
everything served in plate; then we had betel brought
us in fine filligrane boxes made of gold upon large scol-
lopped silver waiters, which we *liked better* than what was
in them, for the betel is a large green leaf which the
Indians chew, of an intoxicating nature, and very disagreeable to the English; but we were forced to comply
with that out of compliment. After this was over we
saw a large silver board brought covered with a worked
carpet, which was presented uncovered to Mrs. Binyon.
There was a fine Moor's coat and a couple of rich veils,
and to each of us a present of a Moor's coat and a gold
veil. The Nabob's lady put Mrs. Binyon's on; so we,
in compliment, put on ours, with which she was pleased;
and we came back to the Governor's in ours, where we
dined and spent the evening. The Nabob's lady sent
an entertainment *after us*, which consisted of *sixty dishes*

all under silver covers, and put up in scarlet cloth bags
made for that purpose; the Governor's lady made a present of an hundred pagodas to her attendants. The
Nabob's lady and her attendants admired us all, but
thought our dress very odd. Two of the ladies examined
my dress till they came to the hoop petticoat, which
they were much astonished at; they much admired my
tweezers and the trinkets that were in them. To conclude all, we were the first English women they had
ever seen; and I doubt not but we appeared as odd to
them as they to us. Their immense riches are all the
enjoyment they have; for she is not suffered to go out
all the year round, and when obliged to travel is covered
up in her palankeen in such a manner that no mortal
can see her—and it would be death for any man to
attempt to see a Moor's lady."

Mr. Dewes to Mrs. Dewes.

Clement's-Inn, 10 March, 1742.

My dear Love,

I had your kind letter of the 5th instant, and am
glad to hear you have so well recovered your journey,
and hope you are now quite well again. I have not yet
parted with any of my teeth, though I have suffered much
from them since I wrote last, but I dined with your
brother on Monday, and he persuaded me against having
any drawn, as they are quite sound.

Mr. Granville is very well, and desires his compliments
to Gloucester. I am very glad the little boy is so stout,
and is such a comfort to you, but hope he has lost his

cough.[1] I don't yet know when I shall be with you, but believe it will be on Saturday se'nnight, so do you order about going home as you see fit. I will not write to Charles, nor give any directions about it, lest I should hurry you from Gloucester before you designed, but whenever you have an inclination to go I'll be ready to attend you,—so you may forecast about that as you please. I dined at Mr. Percivall's on Sunday; they are all pretty well there, and inquired after you. Your brother sent to invite me to dine with him on Monday, which I did, and told him the history of the old Countess[2] (I mean in regard to myself), and he says it is all a joke.

Madam Pen came to town yesterday to see or rather hear the oratorio, and sent me word she should be at home about one, so I went to see her, and we sat and talked or looked at our accounts for about half an hour, and then I came away. She had the headache, I the toothache, so that we were but ill qualified to entertain each other. I find she wrote you word I had been with the Countess since I saw her, but that was a mistake, occasioned by what Mrs. Donnellan had told her; Mrs. Pendarves said I should go see the Countess again before I went out of town, and I seemed not inclined to it, upon which she took me up *pretty short*, as you know she is sometimes apt to do; so then I *drew back a little*, for one you know must give way, and I think I have now learnt to do that pretty readily, though it seemed a little awkward at first; so the argument dropped, but I believe I shall practise in

---

[1] Court Dewes, his eldest son, who succeeded him and inherited the family estates.
[2] Countess Granville.

this particular something of what I have *learnt from
you*, that is, to say little, and then do what I think best.
I am, with the truest sincerity and affection,
Most heartily and entirely yours, J. D.

The Duchess of Portland to Mrs. Dewes.

MY DEAR PIP, No date.

I insisted upon writing to you to-day, which I
think you have no reason to thank me for, as I have
prevented your having a letter from Pen, but I could
not longer refrain giving myself this pleasure, and in
some measure expressing my gratitude to you for your
delightful epistle; besides this must be very short, for I
must dine with Lady Waw,[1] and I expect the Duchess of
Leeds and Mrs. Walters to see my shells, and am
to spend the evening with Lady Bute, if she is not in
labour. Lord Edgecombe[2] has kissed hands, and Earl
Fitzwilliam[3] is made Baron Milton. Poor Mrs. Foley
is very ill, her bad symptoms increase; I am very glad
you are so soon to be happy with Mrs. Granville's company; I hope you will find her soon recover apace with
bracing air. The Duchess of Cleveland's[4] death was

---

[1] "*Lady Waw.*" The only suggestion that occurs as an explanation of this curious abbreviation, is that it was the name by which Lady Wallingford was called by the children of the Duchess of Portland.

[2] *Richard Edgcumbe*, Esq., was elevated to the peerage, April 20, 1742, as Baron Edgcumbe.

[3] William, 3rd Earl Fitzwilliam, in Ireland, was enrolled amongst the peers of Great Britain, by George II., 19th April, 1742, in the dignity of *Lord Fitzwilliam, Baron Milton*, county Northampton.

[4] Lady Henrietta Finch, sister of the Earl of Winchelsea, wife of William Duke of Cleveland. "The Duchess of Cleveland died last night of what they call miliary fever, which is much about; she had not been ill two days."—*Horace Walpole's Letters*, April 15, 1742.

very sudden, some say her own neglect, and others the fault of the physicians; the old woman has got the care of her son again. The children are all very well, beg their loves to Pip. Bill is *the happiest of creatures* in breeches. I shall be late, so adieu, dear Pip, heaven bless you, and believe me,

Affectionately and faithfully yours,

M. PORTLAND.

My compliments attend Mrs. Dewes. My Lord is gone to Cottenham.

Aspasia's Picture, drawn by Philomel, in the year 1742.

You know, madam, that Mrs. P— is of a most agreeable figure, and you may believe that (as it is above twenty years since she was married) the bloom she still enjoys, the modest sprightliness of her eyes, the shining delicacy of *her hair*, the sweetness of her smile, the pleasing air of her whole countenance, must have made her the desire of all who saw her, and her situation (as a widow) must have given hopes to all. She was married *extremely* young to a man who neither by his years, behaviour, nor any quality he was possessed of, was fitted to gain her affection; she had naturally a *great deal of vivacity* and liveliness of temper, with the greatest sensibility and tenderness of heart. *Some* of her nearest relations were ever ready to have encouraged in her every tendency towards gaiety. What could have guarded her in these dangerous circumstances? An *innate modesty*, an *early prudence*, and a *discerning judgment* to know what was right, *with virtue*, and only to follow what her judgment approved,—these were the qualities that have carried her through the gayest companies, the most dangerous scenes, with an unsullied fame, and have made even those who would have undermined her virtue pay homage to it. Her modesty is not that unbecoming bashfulness which is so often mistaken for it—her's is the *modesty of the mind*, which is so far from giving awkwardness to the person or behaviour, that it adds a grace to everything that she says or does. And as her modesty does not proceed from bashfulness, so her prudence does *not consist in formality* or reserve as if she feared both herself or others, but she has a propriety of behaviour in every company that lets them see she thinks she has no reason to fear either herself or them, and by shewing this confidence in herself she takes from others the desire of attacking her; or if there have been some who have had the folly or the assurance to make such an attempt, she has soon made them sensible of the vanity of their designs, and convinced them that the easiness of her behaviour proceeds from the purity of her heart, not the levity of her mind.

I am at a loss what terms to find strong enough to express her general benevolence or her particular tenderness to her friends; her benevolence is so strong it should seem as if she looked upon the whole world as her friends, and her tenderness to every particular friend so great as to fill up the measure of a whole heart. Where can she find this fund of affection? She subtracts it from self-love, that principle that fills the heart of others, and the only person to whom she does not give more than their due is the worthiest that she knows—*I mean herself*. Her generosity naturally flows from her benevolence; she gives as not knowing she gives, and the joy she has in pleasing others persuades one she is more obliged to us for accepting her favours than we can be to her for bestowing them; while the great desire she has to make others happy, never lets her think she has a right either to keep or endeavour at any advantage for herself, if there is any friend she imagines wants or desires it more than she does; and in this examination she is so partial to her friends as to be very apt to cast the balance against herself. I remember a friend of hers said one day to her " she had no merit in doing good, as she had so much pleasure in it;" but surely if we will not allow her a human merit, we must give her a higher one? As her generosity to her friends flows from her benevolence, so does her charity both to the wants and character of her fellow-creatures; the first she relieves with a bounty above her circumstances, and the latter she defends (when decency will permit) with a zeal equal to the amiable principle from whence it proceeds. She does not think that being perfect herself gives her a title to animadvert on the faults or laugh at the follies of those less worthy, but would rather choose to seem to want penetration to find out the first, or wit to ridicule the latter, than to hurt those who can make no reprisals on her.

I need not, madam, to you describe the agreeableness of her manners, the politeness of her behaviour, or the *winning grace* that is in all her words and actions; a small acquaintaince with her makes one desire a greater, and a greater makes one almost wish she was not so agreeable to others that we might have her more to ourselves; so that instead of improving by her example we grow more selfish by knowing her. To this imperfect sketch of her mind I must add something on her many accomplishments and her great ingenuity; and here we should wonder how she has found time to make herself mistress of so many ingenious arts, if we did not consider that dress and the adorning of the person that takes up so great a part of that of most of our sex, only employs so much of hers as the exactest neatness requires, and that she has an activity of mind that *never lets her be idle*, as all her hours are employed either in something useful or amusing. She reads to improve her mind, not to make an appearance of being learned; she writes with all the delicacy and ease of a woman, and the strength and correctness of a man; she paints and takes views of what is either beautiful or whimsical in nature with a surprising genius and art. She is a mistress of the harpsichord, and has a brilliancy in her playing peculiar to herself; she does a number of works and of many of them is the inventor, and all her acquaintance are her copyers—happy for them if they would equally endeavour to imitate her virtues. As these accomplishments are her amusements she treats them as such, and sets no value on herself for excelling in them, but is always ready to teach others and desirous they should excel her, but those wishes are fruitless.

Her house is a little abstract of all sorts of ingenuity, and like her heart is ever open to the virtuous, to the ingenious, or to the distressed—those are the titles to her friendship or protection, and except in one instance,[1] where her partiality has swayed beyond her judgment, she has been as distinguished in bestowing the first as generous in dispensing the latter.

---

[1] This no doubt was intended to denote herself—Mrs. Donnellan.

I could enlarge on all these particulars much more, but I consider I detain you too long from the pleasing entertainment of observing the actions of one whose whole life will better show you that charity and benevolence have been the gales that have filled the sails, and judgement and prudence the pilots that have directed her course.

"*The character*" here given of Mrs. Pendarves, under the name of *Aspasia*, must have been written by Mrs. Donnellan at Bulstrode, for the Duchess of Portland, when the friends were all together, and given by the Duchess to Mrs. Dewes when she left Bulstrode. The delicacy and feeling with which it is expressed, and the exact manner in which all the remarkable points in the history and disposition as well as talents of Mary Granville are touched and described, cannot be read without a conviction of the sincerity of the writer. Mrs. Donnellan here justifies the opinion entertained of her abilities by Dr. Swift, with whom she occasionally corresponded, and by whom she was always mentioned with honour and respect. It must not be forgotten that Mrs. Donnellan wrote this character of Aspasia at a period when the Dean of St. Patrick was continually commenting upon the absence of either good English or anything like an attempt at good spelling in the majority of the fine ladies of the day, and when in alluding to one of his correspondents about the Court, who had superior mental endowments and a very cultivated understanding, he says that "*she wrote and spelt like a Wapping wench.*"

Mrs. Pendarves to Mrs. Dewes (at Mrs. Pendarves's), Charges Street, Piccadilly.

Bulstrode, from my lonely room,
Sunday night.

True love sets one above the scoffs of the world, and whilst I gratify my heart, I bid defiance to the Duke's jokes, Mr. Du Poivré's comments, and the Counsellor's sneer. What!—write when you have been parted but six hours? I did not imagine there was so much in this short separation as I feel there is. You are wanted in the breakfast-room, dining-room, chapel, etc., missed by everybody! What, then, are my thoughts? particularly in my own apartment, which looks like a dark cavern without you. Our most amiable Duchess has indulged me in talking of you, though we have had but little time. It was three o'clock before church was over; *there*, my dearest sister, I called you to my rememberance in a particular manner,—with most ardent prayers for your happiness, and with the most grateful thanksgivings for the great blessing of your friendship. My good wishes extended to every branch that could increase your felicity, and Mr. Dewes and the dear little boy, you may believe, had no small share. I hope your journey was easy; as for entertainment on the road, your remembrance of those you left, and the joy of the dear friend you went to see, amply made up the dulness of your companion, who was not qualified to please, no more than improve. But this is ungratefully said of me, and I have a great mind to blot it out, but that will make a sad blur in my letter, for to give *Cymon* his due, he is *civil* though *not bright*, and I ought only to pity what is a defect in nature, and value him for his good will; but he has taken up almost as much of my letter as he did of the coach. You and I committed a great error in not asking him to dine at my house: I am in hopes you recollected on the road that it would be the right thing, and asked him. I long to know what hour you got to town,—*how you like my house?*—if it is warm and comfortable? I am so unreasonable as to be impatient to know every thought about it: and there is a mixture of *love and vanity* in that wish. I take it for granted I make a considerable figure there; and who can blame me if I glory in it? At breakfast the newspapers employed us all, the Sovereign sympathized with me, and we both indulged a silence more agreeable than speaking. Since dinner we have had the usual circle round the fire, and the dear children, who all asked me for "*Pip.*" Lord Titchfield bid me give you "*his love*" and "*his duty*,"

I have many reasons, you know, to wish for Tuesday-morning; but the strongest is the hopes of hearing from your most faithful and affectionate,

M. P.

My very kind service to Mr. Dewes. Tell Sir John *you are* my letter to him; I will not trouble him with a scrawl, since I shall see him so soon. I hope you have seen my dear Donnellan, and found her well. I am sure she was glad to see you and Lady Sunderland. Don't forget the needles; the hook for the D— is to be bated with an eel; I hope we shall catch a fine dish of gudgeons.

From this letter it appears that Mrs. Dewes had just left Bulstrode, and had gone on to her sister's new abode in Clarges Street.

Mrs. Pendarves to Mrs. Dewes.

From Fidget's[1] Fireside.
(Bulstrode.)

The Duke has been much out of order to-day with the gout, not only in his foot but I fear something of it in his stomach, for he has complained of a pain there and been very sick; that, and Fidget's keeping her room to-

---

[1] Mrs. Montagu, (Miss Robinson).

day, has taken up my time so much, that I am reduced to one poor half-hour to speak to my dear sister in, for I have been nurse to both. The Duke is much better this evening, and our amiable Duchess pretty well, but her gentle spirits are soon discomposed when those she loves suffer. Thanks to you for your letters; I am glad you like my house; you will stamp such a value on it to me, by making it useful to you, that I would not exchange it for the Treasury. I rejoice at your finding my brother Dewes so well; it grieves me to turn him out, but I shall insist on his returning as soon as I have settled my household, for in truth I cannot bear to have you out of my house; but more of this when we meet.

Well—never did plot succeed better than ours; 'tis well we *are legal*, or we might do a wondrous deal of mischief. Mr. *Hachard*[1] swears we all clubbed into it; that *I wrote it out*, and your *clerk* (as he calls him) wrote the *direction;* (for he *is sure* I could not write such a hand). The Senator Elect and the Counsellor were very prim, and said not a word about their packets, but to-night Mr. H. threw a farthing upon the table, and said I blushed at the sight of it, though I stoutly denied it. A word or two has been thrown out of *bobs* and *tyes*, but the letters not produced. The Duke's not being well, and another affair, put us out of sorts to-day, and prevented our mirth from rising very high. A letter came from Lord D——n by a special messenger to desire Lord G. B. to stand candidate for Westminster; many wise ministerial reasons laid down, which staggered his Lordship's resolution, but *a Deborah* stepped in and gave her opinion so wisely and in such strong terms,

---

[1] Mr. Achard, an imitation of the mispronunciation of some illiterate person.

that it was resolved to reject the proposal, and to stand by Droitwych. Don't mention this to anybody but Mr. Dewes, for I don't think it right to spread family news. The particulars of what has passed are too long for a letter; our judicious friend has acted like herself; it was a nice affair, and required skill to manage.

The fair Dash has taken your place in my apartment; she is much concerned at losing your company. I have enclosed you my mother's letter: what can have become of my guinea? I suppose you wrote to her on Monday? I shall write next Thursday. This will not allow me to say more than that all here—men, women, and children—are devoted to you; be very careful of yourself. Make my proper compliments to all friends, and love me ever as I love you.'

Mrs. Pendarves to Mrs. Dewes (at Mrs. Pendarves's), in Clarges Street, Piccadilly.

Bulstrode, Breakfast room fire-side.

The Duke and Lord George[1] are stringing pearl, the Duchess, Dash, and Fidget[2] writing; and I having the temptation of the pen, ink, and paper, the Duke has just done with, so cannot forbear thanking my most dear sister for her charming letter, that warmed me in the midst of snow; but I shall not attempt answering it in full, nor lay you under an obligation of writing me a long letter at a time that you have a variety of affairs on your hands. I am sure my house must please me, since you approve of it; but you don't tell me if it smells of paint. The Duke of Portland had a very good night, and is

---

[1] Lord George Bentinck.   [2] Mrs. Montagu.

much better to-day. I hope the pain will not return, if it should it will be very inconvenient at this time, and may stop there journey; pray send as soon as you can to Mr. Tubbs, and order him to send me down a very good coach and four horses with side-glasses; it must be here on Saturday night, to carry me to town on Sunday. I don't know yet where I am to dine, but you shall have notice in time; the *Gudgeons* have not yet produced the packets, but *whisper* and *simper*.

I have drawn out a very awkward beau in a full bottomed wig, and a man looking over a pedigree, with his three clients at his feet offering him a farthing, which I design to throw on the green table at tea-time; for we shall lose our sport if we do not laugh at them.

Tea is come, I am called, and can only say I am yours ever.

The Honble. *Mrs. Foley to Mrs. Dewes.*

Newport, June 14th, 1742.

I am much obliged to dear Mrs. Dewes for a very kind letter. My design of waiting on you, could I have put it into execution, would have made me very happy; for it really would be great pleasure to me once more to enjoy the conversation of my friends and relations, but in my present situation I must only be beholden to the newspaper; and *could I believe* that *that* intelligence knew more of *my own family* and *bosom-friends than I do* by any other authority, I should now wish my dear cousin much joy of her sister's wedding, which I hope may be attended with all happiness; and I think the newsmonger has reported the *admirer of David* to have acted *like a Solomon!* Whatever name she bears, I hope you'll soon have the pleasure of her company. Perhaps *this news* may be what you mean in part of your letter, "*an extraordinary event has retarded her;*" not that I presume to ask what those are, for as you are not left at liberty to divulge it to me, I am sure on no account you would betray the secrets of another. For I think no crime can be worse than unfaithfulness to the trust of our friends, and I call to mind with great gratitude that in what regards yourself you show me the strongest mark of your friendship by *your confidence in me*, or else *you* would have been married many months before I should have known it. But I was in great hopes when *the secret* was *known* to all the world I might have had a private letter to have *accompanied the newspaper*; and till then I *shall give no credit to the report*. Nor have I mentioned to any mortal even the little hint I have been favoured with, and indeed it caused me some diversion, though I was in a great flutter of spirits, when the paper was opened, to see how Mr. Foley (who poor man met with it first) and his son and daughter stared at each other, and cried out to me, "*You are secret indeed.*" I assured them very truly, I was not worthy of so great a commendation, for I *was never trusted*, which they would not believe, and I got high applause from your cousin Foley for what I really did not deserve. I thank God he is a man of so much honour, that were my inclination ever so bad, I should never dare betray the secret of my friend without forfeiting his good opinion.

Miss Foley desires me to add her brother's compliments to you and Mr. Dewes; my humble service waits on Mrs. Granville; the last I heard from my sister was that in August she would make me a visit. Perhaps I may see in the *next papers that she is married*, for it is several posts since I heard. May all happiness attend *the happy pair*, but not I hope more then to you,
Ma très chère cousine,
G. FOLEY.

The Editor has been unable to find the report of Mrs. Pendarves's marriage, or intended marriage, in any of the papers of the day. But it certainly was a false rumour, for she was not married that year, and there is no allusion to any idea or intention of the sort; although Mrs. Foley had evidently read it in a newspaper, where it must have appeared to be authentic, or she would not have believed it. "*The extraordinary event*" was probably only some joke or jeu d'esprit in which she was engaged at Bulstrode.

The Duchess of Portland to Mrs. Dewes.
June 22nd, 1742.

My dear Pip will, I hope, never think my silence has been occasioned by forgetfulness, for had I wrote as often as I have thought of you, I should have tired you with dull epistles. I have two charming letters by me of my dear friend's, and you know well the hurry I live in, and more particularly for this last month—so many people going out of town, that I have been much taken up. I have hardly had a tête-à-tête with Penny this fortnight. I shall not go to Welbeck till August; I believe mama will be in town in about ten days. Since I wrote this I have seen Pen, and am quite troubled my dear Pip should think my silence long and unkind; I am sure it was not meant so. I am rejoiced to hear *Master* is better, I hope to God he will perfectly recover; I beg you will keep up your spirits as much as is possible; consider what you owe Mr. Dewes and the rest of your friends.

I wish I could tell you anything that could amuse you. Mr. Northey was married on Sunday to the youngest Miss Viner; they made a grand figure. The eldest daughter [1] was much disappointed that she should *dance bare-foot*, and *desired her father* to find out a match for her. With great pains they produced Mr. Pelham, fifty years older than her. He insisted it should be put in the marriage-articles, that she should never come to London or wear jewels, which conditions she readily complied with rather than to be disappointed of a husband. Pen's affair at C— I can't say I like the appearance of at present; I wish Lord C— does not *play the minister* with her which will be abominable if he does, but it is so like their old principles, that one can't help suspecting them.

I am very glad you had the incomparable Princess[2] with you, I am sure her conversation must have been of service, but that *detestable companion* is really terrible to all her acquaintance.

My best compliments attend Mrs. Granville, and be assured, whether I write or not, my mind is still the same

---

[1] Married in June, 1742, William Northey, Esq., grandson to the late Sir Edward Northey, Knt., Attorney-General, to Miss Vyner, daughter to Robert Vyner, Esq., knight of the shire for the county of Lincoln.—*London Magazine*.

[2] The Honourable Mrs. Foley.

to my dear friend. I hope I shall have the pleasure of seeing Mr. Dewes soon.

Your faithful and affectionate
M. PORTLAND.

Mrs. Pendarves to Mrs. Dewes.
Calwich, 10 Sept. 1742.

Most welcome was Thomas on Tuesday night about eight o'clock, when he brought my dearest sister's letter, and a good account of yours and my mother's performance of your journey so far; happy will be the hour that brings us as good news from Gloucester. Our good dear brother bids me make his respects and kind service acceptable.

I will not now indulge myself in lamenting the dissolution of our agreeable society. I will think of it with thankfulness as a blessing bestowed that I had no expectance of, and therefore have no right to murmur at its being past; but at present I have no reason to complain, for, except the want I must always have of your's and my dear mama's company when you are absent, I live just as I could wish to do; have much business, many amusements, a pleasant house, charming fields, and a companion that, you know better than I can tell you, crowns all by his friendly and agreeable manner. I must, for fear of accidents, say 'tis *my brother* that makes me thus happy; for should my letter fall into any hands but yours, it is very likely a brother would be the *last* person thought of! The moment your equipage had whirled you out of sight (for my brother and I watched you from the garden) we trapesed all over *Babylon garden,* went to the *workhouse,* and happily met the smith who brought home the grate for my room; Robin Parker was immediately set to work, and I matched the tiles, so that between us, and in the compass of two days, we have finished a very pretty chimney, my brother overlooking us all. Mr. Prince has finished the cupboard at the end of the closet, but things are reversed to what they were designed, and behold the door openeth into my mother's closet *instead* of the other way, and that which was designed to be a closet at my mother's bed head, is to be one to the *other room*. We have some expectation of the paper coming on Saturday to perfect our works, and if it does, we propose leaving Calwich on Tuesday se'night, the one and twentieth. The new wall is almost built up, and the covings are now putting up in the little parlour, hardly a room in the house, or a foot out of doors, is free from workmen. I propose making a visit at Snellston next Sunday, for we labourers can't make visits on working-days, and on Monday to go to Ashbourne to see Mrs. Fitzherbert, and to go to the Assembly.

Miss Robinson to Mrs. Pendarves.

ye 16th.

If every fault was to have as agreeable a consequence as that which I committed in not writing to you, I am afraid I should make a resolution never to do right again as long as I lived. Had you returned me thanks for a letter *I* had wrote, I should have thought it done out of your wonted courtesy and good-breeding, but this *complaint* I do and will think down right love and kindness; and if it is an error, it tends more to my happiness than any of the few right opinions I have gained, and I will cherish it as the prettiest imagination I ever had in my head. But certainly you love me, for *you say so*, and you are sincere, and I can prove your love to me out of *your* good qualities, though *not out of my own.* " *Madam* " certainly makes a magnificent figure at the beginning of a letter; and " Devoted humble servant," brings matters to a polite conclusion; but " *Fidget* " and " *Friend* " sound more affectionately and much better from my dear Mrs. Pendarves, though with some people *I would be* " Madam," " Honoured Madam," or " Your Reverence," or anything that *assured me* they would treat with the most distant respect they could; but ceremony is the tribute of civility and not of friendship.

You are very right not to anticipate our day; we do not appear at *Phebus's Levér.* After breakfast we employ ourselves as you imagine; we are reading Sir Philip Sidney's famous Romance, which is *far exceeding* the *exceedingness* of the most *exceeding imagination*, as if, the things of which he spoke *exceeded* all imagination, or the imagination with which he wrote *exceeded* all things; so much more *excellent* are the things of which he writes as that the things which he writes are far *exceeding* all other excellence, for art therein does borrow the appearance of nature, and nature the excellence of art, so the eye doth not know whether to praise skilful art or happy chance therein, but surely both together does greatly delight the mind's eye, and work in the beholder a goodly admiration! Seriously it is pity, two such excellent geniuses in Queen Elizabeth's days as Spenser and Sir Philip should write of only such feigned and imaginary beings as fairies and lovers; now that the world is not superstitious and credulous, such personages are not so well received as they used to be. We do not only remember you *in our happy hours,* but the *remembrance* of you *gives us hours!* Surely *by mimicry* I *have fallen* into the style of Sir Philip; but to you I need speak no language but the language of the heart to assure you I am your very sincere and faithful friend,

ELIZA ROBINSON.[1]

P.S. The Duchess desires her love and service, and hopes you and Miss Granville have received her letters. Her Grace suffered much for the little dears; and when *she is grieved I possess no comfort,* and so can bestow none. Thank God, they are now well. I beg my compliments to Miss Granville.

The above letter was evidently in reply to one from Mrs. Pendarves reproaching Miss Robinson for not having written to her, and proposing (with her correspondent's approval as in the case of Ann Granville and "*the Fair Kitty*" Collingwood), to give up "Madam," and to call her "*Friend,*" or "*Fidget.*" The intimacy of Mrs. Pendarves and Miss Robinson was of early date. They

---

[1] The Editor discovered, too late to rectify the error, that this letter ought to have been inserted to 5th August, 1742, at which time she was married to Mr. Montagu.

lived in the same set till the death of the former, who was Miss Robinson's senior, and both were especially intimate with the Duchess of Portland and Mrs. Donnellan. Although it is impossible not to admire the cleverness of Miss Robinson and her power of expression, yet her letters give the impression of sense and reason being often sacrificed to make a *point* or to *round a period*. In the present epistle the well-sounding sentence of "ceremony being the tribute of civility but not of friendship," conveys the idea that there *could* be *no friendship* where ceremony existed: whereas the respectful form of address which for years had been customary between them had been no obstacle to their increasing regard; and experience proves that the flippant and familiar style so often adopted in the present age frequently prevents the formation of any friendship or causes its destruction—whilst the increased disregard to any proper established forms in writing is attended by many inconveniences without any one advantage.

Mrs. Pendarves to Mrs. Dewes.

(Part of a letter, postmark 13, Se.)

(Calwich.)

No letters came by yesterday's post; Tuesday was so rainy I could not walk out. On Wednesday Thomas gave us notice of a *hare sitting*, so out we all sallied with deadly designs, and poor puss was caught in the field next the west field; from thence when our sport was over we went a *moss gathering*, and were caught in a smart shower of rain, came home in a fine daggled condition, but comforted ourselves soon with a good fire and tea. Has not the weather been cold even to you? here it has been very sharp, and we have had fires every day, and if Mr. Dewes had been here he could not have stood by the pond side for three hours together! *The fish leap for joy that he is gone*,[1] and they are the only animals that can have cause to rejoice at his absence. I have not yet wrote one of the twelve letters I was to have written this week. My tenderest love attends you, my most dear sister. I beg my humble duty to dear mama, and my service to Mr. Dewes.

The Duchess of Portland to Mrs. Dewes.

Welbeck, Sep., 20th.

My dear Pip, I was in hopes to have thanked you yesterday for the very kind letter I received that day, but it was impossible, for time is as precious as if I was in London. You rejoiced me greatly with telling me you bore your journey so well; was impatient to hear it, as I must be for everything that concerns your welfare. I am sorry to a great degree that our dearest Pen still continues to have a cough, I wish she would drink asses milk, but I am sure if you can't persuade her it is not in my power to effect it. I am quite of your mind, and heartily wish you may be well in your bed before she gets to you. I must beg you will wear hareskins; they are the most comfortable things in the world. We got here perfectly well. My Lord has had a little fit of the gout, but he is now almost well, and I hope he will have no more returns; the two eldest girls travelled with us, they were very diverting, and the little ones no sort of trouble. I hope to write to Mrs. Duncombe this post, but if it is not in my power I beg you will assure her of my sincerest compliments,

[1] The love of fishing was hereditary in the Dewes' family, who were all anglers from childhood to the third and fourth generation.

and that it has been a cruel mortification not to have done it so long. I, however, love her much, and am very glad she looks so well.

The behaviour of the *Troglodites* exceeds their usual out-doings in ingratitude. I went the Sunday before I came out of town to the *Arch Dragon*,[1] by appointment, to know of her whether the report of our friend's promotion was to be depended upon; and after flattering her pretty sufficiently, she told me she knew nothing of the matter, that she believed there was nothing in it, and that her son was never interested in anybody's business, his whole mind being taken up in *doing good to the nation*, and till the French was drove out of Germany, and Prague was taken, he could not think of such *a bagatelle as that.* I own she put me in a passion, but I was afraid of showing it least I should do mischief; but after expostulating with her that it was doing the *nation service* to put proper people about the Royal family, and how much the C— would be obliged to him, she said, the less it was *talked of the better*, and that her friends should *not mention* it. My own opinion is that Pen should write to Ba,[2] to acquaint him of their whole proceeding, and ask his advice, and be ruled by him, but I fear nobody can do it but the *Troglodites*. I desired Mrs. Don. to write this account to Pen, and my advice, for I had not time upon the road; if she has not, be so good to acquaint her with this, which will save her the trouble of a repetition letter. I think I should be glad that affair of Miss Dodwell was to succeed,

---

[1] Grace Countess Granville.
[2] Lord Baltimore.

for I cannot be more troubled than I am at present. This place is fine and agreeable; and indeed mama's excessive goodness to us would make any place so. Thank God she is very well and in high spirits! My dear Pip, you forgot Lord George was a member of the Hon[ble] House, and my directions about the letter: after you had sealed up my letter you was to write a D. and a P. of each side the seal, and no other direction than inclose it to Lord George.

Adieu, ever yours, my dear friend. May you have a short and happy minette is most sincerely the wish of your ever affectionate

And faithful friend.

My Lord desires his compliments; mine attend Mr. Dewes, Mrs. Granville, and Mrs. Viney, who, I hope, will let me know as soon as you are in your bed, if Pen is not with you.

M. C. PORTLAND.

It appears that the Duchess of Portland was not satisfied with the conduct of Lord Carteret or his mother, Countess Granville, in relation to Mrs. Pendarves's appointment at Court, and that she had confidence in Lord Baltimore's sincerity and advice, although she did not believe his interest was sufficient to carry anything without the sincere co-operation of Lord Carteret, who seems to have been very supine, probably owing to the offence given to Countess Granville by Mr. Granville's taking a lawyer's advice, and not leaving all his affairs in relation to the division of the Albemarle estates to Lord Carteret's management.

Mrs. Montagu writes, October 10th, 1742, to Mrs. Donellan:

"I am glad Mrs. Dewes has not suffered so terribly this time; as for Pen, she is not a daughter of Eve, but of the collateral branch of Enoch, who walked as an angel before the children of men."

Mrs. Pendarves to Mrs. Dewes, at Glocester.

Clarges Street, 12 Nov., 1742.

Your delightful letter made me happy last Wednesday, at Mrs. Percival's, where I was invited to fast, but truly it is one of the last houses one should go to for that purpose, for the company of affectionate sensible friends is the highest feast. However, the day was checkered, my poor Donnellan was very much out of order with sickness and pains; in the evening came your letter, she grew better, and I was happy. She goes next Monday to Twickenham, to Mr. Hoare's for a fortnight. I hope a little good air and change of place will do her good, and that will please me better even than her company.

I am as much perplexed for you as you can be for yourself in regard of my godson, but I think if you can be reconciled to the nurse's house,[1] that the story you have heard can be no great objection, but will rather for the future make her more careful, as she seems to be a good sort of woman. A deaf nurse is not to be endured; the poor dear may make his little moans, and have a thousand uneasinesses that she will hear nothing of. I must desire you to send a chine of pork to Sir J. S., and another to the Percivals' by the return of the next carrier, but remember as I write for them I must pay, or I never will speak to you of what I want again as long as I live. Donnellan was very much pleased with your pretty basons and sweet bag,—they adorn her toilette. Yesterday I went to the play, to Richard the Third, with Lady Mary Colley[2]

---

[1] It was the custom at this period for gentlemen's children to be nursed in the cottages of their wet nurses or in farm houses, and Mrs. Dewes's children were thus nursed.

[2] Lady Mary Hamilton, third daughter of James Earl of Abercorn, married in 1719, Henry Colley, Esq., elder brother of Richard Colley, Esq., who was created Baron of Mornington. Lady Mary Colley had a son, who died in infancy, and two daughters; the younger of whom, Mary, married in 1747, Arthur Pomeroy, Esq.

and her daughter. Garrick acted with his usual excellence; but I think I won't go to any more such deep tragedies, they shock the mind too much, and the common objects of misery we daily meet with are sufficient mortifications. Mrs. Hyet sat just before us in her blue and silver, and with her horns exalted above her fellows. In the evening I go to Bond Street. Yesterday I dined with Lady Sunderland; she is complaining but better than when she went to Tunbridge; to-morrow Mr. Dewes dines with me. A word to *the Princess* before I close: can she forgive my not having yet particularly paid my devoirs? Yes, I know she can; as she has been accustomed to the many hurries and time-devouring accidents of this huge place.

This moment my Lord B.[1] has been with me, and he advises me by all means to get the Duke of Bedford to ask; as if he does, he is sure it will be granted much sooner than if the other person does it, and he would have me send to my Lord Gower, and desire him to request it of the Duke of Bedford. He staid above an hour, looks well, and seems sincere in his way of advising me, and wished me joy of my going to alter my condition. *How can such a report with so little reason be spread so far?* Don't say anything of Guyamore's advice to Princess[2]—I know she will not approve of it, and I am resolved. The fair Maid of Honour, Donnellan, and Mr. Dewes dined with me to-day; the news of the town is, Mr. Doddington owns his marriage with Miss Bean.[3]

---

[1] Lord Baltimore.

[2] Grace Granville (Mrs. Foley) was often called "Princess," and Mrs. Pendarves probably expected her opposition to placing more confidence in Lord Gower than in Ann Granville.

[3] Horace Walpole writes, Novr. 15, 1742:—" Mr. Dodington has at last owned his match with his old mistress," *Mrs. Beghan.* Though secretly

Mrs. Pendarves's allusion to Lord Baltimore's visit and advice proves that they must have been in the habit of meeting again as friends, and previous passages had indicated that they spoke, and that she had acknowledged his civility at Court as an acquaintance; but this is the first instance, at the end of twelve years, of her mentioning his name as "Guyamore." Lord Baltimore was evidently at this time a friend of the Duchess of Portland's, who had confidence in his advice with respect to the contending interests at Court, where a place was in contemplation for Mrs. Pendarves with her own consent and approval; a fact which conclusively establishes the sincerity of her expressions of surprise at the report of her marriage, which can only be accounted for by the supposition that although she was herself ignorant of Dr. Delany's sentiments, yet that he had confided in some friend, who had betrayed his confidence before he had the courage to propose.

Mrs. Pendarves to Mrs. Dewes.

Clarges Street, 29 Nov. 1742.

I have dined two days together in Arlington Street, but heard no other discourse than what tended to the finery of yesterday.[1] My Lord C. was in plain cloth; ('tis well if his heart had the simplicity of his garment,) which was what it *appeared* to be a good, warm, clean, coat. *My lady*[2] was in dark green velvet trimmed with ermine, and an ermine petticoat—a present from her son, but it would have better suited the slender-waisted daughter Fanny, who had a scarlet damask and all her

---

married, he could not own her, as he then did, till the death of Mrs. Strawbridge, to whom he had given a *promise of marriage* under a penalty of 10,000*l.* George Bubb Doddington, (created Lord Melcombe, in 1761; died, 1762.)

[1] On the occasion of the birthday of the Princess of Wales.
[2] Countess Granville.

mother's jewels, was very well dressed, and became her clothes. I have not seen her look so well. Mrs. Spencer was in blue and silver. But our fair Maid of Honour [1] outshone them all; clad in rich pink satin trimmed with silver, more blooming and dazzling than anything there except her own complexion : she was perfectly well dressed, and looked so modest and unaffected, that I think I never saw a more agreeable figure; in the evening I went to Lady North's,[2] where I saw but few people. The Duchess of Montrose [3] was in silver tissue; Lady Scarborough [4] in blue damask with a gold trimming. There were several very handsome flowered silks, shaded like embroidery; but the finest clothes were Lady Caroline Lenox's,[5] gold and colours on white, embroidered by Mrs. Wright. There was a very full Court, and great confusion in getting in and out at Leicester House; the Princesses' ladies were affronted by the Princess of Wales's.

---

[1] "The Honourable Elizabeth Granville, daughter of George Lord Lansdowne is named Maid of Honour in the room of Miss Hamilton, who I told you, is to be Lady Brook."— *Walpole's Letters*, April 22, 1742. Mrs. Pendarves appears to have been at Bulstrode, *as well as* Mrs. Dewes, at the time of this appointment, which accounts for its not being mentioned in her letters.

[2] Francis, 3rd Baron Guilford, succeeded on the death of his cousin, 1734, to the Barony of North. He was born in 1704, and married first, in 1728, Lady Lucy Montagu, daughter of George Earl of Halifax, by whom he had one son, Frederick, his successor, and a daughter, Lucy, born in 1734. He married, secondly, in 1736, Elizabeth Viscountess-Dowager of Lewisham, by whom he had two surviving children. The Baron married, thirdly, Anne Countess-Dowager of Rockingham, daughter and co-heir of Sir Robert Furmese, Bart., by whom he had no issue. Was created Earl of Guilford, 8th of April, 1752, and died the 4th of August, 1790.

[3] Lucy, daughter of John, 2nd Duke of Rutland, married in 1742, William, 2nd Duke of Montrose.

[4] Frances, daughter of George, 1st Earl of Orkney, married Thomas, 3rd Earl of Scarborough.

[5] Lady Georgiana Caroline Lennox, daughter of Charles, 2nd Duke of Richmond, married to Henry Fox, Esq., afterwards Lord Holland.

The story told on their side is this:—The Princesses, attended by their ladies, went to Leicester House, and were immediately carried into the room to the Princess of Wales before the drawing-room begun; and all the ladies of both staid in the outward room. As soon as notice was given that the Princess and her sisters were going into the drawing-room, the Princess of Wales's ladies went on, and shut the door upon the other ladies, saying, "*their Princess's were not there.*" This story, as it is told, is *very black;* but it is, I think, impossible it should be true. There was one lady in the circle whom nobody knew

---

Mrs. Pendarves to the Duchess of Portland.[1]

November, 1742.

There was a quarrel at Leicester House between the Princess of Wales's ladies and the Princesses. Who were *most* to blame I don't know, nor who *got the better*, but Lady Anne Montague[2] and Lady C. Edwin[3] boldly entered the list and *scolded most bravely*, but which of them remained victor is not said.

I have not been at an opera since I came to town, and unfortunately declared before Miss Rich my indifference to the present compositions, who with a very contemptuous

---

[1] The beginning of this letter is wanting.

[2] Ann, eldest daughter of Robert, 3rd Earl of Manchester, married James, 3rd Earl of Suffolk. She was that nobleman's third wife.

[3] Catherine, fourth daughter of Robert, 3rd Earl of Manchester, married Samuel Edwin, of Llanvihangel, Esq., county Glamorgan, South Wales.

smile said "I must not pretend to love music." There are great divisions amongst the critics concerning Garrick's acting.[1] I am glad I am not such a critic as to find any fault with him. I have seen him act once, and like him better than I did last year; but as he is a year older, and the grace of novelty a little abated, he must of course have less merit with the generality of people. Mrs. Foley does not come to town this winter. Miss Granville is at Windsor. The Maid of Honour is much improved, and I have the satisfaction to hear her behaviour commended by everybody; she was very fine on the Birthday, and looked so modest and unaffected that I was extremely pleased with her; she is in *great favour* in Arlington Street.

Mrs. Doddington's owning her marriage, and poor Lady Frances Williams'[2] unhappiness I suppose can be no news at this time to your Grace, and since I have nothing to add that can give you any entertainment I will be impertinent no longer.

I beg my humble service to Lady Oxford, the Duke, Mr. Hays and Mr. Achard.

                I am, madam,
    Your Grace's most obedient humble servant,
                            M. PENDARVES.

I rejoice to hear that Lord Tichfield and the young ladies are well; my affectionate service always attend them.

---

[1] Garrick made his first appearance in Goodman's Fields Theatre, October 19, 1741, in the character of Richard III.

[2] Frances, youngest daughter and co-heir of Thomas Earl Coningsby, married Sir Charles Hanbury Williams, Bart.

Mrs. Pendarves to Mrs. Dewes.

Clarges Street, 6 Dec., 1742.

Since you are upon the wing, my dearest sister, I shall address this letter to you, though in duty bound it ought to have been to my mother, as I am now indebted to her (beside a million of other favours) for the finest of chines and kindest of letters; but when you have left her I will pay my duty regularly directed to her; it ever awaits her with my tenderest affection. I have been this morning with Mr. and Mrs. Percival as far as the farthest part of Cheapside at an auction, the advertisement of which promised us all the varieties of the India coast, but such trash my eyes were never tormented with before; and I am come home peevish and disappointed, and have lost some hours that might have been better employed, though the jumble I believe is wholesome. I dine at home that I may have the satisfaction of writing to you to-day and telling you that Dr. Sandys has wrote to Mr. Phillips, and the letter went on Saturday. Dr. Sandys told Mr. Clark he thought the Bath would be absolutely necessary for the child. Methinks I wish I had the little boy with me here that the most skillful might be consulted, if you and his father approve of it; you know how happy it will make me if my house can any way be of service to you, and if you do not care to come yourself, I shall be your second self in care and tenderness towards him.

I send you Hammond's Elegies on *our friend*, but don't name her when you show them. I pity her; I am sure she *must be touched* when she reads them, and I think it not handsomely done of the person who published them without her leave.

Craik (in his History of Literature and Learning in England) says, that "Hammond, the author of the Love Elegies, who died in 1742, went mad, and eventually to his grave, by love of Mrs. Dashwood, who under the name of *Delia* is the subject of his verses, and who survived him thirty-seven years. Mrs. Dashwood was the intimate friend of Mrs. Pendarves and Mrs. Dewes, and the allusion in the preceding letter confirms the truth of her being the object of Hammond's hopeless passion.

Mrs. Pendarves to Mrs. Dewes.

——— is quite angry that I would not let my room be hung with mohair instead of paper, which I absolutely would not; it would have been ridiculous when I design to cover it with pictures. I have hung up two that I have robbed the cabinet of—*Trevisani's Holy Family* and *Summer*, and the cabinet is better without them—it was before too much crowded; those two pictures and my Lady Weymouth's make the end of my room where my harpsichord stands look very gay. Yesterday I went early to the Duchess of Portland to help to settle her dress for the Birthday: her clothes are brown and gold; she will be a fine figure; her stomacher *all diamonds*, and a bouquet to wear on one side (in the French manner), of all the coloured jewels, which I made up for her yesterday. She is very well and very happy, and sends her "*kind love to Pip*."

Mrs. Montague is on the road to town. At Leicester her sister was taken so violently ill, that she has been forced to stay there a day or two on her account, but is better, and she hopes to be in town on Wednesday night; I feel for her distress having her sister so ill and no good help near her. My brother is very well, his politeness shows well on such occasions. I had almost forgot to tell you that I was making the tea in the cabinet last Wednesday (a card table set in the dining-room, the rest of the company with me), when who should glide in but the Duchess of Queensbury, in a mob and white hood pinned close under her chin, a yellow mohair gown, no ruffles, only little frills sewed to her shift, no hoop, a tumbled apron, and her capuchin dangling round her arm; yet there was *a grace* in her altogether, that shone out in spite of her dress. I believe she was a little surprized at finding my rooms so full; she stopped in the outward room and said, upon not seeing me there, and the room so fine, "*I am afraid I have mistaken the house;*" upon which my brother, who was at cards, got up and introduced her into the cabinet. She was in a very good humour, but it would have been more decent for her to have staid at home till my Lord Essex[1] was buried, though he has been a worthless wretch, and particularly so to her sister.

Now I talk of worthlessness, I must tell you the present discourse of the town is that Lord Euston[2] is certainly going to be married to his sister-in-law, Lady Augustus

---

[1] William, 3rd Earl of Essex, married, in 1718, Lady Jane Hyde, eldest surviving daughter of Henry Earl of Clarendon, by whom he had four daughters. The Countess died in 1724. His Lordship married, secondly, February 3, 1726, Elizabeth, daughter of Wriothesley, 2nd Duke of Bedford, but only a son and two daughters lived to maturity. He died January 8, 1743.

[2] Lady Dorothy Boyle, eldest daughter and co-heir of Richard, 3rd and last Earl of Burlington, married George Earl of Euston, eldest son of Charles, 2nd Duke of Grafton, and died without children the year after her marriage. Upon a picture of Lady Dorothy Boyle, at Chiswick, is the following inscription written by her mother.

"Lady Dorothy Boyle,
Born May the 14th, 1724.

"She was the comfort and joy of her parents, the delight of all who knew her angelick temper, and the admiration of all who saw her beauty. She was married October 18th, 1741, and delivered (by death) from misery, May the 2nd, 1742."

Fitzroy; and that he has made enquiry what the expense will be to keep out of the spiritual Court. *What a monster* he will shew himself to be, and his co-partner in wickedness no less so! If this be true it will confirm every villanous action he has been suspected of. How happy was it for poor Lady Euston to be removed from such a villain! I believe I shall go to-night to see Garrick with Miss Granville and my brother; they are to dine with me. Donnellan is better, though complaining, and is grown a perfect shadow.

The beginning and end of this letter have not been found, and it is not dated, but the death of Lord Essex which took place in 8th January 1743, proves that it must have been written during that month and year. After this date, there is an interval in the correspondence with Mrs. Dewes of more than two months, in which Mrs. Pendarves probably met her sister at Mr. Granville's at Calwich.

Mrs. Pendarves to Mrs. Dewes.

Clarges Street, 23 April, 1743.

My dearest sister, how much in vain is it to say I will sit down and write a long letter in this same populous city, where everybody cuts and carves one's time as they please, without considering the preciousness of the commodity, and that they cannot restore what they rob us of. Monday's post, I hope, will bring me the happy news of my mother's and the little brat's safe arrival at Bradley. Many thanks to you for your last letter. You say Mr. Dewes will come soon to town; he will be welcome when he comes, though I shall soon leave him when he does come. I wrote you word Sir John Stanley had determined to go to the Bath. I wrote to Lady Sarah Cowper to take lodgings, the coach was ordered, the day fixed, and my brother's spirits and mine much elated with the prospect of his pursuing the only method we were assured by Dr. Wilmot could be of service to him; but the wind is changed—he says he has not strength to perform the journey. The lodgings are *unbespoke*, the coach *forbid*, and we are *quite chagrined about it*; but there is no attempting to *alter* his resolution—it *may* of itself, but never on persuasion : such is man!

Yesterday morning Bet Castlemain came and breakfasted with me, and told me all her concerns. She is in fine spirits, I hope with reason ; her prospect is a fair one, and I believe matrimony never appeared with more advantage than it does at present in her eyes. Next Monday is the day appointed, and her *haughty, perverse sister* has not offered to go with her to church. Mrs. Hopkins has promised to go with her (if she is well enough); and if not, I *have promised her I will go*; her brother gives her away ; nobody else goes. As soon as they are married they are to breakfast with me, and go before dinner to Lady Read,[1] aunt to Mrs. Brinsdel, where they stay a week or fortnight. I am to tell you that the servant you recommended to Mrs. Bet Castleman must not depend on her, because she has some thoughts of keeping a *servant* that is now in the family ; but if that servant does not go into the country with her (which she is not sure she will), then she will take the other in case she is at liberty to come to her. So much for Bet.

I dined at Carteret House last Thursday; nothing passed concerning *my affairs*. They were in a mighty

---

[1] *Query*, wife of Sir Thomas Read, and daughter of Sir Ralph Dutton.

hurry preparing for the Hanover journey.[1] Lord and Lady Carteret set out on Tuesday. The old D. *is alive* and *alive is like to be;* she asked me when Mr. Dewes came to town, and said "if he liked to be a commissioner of bankruptcy she could get it for him, but should not look upon that as providing for him, but *would serve for pocket-money in the meantime.*" I hope he will be able to arrange about Welsbourn; I have bought mama's nightgown, and to-morrow Mrs. Foley sets out for Stoke, and will leave it at Gloucester for her. I dine to-day at Mrs. Percival's to meet the Southwells, who are going out of town; in the afternoon we have a musical party at Lady Catherine Hanmer's.

Last Thursday there was a masquerade at Ranelagh, I had a ticket offered me, and refused going, because it was a rainy night; was not that very discreet? Mrs. Wingston is come to town; I had just now a message from her—I had rather she had staid at Bristol. Lady Westmoreland[2] comes to me this morning by appointment, and we shall, I suppose, settle about our Kentish journey; but I am shilly-shally about it in my own mind, as it will be expensive, and *keep me longer from Bradley.* To-morrow Lady North and the Montagus drink tea with me: I dine at Whitehall. Lady Sunderland is pretty well, and was at the Percival assembly; the town is much healthier than it was. Thank God! all our friends are well; and I have not had, nor my brother, the least touch of the

---

[1] "In 1743 Lord Carteret waited on his Majesty to Hanover, who before his leaving St. James', appointed him one of the Lords Justices, and his Lordship attended all the campaign that year in Germany."—*Collins.*

[2] John, 7th Earl of Westmoreland, married Mary, only daughter and heiress of Lord Henry Cavendish, second son of William Duke of Devonshire, but died without issue, August 26, 1762.

influenza: the blustering winds we·have had of late I hope have carried off all unwholesome vapours. My best and affectionate duty to dear mama, kind service to Mr. Dewes, and to yourself say from me all you would say to me.

Instead of an account of Mrs. Pendarves' excursion to Kent, which was in contemplation with Lady Westmoreland at the conclusion of the above letter, circumstances, evidently *totally unexpected by herself*, directed her thoughts into a very different channel. On the very day—possibly at the very hour that she was communicating her doubts to Mrs. Dewes, as to the prudence of complying with Lady Westmoreland's wishes, (because it would not only entail additional expense, but probably prolong her absence from that sister who still continued the chief object of her life,) another individual was writing to herself, who eventually exercised a most important influence over her future existence. The following letter from Dr. Delany to Mary Granville (Mrs. Pendarves) has happily escaped destruction, and may be considered a model letter of proposal as far as words can give unmistakable evidence of deep sincerity, individual humility, and a high principle of honour. In this composition there are no unmeaning phrases. Before he arrived in London, he determined openly to declare the purport of his journey from Ireland, to state simply his consciousness of falling far short of her desert, but yet to admit a hope that the similarity of their tastes and pursuits might possibly induce her to share his home. He enumerates with plain straightforward good sense, details sufficient to prove that she would lose none of the reasonable comforts of life by accepting him, yet this is done in so simple a manner as to be really touching from its unaffected truth; and although no one can peruse it without feeling convinced that Dr. Delany entertained *more fear* than *hope*, yet there is a conscious dignity and a delicate devotion in the feeling he expresses, that he never could be *lowered* by *her rejection* though the chance of her acceptance was worth any effort he could make to obtain it.

The fact of Sir Clement Cottrell Dormer having invited Dr. Delany to remain with him in London, proves that he was an intimate friend, and cognizant of his intended visit to England, and possibly he might have been an indiscreet confidant of his intentions long beforehand, and thus have caused the rumour which had been propagated the previous year, when Dr. Delany had been a widower above twelve months, during which time he had constantly remained in Ireland.

Dr. Delany to Mrs. Pendarves.

MADAM,   Dunstable, April 23, 1743.

I am thus far on my way to wait on my friends in London. I hoped to have reached St. Albans tonight, and Sir Clement Cottrel Dormer's[1] (who has kindly invited me to reside with him) on Monday at noon; but am prevented, partly by the badness of the weather, and partly by the spleen of an humourist—a valetudinarian fellow-traveller. You, madam, are not a stranger to my present unhappy situation, and that it pleased God to desolate my dwelling; I flatter myself that I have still a heart turned to social delights, and not estranged either from the tenderness of true affection or the refinement of friendship. I feel a sad void in my breast, and am reduced to the necessity of wishing to fill it. I have lost a friend that was as my own soul, and nothing is more natural than to desire to supply that loss by the person in the world that friend most esteemed and honoured; and as I have been long persuaded that perfect friendship is nowhere to be found but in marriage, I wish to perfect

---

[1] Sir Clement Cottrell Dormer, was mentioned in former letters as Sir Clement Cottrell, and was Master of the Ceremonies to George II.—his ancestors having been Masters of the Ceremonies from the time of Charles I. Sir Clement died at Rousham, October 13, 1758.

mine in that state. I know it is late in life to think of engaging anew in that state, in the beginning of my 59th year. I am old, and I appear older than I am; but thank God I am still in health, tho' not bettered by years, and however the vigour of life may be over, and with that the *vigour of vanity*, and the flutter of passion, I find myself not less fitted for all that is solid happiness in the wedded state—the tenderness of affection, and the faith of friendship.

I have a good clear income for my life; a trifle to settle, which I am only ashamed to offer; a good house (as houses go in our part of the world), moderately furnished, a good many books, a pleasant garden (better I believe than when you saw it), etc. Would to God I might have leave to lay them all at your feet.

You will, I hope, pardon me the presumption of this wish, when I assure you it is noway blemished by the vanity of thinking them worthy of your acceptance, but as you have seen the vanities of the world to satiety, I allowed myself to indulge a hope that a retirement at this time of life, with a man whose turn of mind is not foreign from your own (and for that *only* reason not wholly unworthy of you)—a man who knows your worth, and honours you as much as he is capable of honouring any thing that is mortal, might not be altogether abhorrent from the views of your humble and unearthly wisdom. This I am sure of, that if you reject my humble and unworthy offering, your humility will not let you do it with disdain; and if you condescend to accept it, the goodness of your nature, and generosity of your heart, will prompt you to do it in a way most becoming your own dignity, and the security of my eternal esteem, and inex-

... gratitude: at all events, let me not be impaired ... honour of your friendship, since it is impossible I ... cease to be, with the truest veneration and esteem, madam,

Your most humble and most obedient servant,
PAT. DELANY.

P. S. I hope to be in London on Monday night, and to have the happiness of finding you either in Clarges Street or Northend on Tuesday morning. I beseech God to guide and guard you.

Ten days after the above letter, Dr. Delany wrote again, and from the tenor of his expressions it was evident that Mrs. Pendarves had declined giving her reply till her mother, her brother and her sister, had been addressed; but yet it may fairly be inferred that Mrs. Pendarves had intimated that her acceptation might follow their approval.

Dr. Delany to Mrs. Pendarves.

May 3rd.

Permit me, madam, to beg to know my fate as far as it depends upon your friends in Gloucester: if it be favourable, be so good as to signify it to me, by *allowing* me the honour to call them *my friends*; I must be theirs, at all events; since I cannot cease to be with perfect affection and esteem, yours.

May every day of your life be as happy as I hope to find this and the next: and may the felicity of making mine such be only yours. Pardon the presumption of this well intended wish, in, madam,

Your most obedient and not wholly unselfish servant,
PAT. DELANY.

Three days after this letter, Dr. Delany wrote again in a manner which clearly shows that Mrs. Granville's approval had not been received, and that Mr. Granville was decidedly hostile, though somewhat mollified by a visit to Sir John Stanley. It also appears that Mrs. Pendarves had made her brother's, as well as her mother's consent a condition, and that Dr. Delany despaired of obtaining that of Mr. Granville, who was well known to have been violently opposed to his sister's marrying a man who had no claim of ancestry to bring forward, or anything to offer in excuse for what Mr. Granville doubtless considered unparalleled presumption.

Dr. Delany to Mrs. Pendarves.

May 6th.

MADAM,

Though I can scarcely hold a pen in my hand, I cannot help attempting to inform you that I apprehend, from a moment's conversation with your brother this morning in the street (for he was gone out before I could reach his house), that his visit at Northend has made some change in his sentiments in relation to me. I beseech you, madam, leave me not to the caprice of any of your friends; and much less to the mercy of every humour of every friend. Where you *owe duty*, pay it; and let me rise or fall by the determination of *duty*; but let not the decision depend upon the fickle, the uncertain, and the selfish. God has blessed you with noble sentiments, a good understanding and a generous heart; are not these, under God, your best governors? I might venture to pronounce that even a parent has no right to control you, at this time of life, and under your circumstances, in opposition to these; and a *brother* has no shadow of right.

Bless me with one minute's conversation before you go, and fix my fate—thus far, indeed, it is already fixed, that I am, and must, at all events, be unalterably yours.

Dr. Delany to Mrs. Pendarves.

Inclosed is a letter to your mother; if you think it such a one as should be sent, be so good as to return it by the bearer with a direction. If you wish anything *added* or *altered* let me know it without reserve, in full assurance, that my greatest happiness is to do everything you wish. Make me happy in one moment's conversation when it may be least inconvenient to you.

From the above lines it appears that a formal proposal was inclosed to Mrs. Granville, requesting her consent.

Dr. Delany to Mrs. Pendarves.

May 12, 6 in the evening.

You are in town, at least I flatter myself that you are, and well and happy. I must not see you! however be well and happy. You have determined on my fate, but I must not know it; perhaps I shall know it too soon. I can endure even suspense for you though I would not endure it for anything this earth calls honour: the hope of the alliance is of a higher species. They say you sleep better, that is the condition of a heart at ease,—would to God mine were so! it must be soon at all events. I awoke early last Sunday morning with these two lines in my mouth :—

> Go half my heart, and half my soul
> Haste home again, and make me whole.

I really cannot say whence they came from,—I wish anybody could tell me: but I wish with much more impatience to know whether *that return* is to repair or to rend me to pieces. I beseech God it may have that effect, whatever it be, in which your temporal and eternal happiness are most interested.

I have the honour of a letter from Mrs. Granville: it is *not unfriendly*; it *leaves* my happiness where I wish it may rest for ever on this side heaven—*at your feet*. Might I hope to have one ray of hope conveyed to me in half a line by the bearer.

Nineteen days had now elapsed since Dr. Delany's letter of proposal, written at Dunstable; and making allowance for all the preliminary steps which were considered proper, as well as the slow pace of the post at that period, and the delay necessary for consideration after a letter on such a subject was received, with the time required to compose and write an answer, it may be considered that Dr. Delany's suit had speeded well to have arrived at the stage of a "*not unfriendly*" letter from Mrs. Granville, and also that he entertained hopes of a favourable decision irrespective of Mr. Granville's consent.

The following letter is the first intimation that there was a complete understanding between Mrs. Pendarves and Dr. Delany, and that she advised him how to act to obtain the concurrence, and thereby preserve the harmony of her family. The "friend" alluded it might be supposed, was Lord Carteret, were it not that there is presumptive evidence, that however partial Lord Carteret was to Dr. Delany previously, he never desired that he should marry a Granville.

Dr. Delany to Mrs. Pendarves.

May 14th, 9 at night.

I have sent the message agreed on to Lady G.[1] by my *friend,* who undertook it with a zeal and a frankness that doubled his merit. He delighted me beyond measure by letting me see he honoured you highly—that is almost half as much as I do; how much that is, I either cannot or dare not say. It is too much presumption to ask, are you alone? it is much more so, to hope to be happy with you one moment? Adieu.

The next link which the Editor possesses of this correspondence, is the following letter from Mrs. Dewes to Dr. Delany, which demonstrates in a remarkable manner her single-hearted and disinterested disposition, and also her entire confidence in her sister's judgment. The date, 3rd of June, indicates that Dr. Delany's suspense and anxiety had then happily terminated.

Mrs. Dewes to Dr. Delany.

Bradley, 3d June, 1743.

SIR,

Though it is very natural to like those persons who are valued and distinguished by a favourite friend, yet I must assure you that my respect and admiration you have had, long before I could imagine there would be any other attachment than what is due to uncommon merit; but I now with great willingness and pleasure will add sisterly affection and esteem, which I dare say must increase upon acquaintance, and as you *make her happy* who is endeared to me by the strongest ties of love and

---

[1] Countess Granville.

obligation. If you find she has not entirely misplaced her friendship and will add yours to it, I shall be vastly glad, and if the most ardent prayers and wishes for your mutual happiness is any degree of merit, then I own I have a great deal, and fear I can claim no other.

The just sense you have of my sister's extreme worth gives me infinite delight, I never thought she could meet with anybody sensible enough of those delicacies in her disposition that complete the most amiable part of a woman's character, but now *I believe she has*; which will greatly alleviate what I shall suffer by her absence. Her absence is a subject I will not mention, for as I now sincerely desire to promote your happiness, I trust in your generosity to deprive me of as little of mine as is in your power to avoid; and shall put Mrs. Pendarves in mind how much joy and satisfaction she retards by staying in London longer than is absolutely necessary.

I hope Mr. Dewes has had the pleasure of being introduced to you; his integrity and good principles are worthy your notice and esteem. I will make no excuse for this long letter, because where the heart is concerned it is impossible to say little. I must return my thanks for the pleasure of your letter, and am,

Dear Sir, your most faithful humble servant,

ANNE DEWES.

My mother's compliments and good wishes attend you. She is sorry her letter had not the designed effect, for she is impatient (as well as myself) to see you at our cottage.

Mary Granville, Mrs. Pendarves, married Dr. Delany (according to the Gentleman's Magazine) on the 31st May, 1743, two days before the date of this letter, and the Editor does not possess any more authentic record, but from various passages in subsequent letters she has reason to believe that the marriage really took place on the 9*th of June*.

There is no doubt that in either case it was very private, and in all probability she would only have been attended by Mr. Dewes, (who was evidently in London), and one female relation. The above letter of Mrs. Dewes still mentions her as "*Mrs. Pendarves*," and if the marriage had taken place when that letter was written, it would prove that even her sister did not know for what day it was fixed, which is highly improbable. It was consistent with the character of Mary Granville, after having obtained her mother's consent, her sister's approval, and Sir John Stanley's acquiescence, and tried in every possible way to reconcile her brother to her marriage, to have no further delay, and at the same time it would have been unworthy of her sincerity to have had the pretence of any appearance of rejoicing. She well knew that Dr. Delany must ultimately stand or fall upon his own merits and qualifications, and having made up her mind as to their value, and obtained the sanction of those who had the nearest claims upon her, she had nothing more to wait for. The only person in her own family who was *intimately acquainted* with Dr. Delany was Lord Carteret, whose dislike to the alliance materially cooled his previous friendship, and whose feelings were certain to be shared by his mother, the old Countess Granville. Lord Carteret's opinions would naturally influence all the rest of the Granville family, had not appearances warranted his objections; as it certainly was a rare exception to the general order of things, that any person who had been born in so different a sphere from that which Mary Granville and her ancestors had occupied for centuries, should have been so endowed as to be a suitable companion for one who stood pre-eminent amongst her own contemporaries for taste, tact, talent, and refinement of manners; and it would have been in vain for her to attempt by reasoning to convince her family and friends that the Chancellor of St. Patrick's, however great his learning, or however virtuous his life and character, could possess those requisites which were necessary to secure her daily and hourly comfort and happiness setting aside all feelings of family pride.

CHAPTER VII.

From November, 1743 to 1746.

The following letter is the first in the Editor's possession written after Mary Granville's second marriage. The interval between June and November had been evidently spent in visits to her mother and sister, and some other friends. and she and Dr. Delany were now apparently on their road from Gloucester to London.

Mrs. Delany to Mrs. Dewes.

Clarges Street, 10th Nov., 1743.

It was a most delightful welcome to my own house to hear so soon from my dear friends at Gloucester. I thank God we have had as good and pleasant a journey as we could possibly have wished for, or our friends for us.

Mr. Dewes has informed you I suppose of his safe arrival in town and adventures on the road. He left Burford about half-an-hour before us. After a good breakfast of caudle we set forward for Cornbury, and sent a messenger forward to ask leave to go through the park, and to say if my Lord C. was alone we would breakfast with him: he sent back an invitation to us to dine as well as breakfast, and entertained us with showing us his house, pictures, and park, which indeed are all as well worth seeing as anything in England, especially when he is there

to do the honours. The house has no regular front; it
is unfinished but newly fitted up with great elegance,
and contains a number of very fine rooms; the lower
apartment is just furnished, and is the prettiest thing I
ever saw, somewhat in the taste of Mrs. Horner's. His
park lies finely to the house and is most charming, and
kept as nice as a garden, and a gravel path quite round
it, that you may walk in any weather. The ground lies
most advantageously, and is planted with great skill and
great variety of fine trees, some thick wood, some clumps,
in short nature and art have done their best to make it
beautiful. I delivered Mrs. Duncomb's message to him;
he pleaded guilty, but asked so kindly after her, that I
believe she will take him again into favour. He *does* live
in Berkeley Square, and they were ignorant who reported
that he had disposed of his house there.

We were much pressed to dine at Cornbury, but that
would have led us too far into the night before we could
have reached Rouseham. I had almost forgot to speak
particularly of the pictures: they are excessively fine, most
of them Vandykes, whole lengths, and a vast number of
them. Either the painter or the persons painted had more
gracefulness than the modern nobility, for they *all look*
like *valets-de-chambre* compared to their ancestors. As
Lord Cornbury led me to the coach, he said he was "obliged
to me that he now belonged to Dr. Delany, and that he
had a right to claim his friendship and acquaintance."

From hence we went to Rouseham, and got there
by two o'clock, just as the family (ten in number) were
sitting down to dinner. We were received with great
friendship, and it seems to be the family of love. Sir
Clement Cotterel is very worthy of the fine place he is

possessed of, for he not only enjoys it himself, but makes
it very agreeable to his family and friends. The house
is very old, and the rooms low, but finished and furnished in the nicest manner; a new library was added
to it not many years ago, a most magnificent room,
and finished with the highest expense. There are two
very large bow windows in it, and nearly five thousand
volumes, and prints that cost between two and three
thousand pounds,—I mean the prints only. The house
abounds with valuable antiques of all kinds such as
busts, statues, bronzes, basso relievos that are enough
to make one wild, besides many very fine pictures
by several of the great masters; so much for within
doors. Then the garden is past my skill to describe; all
I can say of it is that I never saw a garden which
pleased me so well, but the weather was so bad all the
time I was there that I could not see half its beauty.

We left Rousham on Monday morning at seven,
dined at Stoken Church, and lay at Beconsfield, and
found the roads very good; I sent to Peg Bellenden as
soon as we got to our inn, but she was abroad. The
next morning before we set out I made her a visit of
five minutes; for she would never have forgiven me if
I had passed her by in silence: she uttered many a
droll thing, and is *the very individual Peg* you knew her
in Somerset House. We got to Bulstrode by nine
o'clock, the Duchess and Don. were a-bed, but I soon
roused them: we were very glad to meet, and *all talked
out of breath*, asking on both sides an hundred questions,
and not giving leisure for the answering one. I never saw
Don. better than she is now; the Duchess has lost her
cough, but is by no means well; Lady Peterborough is

there, and Lady O's time of making a visit there not yet fixed. We have promised to return as soon as possible; with great difficulty we left them before dinner, and got very well to Clarges Street, as my letter to my mother I hope informed you in time.

That night Mrs. Percival came to invite us to dine with her yesterday, and to go in the morning to Whitehall Chapel to hear Mr. Handel's new Te Deum rehearsed, and an anthem.[1] It is excessively fine, I was all rapture and so was your friend D.D. as you may imagine; everybody says it is the finest of his compositions; I am not well enough acquainted with it to pronounce that of it, but it is heavenly. I dined at the Percivals, many enquiries after you from everybody. D.D. and I made a visit of about two hours to Sir Robert and Lady Sun.; they are all complaining there.

Oh I forgot to tell you I made a visit to the Old Countess, but she looked *so cross* and *so cold*, that I staid but one quarter of an hour, and she received D.D. in *the same way*; great discontents about public affairs. We are just going to Northend—I will finish when I return; Lady S. Cow. is better, she comes to me to-morrow, this afternoon Lady North and the Maid of Honour. Two o' the clock. Sir John Stanley looks and is much better than when I left him, and full of Ward's praises; I am glad he has so much reason to speak well of him. Since our being abroad the Countess has honoured us with a visit, and left word she "*hoped to see us soon;*" I hope she will be in *better humour* when we go next. I like my new maid very

---

[1] The famous Te Deum and Anthem for the victory of Dettingen, were solemnly sung in the presence of the King, in the Royal Chapel of St. James's, on the 27th of November, 1743, after having been rehearsed on the 18th and 25th, at Whitehall Chapel, during the forenoon.

well, she has been come a week, she has a lively look and promises so far very well. Poor Mary had two fever fits on the road, she has a medicine given her of bark and snakeroot that I believe has stopped it. Pray what is your receipt of bark and snakeroot? Let me know exactly how you do, and if you eat and sleep well, and what my brother says more about Calwich, and what you intend to do? I think I must part with Mary soon; I cannot carry her and Betty Wodall also to Bulstrode.

The Lord Cornbury here mentioned was Henry, son of Henry Hyde, 4th Earl of Clarendon, and 2nd Earl of Rochester. He died a few months before his father, after whose death Cornbury became the property of Catherine, Duchess of Queensbury, sister of Lord Cornbury. "The Cornbury Collection, formed by the great Lord Chancellor Clarendon, is (1856) partly at The Grove, in Hertfordshire, the seat of the present Lord Clarendon, and partly at Bothwell Castle, in Lanarkshire, the seat of Lord Douglas."

Rousham (in Oxfordshire) is in the Elizabethan style. Walpole writes, in July, 1760:—" The greatest pleasure we had, was in seeing Sir Charles Cottrell's, at Rousham, it reinstated Kent with me, he has nowhere shown so much taste. The house is old, and was bad; he has improved it—stuck as close as *he* could to Gothic, made a delightful library, and the whole is comfortable. The garden is Daphne in little, the sweetest little groves, streams, glades, porticoes, cascades, and river, imaginable; all the scenes are are perfectly classic. Well, if I had such a house, such a library, so pretty a place, and so pretty a wife, I think I should let King George send to Herenhausen for a Master of the Ceremonies."[1]

---

[1] The Cottrells were hereditary Masters of the Ceremonies from the reign of Charles I.

Mrs. Montagu writes to the Duchess of Portland at this period:

"Pray where is Pen? Will she produce a sprig of bays? It must be a little Master Apollo, or a Miss Minerva, from parents of such art and science."

Mrs. Delany to Mrs. Dewes, at Mrs. Granville's, at Gloucester.

Clarges Street, 18 Nov. 1743.

This was the day appointed for our going to Bulstrode, but Lady O. did not go till yesterday and stays a week, and we choose to defer our visit till that is almost over. To-morrow D.D. preaches for the Bishop of O. at St. James's. Last Sunday we were both there. I believe it is the church I shall go most constantly to,—there is always good preaching. I am very glad my mother and you are come to a resolution about going to Calwich. I pray God send you a prosperous journey, and all joy and satisfaction at the end of it. But you say no more of your little Court than one of your portmantoes. If he could tell his mind, and knew of the fine bowling green he will have to roll upon, he would clap his hands, and crow for joy. This will be the last letter I shall direct to you at Gloucester; my next shall salute you at Calwich, unless you change your mind. If the weather continues as it is now, it will be pleasant travelling, but though I talk so quietly of your going to Calwich, don't think I give up your coming to town, for after three months quiet repose a month of hurry may not be disagreeable; but let that rest at present.

My new maid promises very well, and she has a sprightliness *without pertness* that pleases me well, and wears no hoop—so much for domestics. Foreign affairs stand thus:—We had an invitation to the Troglodite-house to dinner, where we were entertained with many speeches, much rattling, and no food. I had promises, nods, shakes of the hand, and two salutes as usual. I told him I had now *changed my suit*, and that from the merit of D.D. and his friendship to him, I thought I could not fail of what I wished. He smiled and promised, but said nothing to the purpose; but the *vacant Farm* which the *Lord of the Manor* kept to dispose of himself, I am positively assured will not be accepted by the person designed for it. This I have good authority for saying, and have sent *the Bailiff* word of it, and if my intelligence is true without some roguery in the Bailiff I think we cannot fail of being soon put into possession; but my lot is already fallen in a fair ground, and if Providence sees fit to enlarge our dominion I hope to be truly thankful, and to make a proper use of all advantages that may befall me; but my *debt* is *large already*, and I most heartily pray for grace to discharge it as I ought to do.

Yesterday *seven* Cottrells dined with us, but they are such good-humoured people that ceremony is thrown aside, and we passed the day like good country neighbours. I believe Mr. Dewes will think us lost, for we have named three days running for going out of town; he is very well and I shall challenge a day from him before we go. We have all escaped cold and are perfectly well. Poor Lady Sunderland has been under great trouble for Master Sutton, who has lain in a raging fever for several days past; he is now better, and they have hopes of his recovery.

Lady Sarah Cowper is still compliments, but better; if

you have not heard from her it is because she has not been well enough to write. We talk of you, when we meet, till I am forced to change the subject. I really grieve for the loss Mrs. Viney will have this winter and her daughters,—I hope I shall hear from them as soon as you have left Gloucester; I desire the same from Princess, to whom I will write soon. I have a thousand odious fiddle faddle things to do this morning, but will finish this sheet first. I am not sorry the Foleys were so resolute in not coming to you, for at this time it would have been troublesome to mama. Mr. Wise has got the candlesticks and salt-seller, and will obey all commands: Why did you not keep the warm purple-coat to wrap yourselves up in on the road? you might as well have sent it from C. as from G. Pray let Mrs. Brinsden know if you see her (or her sister Skin.) that her parcel was safely delivered to Mrs. Hopkins; the Montagus of Hanover-Square come to town to night. Your dear little stray letter came to town, introduced by the Master of the Ceremonies.

In the midst of all our hurries here, D.D. has found time to settle his sermonizing affairs,[1] and I believe they will all now be finished before he goes to Bulstrode; they have not yet brought forth the dedication. Poor Lady Carteret's body[2] was brought over in the ship with my Lord, who has been dangerously ill, but now he looks well and in good spirits, though they appear to me put on; Lady Dysart is not yet come.

If my brother has no use for his house, why should you

---

[1] "Twenty Sermons upon Social Duties and their Opposite Vices," by the Rev. Dr. Delany. This volume is dedicated to the Countess of Granville, and the dedication is dated Feb. 23, 1743 (old style).

[2] Lady Carteret died at Hanover on the 9th of June, 1743. Her body was brought over in November following, and buried in Westminster Abbey.

not come to it six weeks or so if my mama likes her quarters at Calwich and her landlord resolves to stay in the country. I said I would not talk about this any more, but it lies at my heart, and I cannot help contriving every possible way for our meeting; I hope I shall be able to make my visit in Staffordshire the beginning of April at furthest, but that depends on circumstances.

I was at the opera of Alexander, which under the disguise it suffered, was infinitely better than any Italian opera; but it vexed me to hear some favourite songs mangled. I think I *may say* my pencil has produced a good piece. I have bought a very fine head ruffles and tucker of Mrs. Carter—new fashioned Brussels, it comes to near fifty pounds: is not that extravagant? 'Tis very pretty as well as fine.

Mrs. Delany to Mrs Dewes, at Calwich, near Ashbourne, Derbyshire.

Bulstrode, 27 Nov., 1743.

Our journey was so short that I have nothing to tell you about it, but that we performed it in three hours and arrived here at twelve, met Lady Oxford on the road and found the Duchess better, though she has been very much out of order with hysterics, which has been the reason of her not writing. Don. hopes you have had her letter. She is very well, and so is the Duke, the children, Mons.ʳ du Poivre, and Mrs. Elstob.

To describe to you the charms of Bulstrode is needless; your memory will do it justice, and figure to you the pleasure I enjoy here with my agreeable friends. As soon as I know you are safe at Calwich, I shall taste the joy of my dear friends meeting there in so pleasant a place. It would have been happy for me this winter had the meeting been within my reach, but I must accept of joys as they are dealt to me, and be thankful; it is too much to enjoy every blessing in our own way! We walk every morning—that is we have walked yesterday and to-day, all of us; but to-morrow Mr. Jackson comes, and the Duchess will be shut up in her turning-shop all next week. The Duke and Lord George go to town next Wednesday to the meeting of Parliament and return on Saturday, and Mr. Drummond, your old acquaintance, with them; you know he is very agreeable and entertaining, and after hurrying about as he has done after the camp, he will be glad to sit down quietly in peace within these walls. You'll fancy you are not acquainted with this Mr. Drummond, but indeed you are; it is *not* the banker at Charing Cross, nor Mr. John Drummond, for he is dead.

The Duke of St. Albans sent to the Duke of Marlborough for his interest in an election, the message was carried to the Dowager Duchess, and she sent back word that "*though he was a fool he should not be everybody's fool.*" It is reported that the Duke is disgusted and has laid down. I can tell you nothing of the Troglodite House, for neither D.D. nor I saw them for a week before we came out of town. Master Sutton is dead at last, after a very terrible fever of above a fortnight; I was with poor Lady Sunderland at the time he died, and she was much shocked with it and had suffered a great deal with seeing him endure so much, and is out of order in her own health; but I hope when she comes to consider calmly, and that the natural affection a mother must feel at first for the loss of a child gives way to reason, she will be reconciled to this stroke, for such a child is really no loss. Sir Robert is very ill, and so is Betty Tichbourne, who has nursed herself to death; Miss Sutton bears up very well, and is a support to the rest; I must write to her to-night, and you know hours run away here imperceptibly, I shall hardly have time to write two words.

D.D. preached to-day his first sermon on the Duty of Children to Parents, with approbation. The Duchess's rapture about Matlock continues, and she says the people of Derbyshire and Staffordshire are the best-bred people she ever met with anywhere, and she is quite pleased with Mrs. Bo. How do you like the *pearl fountain?*

P.S. If you should see a paragraph in the newspaper about the Duke of Portland don't be alarmed; he has had the misfortune to break his arm, but thank God is in a good way. He fell from his horse this morning as he was hunting. You may believe what a stroke it was to all, but especially the poor dear Duchess; but the surgeons and Dr. Sandys, who is here, assure us so positively of his being very safe, that I hope the worst is over. He has no fever and the Duchess is pretty well; don't expect to hear next post—the post after you shall not fail. This letter was written yesterday but the accident happened this morning.

Mrs. Delany to Mrs. Dewes, at Calwich, near Ashbourne, Derbyshire.

Bulstrode, 30th Nov. 1743.

For fear my dearest sister should have some anxiety about the Duke of Portland I cannot omit writing this post. He is as well as can be expected; he has no fever, and his arm is very well set; but he must be confined to one posture in his bed some time longer, which is very fatiguing to him, though his patient disposition makes it less an evil than it would be to most people. The Duchess is pretty well,—I apprehended this accident might be of consequence to her. She is very low-spirited, and that you will not wonder at.

Mr. Dewes must have had an account of your journey from your own hand. I came here last Saturday, and hope to-morrow to have the joyful account of your safe landing at Calwich, and that the road and waters between Uttoxeter and my brother's were not so terrific as my mother apprehended they would be; a thousand thanks to my dear mama for her kind postcript, it was indeed an inexpressible pleasure to me to hear of her bearing travelling so well; I believe it will do her a vast deal of good, and am sure make my brother happy. My most humble duty and tender affection to both.

I did not send the work at last to Mr. Dewes, but it shall be ready for you when I go to town; you may have it after that whenever you please. Donnellan is here, and I hope will stay as long as I do; she is very much mended in her health—I never knew her to have so few complaints at this time of the year. You must not expect to hear next post.

We were afraid Lady O. would have come, and her formality would not by any means have agreed with the liberty of this constitution; but she sent Mr. Drummond here yesterday to see the Duke,—and he returned again at noon to her.

Mrs. Montagu[1] to Mrs. Delany.
1st of Dec. 1743 (?).

DEAR MADAM,

None but the *present* Mrs. Delany *can* be *so good as the late* Mrs. Pendarves. By the gentle stroke of humanity and the elegant ones of the pen I know the postscript to be yours; you have saved me from a great deal of affliction though you cannot yet cure me of anxiety for the Duke and Duchess. I had by accident the news delivered to me before the letter. You will imagine how much the paragraph alarmed me; but you say the arm is well set and there is no fever—pray heaven, continue these favourable symptoms and strengthen the poor Duchess, whose spirits are now, I fear, too easily disordered! I hope the Duke will not have a troublesome confinement, but that he will soon be well again.

I ought to make some apology for not having wrote to you on your marriage, which, though custom seems to ordain, I think when a person chooses *such* a companion as you have done, it is almost an injury to interrupt their conversation; and the truth is, not being well when you left London, I let slip so much time before I was aware of it that I was afterwards ashamed to write. I am sure

---

[1] Elizabeth, eldest daughter of Matthew Robinson, of West Layton, in Yorkshire, married Edward Montagu, of Allerthorpe, Yorkshire, Esq., (of the Sandwich family,) Aug. 5, 1742. They had an only child, which died in 1745. Mr. Montagu died in 1775, and she survived until Aug. 25, 1800. This lady was the author of the Essay on Shakspeare, and the chief of "*the blue stockings*" of her day. She gave an annual feast to all the chimney-sweepers in London, and had a room in Montagu House, Portman Square, hung with tapestry made of feathers.

"*The birds put off their every hue,*
To dress a room for Montague!
The peacock sends his heavenly dyes,
His rainbows and his starry eyes."—COWPER.

my good wishes and regard, (and I must say *love*,) for you have had no intermission, though my correspondence has had too much. I hope you will receive me into grace again, and allow me to write to you.

The fine weather we have had lately will have shewn Bulstrode to Dr. Delany to better advantage than places usually appear at this time of the year, and I observed in Dr. Delany (the few hours I had the pleasure of being in his company) a *greater goût* for the country, and a *better taste* for *rural beauty*, than I almost ever met with. In his imagination I could perceive the *poet*, in his reflections the *philosopher*, and *in both the divine*. It is a delightful thing to walk abroad in a sunshiny day and observe the life imparted and happiness communicated to animal life, and the beauty diffused through the vegetable world; each being in the creation, has its portion of happiness; but to our kind is reserved that of rejoicing in the universal welfare. Dr. Delany is happy in a companion like you, who take a philosopher's and an artist's part in the natural world; to a *mind* that *comprehends* you have a *hand that records* and represents its beauties. Your drawing-room boasts of eternal spring—nature blooms there when it languishes in gardens; and not only prospects and landscapes are represented by your art, but even human passions and fugitive thoughts are expressed and fixed by the strokes of your pencil. I cannot help wishing I was within a visit of Bulstrode, though I have one great objection to that place, which is, if one was to live a hundred years there, one should think one went off suddenly. I do remember there was a clock in the breakfast-room, but I am sure I *never counted an hour* there. I cannot imagine how it happens so many *such people* as are now there can have got together; it seems to me like the end of a romance. Sir Philip Sidney would pompously say, "*when the excelling excellency of so many excellent persons was collected in one place it made all other places seem so desolate and destitute of all excellency that desolation itself could not appear more desolate than all other society compared to that excellent assembly.*" I wish you joy of your new nephew, and I hope Mrs. Dewes has well recovered her lying-in. I desire my compliments to Dr. Delany and many kind things to Mrs. Donnellan, who I will epistolize very soon.

   I am, dear madam,
     Your very affectionate and obliged
      Humble servant,
        E. MONTAGU.

Mrs. Delany to Mrs. Dewes, at Calwich, near Ashbourne, Derbyshire.

          Bulstrode, 4 Dec., 1743.

I am infinitely obliged to my dear sister for the great pleasure her last letter gave me; to hear that all at Calwich are well and happy is a true delight to me. I know you would like my brother's improvements, and D.D. is not a little pleased that the *pearl fountain*[1] is *in favour*. Has my brother done anything to the Gothic building yet, or does he reserve that for spring? What room do you lie in? and does the little boy come on with his feet? I think I see him clapping his hands, and hear him crowing all day long at the variety of living creatures that flutter about him. The Duke of Portland is as well as

---

[1] Mrs. Delany was called "*the Pearl*," and Mrs. Dewes "*the pearly* Dews."

anybody ever was under such an accident as he has had, but he is threatened a little with the gout, which will be a sad thing to him in the helpless way he is in at present. The Duchess sends her kind love to you, and begs you will not take her silence ill, but she has been in such a way for two months past, such hysterics have seized her, that it has made her incapable of doing anything. Mrs. Donnellan wrote to you, but I find you have not had her letter, which she is much concerned about, and begs her affectionate service to you; she is pretty well, the Duchess is better, the children very well, and Monsieur du Poivre the *true representative of care,*—for since the Duke's confinement he has hardly allowed himself time for his meals; his eyebrows are arched to the top of his wig, and his sighs are enough to turn a mill. Now the Duke being pretty well again, this continued dismality of Achard's diverts us.

D.D. makes himself agreeable to all, and I have the satisfaction of seeing everybody treat him with that kindness which *I think his due;* he is to preach to-day the second sermon on the Duty of Children; he is quite charmed with the Duchess's management of her little family, and surprized at her *great prudence* and *resolution* in regard to them; Lady Margaret is grown a very pretty girl and in great favour; Mrs. Elstob is pretty well. Yesterday morning D.D., Donnellan, and I went to Windsor to Miss Granville. She was gone to church, where D.D. followed her, but Donnellan and I were so cold we went in, stirred up her fire, and bespoke breakfast; they soon came in, and after breakfast was over, D.D. proposed going to see the pallace; I let him and Don. go together, and staid with Violet, as I wanted to talk with her about her own affairs, which I find are in a very bad way, and her spirits very low. She has wrote to Lord Carteret to desire he would get her a pension; Betty Granville[1] delivered the letter, which he read, and assured her, (in his usual false style) that he " would serve her, but she *must have patience*." It grieves me that so valuable a young woman should be so distressed; the best of her dependance is an hundred pounds a year, paid by the trustees, and when their trust ceases, in all probability her maintenance may. But we must not despond—the hand that overrules all I hope will support her. Mrs. Foley has had a cold and been blooded, but is pretty well again. I have heard of abundance of weddings. I will not say I have good authority for all, but *false news* in the country is matter of *amusement*. Lord —— and Lady Bell Finch,[2] Duke of Beaufort[3] (as soon as the divorce is concluded, which will be soon) and Miss Windham, Will. Leveson[4] and Lady Blandford, Lord Euston,[5] and Lady Camilla Bennet,[6] Ld Litchfield[7] and Lady Mary Tufton. I have not heard from Sir J. Stanley lately, nor from Miss Sutton since I

---

[1] The Maid of Honour.

[2] Lady Isabella Finch, died unmarried 1771, third daughter of the 6th Earl of Winchelsea, first Lady of the Bedchamber to the Princess Amelia.

[3] Henry, 3rd Duke of Beaufort, married, June 28, 1729, Frances, only child of Viscount Scudamore, from whom he was divorced in 1743-4, and did not marry again.

[4] William Leveson, second son of John first Earl Gower, died unmarried.

[5] George Earl of Euston, eldest son of Charles, 2nd Duke of Grafton, married, in 1741, Lady Dorothy Boyle, eldest daughter of Richard, last Earl of Burlington, who died the year after her marriage, and Lord Euston died in 1747.

[6] Lady Camilla Bennet, only daughter of Charles, 2nd Earl of Tankerville. She married first, Gilbert Fane Fleming, Esq., and secondly, in 1779, Mr. Wake.

[7] George Henry Lee, Earl of Litchfield, succeeded his father, February 1742-3. He married Diana, daughter of Sir Thomas Frankland.

came. I wrote to her and begged of her to let me know how Lady Sunderland did; I take it a little ill of her, because it has given me great uneasiness, as I left them all ill and in affliction. It is reported that our great cousin is very *much discontented*, that he will not long maintain his post, and that Lord Chesterfield will succeed him; this does not sound very probable.

Mrs. Delany to Mrs. Dewes, at Calwich, near Ashbourne, Derbyshire.

Bulstrode, 9 Dec. 1743.

The cold I had when I left London was so slight that it was not worth mentioning; the pure air of this place took it off in a day, and I have not the least remains of it. We are all in good spirits about the Duke of Portland—his arm was unbound the day before yesterday, and is very right; in a week more they say it will be quite knit: all send kind greetings to Calwich, where I suppose you are, though you call it "*Bradley*" in your letter. But, my dearest sister, how is your lameness? I know a strain in the calf of the leg is a very painful thing, but I believe and hope not so lasting an evil as a sprain of the ancle; I know you are under the care of an excellent nurse and physician, and I trust they will not only apply what is proper, but will keep you quiet as long as is necessary for you to be so; and the weather is not tempting enough for you to be adventuring: let *your son seek adventures* for you, his youth and spirits can bear the rough salutes of Boreas, and the nipping frost he bids defiance to. We have had no such beautiful icicle scenes as you describe, but have been clouded with continual fogs; about noon they go off, and I have walked or gone in coach or chaise every day. The Duchess, who loves everybody and everything better than herself, will not use that constant exercise that is prescribed for her, though yesterday we prevailed on her to make Mrs. Bellenden a visit at Beconsfield, who is as *bouncing* as ever, and as loud: she made many enquiries after you and my brother. To-morrow we go to Windsor to see Miss Granville. Mr. Drummond was here when I received your last letter, and I made your compliments to him, he returns you his, and many thanks for your kind wishes. Lord Dupplin's son is dead, but his wife alive;[1] happy could he have made an exchange, for she grows more and more intolerable, and sets him at variance with all his family.

I am glad the Shepherd of Calwich has got a good flock without doors, as well as within—everything that adds to his contentment and pleasure adds to my happiness; had I not a very pure disinterested love for you all, *envy* would creep in and make me angry at a satisfaction you possess together without me, but far be that *fiend* from me; I feel all your joys, and wait till the happy hour arrives that will give me my share with you. I am afraid Mr. Dewes will think I am not a woman of my word, I promised to write to him, but you know what a devourer of one's time the Duchess of Portland is when one is with her; I have not written three letters since my being here besides what you have had, and they

---

[1] Constantia, daughter and heiress of John Kyrle Ernle, Esq., married in 1741, Thomas Viscount Dupplin, afterwards Earl of Kinnoul, and had an only child, born August 12, 1742, who died October 14, 1743. The Countess herself died in 1753.

were letters of business. I hope Mr. Dewes will have a good journey, and find you quite *well* of your lameness. I am just come from showing D.D. the Park; we borrow'd the Duchess's chaise; she intends to build a grotto in the hollow that you have a sketch of, and I am to design the plan for it. Her projects of planting and building are as innumerable as her works, but she will be prudent in her execution of them, and not go on too fast; she has this year made some improvements in the garden. I must go to prayers, where my dearest sister will be remembered in my most serious moments, and this must be finished at night.

Night is come, and I was in hopes of getting some news from Lord G., who came to-day from London, but how foolish was I to believe I could gather knowledge! " *To-morrow is to be an important day with the Lords.*"— " About what, my Lord?"—" *About what? nay I don't know, I can't tell; I know nothing of the matter.*"—" I hear, my Lord, that the players have quarrelled, pray how is it?"—" *I don't trouble my head about it—it is no concern of mine, all stuff and nonsense.*" Thus were we informed, and I was resolved you should have your part of it. The clock strikes nine, the supper-bell rings, but before I finish I must obey our kind Sovereign, who desires her " affectionate compliments to dear Pip, and as soon as she can write she will."

D.D. is very busy, looking over his works for the press; as soon as that work is accomplished he will write to the "*pearly Dews.*"

God bless you all! You say nothing of the young park-keeper at Highnam,—I hope his situation agrees with him. The lovely little group here are well, and so is Mrs. Elstob; all send kind love and service to Pip.

Mrs. Delany to Mrs. Dewes, at Calwich, near Ashbourne, Derbyshire.

Bulstrode, 14 Dec., 1743.

I proposed to myself writing my most dear sister a long letter to-day, but behold how my designs are frustrated. This morning I went with the Duchess of Portland, to wait on the Duchess of Kent,[1] and we came home to dinner at half-an-hour past four, and I am now so lazy and tired (though otherwise *perfectly well*) that I cannot say much, but will send you next post a folio sheet. I am very sorry to find your lameness still confines you, and cannot help thinking the accident has been worse than you own. Whatever it is, I beseech you, be not too hasty in walking. The Duchess of Kent[1] has made vast improvements at Old Windsor; I had not a notion of half the beauties of the place; she has made a walk winding up the hill, and a noble terrace-walk at the top that commands a most extensive and delightful prospect. We dropt D.D. at Mr. Bateman's, but found he was expected at the Duchess of Kent's, the servant had forgot to deliver the message, which brings another visit upon us; indeed I am ready to drop asleep over my paper, I must have some coffee to wake me. So adieu.

Lady Sarah Cowper[2] to Mrs. Dewes.

December 20th, 1743.

It will be excusing one fault by another when owning I am ashamed to see two letters from my dear Mrs. Dewes

---

[1] Sophia, daughter of William Earl of Portland, and widow of Henry Grey Duke of Kent.

[2] Lady Sarah Cowper was the eldest daughter of William, 1st Earl Cowper. She died unmarried in 1758.

unanswered. I confess at the same time, that I have broke my word with the physician who attended me in the country, and to whom I promised a faithful account of my health in ten days, which I have not found time for in two months. Three months in debt to Miss Talbot, &c.; and my letter-case is full of demands of the same nature. Writing is scarcely tolerable to me yet, suffering under a thousand complaints, though that of my head is entirely removed. Dr. Hoadley said it was rheumatic, hitherto it only leaves one part to attack another; but I am told I shall be well in time, or what is equivalent pain will become habitual, and I shall *not mind it*; I believe neither of these predictions; my age will not let me hope the one, nor my impatient temper the other. In such circumstances I wish, though in vain, that all my friends were about me which is always a blessing devoutly to be wished,—but in my case would be more particularly so; yet my brothers and sisters and many that I love are absent. *The comfort* I have is in Mrs. Pointz's family; I see them well, and in great joy that the inoculation of the girls has been as successful as that of the boys, and they have one fear less to struggle with.

I had a letter from Mrs. Delany last night,—she does not talk of leaving Bulstrode yet; she was very good to me when in town. I saw her here two or three times, and called upon her one morning; we had not time to look over the drawings and poetry you write of. Nothing convinces me more of *the power Mrs. Delany has over me*, than feeling myself *growing reconciled to the adventurous step she has taken*, but she gives reasons for every thing she does that *I can't but submit to*; I wish her happy; she says she is so, and *I must believe her.*

There is no news but politics, which I never attend to enough to repeat with clearness.

You mention one of your boys only at Calwich. I hope both are well.

Believe me most sincerely my dear Mrs. Dewes,
Your very affectionate and obliged humble servant,
S. COWPER.

My compliments to Mr. Granville.

The Countess Granville to Mrs. Delany.
Jan. 2, 1743-4.

The enclosed is a copy of my letter which I wrote to the Duke of Devonshire as soon as I received my dearest cousin's commands. I wish success may attend all you can desire, and that Dr. Delany and you may see many happy new years together! I am sorry for the Duke of Portland's accident. I hope her Grace and his Grace may now soon be in town, that I may have the pleasure of your company; Fanny [1] begins to return her visits, and will be overjoyed to converse with you both at your house and in Arlington Street, and to wait on you to the opera; but these are no temptations for you to leave the fine place you are in till the family breaks up. My best compliments to all, and my particular and tender respects to Dr. Delany.

I am, dear Madam,
Your affectionate humble servant,
GRANVILLE.

---

[1] Lady Frances Carteret, married, May 25, 1743, to John Marquis of Tweeddale.

This letter from the Countess Granville is a proof that her old feelings of attachment to *Mary Granville* had returned, even after her marriage with Dr. Delany, which had discomposed her very much. Mrs. Delany always seemed to distrust the sincerity of Lord Carteret, but there is no doubt that he was, individually, partial to Dr. Delany, and that he had taken especial pleasure in his society until the marriage which both he and his mother disapproved, though it does not appear that there were any other grounds than inequality of birth; and that, as an individual, both Countess Granville and her son liked Dr. Delany.

Mrs. Delany to Mrs. Dewes, at Calwich, near Ashbourne, Derbyshire.

Bulstrode, 4 Jan. 1743-4.

I am happy in a full assurance of my dearest sister's kind wishes at every season and on every occasion; but I feel strongly the truth of what you say, that when the heart is particularly filled with gratitude to the great Author and Bestower of all our blessings, those friends we love most tenderly cannot fail of our prayers and wishes for their prosperity; nor can we omit our most grateful acknowledgments for the happiness we enjoy in tender valuable friends. My most dear sister knows how nearly she is concerned in what I say on this subject. I do *not expect to hear* from the Squire of Calwich so long as he can have so good a secretary as yourself at his service, nor do I insist on his writing as long as I can have the assurance from you of his being well. I say the same to my dear mama, and beg she will not think herself obliged to write to me because I wrote to her; she is so excessively good to me when she is alone in letting me hear from her constantly that she may well indulge herself now. I am extremely pleased with your hospitable

and rational way of spending your Xtmas. I know
nobody better qualified to make his friends and neighbours happy than your landlord, and I heartily wish we
were with him to enjoy our share of the happiness he
dispenses,[1] but our affairs this winter will confine us to a
spot of less delight, and we must wait for the spring and
sunshine before we can take that share. Must I give up
all hopes of seeing you in town? I hope Mr. Dewes has
entirely lost the disorder in his eye and that he is very well,
pray assure him of my best service. He has had fine
walking weather, and I dare say has made good use of it.

You know by this time how well we agree in our opinion of the Yellow Journal; 'tis really droll and witty.
I believe I told you the judgment of this house about
the Fifth Night;[2] 'tis *not so dark* as some of his former,
but has *not* so much merit as his last, though many
thoughts and lines in it are charming. I am sorry my
godson begins with blotting out "*good,*" but that was
your fault more than his. I suppose by this time he can
point to round O and A, and that I shall find him a
notable scholar in the spring. You bid me not be under
any concern about your lameness—a reasonable request,
truly, and very practicable for me to put in execution; you
may as well charge me not to be cold this weather; but
your letter to the Duchess has lessened my concern and
given her a great deal of pleasure, for which she bids me
give you her kind love and many thanks. Have you

---

[1] This sentence indicates that Mr. Granville had invited Dr. and Mrs. Delany to Calwich, and that there was a certain appearance of amity; but it was very clear that there was a great change in the feelings and conduct of Mr. Granville after his sister's marriage which made her very unhappy.

[2] "Night Thoughts," by Dr. Young, were supposed to have been prompted by the death of his wife in 1741. They were published at different times during the years 1743-4.

seen the comet? All here saw it last night but myself; but I was writing, and by the time I had done it grew cloudy; it is to be seen not far from the south, near the constellations Aries and Pisces, if the air be clear; it is like a small star with a streaming tail, but of a faint light; it was seen here last night about 7.[1]

Now I must tell you what is *more extraordinary* than *any phenomenon in the sky*; upon hearing that Dr. Fletcher, Dean of Down, was to be made Bishop of Raphoe I wrote to Lady G. to desire she would apply to the Duke of Devonshire immediately for it, for that D.D. would like it as well as the bishopric, and in truth it is a better thing. She answered me the third day after I wrote to her in the *kindest manner*, and sent me a copy of her letter which she wrote to the Duke of Devonshire as soon as she received "*my commands*," as she calls them—a very strong, pressing request for the deanery. Well, this is not all the *strange news*.—Lord Carteret has presented the Maid of Honour[2] with a very handsome birthday suit of £3 a yard; I dare say it is all *by way of courtship*, but the *poor nun* of Windsor has no hopes, and they talk of trying to prevail with Lord Weymouth to add to her income, which Miss Granville fears may only do her a mischief with him, but this is to put off trouble from themselves, and they do not consider the bad consequence: however, if, on their application, Lord Weymouth *is disobliged*, it ought to be a strong motive to them to make it up to her.

---

[1] "The head appears bright, equal nearly in magnitude to the star Sirius, the brightest star in our hemisphere. It has a fiery tail about six degrees in length."—*London Magazine*, 1744, p. 46.

[2] The Hon. Elizabeth Granville, with whom it was then supposed Lord Carteret was in love.

The Duke of Portland is very well; they talk of removing the latter end of next week, and will not part with us till the day before they go. Donnellan, D.D., and I went yesterday to Beconsfield, to see Peg, who was excellent, and *entertained us* very much. She enquired after you and my brother very particularly. It is reported that the old Duchess of Marlborough is paying off the Duke of Marlborough's debts, and that she has given orders to her porter not to let that dog of a —— in-law into her doors on pain of losing his place.[1] Miss Hamilton, Lady Brooks,[2] sist (*illegible*) married to Lord Sutton Manners,[3] and Miss Selwyn, the Maid of Honour, very soon to Sir William Irby,[4] who has got by the death of Lord Uxbridge[5] £5000 a-year. She is a lucky girl, for he is a very good sort of man.

D.D.'s most affectionate service and duty attends Calwich. Thank God, he is very well, and I have the happiness to find him loved and respected by everybody.

My dearest sister, ever, &c.

---

[1] This must have been the Duke of Montague.

[2] Elizabeth, eldest daughter of Lord Archibald Hamilton, married in May, 1742, Francis Greville, 1st Earl Brooke and Earl of Warwick. The Earl died July 6, 1773. Jane, second daughter of Lord Archibald Hamilton, married July 24, 1753, Charles, 9th Lord Cathcart.

[3] Lord Robert Sutton Manners, born in 172?, was the second son of John, 3rd Duke of Rutland and of Bridget, only child and heir of Robert Sutton Lord Lexington. He assumed the name of Sutton on succeeding to the Lexington estate, and died unmarried in 1762. On his death, Lord George Manners, his next brother, inherited that estate and took the name of Sutton.

[4] Sir William Irby, born March 8, 1707, created *Baron Boston* April 16, 1761. This nobleman filled several high offices about the court during the reigns of George I. and George II. He married Albinia, (daughter of Henry Selwyn, Esq.) who was one of the Maids of Honour to the Princess of Wales.

[5] Henry, 7th Lord Paget, created Earl of Uxbridge, Oct. 1714, died in 1743, and was succeeded by his grandson, the 2nd Earl.

The following letter alludes to an accident which must have occurred between 4th and 9th of January.

Mrs. Delany to Mrs. Dewes, at Calwich, near Ashbourne, Derbyshire.

Bulstrode, 9 Jan. 1743.

I hope my dear friends at Calwich will make themselves quite easy on my account, for I am as well as it is possible for me to be under my present circumstances; indeed much better than I imagined anybody could be after my accident, as you may conclude from my being allowed to write this letter, which I do with perfect ease to myself. Saturday I got up to dinner and eat boiled chicken very heartily, and yesterday eat roasted chicken; and this morning have sate an hour in the dressing-room, whilst the bedchamber was airing, and to-morrow shall sit all day in my dressing-room, and next day go up to the Duchess's apartment; and on Friday (please God) propose to go to town. It is, I believe, unnecessary for me to enlarge on the kindness and care I have met with from our amiable friend the Duchess and Donnellan; much less reason have I to say anything of D.D.'s tenderness to me. I am sure you have a confidence in my nurses, and hope to find by your letters that you have not aggravated your concern for me by any unnecessary fears. My being able to write so well to-day has robbed you of a letter from D.D.; but next post he will write for me. Direct your next letters to Clarges Street. I received your last dear letter, and hope you will soon recover the perfect strength of your foot. Donnellan hopes to hear from you soon. Adieu, my most dear sister.

In Dr. Delany's handwriting.

I do hereby certify that the above account is the truth, the whole truth, and nothing but the truth.

Pat. Delany.

Dr. Delany to Mrs. Dewes.

Bulstrode, Jan 11th, 1743-4.

I am set down, my dear sister, with the worst pen and ink in the world, but the best good will to write to you, and to inform you that *the Pearl* is, I thank God, as fair and *much more precious* than ever. She has actually forbidden me to say one word of vapours or hysteric headachs; but I am tied to truth, and therefore must own to you that she has had, both yesterday and to-day, complaints of that kind, but without the least symptom of anything that deserves more attention than the inevitable concern which must arise in the hearts of those that are deeply engaged. She is at this moment in high mirth with the Duchess; she eat her dinner with a good relish, has just drunk a cup of caudle, and I think she is well disposed for her supper, and gives hopes of a good night. She is mightily bent on going to town on Friday or Saturday next, and I am at least satisfied she may do so with safety, however, I have this day sent to Dr. Bamber to have the sanction of his opinion whether it may be done with perfect safety.

You who know me, and the treasure under my care, will not be in any way surprised at my solicitude; indeed my whole soul is, and has some time been, divided between prayers and thanksgivings to Almighty God—thanksgivings for the blessing of such a wife bestowed upon me, and earnest prayers for the continuance of it; God in his goodness continue this blessing to you and everybody! with as little alloy as mortality will bear, *as long as I live,* and as *long as you wish,* and *as much longer* as heaven has happiness in store for her.[1] I am got into a spirit of praying, and cannot indulge it more agreeably than in lifting up my heart to heaven for its choicest blessings on you all. Adieu.

In Mrs. Delany's handwriting.

I have promised only to say that I am as well as can possibly be expected; *my head* is much better, and my heart most truly yours.

In Mrs. Donnellan's handwriting.

The good Doctor and our *"dear Pearl"* have given me leave to join my good wishes to all my agreeable friends at Calwich, and to assure them that I think her as well as could possibly be expected, which I know is the most pleasing news I can tell them. I must gratify myself, since I have this opportunity, in wishing dear Mrs. Dewes a happy year, and to Mr. Dewes, Mrs. Granville, and my much esteemed friend Mr. Granville, and the little ones; and in assuring dear Mrs. Dewes that I am her most,
   Affectionate friend and servant,
        H. DONNELLAN.

---

[1] The prayer here uttered was completely fulfilled; Mrs. Delany's life was prolonged far beyond that of her husband and sister, and to the termination of her existence much happiness was granted.

Mrs. Delany to Mrs. Dewes, at Calwich, near Ashbourne, Derbyshire.

Bulstrode, 13 Jan. 1743-4.

I hope the constant and true account you have had of me from hence, has made you and the rest of my dear friends easy on my account, and much more care and caution has been used than I have thought necessary. I did not want any proof of D.D.'s affection and tenderness, but I am confirmed in the opinion of his having as much for me as my best friends can wish him to have; and this I believe *you* are so well convinced of, that it was not necessary for me to be particular in it, but in *justice to him* and my own gratitude, I must indulge myself in repeating it. He wrote you word last post that I had an hysteric headache; it lasted but two days, and is now perfectly well, and I have no manner of complaint.

Yesterday I dined above stairs (you know my apartment is below), and returned to my room at supper-time; going abroad agreed very well with me, and I had a very good night's rest, and would fain have gone to town to day, but D.D. would not consent without Dr. Bamber's leave, and old fusty physicians you know are full of ceremony, and he says though I might travel this week, it is most advisable for me to stay till the middle of next; so the day is now fixed for Thursday. Donnellan is gone to town to-day; she had an account that Mrs. Percival had not been very well, and the Duchess could not prevail with her to stay any longer, and I could not oppose her doing what was so right, though I hope Mrs. Percival's illness is nothing dangerous. I was extremely entertained with your letter, my dearest sister, which I believe drove away my headache yesterday morning:

every testimony of your love and friendship is better to me than gold-powder or sal volatile. I wonder my spirits should ever want a cordial, whilst you so kindly and constantly supply me with your letters, but your foot is still vexatious to you and to me. I believe I have of late been the subject of great conversation round the fire-side of Calwich; and when I know that my dear mama, brother, and sister are satisfied about me, I shall be quite happy, *then* I may say with a good conscience, that I am perfectly well. Our amiable Duchess is but indifferent, she is very busy preparing for her remove, her "kind service to Pip" and compliments to Calwich. We all had the *good luck* to guess Mr. Dewes' riddle; my very good wishes and service attend him and you all, with the addition of duty and love; D.D. joins with me. Don't expect to hear next post, for now I shall fall into my usual train of every other post. I am my dearest sis most

Affectionate and faithful
M. D.

Mrs. Elstob sends her respects.

Mrs. Delany to Mrs Dewes.

Bulstrode, 18 Jan. 1743-4.

Though I hope my dearest sister is quite satisfied about me, I believe you will want to know how I perform my small journey to town; so I prepared this letter for that purpose, that I may to-morrow add that part: and now have not much to tell you but that I am very well and have not the least headache, and walked *in the sun* at twelve o'clock to-day, and got a very good appetite to my dinner. I wrote my mother word that D.D. and I were left in possession of this place; we live in the Duke's apartment, who has left orders that we should be supplied with everything we want, which we are indeed most plentifully. Betty Woodall (my maid) is housekeeper, and behaves herself very well, and I believe will prove a discreet useful servant, and I am really sorry to leave our agreeable retirement. The days have not been tedious; we read to one another by turns, have turned over all the picture-books we could find, talk abundantly, and play sometimes at backgammon. D.D. says he never played before, but he is so quick at it that if I did not know him to be a man of strict veracity I *should not believe him.*

Our retirement has produced a journal addressed to the Duchess of Portland; she was under great concern about leaving us here so ill accommodated, as she was pleased to say, and that she was "sure we should live like hogs," which provoked us to giving her an exact account of our spending our time. You shall have a copy of it when I have time to write it out; but upon my first going to London I shall have abundance of affairs on my hands. You must not expect to hear from me next post. I think myself obliged *to justify* Lady G. to you about the affair of the deanery, she only acted as she was desired; it is a *more advantageous* thing than many of the bishoprics, and would have been *much more agreeable* and convenient to us than the bishopric of Raphoe, for the income is as good, and we should have been more at liberty, and another advantage—we should have been free from ceremony. However, it will not be ours, for

Raphoe is given to an Englishman, Dr. Barnard, Dean of Rochester;[1] and Mr. Fletcher keeps his deanery. The Duchess, &c., got very well to town; I had a letter from her yesterday. So now good night. I will add a postscript to-morrow, as soon as I get to Clarges Street. Duty, love, and service from D.D. (who is now writing to Mrs. Viney) to all at Calwich.

I am, my dearest sister's
Most faithful and most affectionate
M. D.

I am sorry our poor friend Mrs. D. has not been remembered in her brother's will; I had a letter from her this morning. This moment I have received your letter, and must add my best thanks for it, and for all the kind care and concern of my friends at Calwich.

Thursday, half-an-hour after two.

We are, thank God, safely arrived, and I am very well, and find my *own little castle* very neat and comfortable. Mrs. Foley was brought to bed yesterday; she went to church in the morning, and the whole affair was over at eight at night, and before she could get Dr. Sandys. She has got a fine girl. Donnellan and Clarke are come to dine with us. Adieu! D.D. is much obliged to you for your letter, which has just made us happy. So once more farewell!

---

[1] Dr. William Barnard, Dean of Rochester, created Bishop of Raphoe in 1744; translated to Bishopric of Derry in 1747, which see he occupied till 1768.

Mrs. Delany to Mrs. Dewes.

Clarges Street, 24 Jan. 1743-4.

MY DEAREST SISTER,

Pray tell my brother, good wits jump. What he has *kindly hinted* in your letter *has been at my heart* and was proposed to me by D.D., but there are some obstacles in the way which if I can remove *I will* indulge myself in paying a visit to dear Calwich. I have business in town that obliges me to be here the latter end of March, but if I can contrive to spend six weeks with you I will come: the journey is too tedious and the roads too bad to remove for a less time, but that depends on D.D.'s going to Ireland. He waits for an account of the yacht's being at Chester; as soon as he has notice of its being there he will determine his journey, and hopes he *shall not* be an unwelcome guest at Calwich if he drops me there in his way to Chester.

If this scheme goes on I shall not move anything in my house till I return; at that time I shall *be glad of a hurry*, and perhaps you can come and help me, and I may, when all that is settled, and D.D. returns, be at liberty to take another tour among my friends. I have not yet ventured to Northend; the weather has been cold, and I am very carefull. How Sir J. Stanley will take this flight I don't know, but I fear not very well, he complains very much, and is by all accounts much in the same way he was in last year. D.D. made him a visit last Saturday; I am very glad my brother has prevailed with you to send your case to Dr. Bamber; I will get him consulted as soon as possible, but shall not be able to send his answer this post. I believe you should keep your foot warm and be extremely careful not to turn or bruise it.

I was yesterday morning at Mr. Handel's to hear the rehearsal of Semele.[1] It is a delightful piece of music, quite new and different from anything he has done: but I am afraid I shall hear no more music this year, and that will be a loss to me,—but the *harmony of friendship* must make up that loss. As we have a prospect of meeting soon I defer a particular account of it till we meet. Francescina[2] is improved, and sings the principal part in it.

I desire you will recollect all the want that I can supply you with before I leave London, and send me a list of commissions. I fancy we shall hardly leave London before Ash Wednesday. D.D. is engaged to preach on that day for the Bishop of Oxford at St. James's Chapel; but if he has an account of the yacht's being sooner than that at Chester he must go: in a week's time we may be at a certainty. My heart bounced for joy at the news of your good house,[3] pray God give you health and every blessing to enjoy it! I shall have a great deal of lumber that will do for your garrets or nurseries, so don't be hasty in furnishing till I talk to you about it.

---

[1] Semele was given at Covent Garden during the Lent of 1744. The *General Advertiser* of the 10th February, 1744, adds, in announcing it, 'After the manner of an oratorio." It was again performed in the December of the same year.

[2] Madame Duparc, commonly called *La Francesina*, arrived in England at tne end of 1736. On the 18th of November, 1736, she is named as one of a company who sang before her Majesty at Kensington, and met with a gracious reception. "After which, the Francescina performed several *dances* to the entire satisfaction of the Court."

[3] Welsborn, (or Wellesbourne,) near Stratford-on-Avon, Warwickshire.

Our cousin Foley is very well, I drank tea with her yesterday the sixth day, and she was so pert and well that every moment I was forced to silence her. She has got a very pretty little girl, and the boy is well now. I have had a number of visitors—a load upon my spirits, for I must dispatch them all before I leave London, or I shall be abused for incivility. I have not yet been with Lady Granville, but the young ones have *all* been here and the Countess herself. Donnellan is confined with a bad cold. The Sutton house very well, I was there last night. Miss Charlotte Pulteney, who had lost her voice for seven months, of a sudden has recovered it. Haircutter, hosier, visitors, and twenty fiddle faddles have interrupted me. Yours for ever.

D.D. and I join in duty, love, and service. I hope I shall see Mr. Dewes as soon as he comes to town.

From the commencement of this letter, it appears that Mrs. Dewes had communicated a proposal of Mr. Granville's, that Mrs. Delany should visit him while Dr. Delany went to Ireland ; and the joy with which it was hailed clearly proved that she had not expected it: whilst the reply expressing Dr. Delany's hope, that he should not be an unwelcome guest if he dropped her at Calwich on his way to Ireland, proved that he had not been mentioned. The *affection* as well as the *duty*, practically evinced by Mary Granville from her earliest years to her relations, was as uncommon for any age as it was exemplary, and at this period of her history, her brother's society was of less importance to her than it had ever been, and for the first time in their lives she had had a serious difference with him—yet with genuine good feeling she accepted the first advances he made, though with delicate tact she intimated, that if she came Dr. Delany would be with her on his road to Ireland.

Mrs. Delany to Mrs. Dewes.

Clarges Street, 28th Jan. 1743-4.

I must begin with telling you Mrs. Fortescue's[1] letter was sent to her in the country; when I see Lady Westmoreland, (which oh shame for me I have not yet done!) I will ask if she knows anything of it, and I ask your pardon for not mentioning this to you before. I cannot confirm what I said to you in my last, for as D.D. has not yet had any account of the yatch, and that we suppose it waits for the Duke of Devonshire, it is very likely he will not be able to have it, and he has promised me not to venture in any other ship. If *his journey* is postpon'd, *mine* must be so too, and the weather and roads are desperately bad at present; but still I can say nothing till we hear from Ireland, and I now almost wish I had not mentioned coming so soon to Calwich for fear I should not be able to accomplish it. Dr. Bamber was with me yesterday, I sent for him to ask him about your lameness, (for I am, thank God, very well); he says it will be of no bad consequence, and if you had immediately applied vinegar, and kept your bed one week, it would have saved you a great deal of trouble; that the swelling is nothing but the effect of weakness, and is very common after such an accident: he advises one ounce of Castille soap dissolved in half a pint of camphorated spirits of wine, rub your ancle very well with it in the morning, and roll it with a gentle bandage, not too tight; and you must not walk nor keep your leg down so long as the swelling continues. He recommends rest more than any application, and lying abed long in the morning—a prescription

---

[1] Miss Wesley.

well suited to this weather, and easily followed. Dr. Bamber desires his compliments to my brother and you.

Since I came to town I have not made one visit but to friends that are confined—Mr. Montague with the gout, Mrs. Foley lying in, Donnellan with a cold. To-day we are to dine at Mr. Southwell's, and as I must dress I shall make a few visits in the afternoon, for I have a dreadful long list upon my hands. I am sure Calwich is the most comfortable of all places for you at this time. I have not been able yet to go to Northend; poor Sir John complains sadly of this weather. I sent there, yesterday. I have not dared to venture into the City, for it has snowed with us three days without intermission, and I can hardly hold my pen. Mrs. Foley is very well.

I thought to have wrote you a long comfortable letter, but I find that's impossible, so take it *higgledy piggledy* as I can scrawl it.

Your comet. What is *your comet?* *Our's* appears considerably larger than a star of the first magnitude, with a train 300 miles long, and myriads of stars for its pages! I have heard of no astronomical remarks on it, only that it is "going to *fetch fire at the sun*," and will return to us again much more glorious than it is at present. Pray do not let my paltry chair interfere with your more important bed, which I hope you will finish as fast as you can; your hangings must be brown and white flowers, and ought to be the same pattern as your bed; if you can let me have the pattern I will consult *the artist* here about it.

The bed here alluded to is probably one which the Editor remembers to have seen at Wellesbourne as a child: it was the joint work of Mrs. Delany and Mrs. Dewes; the ground was nankeen, worked all over with most beautiful patterns designed separately by Mrs. Delany for each part. The patterns were leaves united by bows of ribbon, cut out in white linen and sewed down with different varieties of *knotting* in white thread—which gave relief, and light, and shade. " *The artist here,*" was probably *herself.*

Mrs. Delany to Mrs. Dewes.

Clarges Street, 7 Feb. 1743-4.

MY DEAREST SISTER,

I wish my letter had had warmth enough to have strengthened and thawed your fingers, then I might have had a longer letter than your last; but I have no reason to complain since I am so happy as to warm your heart: I leave the sun to do the rest, and hope soon he will be powerful enough to drive away the chilling frost. Many things concur now to keep us in town. D.D. has settled his affairs in Ireland for the present, and will escape the dismal journey he had once thought of taking. The Archbishop of Cashel[1] is dead, and it would not be prudent in him to leave this part of the world just as the Duke of Devonshire is coming; now there is a fair opportunity for friends to act.

The long-wished-for sermons are in the press. Twelve are corrected; there are five more to look over: I believe they will be out in a month. D.D. preached a sermon that I think would have pleased you last Sunday at May Fair Chapel, on Friendship and the Love of one's Country. To-morrow he preaches for the Bishop of Oxford at St. James's Church. You desired me an age

---

[1] Theophilus Bolton, Chancellor of St. Patrick's, and Vicar General of the diocese of Dublin, was made Bishop of Clonfert, in 1722, translated to Elphin, in 1724, and to the Archbishopric of Cashel, in 1730; and died in 1744.

ago to send you a pattern for *crackets*, (?) and I have been so negligent as not to do it, but will bring it when I am so happy as to come to you. I have not yet got silks, or worsteds, or answer from Mrs. Shuttleworth; the weather has been so cold I have not dared to go into the City.

As to pasting paper, I use flour boiled in water as smooth as it can be boiled, and paste both the papers very evenly that are to be pasted together. My cold is gone now, but my careful guardian would not suffer me to make any visits as long as the frost and cold weather lasts, so that my debts double and treble upon me. Where is Mr. Dewes? I have been in hopes of seeing him every day last week. I hope he is well and that I shall see him soon. I saw Mrs. Carey yesterday in deep mourning for Mrs. Fairfax; she enquired much after you, but more after my brother. Lady Westmoreland, Lady Cobham,[1] Miss Granville, Mrs. Claverin, Mr. Bateman, made up the number of my visitants. To-day the Misses Granville dine here, and Mr. Grattan, an Irish gentleman.

We have been alarmed about the Brest fleet, nor are we yet satisfied what their designs are; it is thought by most people that they are going to the West Indies, but reported that their design is to join Admiral Torres to guard their galleons home. Lord Cholmondely is to succeed the Duke of Devonshire.[2] I have seen the old Countess but once since I came to town. If the wea-

---

[1] Anne, daughter of Edmund Halsey, Esq., married Sir Richard Temple, created in 1718 Viscount and Baron Cobham.

[2] The Earl of Chesterfield succeeded the Duke of Devonshire as Lord Lieutenant of Ireland, in 1745.

ther grows warmer I propose going to Court next Friday. Lady Egmont is better;[1] she has been in a great deal of danger.

Drapers, hatters, tailors, and a long visit from Donnellan have cut my time so short this morning, that I fear I shall hardly have time to fill this sheet of paper; but I'll go and dress to be ready for my company, and give you all the time that remains. Now I am come again, but can add but little more. Semele is to be performed next Friday; D.D. subscribes for me, and I hope not to miss one of the charming oratorios, except when I give up my ticket to him

I think poor Mrs. Percival in a very declining way; she looks ill and complains often, but can play at cards and visit; Donnellan has got abroad again. Last Saturday I went to Northend, and think Sir J. Stanley much the same as when I saw him last; he asked me when there was hopes of his seeing my brother, which was a question *I could not answer*; he spoke of him with great tenderness to D.D.

The Duchess of Portland has got Sigismunda from him (Sir J. Stanley). He said it was so shocking a picture he could not bear it in his sight, and I carried it from him to the Duchess, who received it with great joy. She has new painted her dressing-room, hung it with green, and turned out the lumbering chest of drawers. It is quite spruce and well, and so is she, and in much better spirits than when she left Bulstrode. My company are at my door. Adieu.

---

[1] Catherine, eldest daughter of Sir Philip Parker A'Morley, Bart., married, in 1710, Sir John Percival, who in April, 1715, was created Baron Percival, and in November, 1733, Earl of Egmont.

The Sigismunda alluded to is in the possession of the Editor; it is painted by Mrs. Delany, and is one of the finest crayon pictures ever seen. Sir Joshua Reynolds was so astonished at its force, that he said his eyes would not allow him to believe it was crayon; on which Mrs. Delany had the glass taken off, that he might examine it closely. It still retains its fine colouring as well as its exquisite finishing. It is believed to have been copied from the Sigismunda in the collection of Sir Luke Schaube, mentioned by Horace Walpole as at Clumber, and as being attributed to Correggio, though in reality painted by Furini. Sigismunda is bending over a vessel on which lies the heart of Guiscard.

Mrs. Delany to Mrs. Dewes.

Feb. 11th, 1743-4.

In return for my dearest sister's last charming letter I can only send her my hasty thanks, for I am but just returned from Northend, and the clock has struck two. Our disappointment in not meeting, I believe, was equal; but on many accounts it is very well D.D. did not go as he proposed: had he been at sea the time we had the alarm about the French fleet I should have been sadly terrified, and now it is necessary for him to wait the Duke of Devonshire's arrival, as he cannot, I think, fail of the promotion which he has so long had a title to.

Last Thursday we dined in A. Street[1] by invitation, and were most courteously received, and a *positive assurance* given of their interest on this occasion; his sincerity will soon be put to the test, and only waits the Duke of Devonshire's coming over, which is deferred for some time on account of the Brest fleet, but I suppose he will be over some time in March. My cold is now

---

[1] Arlington Street, (Lord Carteret's.)

perfectly well. I was yesterday to hear Semele; it is a delightful piece of music. Mrs. Donnellan desires her particular compliments to all *but* to my brother; she bids me say "she loses half her pleasure in Mr. Handel's music by *his not being here* to talk over the particular passages." There is a four-part song that is delightfully pretty; Francesina is extremely improved, her notes are more distinct, and there is something in her running-divisions that is quite surprizing. She was much applauded, and the house full, though not crowded; I believe I wrote my brother word that Mr. Handel and the Prince had quarrelled, which I am sorry for. Handel says the *Prince* is quite out of *his* good graces! there was no disturbance at the play-house, and the Goths were not so very absurd as to declare, in a public manner, their disapprobation of such a composer. Mr. Dewes I understand will be in town to-night, and I hope he will dine with us to-morrow; I shall then talk abundantly of Calwich and Welsborne; I think Lord North's is about eight miles from thence.

The Duchess of Portland has had a cold and kept home; I am to go to her this afternoon, but cannot stay long, for D.D. has got a very bad cold, and I shall not care to leave him long, but he will make me go as I had promised. If my visiting you at Welsborne, and being busy in settling you there, will add to your eagerness and pleasure of taking possession, I see no reason why you should *not* indulge that thought. I am sure I think of seeing you there with vast satisfaction, and hope to spend many happy hours there with you, but shall *expect my visits to be returned.*

Alas! the poor grotto! I grieve for its downfal, but rejoice that nothing was buried in its ruins but the Windsor chairs. The particulars of Miss Lewson? Surely I sent you a long story about her: as how she fell ill, and in the midst of her pains told the Duchess of Bedford (who they say was ignorant of her condition till that moment), that she had been married a year to Lord John Sackville.[1] A wretched couple I fear they will prove; he is ill-natured and a man of no principle, and she has shewn the world that she has little prudence. I was agreeably surprized with Mr. Dewes dining with us to-day, he is very well. The post will wait no longer; my humble duty to my mother and love to my brother; best compliments from D.D.

I am ever yours.

Mrs. Delany to Mrs. Dewes.
16 Feb. 1743-4.

Don't scold, my dear sister, that I begin on small paper, but I fear it is all I shall be able to fill this post. I am very sorry for poor Mrs. Hudleston, and wish we may be able to get the charity money for her. D.D. is not so well acquainted with the people who must grant that petition as to be able to serve her, and the only friend I could apply to has done so much in that way for the Griffiths family (which is Dr. Middleton), that I don't know how to apply to him for more. The first leisure day I have, I will call on Mrs. Underwood, but now my hands and head grow full of business, and I have so much to settle that I am afraid of forgetting what I undertake to do for other people.

I have bought your worsted and silk for my brother's

---

[1] Lord John Philip Sackville, second son of the 1st Duke of Dorset, married Lady Frances Leveson Gower, fourth daughter of John, 1st Earl Gower.

chair that you are to work; pray let me know, how and when I must send it. I could not meet with any workwomen that would do it under two guineas and a half. The materials for working come to eighteen shillings. I have matched the colours to the work that is done; you must fancy them as you think proper. I beg you not to be under any concern for my sky. I would have it clear of clouds, the pink silk must join the hill, and the blue silk next,—about one third silk the other the blue worsted. Mr. Parker dined here yesterday. The Duke of Devonshire is expected soon; when he comes, the Bishoprie will be settled; in Ireland (by report) D.D. is named for Dromore. We cannot guess at our time of going, as it depends on this affair, but he will at least finish the year in England that he took his licence out for. You may imagine how much I talk'd of Calwich and Welsbourne with Mr. Dewes: he is delighted with Calwich, and says he had no notion my brother could have improved it so much in so short a time, but with the genius for improvements that he has, and such industry to execute his scheme, and so much time as he has allowed himself (alas!) in the country, what may he not do? Though I often think with pleasure of the happy society at Calwich, I cannot help wishing another year *than this* had been chosen for it. The loss of my brother's company this winter has been an irreparable loss to me; I can't help *flattering myself* with the hopes of his eloping from you. Forgive me, but I am not used to disguise my hopes and fears from you.

The head-board, tester, and all the inside of the bed must be worked; *my noddle* has thought of a pattern, but till we meet I cannot fix on anything. Did I not tell you,

my dear sister, that I had laid by *Summer*[1] for your new house; it is a picture you used to like. As soon as I am settled in Delville I shall take to oil-painting, and if I can perform tolerably, will send you a copy of my father and mother's picture.

Feby. 16, 1744.

P.S.—Yesterday the King sent a message[2] to the two houses to let them know the Pretender's son was in France, and that they had undoubted intelligence the French design an invasion with the Brest fleet, and it is suspected a great many disaffected people here are ready to join them. What all this will come to God knows, but I pray for peace.

Mrs. Delany to Mrs. Dewes.

Clarges Street, 21 Feb. 1744.

I think, my dearest sister, if *we* are not happy it *must be our own faults*; we have both chosen worthy, sensible friends, and if we act reasonably by them and ourselves, we may hope for as much happiness as this mortal state will afford : *thorns* we *must* all find, but if Providence allows us *roses to our thorns* we ought to be thankful, and make the best of their sweets. You'll say I am in a very moralizing way ; and for fear of dulness I will quit my own thoughts and talk of people and things as they

---

[1] *Summer.*—This beautiful picture in crayons, painted by Mrs. Delany, from Rosalba, is in the Editor's possession. The original picture is now (1859) in the Louvre.

[2] "*His Majesty's Message*" to the two Houses of Parliament, communicating the intelligence that "the eldest son of the Pretender to his crown had arrived in France, and that preparations are making there to invade this kingdom," was delivered on the 15th February, 1744.

go. Your letter though small in size was great in value, as the least mark of your love and goodness towards me will ever be, and I live in hopes that next post will bring me a folio, or an equivalent to one. The warm gentle weather we now have must be an advantage to my brother's works, and make Calwich bloom; my love and tender wishes attend him and all his designs, and my most affectionate duty my dear mama; D.D. is most warmly devoted to all, and wishes nothing more than *to convince* my friends of his sincere and respectful regard to them. He has had a bad cold (colds I may say), for he no sooner lost one than he got another, but thank God he is well again. He preach'd last Sunday at Chelsea; we dined at Dr. Elsmore's,[1] and made a visit to the Coles in the afternoon, who enquired much after you. Captain Cole is much concerned that his friend has not performed his promise yet to my brother's exciseman, but will not fail of putting him in mind. I have a sad tale to tell, but Dick is lost, he has been cried and advertized to no purpose; he walked off above a fortnight ago, and Betty is in a terrible taking about him, but she apprehends he went off mad, for sixteen dogs in the neighbourhood were bit and hanged at the time she missed him. The rest of the animals are all well. I had the pleasure of seeing Mr. Dewes very well last Sunday evening, when we all met at Mr. Percival's.

Semele is charming; the more I hear it the better I like it, and as I am a subscriber I shall not fail one night.

---

[1] Dr. Sloane Elsmere was instituted to the rectory of Chelsea after the death of Dr. King, in February, 1747, and died in 1766. He left behind him a volume of sermons to be published for the benefit of the Girls' Charity School, of which benevolent institution he was the original founder. Dr. Elsmere was a relation of Sir Hans Sloane; in 1752 he married Miss Cotes.

But it being a profane story D.D. does not think it proper for him to go; but when Joseph or Samson is performed I shall persuade him to go—you know *how much* he delights in music. They say Samson is to be next Friday, for Semele has a strong party against it, *viz.* the fine ladies, petit maîtres, and *ignoramus's*. All the opera people are enraged at Handel, but Lady Cobham, Lady Westmoreland, and Lady Chesterfield never fail it.

Now I know you are impatient to have some account of bishoprics, but I can give you none. We dined yesterday in Arlington Street, and Lord C. said there was some demur about the Archbishopric. Price Bishop of Meath and Buscoe Bishop of Limerick were both named, but as there is five thousand pounds *to pay* it made it not quite so desirable; and I am apt to think that Meath will be the Archbishop, Limerick Bishop of Meath, and *your friend* Bishop of Limerick, but this cannot be settled or known till my Lord Lieutenant comes over, and he cannot come over till we have passed the storm that threatens us.

There was a report yesterday that a captain of a ship was come with the joyful news of Admiral Mathews having gained an entire victory over the French and Spaniards; whilst we were at dinner yesterday a message came from Lord Oxford to Lord Carteret to know if there were any truth in the report. He knew nothing of it then, but it is very probable, the French having stopped the mail at Calais, which looks as if they had news they were unwilling we should know; as to the Brest fleet the last account was of their being certainly at Dunkirk; and Sir John Norris has orders to pursue them. There are *some infidels* that suppose all this a ministerial plot;

I suspend my judgment, for such contradictions arise every hour that it is not possible to guess at the truth. Lord C. *does make a great fuss* with Daisy,[1] and some of the family are alarmed at it and treat her very differently from what they used to do, and *I am* in a fright about it, for she can hardly refuse it, and yet I think it would *not* be a *happy* establishment. The son[2] makes but a poor figure, and is not a favourite with any of the family. I have not seen Sir J. Stanley since I wrote last, but I hear he is much as he was; he certainly has less pain and looks much better.

I have just finished a picture which I own pleases me the best of any I have done; 'tis from Paul Veronese— St. Catherine, a head with one hand, as big as the life. I believe my brother remembers the picture. I have finished it as high as possible for me to finish, because it will be a sort of study for me when I can't get better pictures to copy. I went last Saturday morning with the Duchess of Leeds to see Mrs. Waters, a very ingenious obliging woman, a worthy daughter of a very unworthy mother (Lady A.), of whom we have heard many cruel stories; and as she lived so she dies, for she has settled all her fortune *from her daughter* upon my Lord Delawarr and his family. Yesterday as my Lord Winchelsea[3] was going to Court the glass was up and his blind eyes did

---

[1] The Honble. Eliz. Granville, the Maid of Honour.

[2] Robert Carteret, afterwards 2nd Earl Granville. Writing after the second marriage of Lord Carteret, Horace Walpole says of his family: "His only son is gone mad: about a fortnight ago he was at the Duke of Bedford's, and as much in his few senses as ever. At 5 o'clock in the morning he waked the Duke and Duchess all bloody, and with the lappet of his coat held up full of ears, he had been in the stable and cropped all the horses."

[3] Daniel, 7th Earl of Winchelsea, who filled the offices successively of Comptroller of the Household, Lord of the Admiralty, and President of the Council. He married first, in 1729, Lady Francis Feilding, daughter of Basil, Earl of

not perceive it, so that bowing to somebody, and the coach giving a great jolt at the same time, popped his head quite through, and has cut his forehead violently; it is well he did not lose an eye. Lady Dysart is now in good spirits and is as very fine a lady as ever.

I have been for some time in an odd situation about an affair that I have had in my head and at my heart. Our dear worthy Violet's[1] circumstances are such, that if if it were now possible to settle her well it would be doing a good action, and I have had a hint given me that Mr. Gⁿ near Windsor, has thoughts of marrying, but is afraid of the fine ladies, and that it was not impracticable if a judicious friend could be met with, to have her character given him, that such a union might be compassed. I thought of the B. of Gloucester, who is the most intimate friend the gentleman has. I sent for him told him frankly my thoughts, and begged his friendship and assistance, both which he promised me when an opportunity offered; but he feared the gentleman wanted *some money*, as the Earl had not settled the fortune, though the *title* would come to him; but he approved of my scheme, and said he would do all he could, for he thought they were worthy of each other, and *he bears as good a character as she does*; this was three weeks ago, and I have not heard one word. I think you cannot be at a loss to know who I mean if you recollect what Primrose wrote to me when I was at Gloucester I would not mention this to you sooner, in hopes of having surprized you agreeably. I hope my brother will not think I have taken a wrong step; the Bishop of Gloucester is a man of so much honour and discretion that I am sure he may be trusted, and no one else knows it. Well, now I have given you materials enough to think of and talk over for this post, so adieu, my dear sister. When may I have hopes of seeing my brother? We are now tied down till the Duke of Devonshire comes.

Mrs. Waters and the Duchess of Leeds breakfast with me, and are to look over my sketches and drawings; Violet, Primrose, and Daisy dine with me; Portlands and Montagues drink tea with me; I go to the Schaub assembly, and sup in Bond Street. Will not the day be meritoriously occupied? Lady Sarah Cowper is mortified you do not write to her. She is better, and was with me yesterday.

Mrs. Delany to Mrs. Dewes.

Clarges Street, Feby. 25th, 1743-4.

I must make use of your kind indulgence, my dearest sister, this post. I shall hardly have time to say a word, for I painted till the clock struck twelve, and then thought to indulge myself with writing you a long letter, when Sir T. Hanmer came, and he would send for me down, and was so unreasonable as to stay till past one. The Montagus all dine here, and in the afternoon the Duchess of Portland and Donnellan come, so that this present moment is all the time I shall have. The chairs, worsteds, silks, stuff for the bed, seeds, and *tincture of benjamin* all go to the carrier on Monday, and I hope will arrive safe at Calwich in due time. I am glad to hear of the beautiful verdure of the *pearl fountain*, and that you have honoured it with a visit; but I doubt you are still lame, and I hear you have got a cold.

There is a certain account of an engagement between the united fleets of France and Spain and Admiral Mathews, to our advantage; but the particulars are not known, for the French, who know the particulars, will let us know nothing they can conceal, and all the intelligence we can have must come through Germany, as war with France is now declared, that is, France has in effect declared it by falling upon our fleet. As to the Brest squadron, I think we know as little about it as we did three weeks ago; it is generally thought they only meet to divert and alarm us that we may keep our troops at home; you'll smile at my entering into politics, but now one must be dumb or talk of the times.

Well, to change from discord to harmony I will shift my subject, and tell you I was last night to hear Samson.[1] Francescina sings most of Mrs. Cibber's part and some of Mrs. Clive's: upon the whole it went off very well, but not better than last year. Joseph,[2] I believe, will be next Friday, but Handel is mightily out of humour about it, for Sullivan, who is to sing Joseph, *is a block* with a very fine voice, and Beard has *no voice at all*. The part which Francescina is to have (of Joseph's wife) will not admit of much variety; but I hope it will be well received; the houses have not been crowded, but pretty full every night. We went to Northend last

---

[1] Samson, an oratorio by Handel, was first performed at the Theatre Royal in Covent Garden on the 18th February, 1743. It was performed eight times in that year, and twice in the year 1744.

[2] Joseph and his Brethren was written in August, 1743, and was given at Covent Garden during the Lent of 1744. It was performed four times during that year. Signora Galli, a favourite pupil of Handel, made her debut in Joseph.

Thursday and found poor Sir John in great pain; he has complained very much this last week, and says he grows weaker, but I think he looks pretty well. He has given me some very pretty shells for my works, but none fine enough for my collection; but a friend of D.D. in the West Indies has promised me great curiosities. We are still ignorant as to the bishoprics, the grand affairs of war and tumult prevents all thought of anything else: an express came last night from Sir J. Norris, that he was within an hour's sail of the Brest fleet.

I am sorry Mrs. Duncomb comes to town, unless she had a good call, for she will not meet with a kind reception from the old Countess, but *quite the contrary*, and as to the *great man*, if his heart was good towards her he *is now really so much embarrassed* he cannot now think of anything but the state. Sir Thomas Hanmer[1] is determined to prosecute Tom Hervey; the child, they say, is dead that Tom would provide for, and he means to impose one by another person; it is a most villanous affair, and I heartily wish Sir T. may get the better of his wicked adversary. The Rev. Mr. Hervey[2] made a recantation sermon at St. George's church, acknowledging his errors and purposing a thorough reformation. It was thought that the £4000 a-year he has got by the death of Sir Thom. Aston would have made him throw off the gown, but he declares he will not, and that 'tis the

---

[1] Sir Thomas Hanmer married, first, in 1698, Isabella, Duchess-Dowager of Grafton; and secondly Elizabeth, only daughter and heir to Thomas Folkes, Esq., who eloped with the Honble. Thomas Hervey, second son of John, 1st Earl of Bristol. Walpole in 1741 calls Mr. Hervey "quite mad."

[2] The Honble and Revd. John Hervey, D.D. fourth son of John, 1st Earl of Bristol, married Catherine, eldest sister and heir of Sir Thomas Aston, Bart., who died 17th February, 1744.

life in the world he shall choose, and will follow. Betty Carter is in great grief for her mother. She had last post an account of her death, which was very sudden: when she went to bed she complained of a little cold, in the night the person that lay with her heard her give a sigh, she asked her how she did, she did not answer, but soon gave another sigh, upon which the person that lay with her got up and found she was dead! A happy ending for a good woman. I have put Mr. Bateman in mind of the bracket he promised, which I hope to have soon. Pray send Mrs. Godineau's receipt for the baked fillet of veal.

Mrs. Delany to Mrs. Dewes.

Clarges Street, March 1, 1743-4.

In vain is it to purpose doing anything. I was as much determined to write my dear sister a long letter by this post as ever I was to do anything in my life, and behold I am reduced in time to past ten o'clock, but will say the most material things I can in the time. I am very much concerned for my dear godson, but hope before this reaches you that his ague will have left him. Two *infallible receipts* I must insert before I proceed further.

1st. Pounded ginger, made into a paste with brandy, spread on sheep's leather, and a plaister of it laid over the navel.

2ndly. A spider put into a goose-quill, well sealed and secured, and hung about the child's neck as low as the pit of his stomach. Either of these I am assured will ease. *Probatum est.*

Letters from Marseilles by a Jew, and from Admiral

Mathews' agent, have brought an account of our having gained an entire victory after three days' desperate fight,—such a fight and such a victory as they say has not been known on the seas.

The post bell calls. Adieu.

M. D. & P. D.

Although the prescription of the spider *in the quill* will probably only create amusement from its apparent absurdity considered merely as an *old charm*, yet there is no doubt of the medicinal virtue of spiders and their webs, which have been long known to the Celtic inhabitants of Great Britain and Ireland. Some interesting anecdotes and facts relative to this subject may be found in 242nd number of Notes and Queries, where particulars are given of the efficacy of spider's webs rolled up like a pill, and swallowed when the ague fit is coming on. Dr. Graham[1] prescribed spider's webs for ague and intermittent fever, and also named powder made of spiders given for the ague, and mentions his knowledge of a spider having been sewn up in a rag and worn as a periapt round the neck to charm away the ague. This no doubt arose from the practical knowledge of the efficacy of the internal administration and ignorance of its medical properties, which resulted in the belief that *the insect* (spider) would work a charm if hung round the neck bodily. The black spider (Theridion) of Curaçoa is used for sea-sickness; spiders or cobwebs given on brown sugar are still given in some agueish localities in England, and the great black barn spider is the sort used for medicine in Britain.

Dr. Donaldson in a letter in "the Indian Lancet," recommends the web of the common spider as an unfailing remedy in certain fevers, which was used a century ago by the poor people in the fens of Lincolnshire, and by Sir James M'Gregor in the West Indies.

The *Aranea Diameda*, the largest English spider, found in birch trees, is a remedy well known in Homeopathic medical practice.

---

[1] "Domestic Medicine."

Mrs. Delany to Mrs. Dewes.

Clarges Street, 6 March, 1743-4.

It is impossible for me not to be uneasy, when I know my dear little godson is ill, and what you and my mother must suffer when he is so, though an ague is so common to little children, and not of dangerous consequence. I hope before this arrives he will have lost every symptom of complaint, if not, it is best to give him bark in the only way children can take it, which very seldom fails. I have sent a prescription from Mrs. Montague and Mr. Clark. Everybody agrees you should give the child meat now; he may eat meat three times a week, and pudding or panada the other days. Sometimes sheep's totters, which are both innocent and nourishing; and make him to be jumbled about a good deal for fear of falling into the rickets, and throw away his wormwood draughts, for they *signify nothing* for an ague. Have an attention to him about worms, which are the cause of most children's illness; pray God bless the dear boy, and send you many years of joy and comfort with him!

And *now* having finished my paragraph about him, *like a good old fashion'd godmother*, I leave him for this post. Mrs. Duncomb came to town last Saturday. I called on her on Sunday, she looks thin, and I am afraid she will not meet with anything here to fatten her up; for those that might make up to her her brother's unkindness *seem not at all* disposed to serve her.

We have had at last good news from Admiral Mathews, though very different from what I sent you before. He has beaten the Spaniards, and the French have run away. The storm we had on Friday se'nnight stranded 12 of the French transports at Dunkirk, and lost them 600 men. Sir J. Norris' fleet received small damage from the storm.

You must not expect I shall lament with you my brother's leaving Calwich, for I own sincerely I am overjoyed at the thoughts of seeing him. Oh what a joy it would have been to have seen you all together! We dined last Sunday in Arlington Street: prodigiously gracious!

Lady Wescombe[1] died last Saturday—a six weeks mourning for my mother and three for us, but as she is not known in Staffordshire, I think it of no consequence to put it on there. The Bishop of Gloucester has just been with me, he has had an opportunity of talking to Mr. G., he asked him if he had ever had *such* a query proposed to him? that her fortune was *so and so*, and her character a most extraordinary one from everybody. The gentleman agreed she had an excellent character, said she never had been mentioned to him, and made no objection; but gave no encouragement for the Bishop to say more. Is this good or bad? But as he says he designs marrying, and is a very reasonable man, and has no other person in view, the more he considers this affair the better he must approve of it. *She* is gone out of town this morning; I wish there could be an acquaintance between them, but he knows none of her friends; the Bishop of Glou-

---

[1] Anna Maria Calmady, wife of Sir Anthony Westcombe, Bart. was baptized February 10, 1701. She was the only child and heir of Josias Calmady of Langdon, Esq., and of his 2nd wife Jane Rolt, daughter of Sir John Rolt, of Milton, Devonshire, Knt.: Anna Maria Calmady, married Sir A. Westcombe, April 6, 1736. The order subsequent to her death for her heraldic achievement in the Heralds' College, bears date March 7, 1743-4.

cester has promised to watch and do all the service he can; he seems really to enter with zeal into the affair.

Where do you think we dine to-day? Why truly at Sir Thomas Hanmer's! In the evening I go to the dear Duchess, who has been confined, and ill with a cough and soreness on her chest this week or ten days; and after what she suffered with a cough last year, I own I was greatly alarmed for her. I dined yesterday at Sir Robert Sutton's; poor Lady Sunderland is very complaining, the rest are all well.

Mrs. Delany to Mrs. Dewes.

Clarges Street, March 10, 1743-4.

My dearest sister's last letter gave me a great deal of pain for my dear boy, but a note Mr. Dewes sent me this morning has revived my spirits. My brother did not come to town till yesterday at two; he is very well, though he was yesterday much fatigued with the ways and weather, yet alert enough to dress and go to the oratorio, which was *the first place* I saw him in. I sent to his house to beg he would dine with me, or at least come to me as soon as he had dined, and I would carry him to the oratorio, but he *would do neither*; he came home with me, but would not stay one moment, and to-day he is gone to Northend. D.D. and I dine at Leicester House with Mrs. Claverin, who is in waiting; the Percivals meet us there. Yesterday Mr. Dewes dined with us; he made my brother a visit in his way, and they are to meet on business next Monday. I went yesterday morning into the City to buy myself a white satin manto and petticoat, but did not meet with one to my mind, so I shall wait some days longer. I have now two cousin-germans to mourn for—Lady Wescombe and Sir William Carew,[1] who died last Monday.

Did I write you word of our Princess's being in town? Yes, I did; and you knew it before me by the letter you enclosed for her, which I delivered safely to her last Wednesday: she and Lord Belfield[2] dined here. You remember his unfortunate story? He is a sort of son-in-law of mine; his name is Rochford; his first wife was the eldest Miss Tennison, his second, my Lord Molesworth's daughter. He discovered an intrigue, and they say he has come to England in search of *him*, to kill him wherever he meets him; but I hope his resentment will cool, and not provoke him to so desperate an action, and he does not appear to have any such rash design, but is more cheerful and composed than one could expect him to be; he is very well-bred, and very well in his person and manner; his wife is locked up in one of his houses in Ireland, with a strict guard over her, and they say he is so miserable as to love her even now; she is extremely handsome, and has many personal accomplishments.

> "A fairer person lost not heaven; she seem'd
> For dignity compos'd and high exploit:
> But all was false and hollow."

I have no public news. It is now said that there has

---

[1] Died, March, 1744, Sir William Carew, of Antony, in Cornwall, Bart., one of the knights of the shire for that county. He was succeeded by his only son, Sir Coventry Carew, Bart.

[2] Robert Rochfort, created Lord Belfield, in Ireland, 1737, Viscount Belfield in 1751, and Earl of Belvedere, in 1756. His second wife, whom he married in 1736, was the Hon. Mary Molesworth, daughter of Richard, 3rd Viscount Molesworth.

certainly been an engagement in the Mediterranean, and that we have had the advantage, but farther particulars have not yet come. To-morrow we dine in Arlington Street; what stay do you propose making at Calwich? By the time the roads are tolerable I hope I may be able to come to you in Staffordshire; it will not be in my power to make the tour of Gloucester and Bradley in my way to Chester; and you cannot be settled at Welsbourne before Midsummer, so that, though I may call there in my way to Calwich to *see the place,* there is no possibility of our meeting there till next year. I have got an old broken Indian chest for you, some scrub chairs, a sofa and couch—(the couch is precious because covered with a gift of my mother's, but it is so lumbering a thing I can't take it with me,)—a clock, and a few pictures; let me know where these shall be deposited when I pack up, not that I have yet made any preparations for it, but I must settle by degrees, that the confusion may be less at the time of moving. I think it fortunate for us both, that we shall be in a bustle this summer; and when we consider that we are not only settling ourselves in a happy and reasonable situation, but are preparing pleasant apartments to *receive each other by turns,* I think we may find great satisfaction in the employment. I shall wait with impatience for to-morrow's post, in hopes of a confirmation from you of the dear child's being well again. I think, in case of a return, you are now well provided with remedies.

The oratorios fill very well, notwithstanding the spite of the opera party: nine of the twelve are over. Joseph is to be performed (I hope) once more, then Saul, and the Messiah finishes; as they have taken very well, I fancy Handel will have a second subscription; and how do you think *I have lately been employed?* Why, I have made a drama for an oratorio, out of Milton's Paradise Lost, to give Mr. Handel to compose to; it has cost me a great deal of thought and contrivance; D.D. approves of my performance, and that gives me some reason to think it not bad, though all I have had to do has been collecting and making the connection between the fine parts. I begin with Satan's threatenings to seduce the woman, her being seduced follows, and it ends with the man's yielding to the temptation; I would not have a word or a thought of Milton's altered; and I hope to prevail with Handel to set it *without* having *any of the lines put into verse*, for that will take from its dignity. This, and painting three pictures, have been my chief morning employment since I came to town. I must write two letters more this post.

D.D. has been much concerned for the little boy. But as

An ague in the spring
Is physick for a king,

we hope he will find no bad consequences attend it.

The letters of Mrs. Delany after her second marriage, gradually unfold the effects of the constant cultivation of the uncommon talents, which she had through life taken every opportunity to improve quietly and unostentatiously; but there is no doubt that the pride and pleasure which Dr. Delany took in her favourite occupations, gave her fresh spirit and fresh zeal. She here mentions finishing three pictures, besides the remarkable fact of her having arranged a drama for an oratorio by Handel from Paradise Lost. It does not appear that this oratorio was ever brought forth in Handel's life-time; but an oratorio under this title was published as Smith's, after his death, which was most probably Handel's own composition.

Mrs. Delany to Mrs. Dewes, at Calwich.

Clarges Street, 15 March, 1748-4.

It grieves my heart that the poor dear little boy should have a return of his ague, but I hope you have given him the bark before now and at the time you laid on Clark's plaister. How unfortunate I am always to be from you in your distresses! but absent from or present with you I must mourn when you mourn, and rejoice when you rejoice. Agues though frightful are *not fatal*, and I have strong faith in the bark *where it can be taken*, and in nothing else.

I shall be glad to leave the Duchess of Portland safe in her bed before I come to you, and when I shall have that happiness the Duke of Devonshire only knows, for till then we must not move. If it were not for the giving up my house, packing off my trumpery, which I must do myself or may sustain great damages, I should leave D.D. and fly to Calwich; but you must not let the uncertainty of my affairs disturb the order of yours, and when it is convenient for you to go to your house at Bradley, don't let me detain you at Calwich: but I fancy you will hardly think of doing that till the roads are good, and now I believe they are worse than they have been for some years. B.[1] is in very *good humour*, and seems mightily pleased with my mother and your being at Calwich, and speaks very kindly of the little boy, and with much concern at his having a return of his ague. How long he stays I don't know (nor ask), but he told the Percivals a fortnight.

---

[1] "*B.*" Bernard.—This proves that Mr. Granville was then in London, and "in *good humour*," having left his mother and Mrs. Dewes at Calwich.

We went together last night to Joseph. 'Twas the last night, and I think I prefer it to every thing he has made, except the Messiah. I have collected the oratorio for him out of Milton's Paradise Lost, which I hope will do. The Duke and Duchess of Portland dine with me to-day. D.D. is affectionately yours; his best duty and mine to dear mama, and our tender wishes to the little boy.

I am, my dearest love, ever yours,

M. D.

How is your foot? For God's sake take care of *stumbling!* The charming *thread* is come, and is more precious than threads of gold. The Brinsdens are in town; we dine there on Thursday next.

Mrs. Delany to Mrs. Dewes.

Clarges Street, March 22, 1743-4.

In hopes of performing my promise to my dearest sister I begin on a folio sheet of paper, my eye being now well enough for such an undertaking. I most joyfully congratulate you and my dear mama on my godson's having lost his ague and gained a tooth. All your letters make me happy beyond expression, and D.D. takes a particular pleasure in our friendship for one another; he knows the human heart was formed for social affections, and that the friendly communion between sisters and friends no way interferes with that of husband and wife; for can we suppose that Providence should make it our duty to love our relations, and that the performance of that duty should be an *injury* to *one another?* It was ever my opinion, that this could not be: tis now strengthened by experience, for I never loved my dearest sister with more (if with so much) warmth and tenderness as at this moment. Pray give my most affectionate duty to my mother, and a thousand thanks for her charming letter. I hope she will be so good as to forgive my not answering it this post.

There is yet no account of the Duke of Devonshire coming, which will occasion D.D.'s taking out a licence for another quarter of a year; you may imagine, a longer stay amongst my friends than I expected will not be unwelcome, but I am afraid it will be attended by some inconveniences in his affairs, and be a detriment to his parishioners, but we are not to blame, and we must endeavour to make them amends when we get among them, and in the mean time we will be as happy as we can.

The moment I can guess about what time we shall be at liberty I will let you know; but I think it will not be possible to move till the latter end of next month. I wish you had the reforming of the present family[1] you are in, but tis *only a wife* can do those things; there is no sister in the world can act as freely for a brother as for herself. *I wish Mrs. Dean was translated*—can't you persuade her to give my brother warning? He never names domestic affairs to me; if I heard of a clever woman that I thought would manage well for him, I would recommend her, for he *cannot have a worse* than his present manager. Now I am talking of these affairs, I must let you into a secret which I suppose cannot long remain so. Father Fo[2] is going to be married to Mrs.

---

[1] Mr. Granville's household.

[2] The death of the fourth Mrs. Foley (Elizabeth Unett) the friend of Ann Granville, not having been previously mentioned, it must have occurred when the sisters were together.

Gwyn, a maiden gentlewoman of thirty-six, plain enough and two thousand pound fortune; her brother is a great friend of the Fo's, perhaps you may have seen him; don't mention this even to Mr. Dewes, for my coz Fo. told it me in *great confidence*. The family are not at all pleased with his marrying, *except the daughter*, and she thinks it will be easier to her than the management of the family. I thought he would marry again the first woman that would have him. The Bishop of Gloucester was with me three days ago, but with no good news, he has twice mentioned what was desired, but nothing was said that could be interpreted to her advantage; the Bishop wishes there may be interviews this summer, which perhaps (as he is unengaged), may bring him to some resolution.

It has been confidently reported for some days that Lord Carteret was to be married to Lady Sophia Fermor, Lord Pomfret's daughter.[1] Nay they went so far as to say they *were certainly married* on Tuesday night; but I believe there is no ground for the report; she is a handsome woman, but I know no more of her. Last night, alas! was the last night of the oratorio: it concluded with Saul: I was in hopes of the Messiah. I have been at ten ten oratorios, and wished you at every one most heartily.

I have not seen Lady Sunderland this age: she is but indifferent, but the oratorios took up two days in the week, and I seldom go out on a Sunday. Last Monday we dined at Mr. Percival's; B. was invited, but would not come, which gave great offence, and vexed me. Mr. Dewes was there; to-day we dine at Mr. Brinsdens'[2] in

---

[1] Lord Carteret married, secondly, in March, 1744, the Lady Sophia, eldest daughter of Thomas Fermor, Earl of Pomfret.

[2] This was probably the husband of "*Mrs. Bet Castlemain*" whose marriage was before alluded to.

Rathbone-Place; did I tell you she came to ask me where my silversmith lived, for she wanted some plate? I recommended Mr. Crapin, who had made all the plate I ever *purchased*, viz., a silver ladle! Mr. Dewes is invited to meet us, and my brother, but the latter I believe will *slip his neck out of the collar*. I made a short visit to our dear Duchess yesterday morning after prayers; she is in pretty good spirits, and desired her kind love to you. She expects Lady Andover in town every day; she comes to lye-in, and I fear they will come at the same time: I hope not the same day, as they both employ Sandys. Let me know, my dearest sister, particularly how you do.

Did I tell you how I was pleased with Mr. Bevern the Quaker, who dined with us about a fortnight ago? He is a most extraordinary man, very sensible, smart and polite in his manner: he has taken to carving in ivory for his amusement, and cuts likenesses of people that he has not seen for many years. I have packed up a box of work for you; the great chair that was begun so long ago, with all the worsteds and silks that belong to it, which at your leisure I hope you will finish, and that I shall have the pleasure of sitting in it by your fire-side at Welsborne. I shall not send it you without your orders, but leave it to be packed with the rest of your trumpery affairs.

D.D. is at St. James's Chapel, and I can't leave my letter open till he comes home, because I must go and dress—but I know he is faithfully yours, and I am just what I wish you to be ever to me. Lady Dysart has got another son, and is very well.

Mrs. Delany to Mrs. Dewes.

Clarges Street, 30 March, 1744.

Though to-morrow is the post day I must begin to-day, for fear of not being able to say all I would say to my most dear sister D.D. wishes you would *set about* the ballad on leaving the *old oak of Bradley*; he is sure you will succeed incomparably well. I hope we shall make a party together for visiting the sacred Druid's habitation, though not this year; in the meantime we will recal every pleasant moment we have past together, and lay schemes for their renewal. I thank God we have happily executed many a delightful scheme, and if we keep them within the limits of reason and discretion we may always indulge ourselves with the hope (at least) of success. I am glad the weather favours all your works. I have sent you by Mr. Dewes some garden seeds from the Oxford physic garden; you are to divide with my brother those that are for the natural ground, and those for hot-beds are all your own, and some of the produce I bespeak for Delville, and hope you will sow them there with your own dear hands. My brother talks of staying till the latter end of April; it is not unlikely but we may travel together. I don't think there ever was a happier creature than Mrs. Brinsden; I wished you with me (*and was not that strange?*) the day I dined there, to see with what joy she pulled out of her Indian chest fragments of good things, and some whole pieces of velvet and silks. She has an honest good heart, and I am pleased to see how she enjoys the blessings that she has. Nothing hurts me more than the repinings of some of my acquaintance (at least their *insipid possession* of good things), when, if they had the gratitude to Providence they ought to have, their whole lives should be spent in thanksgiving instead of murmuring; this makes me often check a rising sigh, and sets me recollecting the many blessings that I possess; and *I hope* I shall maintain this temper of mind, for the sake of my friends as well as my own advantage. I have been in a little bustle with my servants. Thomas Rogers, that Mrs. Chapon recommended to us, and promised to be an excellent servant, says he will not go to Ireland, and we have discharged him, Barrow has mishaved himself so much that he *must go*; Margaret and I had almost parted, but at last I have agreed, and she goes to Ireland as housemaid.

The Duke of Devonshire is now expected soon, some say he will be at Chester next Sunday. Lord Carteret has hurried Lady Sophia Fermor's spirits into a scarlet fever, and she was in great danger for twenty-four hours, and she has thrown him into the gout, with which he has been confined this week; I believe I writ my mama word all the particulars of the settlements and so forth. D.D. preaches on Sunday next before his Majesty; it is unlucky for him that my Lord Carteret will not be able to attend in the closet, for he had determined to have said something in his favour. This was written in the morning. At eleven we went to Northend; at my return I made a visit to the Percivals, dressed and dined at Whitehall, made visits in the afternoon, drank tea with Lady Andover, who is come to town to lye in, and, poor thing! has had a fever. Cousin Fo. came to town to-day, I sat an hour with her in my way home, and am now by my fireside with my own D.D., who bears all my flirtations and rambles with *unchangeable good humour*, and only makes me regret every hour I spend from him. To-morrow Sir Anthony Wescomb calls for us in his coach (my brother is to be of the party) to carry us to his villa¹ that he purchased last year on Chelsea Common; he is to come back with us and dine here, so we shall pay our court to the Black Knight, who ought not to be neglected, but I suppose he *will take another!*

Mrs. Delany to Mrs. Dewes.

Clarges Street, April 3, 1744.

Though I cannot hear of my dearest mama's suffering pain without feeling it myself, I hope and believe this fit of the gout will be a blessing to us all, by prolonging her life; for where there is a disposition towards it, it is safest when it gives pain in the limbs: pray God keep it from her stomach! If she could take the Rawleigh Cordial, it is the best thing to prevent its coming into her stomach, and to give her rest.

Our next care at present, the dear Duchess, is as well as can be, and the child also though a little tiny boy;

---

[1] Blacklands is in the Marlborough Road, Chelsea, formerly called Blacklands Lane. Bowack in his *Antiquities of Middlesex*, (1706), says:—
" William, Lord Cheyne, Viscount Newhaven in Scotland, has two good seats in Chelsea. The first is the mansion house, where Queen Elizabeth was nursed, east end of the town near the Thames. The other some distance north of the town, called Blacklands House, both (1705) let to French boarding schools." It is now (1860) a lunatic asylum, and adjoins the old Manor House at Chelsea, which forms part of the premises of Messrs. Scott and Cuthbertson (paper manufacturers), called " Whitelands." Blacklands has still a good garden, old iron gates, and the centre of the house is evidently part of the original structure.

but Elias the porter says "'tis a *parfict Dimont.*" I have not yet seen her, nor will these two days, for you know my caution about lying-in ladies.

Well, the affair of preaching before his Majesty is over,[1] to the great ease of mine and D.D.'s mind. He was as anxious about it as if he had never spoken in public, but he came off with applause. The King attended and commended his sermon; the generality of the congregation were gaping for a flattering discourse, and thought that he would preach for a bishopric, but found he thought more of acquitting himself like a good Xtian orator, than of gaining promotion by a fawning, fulsome discourse; which in truth would not only have been below his own dignity to have uttered, but an affront to his royal audience. His text was the 4 Chap. of St. Paul to the Galatians, part of the 8th verse:—"*But it is good to be zealously affected always in a good thing.*" Lord Carteret is still confined with the gout, and could not be there; but I mistook in saying he would tell the King that he "might be *amused*;" his *joke* was, that "perhaps he might be *abused!*"

I have just had Hele with me, and shall pack up your affairs and send them to Welsborn. I don't know where we can meet if we do not at Calwich; it is there I propose our meeting shall be; and as my stay cannot be very long, I hope the neighbours will be so indulgent as not to expect any visits from me. I design to ask my brother to-day when it will be most convenient to him for us to go; but my Lord Lieutenant is not yet arrived, and our motions must be regulated by him. My heart and thoughts

---

[1] Dr. Delany's preaching.

have long been with you, and I shall have no joy till my body follows. D.D. is as impatient to be with you as I am, and treats me with such tenderness on the subject, that it lies most on my mind that you will love him better than ever; and I assure you he loves and admires you extremely. We have this day dispatched Barrow to Dublin to take out a new license; the old one will be out on the 14th, and we must not run the hazard of the post, for fear of accidents.

To-day I shall have a treat that I shall most ardently wish you and my mother your share of. Handel, my brother, and Donnellan *dine here,* and we are to be entertained with *Handel's playing over Joseph to us.* How often and how tenderly shall I think of *my Benjamin!* I shall be impatient for to-morrow's post, to know how my mother does: the very sharp moist weather we have, I fear may increase her pain. I love my dear little godson for calling for me, and desire you will tell him "I am coming as fast as I can." When the *great wedding* will be, I don't know; I have given myself very little trouble about them; the courting, I assure you, is much more on their side than ours. We dine there once a-week, or once in ten days, and I come away, and so does D.D. as soon as dinner is over.

Wish me joy and wish Donnellan joy; for Captain Bury,[1]

---

[1] "About the end of last month we had an account, that on *Feb.* 26, was brought into *Gibraltar,* by his Majesty's ship the *Solebay,* commanded by *Capt. Bury,* the *Concordia,* a *Spanish* register ship of 22 guns and 142 men, including passengers, taken the day before off Cadiz, after five hours' engagement. She is the richest prize that has been made in the present war with *Spain,* having on board 180,000 dollars, 12,000 serons of cochineal, 500 of indigo, and several other rich goods; the whole computed at a million and a half of dollars. A little before, *Captain Bury* took a Spanish privateer of four carriage guns, ten swivels, and seventy-five men."—*London Magazine Chronologer,* for April, 1744.

for whom we applied last year to the Admiralty, and made him captain by our interest, has got a vast rich prize; his own share, they say, will come to fourscore thousand pounds; and he is an honest, valiant young man, and deserves his good fortune; you may imagine how pleased and proud his patronesses are on this occasion. You ask me how many pounds of thread I have got for you; do you mean knotted or unknotted? I hope I shall not forget the cornice of your bed, but please God I shall make you a visit at Welsborne long before you will be ready for the cornice. I wish I may be able to get a recommendation for poor Mrs. Lander: I have not yet been able to meet with a subscriber.

I believe I have burnt this week an hundred of your letters: *how unwillingly* did I commit to the flames those testimonies of your tender friendship! but I *have preserved* more than double their number, which I shall take with me as so many charms. I thought it prudent to destroy letters that mentioned particular affairs of particular people, or family business. Don't expect to hear from me next post, for the Duchess is, I thank God, so well you may be easy on her account, and I am to go out early on Thursday upon business, and shall hardly find time till Saturday to write; but if I can I will. My most humble and affectionate duty to dear mama, and D.D.'s love to "sister Ann." The Sixth Night has been in my house three days, and I have not had time to read it!

Upon second thoughts, I believe the clock can't go to Welsbourne till I go away, for we shall want it; but I will see it packed up safely the day before I go.

with good courage, and when we meet I shall be recompensed the anxieties I have had; and the word *going*, let it not be named, that is, not the time hinted at, be sure we will stay as long as in *prudence* we may—indeed, I fear we have a little trespassed on *that boundary* already. My dear mama's pain I feel at this distance; the sickness I believe proceeds from the pain: cannot you prevail with her to take palsy drops? she used to do that, and they are very proper. It is vastly good in you to write constantly; it is impossible to be easy without knowing punctually. Pray God give her ease, all her children pray most heartily for her relief. I fear I have communicated too much of my pain to you, by telling you how uneasy I was on B——'s account, but I think of late his humour is mended: he *has dined* once or twice *here lately*, and been very cheerful.

We all dined yesterday at the Duke of Portland's, and went together to Sullivan's benefit; a most stupid entertainment on the whole, but there was one scene of tolerable humour, which made us laugh, of the King and Queen of Spain and Farinelli.[1] B. came home and supped with us: he is much concerned about my mother's being ill, but I hope this severe fit of the gout will be a means of her having better health hereafter. I cannot express to you the satisfaction your last letter gave me; it has given *a new turn to my thoughts*, and I believe I shall now go through all I have to do with great fortitude. I hope my dear mama will take Mr. Rogers' draught, if there is occasion.

---

[1] The Queen of Spain; or, Farinelli at Madrid. Mus. Ent. by James Worsdale. Acted at the Haymarket, 1744. Not printed.—Baker's *Biographia Dramatica*.

Well, now for business. Your nightgown I bought yesterday—blue and white; more a winter suit in substance than a summer one, but so great a penny-worth I could not forbear, though it cost eight shillings a yard. I shall take your advice and bring nothing with me but nightgowns, and Margaret shall have the great honour of being your slave and servant. The Duke of Devonshire came to town last Tuesday, and in a few days our fate must be determined. I have wrote a letter to Sir Clement Cottrel to shew Lord Carteret, wherein I name the Bishopric of Meath, and I have laid it to his conscience whether *D.D. and myself* have not merited that favour at his hands. But now the happiness of a bridegroom, I suppose will so engross his attention, that it will not be easy to fix him on any other subject, and I have more dependance on the Duke of Devonshire than the other. The wedding was last Saturday evening; they were married at Lord Pomfret's: Lady Granville was invited, but did not go; the daughters my Lord would not invite, for fear it should affect them too much, and *he has indeed* acted with a tenderness towards them that I did not imagine had been in his nature. At 12, bride and bridegroom came home, attended by Lady Pomfret and Lady Charlotte Fermor the sister; Lady G. and Miss Carteret were gone to bed, but Mrs. Faver was there to do honours and help to undress the bride. Have you a notion of that? I really thought Faver had loved poor Lady Carteret; but if she had, was it possible for her to go through such a scene? but she was

---

On April 14, 1744, Lord Carteret married his second wife, Lady Sophia Fermor. She was the eldest daughter of Thomas, 1st Earl Pomfret.

trained up in the school of indifference for others and love of self. The next day all the Pomfrets dined there, and nobody was admitted. I left my name at the door *with the crowd*, and shall wait *till I am sent to*. They have furnished the town with conversation in abundance, all which tittle-tattle I reserve for talk at Calwich.

I go to-day at 12 to Whitehall to our Duchess. When you write to her say nothing of the day I have fixed for my journey: she is very well and all the little ones. Mr. Percival has had the gout, and has it very bad; the rest are well. Have you the Minute Philosopher[1] and Derham's Physico-Theology?[2] I hope I shall be able to get the fringe, but Mrs. Littleton (who was to get it for me) and I have not met; I will send her a message by Lady Westmorland. I have not seen Lady Sarah Cowper a great while, but she has been much out of order all this winter.

Next Thursday we go to Paul's to hear the music for the Sons of the Clergy—Donn. Mr. Brinsden, D.D., my brother, and I. Dr. Young dined yesterday at Whitehall; he is vastly broke, but he and D.D. took very kindly to one another. Princess is very well and in high favour in Arlington Street, but I am sure they will do her no substantial favour; however, as it keeps up her spirits to be well received there, I am glad she is. Mr.

---

[1] "The Minute Philosopher," a series of dialogues, written in 1732, by Dr. George Berkeley, with which Queen Caroline was so pleased that she had him promoted to the Bishopric of Cloyne.

[2] William Derham, D.D., Chaplain to George I., and Canon of Windsor, born 1657, died 1735. He devoted himself to philosophical pursuits. In 1713 he published his "Physico-Theology," being the substance of his Boyle's Lectures, with curious and instructive notes. He also wrote "Astro-Theology," "Christo-Theology," &c.

Foley[1] will soon be married; he is all flame and impatience.—I wish she may prove a discreet woman, for Miss Foley's sake; Matrimony is much in fashion, but I have neither time nor memory at present to recollect them, so they must go into the bag of chatter that is to be opened at Calwich; I shall think the time long till the post comes in to-morrow; enclose no more to Mr. Foley.

I hope you received the paper about Mrs. Huddleston: I have at last recollected her direction, and shall by this post send one, for fear of losing time, for next Tuesday is the day the paper must be returned.

Mrs. Delany to Mrs. Dewes, at Calwich.

Clarges Street, 21 April, 1744.

I shall have no real comfort in writing to my dearest sister till I can positively say our day of leaving this place is settled, but uncertainty is the lot of mortal man, and I can only say I hope we shall be able to keep to the time I named. But my Lord Carteret's marriage and the Duke of Devonshire's hurry upon first coming over, have I suppose not given them leave to settle about Irish affairs. D.D. was at the Duke of Devonshire's levee; his favorite chaplain the Dean of Down they say stands fair for a bishopric; if so his *betters must wait* till another vacancy. This week must determine it, and I am sure it will finish my patience if it does not finish this affair; we dine to-morrow in Arlington Street. I have not yet

---

[1] "Married, May 1744, Thomas Foley, Esq, knight of the shire for the county of Hereford, to Mrs. Catharine Gwyn," his fifth wife!

seen bride or bridegroom, but have seen all the rest of the family. Yesterday Lady Carteret was presented at Court, vastly fine in gold brocade and jewels. In the evening Lady Dysart's son was christened; the King stood in person, the other gossips Lord and Lady Carteret. So much for the great and magnificent. Lady Oxford comes to town to-day, which will rob me of some happy minutes. The Xtning is to be next Thursday, the name Edward, the gossips Lady Oxford, Lord Limerick and Lord Foley. Last Thursday Don, D.D., my brother, Mr. and Mrs Brinsden, and myself, went to St. Paul's and got very good places in the choir, and I never was more delighted with music in my life. After it was over my brother proposed our dining at Pontack's, which we accepted you may believe, and passed a pleasant day: my brother was in good spirits, and very obliging, and you know how very delightful that is to me. Mrs. Delahay has brought my new gown to try, yours is made up without a lining, the wrong side is as good as the right, and it will be too hot for summer if you line it. The Duke of Portland, Mr. Drummond, Mr. Achard, two Mr. Delanys—(relations of D.D's.,) and my brother, dine with me to-day, and this morning I expect Lady Bridget Bastard[1] to see my house, and take it I hope. So all I can say more is our affectionate duty, love, and service attend the dear inhabitants of Calwich.

A letter without signature, at this period, but evidently from Mrs. Foley or one of her sisters, gives a curious account of the wages of the ladies' maids, or waiting-women of that time. The writer says that a person who wishes for the place of her own woman,

---

[1] Pollexfen Bastard, of Kitley, Esq., married Lady Bridget Poulett, daughter of John, 1st Earl Poulett.

says, she has had £4 a-year, with an addition in other ways of the value of £4 more, but that she "can only wash head-things and aprons, and has never washed larger things, but would learn to do the additional things necessary;" and the writer asks Mrs. Dewes "*if it is possible* that a person who had received such high wages *could have done so little?*" She also mentions a letter from Lady Fanny Carteret, saying that Lord Granville "designs to carry his consort into Bedfordshire for a fortnight, just to show her the beauties of Hawnes," and adds, "*Poor Lady Carteret* did often wish for such a journey *without her Governess*, but never did obtain it! but I hope in the regions she is now in she wants no change or liberty."

Mrs. Delany to Mrs. Dewes.

Charges Street, April 26, 1744.

Our day was fixed for leaving this place next Wednesday, most of my things packed up, but the affair not being decided, my brother and other wise politicians say it would *be absurd* to go out the way just at the time that there is a struggle between the Duke of Devonshire and Lord Carteret. Which will get the better cannot so much as be guess'd at, but I fear our friend will be defeated, though surely next week we shall know our doom and be set at liberty, and then I shall fly to Calwich and be happy. You can very well imagine how perplexing these delays have been to me, but I will name no more days, nor do you think of any, but as soon as I may come you know I shall. We have been this morning to see Sir John Stanley, whom we found pretty well. Mrs. Brinsden came to me at nine, then Mrs. Delahay, then Miss Yate—her sister is married to Captain Elton[1],

---

[1] Caroline, youngest daughter of Charles and Elizabeth Yate, of Arlingham, in the county of Gloucester, married Jacob, second son of Sir Abraham Elton, Bart.

and we dine at the Percivals. Reading *this* is enough
to put you into a hurry of the spirits, what was it to me
in the operation? Our dear Duchess is very well, and
on Saturday night all her ceremonies will be over, but
she is so good and careful as never to go out till the
fifth week. Sir Clement Cotterell called here this morning
when we were out, very likely he had some news to tell us.
Take care of riding, as now you are a little cowardly it
may be dangerous.

I am come home to take care of my dear D.D.
who is not well; he complains very much of his head,
and is just going to take hartshorn and sack whey, and
go to bed; I hope a good night's rest will cure him. I
am very well. Yesterday my brother gallantly attended
Mrs. Donnellan, Miss Dashwood, and myself to breakfast at
Ranelagh, the day was clear but cold : there was a great
deal of company. D.D. was obliged to go into the City,
where I believe he caught his cold; I invited my brother
home with me; he was in a very easy good humour, and
staid till past seven.

Good night, all health and happiness attend you. Duty,
love, and service to Calwich. I am glad my dear godson
continues well. I am, more than I can express, yours.

Ranelagh, a public garden, opened in 1742, on the site of the
gardens of Ranelagh House, eastward of Chelsea Hospital; and
originally projected by Lacy, the patentee of Drury-lane Theatre,
as a sort of winter Vauxhall; the Rotunda, 185 feet in diameter,
had a Doric portico, an arcade and gallery outside. There was also
a Venetian pavilion in the centre of a lake, upon which the company
were rowed in boats; and a print of 1751, shows the ground
planted with trees and *allées vertes*; the several buildings were
designed by Capon, the eminent scene-painter. The interior was
fitted with boxes for refreshments, and in each was a painting; in

the centre was an ingenious heating apparatus, concealed by arches, porticoes and niches, paintings, &c., and supporting the ceiling, which was decorated with celestial figures, festoons of flowers, and arabesques, and lighted by circles of chandeliers.

The Rotunda was opened with a public breakfast, April 5th, 1742, Walpole describes the high fashion of Ranelagh:—"The Prince, Princess, Dukes, much nobility, and much mob besides were there." 'My Lord Chesterfield is so fond of it, that he says he has ordered all his letters to be directed thither." The admission was one shilling; but the ridottos, with supper and music, were one guinea. Concerts were also given here—Dr. Arne composed the music, Tenducci and Mara sang, and here were first publicly performed the compositions of the Catch Club; fireworks and a mimic Etna were next introduced; and lastly masquerades, described in Fielding's "Amelia," and satirized in the "Connoisseur." But the promenade of the Rotunda to the music of the orchestra and organ declined.

The peace fête took place here in 1803. Ranelagh was then deserted, and in 1804 the buildings were taken down.

Mrs. Delany to Mrs. Dewes.

Clarges Street, 8 May, 1744.

Well, my dear sister, I told you that I should not write to you this post, and I should have been as good as my word but that the *Dean of Down* desires me to make his compliments to you, and to present his humble duty to my mother. He has a most sincere regard for you, and only wishes and waits for an opportunity of telling you so in person; in the mean time hopes you will accept of his *devoirs* from *my hand*, and I believe there is nobody in England excepting myself (and D.D. is not jealous I assure you) for whom he has a greater value, and we have had several private conferences on that subject as well as many others. I am very glad to find, by your letter to my brother, that you did not apprehend D.D. to be as bad as he really was: but I suffered greatly, for nobody for the time could suffer more than he did, but I thank God he mends very fast. Yesterday he din'd in the parlour, and just as dinner came upon the table, Lord Carteret came to the door and came in. He desired we would send the servants away, and when they were gone, he told D.D. he was come from the Duke of Devonshire to offer him the Deanary of Down,[1] and that the first small bishoprick that fell in he might have if he cared afterwards to quit Down; but the deanry is a much better thing than any small bishopric, and we are well pleased with the possession of it. As soon as D.D. is well enough to go abroad he is to kiss hands, but that cannot possibly be till the beginning of the week, which will put off the happy hour of our meeting still longer. Our dear Duchess raps at the door, and this cannot be finished 'till she is gone: she is pure well,—but has staid so long I can say but little more. I shall send to my brother your new gown to send because you may want to wear it; and two prints for you of the Giant's Causeway, which I desire your acceptance of, they are curiosities. Well, good night, I must sign and seal.

I am yours, my dearest sister,
With the utmost tenderness,
M. D.
Duty, love, and service as due.

---

[1] Among the ecclesiastical preferments recorded in the "London Magazine" for May, 1744, is the following entry—" Dr. Thomas Fletcher, made Bishop of Dromore, and Dr. Patrick Delany, Dean of Down in his room."

After the letter of 8th of May, a period intervenes of more than five weeks, probably spent at Calwich with her mother and sister—the next date being Chester, where Mary Granville once more found herself, after an interval of thirteen years since she had passed through that city on her way to Ireland, determined to conquer her attachment to Lord Baltimore. How well those years had been employed in maturing her judgment, strengthening her principles, and cultivating every opportunity of improvement, her letters fully prove, till she again landed in Ireland with a companion who knew how to value the superiority of her mind, and the versatility of her talents.

Mrs. Delany to her Mother and Sister.

Chester, Wednesday, 18 June, 1744.

I dare not trust myself with saying anything on the subject my heart is fullest of, but will endeavour to satisfy my dearest mama and sister with an account of our travels, which have hitherto, I thank God, been prosperous. The weather was yesterday excessively hot, and we wanted the comfortable breezes of Calwich. We breakfasted at Cheedle, (your good cake we eat in the coach,) and arrived at Trentham, where we dined, about half an hour after twelve: there we both had courage to name our friends at Calwich, but till then I could not venture to mention you—*that* wants no explanation to you. The roads were very good, for we had no occasion to get out of the coach the whole way; we did not get to Nantwych till near nine, the road rocky, and the miles Worcestershire miles; our inn was a poor one, but your excellent chicken furnished us with an admirable repast, for which we were not ungrateful. We had a good bed and civil landlady, and got to

Chester to-day at twelve o'clock, where we have a good
lodging and provision. The yacht is to sail to-morrow
at eleven, at which hour please God we shall be at the
water-side. Mrs. Henery, the lady that was to have
gone, does not go yet, so the yacht is to return for her, and
the weather is so good the captain says though the wind is
not directly fair he does not fear making a good passage.
I have also sent you the Bishop of Cloyne's book on tar-
water, for your amusement, and two volumes of enormous
size for my lovely godson: I could not get the second
without the first, and thought he might be gallant and
make a present to Miss Jenny of one. I shall keep Frank
till we are on board, as you desired me to do, and shall
have no time to-morrow morning to add to my letter, but
must refer you to Frank to tell you all that happens
to-night. Since dinner we have taken a nap, made up
our accounts with our fine landlady, walked round the
town, and seen the library, which is a beautiful Gothic
building. The poor Dean has had the headache all day,
but is now better; his best respects and kind wishes
are your constant attendants. It is unnecessary for me to
tell you he exerted himself to keep up my spirits, and
indeed his own wanted some support; and I must say
I saw it with satisfaction—for to have the friends I
love best, love one another, is the height of happiness
to me. So, my dear mama and sister adieu; I am very
well and in surprising spirits, and beg you will have no
anxiety about me. I will write as soon as I get to
Delville, but as the winds are concerned you may not
receive it so soon as your impatience will wish for it.
William Curl is here and is grown prodigiously. Supper

is coming, and once more adieu. No words can say how much and how tenderly

I am yours,
M. D.

Friday nine o'clock, Chester. As it is now likely we may stay here some time, I cannot keep Frank any longer, and as I know you may in all probability hear the occasion of my staying in a way that may alarm you, I think it best to acquaint you with D.D's illness by my own hand. I thank God he is much better, and the worst I hope is over. He was taken ill on Friday night after I had wrote this letter; he complained of the headache all day, and in the evening had a direct fever fit which lasted the greatest part of yesterday. I sent for an apothecary, but I would not venture any farther without better advice, and so sent for Dr. Gore, a physician in great repute here, who gave him the bark as soon as he found his fever would allow of it. He is free from fever this morning, and I hope in God he will have no return of it! the doctor thinks he will not. I have sent for Dr. Barber to come over to us from Ireland to attend him for the voyage, but the yacht will not be back till the 20th of this month. All events are guided by the Great Disposer of all things; so I keep up my own spirits and am very well, and hope by Saturday's post to give you a good account of my own D.D.: in the meantime I entreat you and my dearest mama not to be too anxious about us, but hope for the best as I do. As ill news flies apace, I feared you might by some means or other hear this, or I would have spared you the pain of knowing it till it had been quite over. Write to me by the post and direct for me at Mrs. Kenna's, Chester; and if I should be gone, Mrs. Kenna will send it after me; she is a very pretty kind of woman, and we are fortunate that this unhappy delay happened in so good a house.

Mrs. Delany to Mrs. Dewes, at Bradley, Worcestershire, to be left at Mr. Phillips', Apothecary, in Droitwich.

Delville, 28 June, 1744.

I much fear my dearest sister has had some anxious hours if not days on our account. How impatient have I been to let you know how happily and well we have performed our journey; and to crown all I was welcomed to Delville by your dear letter of the 14th instant— *a fortunate omen.* I wrote to you from Chester on Saturday last the 23rd, and sent that letter round about, for as yours did not come to me as it ought to do in time by the cross-post, I would not venture it that way. On Sunday evening we removed from Chester to Park-Gate, in hopes of sailing next morning early, but the wind was contrary, and we were obliged to remain there all Monday. We were so lucky as to get a very clean, good lodging, and on Tuesday morning went on board the yacht. Though the wind was not very fair, the weather was so good that the captain said we might make our passage very well, which I thank God we did and landed yesterday between eight and nine. We did not come directly to Delville it being so late, but packed away bag and baggage and went to Mrs. Forde's, who expected us to lie at her house: she is a very wellbred, friendly, agreeable woman, and I was perfectly easy with her and had a most comfortable bed. On Tuesday the day was so fine that I sat on deck the whole day and eat a very good dinner and an egg for my supper, and worked and drew two or three sketches; nothing could be more pleasant; you would have been pleased and not the least afraid: but we went on slowly not having wind enough. In the evening the weather grew more favourable for our sailing, but made the ship roll, and we were very ill all night, and the next day till about 5, that they came to the cabin and said we were just entering the bay of Dublin; upon which we got up, and were soon cured by the good weather and fair prospect of landing soon.

This morning after breakfast we called on Barber, who was truly transported with seeing us; she looks tolerably well, and enquired very much after you and all my friends. My impatience to see Delville and read my dear sister's letter shortened my visit there, and we arrived at our own pleasant dwelling by 11,—and never was seen a sweeter dwelling. I have traversed the house and gardens, and never saw a more delightful and agreeable place, but particulars must come by degrees, and I have now the joy of seeing the kind and generous owner of it perfectly well, and well pleased to put me in possession.

We are just going to dinner, and I must get all my letters ready to send before dinner, so that it is impossible for me to say the hundreth part of what my heart is full, and to thank you as I wish to do for your letter that met me here, but I hope to have leisure when my head and affairs are not so confused as they are at present to make a better return. Every tender word of my dearest sister's touches my heart, and is most faithfully returned with the sincerest love,—a love that has increased with our

years, and must and will still increase. Do *not say* I am
"*lost to you*"—I *cannot bear* that expression, for I am
everywhere yours, and ready to assist and advise you on all
occasions to the best of my power; when absent, by the
blessed means of writing we may assist each other and be
a mutual support and delight, and many days and months
I hope we shall spend together. As soon as I examined
my house to-day I laid out an apartment for you, and I
hope soon you will provide the same for me at Welsborne.
I shall wish to have you settle all affairs there, and to
hear of your safe arrival at Gloucester. I hope my mother
has not left you yet, but for fear she should I shall write
a word or two to Mrs. Duncomb to let her know of
my safe arrival, that she may communicate it to my
mother, to whom I shall write as soon as I know she is at
Gloucester. My love and blessing to the dear, happy boy,
that flourishes under your care; I don't apprehend you
will be too indulgent, and you know the way to save yourself pain is to have *a thorough command of your children*
when they are *very young*. My very kind service to Mr.
Dewes and best duty to mama: the Dean joins with me
in all I say, and is yours most affectionately.

Mrs. Delany to Mrs. Dewes, at Bradley.

Dublin, 12 July, 1744.

I begin to my dear sister before my usual day, as I
intend to enclose it to the Duke of Portland, and he is
at Bulstrode, which will make this letter a day or two
longer in its progress. I am now in Dames Street
waiting for the raree show of the city militia, who are
all in their regimentals, and, they say, make a most
gallant show; but I am willing to secure a real pleasure
to myself, therefore take this interval to write to my dear

sister in the midst of so great a noise and hurry of people and coaches that I hardly know what I write. Before I left Delville this morning I wrote to my mother, and have directed it to Gloucester, supposing her by this time settled there, and I hope you are on the wing to Welsbourne.

Last Sunday I made my first appearance at St. Warbor's church. (I refer you to my mother's letter for more particulars). In the afternoon I had a great deal of company: the Bishop of Down[1] and his lady; Mrs. Kelly (Mr. Kelly's wife, nephew to Sir John Stanley), an extremely pretty lively woman; the eldest Miss Forth, and Miss Monck, sister to Harry Monck; a Mrs. and Miss Fowkes; and Mrs. Cope, a young widow. Monday morning waited three hours for the upholsterer, and settled some of my shells and papers. Miss Parker (the Curate's sister), and Miss Delany, a niece of the Dean's, dined with me; both very modest pretty sort of women. I dressed *in my airs* for formal visits, and just as I was setting out Mr. and Mrs. Donnellan came in; they made their visit short, and when they went away I made my visits in Dublin. I wish you had just such a chariot as ours, because I never went in so easy a one. Yesterday morning (for Tuesday I spent the whole day in settling shell and papers) my upholsterer came, and my new apartment will be very handsome. The drawing-room hung with tapestry, on each side of the door a japan chest, the curtains and chairs crimson mohair, between the windows large glasses with gilt frames, and marble tables under them with gilt frames; the bedchamber within hung with crimson damask, bed chairs and curtains the

---

[1] John Ryder, Bishop of Down and Connor, in 1743, translated to Archbishopric of Tuam in 1752. Died 1775.

same; *the closet* within it is most delightful, I have a most extensive and beautiful prospect of the harbour and town of Dublin and a range of mountains of various shapes. This bedchamber and closet are on the left hand of the drawing room; on the right is a very pretty square room, with a large dressing room within it, which I hope will be my dearest sister's apartment, when she makes me happy with her company.

I have described my house very awkwardly to you, but to be regular: it stands on a rising ground, and the court is large enough for a coach-and-six to drive round commodiously. The front of the house is simple but pretty— five windows in front, two stories high, with a portico at the hall door, to which you ascend by six steps, but so well sheltered by the roof of the portico that it is secured from rain. The hall is 26 f. by 22, and 12 f. and $\frac{1}{2}$ high, the ceiling finished in compartments, with a Doric entablature in stucco round the room. On the right hand is the eating parlour, 26 f. long and 16 f. and $\frac{1}{2}$ wide, with a projection in the middle, which opens thirteen foot and is eight foot deep, with three windows, and large enough for two side-boards, one window between the tables and one at each side, which lights the room very agreeably: it is a very charming room, cool in summer and warm in winter; the chimney is at one end and a window over against it; on the left hand of the hall is another large room, which at present is unfinished, but is designed for a chapel when we are rich enough to finish it as we ought to do. At the end of the hall is a very neat stone stair-case, well finished with stucco, which leads to the apartment I have described above. Beyond the stair-case, below, is a little hall; on the right hand is a small parlour, where we breakfast and sup, out of it our present bedchamber and a large light closet within it; it is but a small apartment, but very pretty, and lies pleasantly to the gardens, and as we sit by the fire-side we can see the ships ride in the harbour. From the door of the little parlour are about ten steps that carry you to my English room, and another flight of the same stairs lead to the rooms over the little parlour, and bedchamber and the maids rooms, and serve for back stairs to the great apartment. I have been three times called from my letter to look at the militia, and really they are a noble sight, very well-looking men in regimentals; three regiments well mounted and three of foot. It is a satisfaction to see so many brave men well prepared to defend us in case we stand in need of their assistance; but if the news is true of Prince Charles of Lorraine's victory over the French and Hessians they may sheath their swords in peace. My head turns round with the tumult, and I am obliged to defer my description of the gardens till I have a better opportunity; but I can never be so much taken up but I shall find time to tell my best and dearest of sisters that I am, with the greatest warmth of affection, ever hers.

I forgot to add, that out of my English room you go into the library, which is *most plentifully filled*, and D.D. has filled up the vacancies of my shelves with the modern poets nicely bound.[1]

Mrs. Fortescue (Miss Wesley that was[2]) came in by

---

[1] The Editor read this account of Delville to a lady who knew it well, who had been there in July, 1860, and who stated that it might still serve for a description of that place; also that she had seen quantities of shells in heaps, which had evidently been pulled down to repair or alter buildings; but that the former possessors, Mr. and Mrs. Mallet, had with great care preserved some rooms as they were.

[2] Elizabeth, eldest daughter of Richard Wesley (afterwards created Lord Mornington), married, in 1743, Chichester Fortescue, of Dromisken, county Louth, Esq., ancestor of the present Lord Clermont, 1860.

accident to the house where I was this morning to see the show, we were very glad to meet again. She came to town just to see her son, and goes again to-morrow. She looks very well, and asked very particularly after you.

The following letter is one of the very few found of Mrs. Granville's, and is interesting from the insight given into the nursery system of that day. The little Bernard alluded to was then at a farm or cottage with his nurse, whether he was weaned is *doubtful*, but as he dined on *buttered turnips* it is not a matter of astonishment that he was often ill.

Mrs. Granville to Mrs. Dewes.

Friday, 10 at night.

I hope my dearest Nanny that your next letter will be dated from Welsbourne, that you'll soon dispatch your affairs there, for I long to have you with me where I hope you'll be cosy and free from bustle and fatigue, which at this time you should not have, and then we shall be a comfort to each other whatever disorders attend us. I have had Dr. Capell with me two or three times, and have been taking some medicines he prescribed twice a day. Yesterday I had the pleasure of seeing my little Banny who is the fairest thing I ever saw, and very lively; he was with me by nine o'clock, and staid till five, eat *buttered turnips* for *his dinner* heartily, and a mess of milk and bread before he set out again. In my opinion he is not like father, mother, or brother, but the picture of your poor brother Bevil; he is but a small child but tall and well-proportioned, the finest skin I ever saw, and of his hair I shall enclose a lock for you to see. Mrs. Peters and the nurse send their duty, and the former says she (and her husband) *dread the time* of your taking him away from them. Mrs. Pitt's child was made a Xtian at the bishop's palace to-day, his lordship was godfather, Mr. John Webb the other, and little Mrs. Webb godmother.

Mrs. Viney made me go from church to-day to dine with her, which is the first visit I have made to anybody, she is heartily yours, so are her daughters; Mr. Hays was there and Smith, and we had a good deal of music vocal and instrumental. Mrs. Duncomb was here yesterday, and *cards the entertainment*. Mrs. Gaudinau has quarrelled with the H's, so they don't now meet at all, and they are sadly *put to it* for parties *at play*.

Saturday.

Mrs. Peters has been here, and tells me your little boy got home safe, and is very well. I thank you for our "*dear Pearl's*" letter with the welcome news of health, which she shows by the spirit she writes with; by her discription Delville is a charming place. And now I can add no more, but beg you to make haste to her that cannot express with how much affection she is

Yours,

M. GRANVILLE.

My compliments to Mapleborough, who I hope are well; you surprised me with the wedding that is to be at your house.

Mrs. Delany to Mrs. Dewes, at Bradley.
Delville, 19 July, 1744.

I have received my dearest sister's letters dated the 30th of June, the 6th and 7th of this month. It is not to

be expressed how happy they have made me, especially as
I have the satisfaction of knowing your fears are over
for me; for I could have no real enjoyment of any
thing while I thought you were anxious about me.
I wish you were at Gloucester, for I think you have
deferred going to Welsbourne a vast while, and fear
the fatigue will be too much for you; don't *settle* any
part but *one room for yourself*; the rest you may do at
your return. I want to know a million of particulars
about it, but desire you to defer that for your winter
evenings' amusements. I must now write to my mother
and the old Countess, who has wrote two *very kind* letters
to me, and I expect the upholsterer every minute to put
my furniture in the new apartment. I wish I had sent
you more, for this house is so full it will hardly hold what
I have brought. You may have seen D.D. mentioned
in the newspapers for the bishopric of Ferns, but I hope
it will not be offered him, at least not these two months,
for till then he will not be entitled to the rents of Down,
and it will do us more harm than good, and the income is
not better. I wrote to my brother last post a very long
and kind letter, with an account of things here, and an
invitation to be *a witness* and *sharer of my happiness*—
(such a letter as you may imagine) but I should not
have wrote *after what is past* without the consent of
D.D., whose generosity and tenderness for me will not
let him oppose any thing that gives me satisfaction:
it is the second letter I have wrote to my brother, but I
have not yet received one line from him.[1]

---

[1] This sentence, and those which precede it, prove that Mr. Granville had not got over his objections to his sister's marriage with Dr. Delany, and that although they were on speaking terms, and met in London, that there was no

I believe I have received all your dear letters safe; those directed to Chester were all sent after me. I hope mine have had as good success in their progress. I have had letters from almost all my *considerable correspondents* in England, which furnish me with abundance of employment. I shall be glad when I have time for sketches, but I believe that can hardly be this year; I have had twenty visitors already, and have returned but two. I wish I could give you an idea of our garden, but the describing it puzzles me extremely; the back part of the house is towards a bowling-green, that slopes gently off down to a little brook that runs through the garden; on the other side of the brook is a high bank with a hanging wood of ever-greens, at the top of which is a circular terrace that surrounds the greatest part of the garden, the wall of which is covered with fruit-trees, and on the other side of the walk a border for flowers, and the greatest quantity of roses and sweet briar that ever I saw; on the right hand of the bowling-green towards the bottom is placed our hay-rick, which is at present making, and from our parlour-window and bedchamber I can see the men work at it, and have a full view of what I have described; and beyond that pleasant meadows, bounded by mountains of various shapes, with little villages and country-seats interspersed and embosomed high in tufted trees: to complete the prospect a full view of Dublin harbour, which is always full of shipping, and

---

cordiality, and that Mrs. Delany considered Dr. Delany so much aggrieved that she would not have written to her brother without his sanction. The letter from Chester did not contain any message to Mr. Granville, though she and the Dean had been at Calwich to visit her mother (Mrs. Granville) and Mrs. Dewes. It is therefore evident that Mr. Granville was absent, and that fact might of itself account for her allusion to the "*past.*"

looks at this instant beautiful beyond all description: these are the views from the house *next* the gardens. On the left hand of the bowling-green is a terrace-walk that takes in a sort of a parterre, that will make the prettiest orangery in the world, for it is an oval of green, planted round in double rows of elm-trees and flowering shrubs, with little grass walks between them, which will give a good shelter to exotics. The terrace I just mentioned is bounded at one end by a wall of good fruit, in which there is a door that leads to another very large handsome terrace-walk, with double rows of large elms, and the walk well gravelled, so that we may walk securely in any weather. On the left hand, the ground rises very considerably, and is planted with all sort of trees. About half way up the walk there is a path that goes up that bank to the remains of an old castle (as it were), from whence there is an unbounded prospect all over the country: under it is a cave that opens with an arch to the terrace-walk, that will make a very pretty grotto; and the plan I had laid for my brothers at Calwich (this being of that shape, though not quite so large) I shall execute here. At the end of this terrace is a very pretty portico, prettily painted within and neatly finished without; you go up a high slope to it, which gives it a mighty good air as you come up the walk: from thence you go on the right hand to the green terrace I mentioned at first, which takes in the whole compass of this garden; in the middle, sloping from the terrace, every way, are the fields, or rather paddocks, where our deer and our cows are kept, and the rurality of it is wonderfully pretty. These fields are planted in a *wild way* with *forest-trees and with bushes*, that look so naturally you would not imagine it the work of art. Besides this, there is a very good kitchen-garden and two fruit-gardens, which, when proper repairs are made and they are set in order, will afford us a sufficient quantity of every thing we can want of that kind. There are several prettinesses I can't explain to you— little wild walks, private seats, and lovely prospects. One seat particularly I am very fond of, in a nut grove, and "*the beggar's hut,*" which is a seat in a rock; on the top are bushes of all kind that bend over: it is placed at the end of a cunning wild path, thick set with trees, and it overlooks the brook, which entertains you with a purling rill. The little robins are as fond of this seat as we are: it just holds the Dean and myself, and I hope in God to have many a tête-à-tête there with my own dear sist^r ; but I have had such a hurryof business within doors, and so many visitors, that I have not spent half so much time in this sweet garden as I want to do.

I am afraid this will prove an incomprehensible description; but if it does but whet your desire of seeing it, that is sufficient for me. Monday I invited all the Barber[1] race, and our good old friend, though she had the gout upon her and was forced to be lifted out upon men's shoulders, came, and was delighted with my new room, and seemed very happy to see me mistress of this charming place. She has a true sense of your worth, and we never meet but she talks incessantly of the "*lovely pearly Dewes.*"

Poor Mira (Barber) is a melancholy drooping young woman, and I wish a prospect of her being well settled;

Mrs. Barber, of Glasnevin, was the same Mrs. Barber so often mentioned as the poetess so much patronized by Dean Swift, who visited England to obtain subscribers for her productions.

but I hear of none. To-day I expect a niece of Dr. Delany's, his brother's daughter; I have asked her to spend a few days here; she seems a pretty sort of young woman. I am amazed already to be come to the eighth page, and I could most willingly add eight more, but time will not serve, and I must finish with assuring you of D.D.'s tender regard and my everlasting love.

M. D.

I hope you received my letter of last Thursday (militia day). I am uneasy not to hear from Sally; I hope she is well. She will want an account of Delville; I have not time at present to send her one. If you see her read her what you think will entertain her. Adieu.

Mrs. Delany to Mrs. Dewes, at Bradley, &c.

Delville, 26 July, 1744.

My dearest sister, who warms my heart every moment of my life, must know how precious this day[1] is to me; how ardent my wishes are for her happiness, that I may long be blest with such a friend, and that length of days may be a blessing to her! D.D. and I have solaced ourselves with discoursing of you early this morning, and joined in kind thoughts of and wishes for our loved and lovely *Pearly Dewes*.[2] I was rejoiced with your last dear letter of the 12th July, last Tuesday the 24th, which had the winds favoured my impatient wishes, would sooner

---

[1] July 26, Ann Granville's wedding-day.
[2] *The Pearl* was a name given to Mrs. Delany by the Dean. And *Pearly Dews* (or Dew Drop) was a name they both applied to Mrs. Dewes, whose portrait gives an idea that the countenance and complexion well deserved such an appellation.

have reached my hands. A thousand thanks for the particular account you give me of yourself. I am very glad you have been blooded,[1] for with so much bustle as you must go through the blood cannot but be a little heated. I am impatient for a letter from Welsbourne. Some of your questions I have already answered. The solitude of Bradley was really *too much* for a sociable spirit to bear, and I shall be happy to have you in a neighbourhood where you may have some conversation a little better suited to your own, which I hope will be the case at Welsbourne, at least you will have a comfortable house, and that is a main article for happiness to those who know so well how to enjoy home and make it pleasant to your friends.

D.D. had institution last Tuesday from the Bishop of Down, and has taken out his patent, so now he is a Dean in all the forms; we propose setting out for Down on Monday se'night, please God he is well. I hope we shall have a pleasant jaunt, but I believe it is too late, and the days will be too much shortened, to think of going so far northward as the Giants' Causeway, which is above fifty miles from Down. Miss Forth (that lived with Mrs. Clayton), is now with her sister Hamilton; they are in our road to Down, and we design making them a visit in the way. To-day we are to dine with Mrs. Ford. We have killed a second buck—I never saw finer venison; it would have grieved me to have any of my pretty herd killed, had they not been two mischievous old rogues that have almost killed the rest with their great unruly horns. What a thing must Miss Knightly be that could be enamoured

---

[1] The constant bleeding that was resorted to at the period of these letters, renders it almost marvellous that anybody ever passed the age of forty, and prevents all surprise at the frequency of deaths after illness.

with *Scarebrains?* The pleasure you take in "*Y͡ᵉ Oak*"[1] pleases the Dean excessively, who is never happier than when he contributes to the pleasure of his friends. I have at present no folio paper in my possession but what is so thick it is not fit for carriage; but I write my words so much closer than you do, that I believe I have as many words in a quarto as you have in a folio, and I am sure I have not wrote above three sides to any one besides, and those in *my large hand.* I expected a great deal of business, but not so much as I find; I have workmen of all sorts in the house—upholsterers, joiners, glaziers, and carpenters—and am obliged to watch them all, or their work would be but ill-finished; and I have not been one day without company since I came. I have a young woman now in the house with me, Miss Delany, very lively and good-humoured, and very ready to assist me in anything I want to have done. I propose having her a good deal, as I believe it may be some advantage to her, and at present I see nothing in her but what is very agreeable. Friday and Saturday last I visited, and Sunday we had company dined with us, and in the afternoon Lady Bell Monck,[2] Mr. Monck, and Miss Kelly came to make us a visit; they came twenty miles to pay us that compliment; Lady Bell is handsomer, but has the same pert *Miss Notable* behaviour she used to have, but was very civil; they walked in the garden, and she had no eyes nor understanding to see that it was *not a common vulgar garden,* and she did not commend anything she saw —all the pearls were thrown away! On Monday eight

---

[1] Probably an allusion to some poem of Dr. Delany's on the old oaks of Bradley.

[2] Lady Isabella Bentinck, married in 1739 to Henry Monck, Esq.

gentlemen dined here, old friends of the Dean's. Mr. Steward was one whom I mentioned to you at Chester, and a Mr. Ludlow, a very ingenious gentleman with a vast deal of humour, but so reduced by the gout that he was carried in and out on men's shoulders: he is very musical and understands painting, and D.D., who displays all my little talents to their best advantage, drew many compliments from him on my score. Last Tuesday we dined at the Bishop of Down's: Mrs. Rider, his lady, is a very pretty sort of woman, and a great friend of Lady North's. I am always in haste to fly home, and as soon as we return put on my walking-dress and away we go to the garden, and though you complain so much of the weather in England, there have past few days but what we have been able to spend some time in the garden. Yesterday I indulged myself at home all day, and had our neighbours the young Barbers. Mr. Parker and his sister came to eat venison with us, they were kept for the evening, and sung and were very merry. I remembered it was the eve of one of my great festivals;[1] and I kept it with a double pomp of gladness. Adieu; every tender thought and wish of the most affectionate heart attends you.

Mrs. Delany to Mrs. Dewes, at Wellesbourn, near Kineton, Warwickshire.

Delville, 28th August, 1744.

What joyful news was it to me to hear of my most dear sister's safe arrival at Welsbourne, where I hope she will enjoy every blessing her heart can wish for and be as happy as she makes all around her! I am at present in

---

[1] "*My great festivals.*" Alluded to Ann Granville's marriage.

a great hurry, for at last we are obliged to go to Down. The Dean thought his presence might have been dispensed with, but upon examination finds there are forms that cannot be done by proxy, so to-morrow, please God, we set out for Down. The roads are excellent, the weather very good for travelling, and I hope the journey will be pleasant; the seeing of new places is entertaining, and we are going into such a hospitable country, that we shall not lie at an inn all the way. To-morrow we lie at Dunleer, which is twenty-five miles from hence, at Mr. Hamilton's, that married Miss Forth; and her sister Miss Mary Forth, that was with Mrs. Clayton, is now with her, which will be very agreable to me. There I believe we shall rest a day. We are to take up our residence for the time we stay in the North, at Dr. Mathews's a clergyman of a very singular good character, a most hospitable generous man : his house is near Down ; and Mr. Forde, Mrs. F.'s eldest son, lives in that neighbourhood. If I could be reconciled to leaving Delville I should be very well pleased with this little pilgrimage, but I own I leave it for a day with regret. We shall take this opportunity of having our house whitewashed, and some part painted, and many other finishings which we are now very busy in giving directions about. We don't propose making a longer stay than a fortnight, but as it is above seventy miles from hence our letters may be a little tedious in their passage, so I beg you will not be uneasy if you don't hear as regularly as you used to do. By the time you receive this and answer it, I hope to be at home again.

Mrs. Delany to Mrs. Dewes, at Gloucester.

Mount Panther, 10 Sept'., 1744.

After many tedious days' expectation arrived my dearest sister's letter dated the 19th August finished on the 20th. This letter I hope will find my dearest sister safely reposed at Gloucester; I believe it is time you shou'd be there, but I could not expect it much sooner as you have had so much to settle. Your house describes agreeably, and when it is graced by your presence and your good fancy, it will be delightful. Happy will be the hour when my eye sees what now I only can have an imperfect idea of, but I am glad to know every corner of your house and how you appropriate it, that I may follow your steps from place to place. Your orchard is charming, and so is your walk to church. I shall take it extremely ill if you rob Court[1] of his pictures; *all but* Summer and Faustina's pictures *are his*, and to be hung up in his nursery. I wrote to you the Saturday[2] I arrived here, which was this day se'night—with an account of our having been at Down Patrick. Last Monday we dined at Mr. Forde's, three miles from hence, a very pleasant place and capable of being made a very fine one; there is more wood than is common in this country, and a fine lake of water with very pretty meadows. The house is situated on the side of a hill, and looks down on his woods and water. The house is not a very good one, but very well fill'd; for he has *ten children*, the youngest about 10 years old,—but that's a *moderate family* to some in *this country*. In the afternoon came in two

---

[1] "*Court.*" The eldest son of Mrs. Dewes.
[2] "*The Saturday I arrived here.*" This letter has not been found.

ladies who had been to see me at Dr. Mathews's, and missing me followed. One is a Mrs. Annesly[1] (a relation to the present disputants), she is daughter to my Lord Tyrone, such another slatternly ignorant hoyden I never saw, and the worst of it is she is very good-humoured, but *will be familiar*: her husband is very like the Duke of Bedford, and well enough. The other lady is a Mrs. Baylis, a handsome sprightly woman, well behaved, with a little dash of a fine lady. Her husband, a genteel agreeable man, brother to Sir Nicholas Baylis, that married the Paget, a clergyman very well esteemed in the neighbourhood. On Tuesday the Fordes dined here; and on Wednesday Mr. and Mrs. Mathews of Newcastle, about six miles from hence. The whole family of the Fordes are religious, worthy people. On Friday we dined at Newcastle at Mr. Mathews's: it is situated at the foot of a range of mountains so high that they are at top seldom free from clouds, and the water has made a winding channel and falls down in a cascade; the main ocean bounds them on one side and is so near them that the spray of the sea wets them as they stand at the hall-door. On the other hand of

---

[1] Lady Anne De la Poer Beresford, married in 1738, William Annesley, 1st Viscount Glerawley. Sir Marcus Beresford, Bart., married, July 16, 1717, Catherine Poer, Baroness de la Poer in her own right, only child and heir of James, 3rd Earl of Tyrone. Her husband was created in 1720, Baron Beresford, Viscount Tyrone, and in 1746, Earl of Tyrone. He was the ancestor of the Waterford and Decies families. His eldest daughter, married, in 1738, William Annesley, 1st Viscount Glerawley, and ancestor of the Earls of Annesley. When a commoner, he was a claimant for the titles of Earl of Anglesey and Viscount Valentia.

[2] Sir Nicholas Bayley, Bart., of Plâsnewydd, Isle of Anglesea, North Wales, married Caroline, daughter and heiress of Brigadier-General Thomas Paget, grandson of William, 5th Baron Paget. Plâsnewydd is now the property (1860) of the Dowager Lady Willoughby de Broke, daughter of Sir John Williams, of Bôdelwyddan, Bart.

them are hills, fine meadows, winding rivers, and a variety of pretty objects for so bare a country of trees, though on the side of the mountains there are scattering shrubby woods which make the view pleasant. This country is famous for the goat's whey; and at the season for drinking it, which is summer, a great deal of company meet for that purpose, and there are little huts built up for their reception, and they have music and balls and cards, and happy are the family at Newcastle[1] when that season comes, for there are thirteen sons and daughters, most of them never out of that part of the country. Mr. Mathews is an attorney, has a very good fortune, is a good sort of man; his wife a sensible agreeable woman, and has brought up all her children extremely well—they are as decent and as healthy a family as ever I saw; and to make up the company, at the head of them are placed both Mr. and Mrs. Mathews's mothers; old Mrs. Mathews is eighty-seven years of age, and the most venerable fine figure I ever saw, and as apprehensive as a woman of five-and-twenty. A lady that went to see her this summer found her darning fine cambrick; her hearing is a little impaired.

There was something so extraordinary in the appearance of the family, and the situation of the place, that I was extremely entertained with my visit. Mr. Mathews waited for us at the door with his fishermen, and as soon as we arrived had the net thrown into a river near his house and took a large draught of fine salmon trout; the sun shining on them made them quite beautiful.

On Saturday we dined at Mr. Annesly's;[1] it was *a mere*

---

[1] "On the south side of Dundrum Bay is the watering-place of Newcastle, formerly called Black Rock, adjoining which is the residence of the Earl of Annesley."

rabble rout. Yesterday the Dean preached at Down, and we women went to Dr. Mathews's church two miles off, —a very pretty church and full congregation. We were invited and dined at Mr. Baylis' about a small mile from hence. They live in what is called in this country "*a cabin*"—that is a house of one floor and thatched; it is situated very near the sea, with a pretty neat court before it: the outside promises very little, but the inside is quite elegant, as much as I saw of it, which was the hall, a large parlour, drawing-room and bed-chamber. We were very handsomely entertained. There is a Mrs. Murray, a cousin-german of Mrs. Baylis, that is now with them,— a very sensible agreeable woman, and a great proficient in miniature painting; the likeness of her portraits, of which she showed me a great number, I was no judge of, I did not know the persons for whom they were drawn, but they are prettily pencilled, and some of her *landscapes* are really fine.

The weather is so excessively bad that I don't believe we shall be able to set out to-morrow for home as we designed; not that we have anything to apprehend from the roads, for I never travelled such fine roads as are all over this country, but I shall be afraid of the Dean's travelling in damp weather. D.D. is very busy in making a plan for the Deanery House. He is very much shocked at the present jail at Down, and is determined to have it altered, and to have one built with different apartments for men and women, and a chapel; he gives a hundred pounds towards it, and endows the chapel with twenty pounds a year for a clergyman to give them divine service, and is finishing and beautifying the church, which will be very handsome when done. I shall be very well pleased to have him continue in this scene till he has accomplished all his good designs; I must dress, company dines here.

In 1849 Frazer gave the following account:—" Proceeding from Castlewellan to Downpatrick, there is an undulating country, and at three and a half miles Mount Panther, the residence of J. Reed Allen, Esq., and five miles further the village of Clough—a mile north from which is the village and demesne of Seaford, the latter the fine residence of Lady Harriet Forde. Downpatrick, the county town of Down, returns a member of Parliament, and as the name imports *the hill of St. Patrick*, is said to be the most ancient town in Ireland. It is situated near the head of Lough Strangford, built on an undulating surface, and encircled by a series of low hills. "Slieve-na-griddle (414 feet) is about two miles and a half east from the town, and not far from its base are Struel, or as they are sometimes called St. Patrick's Wells, where at midsummer many persons resort from various parts of Ireland to do penance, and to partake of the supposed sanative qualities of the waters. St. Finian's Well is near the race-course, on the south of the town. A little to the west of Downpatrick, near the road to Clough, is Holly Mount, the seat of Mr. Forde."

The following original letter from Dr. Salter[1] is here inserted in its chronological order.

Mr. Samuel Salter to Mrs. Dewes.

MADAM, September 11th, 1744.

I have seldom met with a more pleasant request, in whatever light it is viewed. I am the gayest man upon earth. I come hither for two months, only three-fifths of which time is gone. I shall leave Glocester the first day of October, and fly on the wings of impatient love

---

[1] Samuel Salter, D.D., a learned divine and a prebendary of Gloucester. He published several sermons, &c., and died 1778.

into Lincolnshire. I shall not be here again this twelve-month be sure, perhaps not these two years ; and you ask *the gay man* for *grave books;* you suppose the man whose stay is only two months has his whole library with him, and you expect to borrow of one whom you cannot see again for so long a time. But there is something so wild in your note that I consider it as a burlesque only upon mine ; for if you want books, who so able, so ready, or so willing to supply you as our friend Jack Newton? You are again mistaken in me, and seem to have heard but half my story, which is a wonder too ; for I have taken a deal of pains, or rather a deal of pleasure, to tell it all. The verses I quoted are only applicable to a lover in doubt and fear; *I am safe in port,* and when I go from hence I go to be married. The joy, therefore, which lightens from my eyes never sickens with desire and dies, but, on the contrary, brightens with the assurance of success and the prospect of possession, and lives and acquires fresh brightness and spirit every hour, every moment, as witness my hand this 11th day of September, 1744.   Samuel Salter.

P.S. Seriously, I have gotten only three books which I can make you an offer of: one is Fontenelle's Dialogues of the Dead (Fr. prose), another Fontaine's Fables (Fr. verse), and the third is entitled A Wedding Ring fit for the Finger, or the Salve of Divinity on the Love of Humanity; laid open in a Sermon at a Wedding, by William Secker,[1] &c. This last I am fallen

---

[1] " A Wedding Ring fit for the Finger ; or, the Salve of Divinity on the Score of Humanity :" a Sermon at a Wedding, by William Secker, preacher of the Gospel at Tewkesbury. Published in 1658.

in love with upon two accounts: the subject is particularly interesting to me at this time, the manner of handling it is most entertaining, and which is better than all, the author is of the *same name and family* with the lady who has already made me the happiest man on earth, and will soon make me the happiest in the universe. If you would see this last pray let me know it, and you shall have it for a day or so, but I will not trust it out of my hands longer; and indeed if I did not know how to spend my time much better than in reading when I am happy in the company of ladies, I should insist on reading it to you myself. I am, with compliments and respects of every proper kind, and the wishes, moreover, of the season to you, madam,

Your most obedient humble serv^t,

S. S.

P.S. 2nd. 'Tis a sign you know me very little that you will dare write to me, for none dare but they who know me very much and they who scarce know me at all.

P.S. 3rd. Either of the French books you may have for as long as you please. This letter has three postscripts.

I must add a 4th P. S. by way of remark on your last words, which are *so curious* as to fetch *more last words out of me.* You *can bear* Night Thoughts, you say, and bid me remember it. Oh! there is no sort of danger of my forgetting it while the request preferred in your last remains in my memory, for I can hardly think you were all awake when you thought of it. I do insist upon it, the expression in the Night Thoughts is *affectedly labored into obscurity;* that the sentiments are but *pompous trifling* and *magnificent commonplace,* and that the morality of them *is false* and highly unbecoming a philosopher and a divine to inculcate, and nothing could excuse him on this head but the *piety of his conclusion,* which, however, is very *ill built on his premises.* It is not true nor right to argue thus : " This world is a scene of misery, therefore let us look for another and better ;" but it is both right and true to say—" Let us look for another and better world, and then we *shall be able* to go through this with *comfort and content,* even though *it should prove* to be a scene of misery and a vale of tears !" You made me miss church, so I wrote all this side out of spite.

Mrs. Delany to Mrs. Dewes, at Gloucester.

Delville, 23 Sept. 1744.

I thank God, my dearest sister, that you are safe at Gloucester, and I trust with a thorough confidence that I shall hear more happy news of you by the beginning of October. I am rich with three folios of your precious letters, but am poor in time; for upon my return home visitors, and tradespeople have encompased me, and I can't say an hour is my own : but by my next turn of writing I hope to be at leisure to reassume a folio-sheet of paper.

I am excessively obliged to you for your particular account of your house and all its appurtenances, and your neighbourhood, all which gives me great contentment, and will afford you I hope many years of satisfaction. You cannot more eagerly wish to see the Magician and his Nymph at Welsbourne than they wish to see it, and they will both be ready to enter into a consultation to improve a place so well inhabited ; and as we are both in our natures busy people, it will be impossible not to scheme where there are such good materials to work upon. We returned from the North on Thursday; dined and lay one night at Mr. Hamilton's: I was sorry to make so short a visit to such an agreeable family, but our workmen were waiting at home for us. My English room is quite unfurnished again and under the painter's hands. I have had it painted a sort of olive, somewhat lighter than my brother's, for the sake of my pictures, and because the room is very light. I have had the frieze painted with festoons of flowers and shells alternate, and you can't imagine what a pretty effect it has; as soon as the room is dry, which will be about a fortnight hence, I shall be very busy in replacing my goods. We now live in our great parlour, which is a most comfortable room. Oh that I could bring you and our dearest mama, etc. to this dwelling with a wish! You should have a very snug apartment for your purpose, and I should have the happiness of attending you as usual, but this is chimerical and at present impossible. I am very glad my mother is so much better. I pray God give her many happy years! I shall not answer her dear kind letter yet, because I would have her quite easy about not writing to me. She has been excessively good, and I am sure I am with the tenderest affection her most obedient daughter.

The Dean bids me say in answer to your challenge that the author of Tar Water [1] is so well qualified to deal with

---

[1] "Siris, a Chain of Philosophical Reflections and Enquiries concerning the Virtues of Tar Water. By Dr. Berkeley, Bishop of Cloyne. Sold by M. Cooper, price 1s." (1744). Bishop Berkeley declares it to be a sovereign remedy against all the ills that flesh is heir to. His receipt was, 1 gallon of cold water to 1 quart of tar, stirred well with a ladle for three or four minutes, then left to stand forty-eight hours, and the clear water poured off for use, no more being made from the same tar. In a pamphlet from the author of *Siris* to T. P., Esq., he

his adversaries that he wants no second, and so poor an epigram can only bring a reflection on the silly publisher. His most affectionate service attends the Pearly Dewes, with his constant prayers for her welfare. As to your question about the northern journey, he says I was the occasion of its being put off; but it was to comply with my fears about his health, and not on my own account. He has been very busy all this morning in cleaning and trimming the *Pearly Dewes's Bower.* It is provoking to have so many charming letters of yours to answer and not have time to say a word more. *I have had a letter from my brother;* he is mightily delighted with Gleg: and I have had a letter from my dear Princess. Now I finish with duty, love and service, as due, from your ever affectionate

---

Mrs. Delany to Mrs. Dewes, at Wellesbourne, near Keinton, Warwickshire.

(A fragment,) without date.

"How I could run on, but must not. I am called to range dishes on my table, which is a long one, and consequently easier to set out than a round or oval one. The table takes seven dishes in length. Here follows my bill of fare for to-day; is not this ridiculous? but if you *wander still unseen,* it may serve as an amusement in your retirement.

First Course.	*Second Course.*
Turkeys *endove*[1]	Partridge
Boyled neck of mutton	Sweet breads

---

says, "As the old philosophers cried aloud from the house-tops, '*Educate your children,*' so I confess, if I had a situation high enough and a voice loud enough, I would cry out to all valetudinarians upon earth, '*Drink tar water.*'"

[1] Query *Endive.*—Turkey with Endive.

First Course.	Second Course.
Greens, &c.	Collared pig
Soup	Creamed apple tart
Plum-pudding.	Crabs
Roast loin of veal	Fricassee of eggs
Venison pasty.	Pigeons.

No dessert to be had.

The arrangement of the above bill of fare is very curious, as well as the combination of collared pig and venison pasty with hot meats for dinner. This list of viands for an ordinary dinner is probably a fair sample of what Mary Granville in her first visit to Ireland alluded to, when she mentioned "*always seven dishes of meat,*" or "*eight dishes of meat.*"

The Duchess of Portland writes to Lady Throckmorton, dated "Bulstrode, Dec. 15, 1744," to say that her spirits had been much sunk by Lady Oxford's illness, who, however, was then recovered. She also gives the news that the Duke of Bedford was to be head of the Admiralty and the Duke of Somerset to be made Earl of Northumberland, to descend to Sir Charles Windham with the estate the Duchess of Somerset[1] settled upon him.

An interval of three months here occurs, during which period Sir John Stanley died.[2]

Mrs. Delany to Mrs. Dewes.

Delville, the third day of the new year,
1744-5.

It is needless to repeat how warmly my heart wishes you, my dearest sister, all happiness this year and many succeeding ones. The Dean joins me in every tender

---

[1] Lady Elizabeth Percy,

[2] Died, December, 1744, Sir John Stanley, Bart., one of the Commissioners of the Customs, aged 85.

wish. Your letter of the 16th December is come safe. What you say of Sir John Stanley is very just. I *have* the satisfactory consciousness of having acted *a right part towards him*; I have from my childhood received many favours, and to the day of my death shall gratefully remember him; but my brother has had it more in his power to shew his regard, and for many years we know gave up the world for his sake, and I own *he deserved* to be more distinguished. There can be no mistake in the hundred pound left you, for Mr. Charles Monck sent me a copy of the will, where he says he leaves that sum to "*Miss Ann Granville, sister to Mrs. Pendarves.*" W.M. had not the manners to give my brother notice either of Sir J. Stanley's sickness or death, or me; he will be obliged to sell Northend; I wish it may be bought by somebody I love, but I would rather have it in the possession of anybody than W.M. You may remember that the basons and covers that are left me had dishes belonging to them; I suppose poor Sir J. did not think it necessary to mention them, as they belonged to the dishes, but W.M. told my brother the *basons* were left me, but *not* the dishes, it will be in character if he separates them, as I don't doubt he will.

Who is at Bradley, and how are all your friends at Mapleborough? I have had a long letter from my mother; I find she is very weak in her limbs, and fear that is an infirmity will increase upon her. The ingenious and agreeable Letty[1] is still with me, thanks to the winds that have kept back her clothes; as soon as they arrive away she flies into the country sixty miles off to

---

[1] Letitia Bushe, often mentioned in Mrs. Pendarves's first visit to Ireland.

Lady Anne Magill,[1] a sister of Lord Darnley's. She will be a great loss to me; she is one of the few who is perfectly qualified for an agreeable companion in a domestic way; her sweetness of temper makes her give into all one's ways as if she chose to do whatever is proposed; her other agreeable and engaging talents you have long been acquainted with; she paints for me in the morning and draws in the evening, which with reading, prating, walking, backgammon and puss in the corner employ the hours of the day and evening so fully that we do not feel how fast they fly. Our concerts are begun again and are to be continued every Tuesday.

Mrs. Delany to Mrs. Dewes.

Delville, 10 Jan. 1744-5.

Bushe is still with me, and Miss Parker and a little girl a friend of Miss Delany's. This is by way of preface to a short letter; as you know when one's house is full of company, time is unaccountably swallowed up. Besides, I have been for two hours writing out a long list of affairs for D.D.'s lawyers. Yet I must write to my most dear sister, and thank her for her delightful letters, dated the 22nd and 29th Dec.! Such stormy weather we have had for two days past, with violent snow driving at such a rate, that it has penetrated through the roof of the house, almost into every room. I never remember anything like it; and yesterday D.D. was engaged to preach

---

[1] Anne, second daughter of John, 1st Earl of Darnley, married, first, 17th September, 1742, to Robert Hawkins Macgill, Esq., of Gill Hill, county Down; and secondly, in December, 1748, to Bernard Ward, Viscount Bangor.

at St. Warbor's. My heart ached for him, for it was a *most hazardous undertaking*, but he was so discreet as to come home in a sedan-chair. We went at two to Mr. Wesley's, and were *one hour* driving, and we used to be only twenty minutes, but such hills of snow and dales of mud were in our way, that we made our passage with great difficulty.

Mrs. Fortescue is following your example, and producing another child; her boy is very handsome and stout, all the family look happy, and Mr. Wesley has *smoothed his brow*; they are a very agreeable, good-humoured set of people, and Mr. Fortescue a very pretty man, and has an extremely good character from everybody. Our little hop which I promised Bell was appointed for Wednesday, but that proving the Fast-day, it is to be this evening; the dancers are to be your humble servant and Mrs. Hamilton's eldest son (a very sober, well-behaved youth), his sister and Mr. Ford: how the rest will be coupled I can't tell; but these are the rest of the hoppers—two Mr. Swifts, young men of this village, Mr. Parker, and a younger son of Mrs. Hamilton's; Miss Delany, Mrs. Barber[1] (the Dean's niece), Miss Parker, Miss Green; we begin at five and end at nine, tea, coffee, and cold supper; and beds for those that will accept of them. Did I not write you word of an humble servant of Miss Delany's, a Councellor Green? he has been here and has made his proposal, and is accepted; he is really a very handsome, agreeable man, modest, and has long had an affection for her, and I think she will

---

[1] "Mrs. Barber, the Dean's niece." This was not Mrs. Barber the poetess, though it is possible it might have been the wife of one of her sons, perhaps of Dr. Barber the physician.

make a very proper wife for him : without being at all handsome, she has something engaging in her looks and very proper in her behaviour: so now my thoughts are busy about her. Her uncle gives her her fortune and her wedding-clothes; I hope we shall settle her happily, but she will be a great loss to me at home, for she is very useful and diverting, and gives us many a hearty laugh.

Saturday 12th January.

The little rout is over? we had four hours of smart, clever dancing; and broke off a quarter before nine; supped, and were all quiet in our nests by twelve, and the Dean seemed as well pleased with looking on as we were with our dancing.

I think my Lord Gower might be of use if he were properly applied to, and you know I am ready with heart and hand to make any application that can be serviceable. My first thought was for poor Miss G.; for on hearing of Lord Weymouth's illness, and knowing how precarious her small income is, (which depends upon his *life and pleasure,*) I wrote to my brother to know if it would be right for me to write to Lord Gower in her behalf: since that I have had a letter from her, to tell me she had written to the Duchess of Bedford, to ask her interest with her father; and if my brother thinks it proper I should write to back her request I must. Lord Chesterfield comes to Ireland after his negotiation to Holland. I am sorry I have kept the story of the young lady so long from you, but I have not had an opportunity yet of seeing her, and I was willing to give you the story first from her own mouth. Mr. Brook's play is called The Patriot; I don't find it greatly approved of, but they say it is miserably acted. He will not print it till it has made its appearance on the English stage. I am sorry Mr. White is not on better terms in his neighbourhood; but every place has its parties and partizans.

Mrs. Delany to Mrs. Dewes.
Delville, 19 Jan., 1744-5.

I must own I am greatly pleased at your present situation. I could not bear your being buried in such a solitude as Bradley, and I am heartily glad Mr. Dewes enjoys the pleasure of cheerful society and a pleasant dwelling: his own cheerfulness and good-humour makes him worthy of it, and may you both long enjoy every blessing that human nature is capable of! I am so happy as to have the lovely and ingenious Letty Bushe with me still; the winds that have crossed our wishes often have been kind to me on her account, and by detaining her clothes kept her under my roof, but now she talks of leaving me, and as I have always made it a rule in any friendship never to be a monopolizer, I must give her up. Lady Anne Magill is a sister of Lord Darnley's, a young lady of a very good character, and a great friend of Letty's; they are engaged to spend the winter together, and I must yield to the first engagement, though my loss will be irreparable, as I *can have nobody with me here* that can give me so much pleasure; for besides her ingenuity, she has a turn for conversation that is not common, and her good-humour is inexhaustible, but her constitution is tender, which must be an allay to the pleasure she every other way gives.

You say you wish the Bishop of Gloucester *knew* Lord Weymouth had settled £4000 on ——. Are you sure of that? Mrs. F. writes me word she is not certain of it. In my last to you I think I said I waited for an answer from my brother before I could write to Lord Gower, but as I do not love to lose time, if I may by any means advance a friend's interest, I wrote him a comical letter last Tuesday; my preamble was compliments on his promotion, and that it was the tax of men of power to be importuned, but I said I was *so* reasonable I had *but three petitions* to prefer *at a time*; my letter was a long one, and I have not time to transcribe it, but sometimes a letter of that kind is better remembered and listened to than a more serious one. D.D. thinks Mr. W. has *not authority* for what he did in relation to the Xtning, not but that in the main it was right and may be a means of putting the common people in mind of a duty too much neglected.

If *we* are promoted I hope in time something may be done for Mr. Chapon, but at present D.D. has old friends and relations to provide for that claim the first right to his interest. The Chapons talk of sending Harry to study in our college,—I think if they can afford to bring him up in that way, it will be better and cheaper than the universities of England; here he may be maintained and educated in that way for £40 a year, and be upon the same footing as the best gentlemen's sons.

I ask a thousand pardons for not sending the story of Miss McDermot sooner. Last Thursday was se'night we dined at the Wesleys (great enquiry after you), and the day following we had our ball which I have already given you information of, as also of the wedding in hand which goes on very well; and next Monday I go to Dublin to buy the clothes. D.D. gives her five hundred

pounds for her portion, and sixty pounds to buy clothes;
I believe the knot will be tied about the middle of next
month. I hope she will be happy; the prospect is fair, and
she has engaged my good wishes by her very obliging
behaviour; I am going to fit up my only room that is
still unfurnished; it is to be hung with tapestry, a rich
green damask bed, chairs, and window curtains, which
apartment I hope will be honoured by my dearest sister
when she can make me happy with her company."

Mrs. Delany to Mrs. Dewes.

Delville, 31 Jan., 1744-5.

Did I tell you of another wedding in hand here? a
nephew of D.D's, who is a kind of steward to us, and a
sober good sort of young man bred up to farming affairs.
He is going to be married to a very clever girl, bred up
in the same way—a niece of Mrs. Barber's; the Dean
gives them a very comfortable farm about twelve miles off,
and they are to supply us with all farming affairs. When
this is done the Dean has not a relation left that he has
not portioned or *settled* in some comfortable way; and if
I were to tell you all the particulars of his benevolence
and his goodness towards them you would be astonished
that his fortune had answered so well the beneficence of
his heart, but these are the things for which he has
been blest. " *His leaf shall not wither, and look whatsoever
he doeth it shall prosper.*"

The pretty enclosed drawing is from the ingenious
Letitia, invented and executed by my side.

Mrs. Delany to Mrs. Dewes.

Delville, 2nd March, 1744-5.

I gave you a short account of our wedding-day, which passed off as well as such things generally do. They are still in the house with us, and will stay till the beginning of May that we go to the North. Mr. Green is an agreeable man to have in the house, as he is very well bred and easy, conversable, and reads to us whilst we work in the evenings, so that we spend our time very pleasantly. Miss Harman, a cousin-german and friend of Mrs. Green, is now with us—a modest young thing, obliging and good-humoured; and you know I like to indulge friends, as I love to be indulged myself; we have had a good deal of company on this occasion, and next week we return visits and have many dinner-invitations on our hands. The Councellor Green has three brothers, the two eldest great sugar-bakers, and one of them made a present to the Bride of a bill of fifty pounds the day after she was married.

The account you give me of your walking through frost and snow with your little boys, delights me. You say you want a little "*good conversation;*" why that is certainly the most rare of all rarities, and were you not yourself richly endowed with the talent of conversing, you would *not feel the loss of it* so much, but a little lively talk and chit-chat must be accepted, and for more solid and useful thoughts your own breast and your library can supply you. The insolence of the Duchess of Bedford towards our worthy cousins fills me with indignation whenever I think of it.

My Lord Salisbury's[1] match did not surprize me; his steward perhaps may be a gentleman of as good a family as himself, and a woman of rank and knowledge of the world would not have accepted of a *coachman* although he *was a peer of the realm!* The Duke of Chandos's[2] choice is a more extraordinary one, but I own I am well pleased with both, as I take it to be a strong proof of the virtue of both these women, who would hardly have been raised to the rank they are now in had they *not been virtuous;* and as *virtue is now more scarce* in the world than *nobility,* I can't help rejoicing at every instance of it.

You say Mr. Yate *is very gay, and well pleased with the good fortune his cousin has left him.* Pray what is it? you never mentioned it to me. I am glad he *had it not* some years ago, for I am now well assured I could not have been so happy with any man in the world as the person I am now united to; his real benevolence of heart, the great delight he takes in making every one happy about him, is a disposition *so uncommon* that I would not change that one circumstance of happiness for all the riches and greatness in the world. This evening we have a concert; next Tuesday should have been the day, but we are to dine abroad. I wish Miss Tracy was well married for her sake and for her mother's, who would finish her days with more content could she leave that good young woman well settled. Is there no talk of Miss Dodwell's marrying? I am sorry the poor Chapons are under trouble of any kind; in time I still hope I

---

[1] James Cecil, 6th Earl of Salisbury, married, in 1743, Elizabeth, sister of the Rev. John Keet, Rector of Hatfield.

[2] Henry, 2nd Duke of Chandos, married his second wife, Anne Jeffrys, in 1745.

may do them some more considerable service than I have yet done, but my designs hitherto for them have never succeeded.

Have I told you of a pretty tortoiseshell puss I have? the sauciest and prettiest, most indulged little animal that ever was everybody's favourite. After this important sentence I have no more to add, but that I am with the utmost tenderness yours.

Mrs. Delany to Mrs. Dewes.

Delville, 9 March, 1744-5.

I have of late been happy in receiving my dearest sister's letters regularly. Dr. Barber is generally a person sure of a sincere welcome; indeed he is always welcome on his own account as a very good sort of man, and I believe a very good physician; but in that capacity I hope we shall have but little use for him. I thank God we are both at present in very good health, and yᵉ few warm days we have had, have given an air of cheerfulness and spring that revives all one's senses, Delville begins now to open its sweets, and yesterday and the morning before I spent two hours in my garden and paid my affectionate homage to the "*Pearly Bower.*" D.D. is restoring some winding walks that the encroaching weeds had almost smothered. The birds sing melodiously, and there is one chaffinge and two robins that eat out of his hand; I wish they may not grow quite wild again before we return from the North; but cold and want will bring them to hand again—the great tamers of the human as well as the animal kind. I think Lady G. S.'s conduct was very odd and not at all well-judged towards Lady

Sunderland, but if it succeeds we have reason to be glad of her indiscretion.

I had a very long letter from my brother two packets ago, with an account of a long conference he had with Lord G—[1] who told him he had a very handsome letter from me, and that he had desired Lord Cornbury to make his excuse for not sooner answering it. My brother talked of Miss Granville; I fear her prospect is but indifferent; Lord G. asked what could be done for Mr. Dewes, for he supposed he would not care to quit his profession, and asked several questions about him. My brother told him he was a younger brother, but of a very good family in Warwickshire, and had very good expectations. He asked what Lady Granville proposed to have done? My brother gave him as good an account as he cou'd recollect, which Lord G. said was "*very like the old Countess.*"[2] This was all that passed, and you'll say a great deal for my brother to repeat; but *his heart* is set on doing something for Miss Granville, as he thinks her situation a very precarious one, which prevents his entering more into Mr. Dewes's affair.

There is something very odd in poor Sr John Stanley's late behaviour,[3] but I try to forget it, for it *grieves my heart.*

Well, we have eaten etc. *such feasts—such routs,* but thank God all over, and most of my formal visits returned. So I feel a free woman, and shall return to my pencils and shell-works; the new-married couple stay with us till

[1] Lord Gower.
[2] Grace, Countess Granville in her own right, died October 18, 1744, on the same day as Sarah Duchess of Marlborough.
[3] From this sentence it is probable that Sir John Stanley continued dissatisfied with the marriage of Mrs. Pendarves to Dr. Delany, though not so much so as Mr. Granville.

we go to the North, which I hope is as agreeable to them as it is to me.

Mr. Phipps is come to Ireland to put in his claim, and carry off, if he can, the estate so long contended for between Lord Anglesey and Mr. Annesley,—it will be fine harvest for the lawyers; I have been to wait on Mrs. Phipps;[1] you know she was Lord Hervey's daughter: she was not at home—they are soon to dine here.

Was there ever such an infatuation as now reigns amongst the nobility of England! *Are all* the *strange* matches *true?* I am not apt to believe scandal, and don't know how to credit such extraordinary reports. The Duke of Beaufort's[2] death is not to be lamented—he was unhealthy in his constitution and unhappy in his circumstances, though possessed of great honour and riches: his brother is qualified to make a better figure, and his wife I *hope* will prove an honourable and virtuous Duchess of Beaufort. The sun calls me abroad and the Pearly Bower has not been visited to-day.

Mrs. Delany to Mrs. Dewes, Wellesbourne.

Delville, 23rd March, 1744-5.

It is comical enough that we should give each other a relation of my brother's transactions, I believe on the same day; but as he *sometimes is taciturn,* I chose rather to

---

[1] Lepoll, eldest daughter of John Lord Hervey, married February 26, 1743, Constantine Phipps, Esq., who was created Lord Mulgrave, September 3, 1767.

[2] Henry, 3rd Duke of Beaufort, married Frances, only child of Viscount Scudamore, from whom he was divorced, died without issue February 24, 1745-6, and was succeeded by his brother, Charles Noel, 4th Duke, who married, 1st of May, 1740, Elizabeth, daughter of John Berkeley, Esq., and sister of Norborne Lord Bottetourt.

trouble you with a repetition than not tell you all I know. It is reported here that Mr. Chenevix has more mind to the Deanery of Down than the Bishopric of Dromore; if he has, let him take it. Mrs Montague, of Hanover Square, writes me word the Duke of Cumberland[1] is certainly to be married, and that Lady Wallingford is named for a lady of the bedchamber to the Duchess, and Miss Granville as bedchamber woman; and though I suppose it will be no great matter, it may bring her into the way of something better in time.

I wrote to Will Monck about the pictures, and desired him to send the basons with their covers and dishes belonging to them to my brother, that Sir John Stanley had left me. He wrote me an answer to say " the pictures must go with the house or it might be a detriment in the disposing of it, *and that the dishes were not devised to me, only the basons and covers.*" My answer was as follows:—

Sir,—I should not have had the assurance to mention the dishes to you had I not apprehended they belonged to the basons, and it was natural for me to imagine Sir John Stanley did not mean to separate them; but whatever his meaning was, I perceive the letter of the law gives me no claim to the dishes the basons stood upon, and therefore (if it will be no detriment in the sale of the house) I desire you will let a price be set on the dishes, and I shall willingly pay it, as the basons are no more complete without them than a flower without a stem. If you have sent the frame belonging to the fruit piece with it, I am indebted to you for that, and

---

[1] William Augustus, Duke of Cumberland, youngest son of George II., born 15th April, 1721; died unmarried in 1765. He was a Field-Marshal and Commander-in-Chief of the Forces, and commanded the English forces at Culloden and Fontenoy.

desire to know what I must pay, for I don't find that was "DEVISED" *with the picture.*

I have seen Miss McDermot, and had her story from her own mouth. At half an hour after seven I sat for the finishing my picture in enamel; at ten went to painting; company came at two and dined here; and till this instant (half an hour after eight) I have not had the least moment to myself.

Mrs. Delany at Mrs. Dewes, at Wellesbourne.

Delville, 20th May, 1745.

I told you in one of my letters that Miss McDermots *had sent* to speak privately to D.D., and that I was in hopes it was on a religious account; thank God! so it has proved, and last Sunday they made their recantation in our church. They had not been at mass these twelve months, and their brother died a Protestant. They had several conferences with the Dean, and he collected texts of Scripture for them. What they most stuck at was transubstantiation, but I believe they have been thoroughly convinced of their error in that point. Miss McDermot said "though she had been so barbarously treated among the Papists she should *not* leave them were not her reason thoroughly convinced of their errors;" she has on the whole occasion showed herself a reasonable woman. They dined with us on Sunday; the ceremony of their making their recantation is their reading a paper signed by them, wherein they renounce all the errors of the Church of Rome; the minister (when they have read the paper aloud in the midst of the congregation, just before the Communion Service) lays his hand on their head and receives them into the Church as converts, and then prays for them. There is something very awful in it, and the poor ladies were under great confusion, but behaved themselves very well, and seemed extremely glad when it was over. I thought they would have been here very private and quiet, but eight persons that I did *not expect* came to dinner beside themselves, still there could not be too many witnesses of so good an action. All the company came to church as well as to dinner, and we all went again in the afternoon; you can't think what a gay appearance we made as we walked through the garden to church, attended by all the servants, who were pretty numerous.

I have now every thing packed up for our journey, which is put off to next Monday. We shall lie the first night at Mr. Hamilton's at Dunleer, the second at Newry, and dine the third day at Mount Panther; at Dr. Mathews's, where we were last autumn, and where we propose staying some days till my domestics are settled.

The Dean and I travel in our chaise, which is easy and pleasant; Betty and Margaret, the cook and a housemaid in the coach and four, and Peg Hanages (who I am breeding up to be a housemaid) in a car we have had made for marketing, and carrying luggage, &c., when we travel. Our new coach will be ready when we come home, but now we hire one for the northern expedition. Yesterday we dined at Arteen, at Mr. Donnellan's, and were met by Mrs. Marly and Letty Bushe. To-day we dine at Mrs. Conolly's, and in the afternoon are to meet Miss McDermots and Letty Bushe at Mr. Taverner's, and to have a concert of music. But the sad havoc that has been abroad damps all one's pleasures at home.

The History of Miss Macdermot, written by Mrs. Delany.

The principal heroine of the following story related it to me herself about half a year after it happened. Previous to the affair, Dr. Delany received a very sensible letter from Miss Macdermot out of Connaught, expressing her desire of recanting her religion; she was of an old Irish family. She and her sister Miss Maria, on the death of their only brother, were left heiresses of a large estate (their father and mother had been long dead). The oldest daughter was entitled by the settlement to a double share of the estate left to her and her sister; they had both resolved to make their public recantation if she survived their brother, who was a great bigot. On his death they wrote to Dr. Delany; his answer gave them so much satisfaction, that they fixed a time to go to Dublin to talk with him further on the subject, which though they had not declared to those they were nearest connected with, was suspected, and they received an invitation from their Uncle Flinn, their mother's brother, (who had an only son, who had made proposals to the eldest sister, and had been rejected about this time,) which they could not well refuse, as they had always been on good terms, though not on intimate ones. The distance allowed of their going and returning back the same day; a day was therefore named, and they went early in the morning, and ordered their chaise to be ready for their return soon after dinner. When the hour came they went to take leave; their uncle insisted upon it they should not go back that evening, but they refused with all the civility they could, pleading that business obliged them. This availed them nothing, for on enquiry about their equipage, with a firm resolution to go, they were told that the chaise and servants were gone, and would return the next day: so they were obliged to submit, though very unwillingly. Miss Macdermot told me that she was seized with a horror that something bad would happen (she was not handsome, tall and rather large, but her person altogether very well; she had a very sensible countenance, with spirit, a sweet voice, with great gentleness of manner when she spoke). The terror which first seized her upon being obliged to stay continued, and not without reason, for as they were seated down to cards in the evening, in rushed four men in masks into the room. Miss Macdermot, terrified with the appearance of these people, started up and ran into the next apartment. One hid herself under the bed, and the other behind it, not finding any way out but the door by which they entered, but not quick enough to escape being seen by the principal person masked, who first seized Miss Maria who was behind the bed, but on viewing her said she was the wrong sister, cursed her heartily and quitted her, and then laid violent hands on Miss Macdermot who was under the bed. She fought manfully to avoid him, and he could not take hold of her to take her away till all her clothes were torn off except her stays, her pockets, and underpetticoat. She then endeavoured to throw herself upon her knees, to implore his mercy, but he seizing her by both her arms, dragged her in that posture through the room they had left, where nobody remained but her uncle, who stood upon the hearth before the fire with his hands behind him, with the coolest indifference at what he saw. Miss Macdermot asked him how he could be

such a villain to see her treated in such a way in his own
house, and begged for God's sake he would rescue her.
Pleading was to no purpose, and when he had dragged
her into the hall, it was crowded with desperate-looking
men; and about two hundred of the same sort were
assembled about the door, where was a horse and pillion
ready to receive them; and whilst others of the gang were
tying her hands and feet, this desperate man mounted
the horse and she was placed behind him, and tied on as
fast as possible. They tried to gag her, but she eluded
all their force, and they were in haste to carry her off.

When they had gone about a mile from the house, she
had struggled so violently as to get her hands at liberty
and threw herself off the horse. They were all armed with
bludgeons and great swords, one of which she seized as
they were endeavouring to replace her on the horse, and
finding herself at liberty to walk, she sprang from them
and got against a tree—for though it was a dark night,
they had a number of lights with them. She fought for
some time and kept her station, till one of the cruel
gang run a sword up her arm, from her wrist to her elbow,
in such a manner that obliged her to drop her weapon;
as she could no longer defend herself and was almost
fainting from pain and anguish, she again fell into their
barbarous hands, and their numbers were constantly
increasing.

They proceeded on in this manner for some miles, and
then stopped at a cabin, where they took Miss McDermot
off the horse, and carried her in, and gave her into the
care of the woman that belonged to it, with a strict charge
not to let her stir, for her life would answer for it if she
did. With this order they left them together locked in,

when it proved, this woman had formerly been Miss M—'s nurse, which circumstance she hoped would make her feel more compassion for her present unfortunate situation. She instantly threw herself upon her knees, and begged the woman for God's sake to save her life from these villainous wretches, who were carrying her off by force, and entreated her if she had no better way of concealing her, she would let her go out of the window, and she would take her chance for making her escape. She took a £5 note out of her pocket, which fortunately they had not found, and offered it to the woman, who looked terrified and at a loss what to do ; when the door opened, and in came the chief person, Mr. Flinn, with three or four other men, and one that was a priest, who immediately laid hold of her, and said if she would submit quietly to the ceremony of being married to Mr. Flinn, she should be treated with all manner of kindness and respect ; if not, he was resolved to make her his wife by force.

Finding she was resolute in not complying with his request, but vehemently asserted that she would rather die than be united to such a monster, on their laying hold of her to put the ring on her finger, she threw it off whilst the priest was muttering over the marriage ceremony, and springing from them, snatched up a mug of milk, which she had accidentally laid her eyes on, standing by the fire, and threw it full in the priest's face. At that moment some of the party came in and spoke to Flinn in Irish (which *they supposed* she did not understand), and told him that the country was raised and in pursuit of them, which gave her a gleam of hope and supported her in this dreadful calamity. After they had whispered with one another some time, more of the party came into the room in order to secure her, but they grew alarmed at finding that the wound she had received in her arm bled profusely, and they could not tell what might be the consequence. Fresh alarms coming in, made them immediately carry her off, and they took her to a bog and plunged her up to her shoulders in mud, placing a man on each side with pistols (for they were armed with all kinds of weapons) to prevent her making her escape. But they were soon discovered by her friends, who came from every part to her relief, and put her enemies to flight. They immediately carried her to a relation's, a gentleman of considerable fortune in that country, where with the help of the best medical advice and kind treatment, it pleased God to restore her (beyond expectation) after having lain twenty-one days in a violent pain, and doubtful whether she would live or die.

It was thought horrible, but it appears that the plunging her in the bog stopped the bleeding, and by that means saved her life. The poor sister made her escape from her uncle's house early the next morning in the deepest distress, and immediately raised the country, all the way as she went home, to go in pursuit of her sister, and try to recover her, which was (through her) effected as above, and she sent for her to the gentleman's house where her sister was recovered with so much kindness. It was some months after before they could put in execution their religious scheme, for which purpose they came to Dublin to make their recantation in Glassnevon church (a parish belonging to Dr. Delany, in which his house at Delville was situated, out of the garden of which there was a door into the churchyard).

Dr. Delany was perfectly satisfied that they renounced their former religion upon the best principles of conviction; and they thought themselves happy to obtain the direction of a person so well able to satisfy all their doubts. They were unwilling to make the sad affair which had commenced at their wretched uncle's more public, but that was impossible, as they were obliged to prosecute and appear in open court against those who had so cruelly treated them. Miss Macdermot, who was a very sensible woman, and had great presence of mind, gave her deposition to a person eminent in the law (I think Dr. Foster), in so clear and proper a manner as to be universally approved of, but why it never came to an issue I never heard. Soon after this they retired into the country, and returned no more to Dublin, which deprived me of further acquaintance with them.

Lady Sarah Cowper[1] *to Mrs. Dewes.*

Midgham, June 5th, 1745.

Your letter, my dear Mrs. Dewes, came to me last night, and I can't thank you enough for letting me hear of you (which I very much wished), and giving me encouragement to renew our correspondence. It is very true that awkwardness and shame of my long silence would have continually prevented me writing again, and this I had experience of; for upon confessing my fault about two months ago to Miss Pointz, and telling her that I could not now have the assurance to write, she threatened

---

[1] Lady Sarah Cowper was the eldest daughter of William, 1st Earl Cowper. She died unmarried in 1758.

to teaze me till I got the better of my *mauvaise honte*, and has so far kept her word that I think I have not escaped one post being asked " have you writ to Mrs. Dewes ?"

I once thought the action in Flanders[1] gave me a pretence of writing to you, but the first letters were so imperfect that I waited for others, and the whole was made public in the papers as soon as these arrived; but if you know no particulars except from the papers, perhaps the gleanings of conversations in town, from a great variety of private letters, may furnish something new to you, and I will give you all that occurs to me; only warning you to remember that I don't vouch for the truth of *all* particulars, and so don't care to be named as the author of them.

Some circumstances of the Duke's behaviour delight me more than his bravery; Coll. Russel writes that himself with other officers were in the advanced guard the day before the battle, where they were to undergo a good deal of fatigue, and had made no provision for their refreshment. His R. H., (*whose care was universal*), thought of this, and sent some of his own servants with the provisions they had brought *for himself* to furnish these gentlemen, and attend on them the whole day. His exhortations and example supported the fight while there was any hope of success: he was in every part of the field where he saw the men dispirited and giving way, calling out, "Don't you know me, my country men? Will you leave me? I don't ask you to do anything without me; all I beg you is to *share my danger*."

---

[1] The battle of Fontenoy was fought between the allied army and the French on the 11th May, 1745.

When the retreat was determined he showed the same spirit and diligence to preserve the order of the march, and to give all possible assistance to the wounded. He was one of *the last* that left the field, so that he did not reach the camp till three next morning, and great part of the army did not know what was come of him. While the army was retreating, and he looked round and saw the numbers lost in the action, and had accounts brought him of particular persons killed or wounded, he lost all command over his passions, and burst into a violent fit of crying! I own these tears of generosity and humanity make him appear *much greater* to me even than all the instances of his courage. 'Tis said the French king, looking upon the English that were killed, said, " Ma foy ces gens meritoient de vivre." And Marshal Saxe said, " Cette poignée de gens m'a fait plus de peine que tout le reste." It was certainly a glorious effort that the Allies made to raise the siege, and though the inequality of numbers made it hazardous, yet if they had stood by and seen the town taken without giving a blow it would have been called tameness and cowardice; and indeed all accounts agree that if *all parts of the army* had behaved *equally well,* it would have been a *complete victory* on the side of the Allies. It was once so near it, that Marshal Saxe confesses he was in the utmost pain how to dispose of the French King and the Dauphin; and even at last the French would have fled, had it not been for the obstinate resistance the Irish regiment of Buckley made to the English attack, and that decided the affair. I say nothing of Ingoldsby; the reports of his conduct are so contradictory, that nothing was ever more mysterious; but I suppose it must be cleared up soon. The general opinion is that the Allies are *not strong* enough, even with the reinforcement they have received, to venture another engagement at present; though if an opportunity should offer it certainly won't be neglected. The soldiers have spirit enough to undertake anything, and say that they don't doubt of "*winning the rubber*," that Dettingen and Fontenoy are "*only game and game*."

The only relation I have in the army is Mr. Madan, he, thank God! came off unhurt, and so did Mr. Colleton's[1] brother. Three young men are killed whom I am much concerned for, Mrs. Sabine's second son, a very brave and fine young man, and Shaw Cathcart, a *true romance hero*, insensible of danger—these are a loss to the public; but I am *much more touched* with little Molesworth's death. I have known him ever since he was five years old; he was a youth of sixteen, a very sober boy, and a good scholar, and capable of making his fortune in a learned way, but nothing could persuade him from being a soldier. I saw him at Mr. Pointz's the day the Duke gave him his commission; he was quite fuddled with joy, his father went abroad with him. It happened there was a vacancy in the guards, and the Duke advanced him to it the day before the battle. Just before the engagement, Lord Albemarle said to Molesworth, "*Keep your son at home to-day*; his commission is *not signed*, so that he really *has no post in the guards*, and it will be no disgrace to him that he is absent; he may avoid the danger of this battle, and will gain some experience against another:" the boy *cried*, and said "*if he was not fit to fight he ought not to have a commission*," went to

---

[1] James Colleton, of Haynes Hill, Esq., co. Berks, married 1731, Lady Anne, second daughter of William, 1st Earl Cowper.

the battle, and after it was missing. After several days' search his father thought him dead, and was returning home, when a note was given him on the road, with these words: "*Robert Molesworth is living*, slightly wounded, and a *prisoner at Lisle*." Mr. Molesworth writ this to his wife, and afterwards a further account came that he was fallen into the hands of a French Colonel, who was very humane, mightily pleased with him, and treated him like his own child; the mother was transported with this good news. Mr. Molesworth went to Lisle, had leave to take care of him, found the wound they thought so slight had proved incurable, and the boy, after lingering a week, *died in his father's arms!* Captain Wade, son of the Marshal, was dangerously wounded by a very odd accident: his horse's head was taken off by a cannon ball, and thrown with such force against Wade's side, that it broke several of his ribs. Lord Albemarle was thrown.[1]

Mrs. Delany to Mrs. Granville, at Welsbourn.

Holly Mount,[2] 8th June, 1744-5.

DEAREST MADAM,

Though I did not expect it, (nor do I desire, though you have a secretary, you should do what I know is not agreeable to you,) the sight of your hand gave me a great deal of pleasure, and my sister must wait till next post, for I can no longer defer making my best acknowledgments to you, madam, for the favour of yours; but you overwhelm me with shame when you make any acknowledgment of thanks to me, you make me feel

[1] The end is missing.
[2] The place the Dean and Mrs. Delany inhabited before they went to Mount Panther.

how much more I owe you, than I can ever pay; and all I can do is to take every opportunity I can of shewing you I gratefully remember your goodness, though I am unable to make a sufficient return. I return you many thanks for your kind wishes on the 14th of May.[1] I enjoy too many blessings not to be thankful for the return of that day.

I don't at all doubt my sister's notableness; I think she has blended in her composition, beyond any body I know, the *excellences* of a good economist with the *elegance* of a fine lady, without any of the foibles.

Mrs. Viney is *too sensible a woman not to feel in time* the blessedness of her present condition, to be rid of a tyrant, that would not suffer her to have any enjoyment of her friends (or even of her children) at home or abroad. Surely she ought to be thankful: I own I cannot help being thankful for her.

I gave my sister an account of our journey as far as Mount Panther, which is six miles from hence. We came here last Tuesday and brought all the family with us, and found the house in very good order, and a good dinner ready. The house is very indifferent, but the situation pleasant.

The Dean has agreed for the building his new church, and is very busy visiting *all the families in his Deanery*, which will be a laborious work, but what he is determined to do. It is very strange, but the poor have been so neglected here, they say they *never saw a clergyman in their lives but when they went to church.*

---

[1] The 14th May was Mary Granville's birthday.

Mrs. Delany to Mrs. Dewes.

Hollymount, June 11th, 1745.

Though I have settled Saturday to be the day dedicated to writing, as I have several letters to write for D.D. as well as myself, I will not postpone this, but must thank my dearest sister for hers of the 22d May, which I received at Mount Panther the day before I came to this place, and is the only letter I have had from England since I left Delville. Never did any flock want more the presence and assistance of a shepherd than this Deanery, where there has been a *most shameful neglect;* and I trust in God it will be a very happy thing for the poor people that D.D. is come amongst them. The church of Down is very large, but it is not a *quarter* filled with people; the Curate has been *so negligent as never to visit any of the poor* of the parish, and a very diligent and watchful dissenting preacher has visited them on all occasions of sickness and distress, and by that means gained great numbers to the meeting. D.D. has already visited a great number, when he has been with all the *Protestants* he designs to go to the *Presbyterians,* and *then to the Papists;* they bless him and pray for him wherever he goes, and say he has done more good already than all his predecessors; the last Dean was here but *two days in six years!*

Your account of our dear mama's being so well was a great joy to me. I don't wonder your neighbours are charmed with her, for she is—(but I dare not say what she is as she will read my letter,) you can much better comprehend what I would say when I wish to do justice to her excellencies than I can express.

I know no more than you who they mean by "a son of my Lord Hervey's;" they must mean a *brother* of the present Lord's, though he may be *fashionable enough* to have a son without a wife! This is really a sweet place, the house *ordinary* but is well enough for a *summer house*. Two rooms below, that is a small parlour and drawing-room, and within the drawing-room a little room in which there is a bed, but the Dean makes it his closet. Above stairs four pretty good bedchambers and a great many conveniences for the servants. I have a closet to my bedchamber, the window of which looks upon a fine lake *inhabited by swans*, beyond it and on each side are pretty hills, some covered with wood and others with cattle. On the side of one of the hills is a gentleman's house with a pigeon-house belonging to it, that embellishes the prospect very much. About half a mile off is a pretty wood which formerly was enriched with very fine oaks and several other forest trees (it covers a hill of about twenty acres); it is now only a thicket of the young shoots from *their venerable stocks*, but it is very thick, and has the finest carpeting of violets, primroses, and meadow sweet, with innumerable inferior shrubs and weeds, which make such *a mass of colouring as is* delightful. But thorny and dangerous are the paths, for with these sweets are interwoven *treacherous nettles* and *outrageous brambles!* but the Dean has undertaken to clear away those usurpers, and has already made some progress: it is called Wood Island, though it is no more than a peninsula; the large lake that almost surrounds it is often covered with threescore couple of swans at a time. On the other side of the lake are hills of various shapes, and on the side of one of them the town of Down.

The ruins of the old cathedral are on an eminence just opposite to Wood Island, from whence I have taken a drawing. D.D. is making a path round the wood large enough to drive a coach; in some places it is so thick as to make it gloomy in the brightest day; in other places a view of the lake opens, and most of the trees are embroidered with woodbine and the "*flaunting eglantine*." Four extraordinary seats are *already made*, one in an oak the other three in ash-trees. This afternoon we proposed spending some hours there, but the rain drove us back again; on the beach of the lake are a great many pretty cockle shells,[1] which will not be neglected when the weather will permit me to go to it.

This has been our chief entertainment abroad. At home, on Sunday last, it being the 9th of June[2] (a day I have great reason to celebrate), we had Dr. Mathews's family and Mr. Bayley's to dine here; they are the best of our neighbours, and I was not a little pleased to find that we have none nearer only some good plain sort of people at Down, that don't *set up for visitors*. As Down is three miles from hence, and we cannot go to prayers in the afternoon if we dine at home, the Dean designs to dine every Sunday at Down. There is a public-house kept by a clever man who was butler formerly to one of the Deans; he has a very good room in his house, and he is to provide a good dinner, and the Dean will fill his table every Sunday with all the townsmen and their wives *by turns*, which will oblige the people, and give us an opportunity of going to church in the afternoon without any fatigue.

---

[1] *Query* fresh-water mussels?
[2] "*The 9th of June*" is here mentioned in a manner which confirms the Editor's belief that it was Mrs. Delany's wedding-day.

We rise about seven, have prayers and breakfast over by nine. In the mornings D.D. makes his visits, I draw; when it is fair and he walks out I go with him: we dine at two; in the afternoon when we can't walk out, reading and talking amuse us till supper, and after supper I make shirts and shifts for the poor naked wretches in the neighbourhood. I have begun to copy an old picture of Mary Queen of Scots, which is but indifferently painted but the face pretty; and to indulge the Dean, who is smitten with it, I have undertaken to copy it. I wish you would write down every day, whether foul or fair, I'll do the same and compare when we meet. Pray let me know how near you are to Meridan.

Mrs. Delany to Mrs. Dewes.

Holly Mount, 21 June, 1745.

I have two dear charming letters of my dearest sister's to answer; last post should have been the day, but twelve people that came to dine here prevented me. The Dean wheedled me away to *his wood* in the morning as soon as breakfast was over. I returned before twelve, in hopes of having time to write my letter; but just as I was preparing materials, Dr. Mathews and his family came; so I chose to defer, that I might send a long letter. They were all the company I *expected*, but there were added to them by dinner-time, Mr. Johnston, a very good sort of man (agent, that is, rent-gatherer, to the Dean); his wife and niece, both *fine ladies!* the sheriff of the county; and *three persons* of very different characters—Mr. Hall, a crafty, mercenary man, not at all esteemed or countenanced by the good people of this country; Mr. Ward, a plain, honest curate; and Mr. Cornabée, a Frenchman by birth, who has a living in this neighbourhood—a polite, lively, entertaining man, just come from the Queen of Hungary. He was chaplain some years abroad to Mr. Robinson the envoy, and much esteemed by him; he is a particular friend of Lady Colladon's, and has been recommended to the Dean by her; he is agreeable and well-behaved, but as for any other merit he is too great a stranger to make any other judgment of him.

Wednesday I went to Down with the Dean, and whilst he was visiting the poor, walked round the ruins of the cathedral, which has been a fine Gothic building; it is situated on an eminence just above the town, and commands an extensive view of mountains and lakes. I was called from my attention on this venerable ruin, by the bell that rung for prayers, after which we went home, and as soon as dinner was over we walked to Wood Island, where the Dean amused himself with his workmen, and I at my work under the shelter of a young oak in which D.D. has made a very snug seat. When he had discharged his labourers we set forward for adventures; and as bold as Don Quixote, he undertook, armed with a stout cane instead of a lance, and I (with my shepherdess's crook) followed intrepid, to penetrate the thickest part of the wood, where human foot *had not* trod *I believe for ages*. After magnanimously combating brakes, briars, and fern of *enormous size* and thickness, we accomplished the arduous task, and were well rewarded during our toil by finding many pretty spots enamelled and perfumed with variety of sweet flowers, particularly the *woodbine and wild rose which grow here* in great abundance. We came home as weary and warm as we used to do frequently at Calwich, and enjoyed the refreshment of an easy seat, and the pleasure of talking over our toils, as you and I and our dear brother have often done there, and hope we may often again.

I hope this letter will salute you together at Welsbourne; I wrote him a long letter last post, and directed it to Calwich. The death of the Bishop of Clogher[1] may make an alteration in our affairs, and if it does, I fear it must in our schemes; for should D.D. be made a Bishop, he must attend the Parliament this winter, and our journey to England cannot be undertaken till the spring, as the bishopric must be taken if offered, or it may not again be offered; though a small one will not be accepted. I believe *he* will be condemned in general for this, but I own I think him *quite in the right;* and I am better pleased to have him remain Dean of Down, than have him at the fag end of all the Bishops! If they give us Kildare I shall be at the height of my wishes as far as they regard *any worldly preferment;* though Clogher is more considerable by five hundred pounds a-year; but the Deanery of C. Church being annexed to the Bishopric of Kildare obliges a residence in or near Dublin, and so *Delville* might be our palace. The deferring the pleasure of seeing my dear friends in England this year, will be a vast disappointment to me, but if this happens, I shall have the joy of being with them a whole year instead of half a year, for if D.D. continues Dean of Down, he must be here next summer to finish the good works he is now laying the foundation of, and we shall hardly be able to leave this place till towards September.

You ask me "*was not the standish adorned with poetry?*" It was not,—a long bill in Chancery *to answer* frightened

---

[1] Dr. John Sterne, Bishop of Clogher, from 1717 to 1745, when he was succeeded by Dr. Robert Clayton, Bishop of Cork and Ross.

away the muses. D.D's constant attention to me, his indulgence on all occasions, his tenderness, and the regard he has for *all those I love*, testify his affection with more force than the muses can dictate; *they* indeed help to illustrate a growing passion, but when once it is arrived to the dignity of a settled friendship *their aid* is not wanted, though at all times their company is desirable and agreeable. Poor Betty Winnington[1] was at her last prayers, indeed. What a match for her!

In your letter dated the 29th of May, you say *Newport goes to Cal. next month*; in that of June 5th, that you are in hopes of seeing my brother in a fortnight;—by that I suppose our cousins have made their visit.

I am very sorry to find here and everywhere people *out of character*, and that *wine* and *tea* should enter where they have *no pretence to be*, and usurp the rural food of syllabub, &c. But the dairymaids wear large hoops and velvet hoods instead of the round *tight petticoat and straw hat*, and there is as much *foppery introduced in the food* as in the *dress,—the pure simplicity of ye country is quite lost!* The Dean is much obliged to you for your caution of not over-fatiguing himself; but he served you as he is often served,—he hears you *preach* and owns your doctrine *good*, but does *not practise*; the truth is he cannot, for he finds there has been such a *total neglect of a partial minister's duty* here, that it has cut out a great deal of work for him; but as it is a work worthy of a good Xtian, I don't doubt but he will be enabled to go through it.

Yesterday, Mr. Bayles and his lady and Mrs. Murray

---

[1] Elizabeth, second daughter of Francis Winnington, Esq., married, Reginald Wyniat, Esq., of Stanton Hall, Worcestershire.

(a lady painter), who live five miles off, dined with us. We dine with them to-morrow, and as soon as the weather is settled enough for an expedition, we are to meet at Arglass, about seven miles off, where there are fine ruins, to carry cold meat, and make a merry day of it; and I am to provide paper and pencil for taking views: I have taken two of Down, and they are placed in the book, which will travel with me to England—*but when?* that the $L^d L^t$ must determine. I feel very oddly about it, and cannot tell *how to wish heartily* for this bishopric, and yet I do wish for it too, for if does not come now, it never will come.

How near are you to Meridan? Pray ask my brother for the account of the travelling bog.

Mrs. Delany to Mrs. Dewes.

Holly Mount, 28 June, 1745.

I am very sensible of the pleasure my dearest sister must have in seeing my brother at Welsbourne. The meeting of friends is everywhere a delight, but to receive them in one's own home gives the most pleasure,—a happiness I languish for, and must, till time and their convenience bestow it on me. I have now for the *greatest* part of my life been the visitor, and though I am possessed now of a pleasant and commodious dwelling, where I could receive my friends with great joy, I am debarred that blessing, but hope I shall find, *in time,* that there is *no more hazard or inconvenience* in *their coming to me,* than in my going to them! God knows whether we are to meet before spring or not!

Lord G. went to my Lord C. as soon as he was told

of the Bishop of Clogher's death, and *demanded* that Bishopric for D.D. Lord C. said it *was engaged to a Bishop*; but explained no farther (I suppose the removes not being yet settled), and added he should "*not forget his friend.*" If the Bishopric is to be given to a Bishop, it will of course occasion removes. I heard some time ago that Lord C. had declared that whenever he had a good Bishopric in his power he would give it to the Bishop of Cloyne (Berkeley); and *if he does* I shall honour him for distinguishing a man of so much merit, and may then have reason to hope D.D. will have a fair chance of being preferred as he deserves. Cloyne is a middling Bishopric, not to be refused, but I own Kildare *alone* is what I *wish for*. I hope my brother may be with you still, though I know he does not make long visits.

Never do I remember such a season! if it continues, this country will be undone; though now there is as fair a show of corn as ever I saw in the vale of Evesham.

Last Monday there was a fair at a town four miles from hence called Clogh, where Dr. Mathews's family were to have met us, and we proposed it a day of mirth; but it proved so wet and cold, we sat by the fire all day. I am sorry for the accident to Lady Stanley's picture; but I believe it can be easily repaired. I have drawn a good deal since I came here, taken three views, and finished some I had sketched out. I have borrowed a fine picture of the old Duke of Ormond's, done by Sir Peter Lely, which I hope to copy; but we are going a little progress next week. D.D. is to preach the visitation sermon for the Bishop of Down at Lisburn, twenty miles from hence. They say that part of the country is very pleasant, and the Dean will not go without me; so on Monday we set forward, and shall return on Saturday. We are to be at a clergyman's house (a nephew of Mrs. Mathews's) Mr. Geer by name; he lives within two miles of Lisburn. Our best love and service salutes Welsbourne.

We have got an Irish harper in the house, who plays a great variety of tunes very well; he plays to us at our meals, and to me whilst I am drawing. Lady Sarah's letter is not come yet.

Is Lady Archi. Hamilton really deposed?

Mrs. Delany to Mrs. Dewes, at Calwich.

Holly Mount, 13 July, 1746.

Your letters, dated the 18th June from Welsbourne, and the 22nd from Calwich, now lie before me. I don't at all wonder at your taking such a flight, when you could leave your boys under so good an inspector. To see a friend one loves there are few difficulties in the way that cannot be removed; and when we consider how precarious our enjoyment of earthly blessings are, *'tis wise to seize* every reasonable opportunity of gratifying ourselves in what is laudable. Never did heart yearn more than mine did to have added to the society at Calwich, where so many of my friends were met, and to have made up the group of *Granvilles,* of which *so few are now remaining!* The Dean wished as heartily as I did, but duties call him another way; and he has found so much to do here, by the unworthy and negligent behaviour of his curate, that he has hardly an hour in the week to himself: it is a vast parish, and he is *determined to visit it thoroughly.* If he can have finished that important work by the time of the assizes, as soon as they are over (which I fear will not be till the middle of August), we shall go to Delville; and if the Bishopric is then filled up, and we are overlooked, we shall hasten to England with all expedition.

I have a very good notion of my brother's improvements at Calwich: his good taste, and the natural beauties of the place, must make it very delightful. But there is something more to make it so *to us*—the person it belongs to! His tenderness to ye *penny flowers*,[1] brought the tears into my eyes, and gave my heart that sort of sensation which can only be raised by the delicacy of true friendship—something not to be exprest. I have three drawings of Calwich which I look at every day; when I return to Dublin I will endeavour to contribute to his grotto. D. D. has almost finished all he designs doing in Wood Island, which is really a very pretty spot; and we walk to it sometimes twice in a day. I am now very busy copying the fine picture, after Sir P. Lely, of the old Duke of Ormond, and hope I shall make it like, I paint it in oil. Your pictures were not dry enough to send when I left Dublin; you shall have them as soon as I go home.

Mrs. Delany to Mrs. Dewes.

Holly Mount, 20 July, 1745.

Whether this letter will salute my dear sister under the dear Calwich tent, or within her own walls I know not, but as I shall write to my mother at Welsbourne, I choose to direct this to Calwich, that you may not fail

---

[1] "*Penny flowers.*" This probably alluded to the care Mr. Granville had shown for the plant called "Penny-leaf," at Calwich, which was associated with his sister and her former name.

of hearing of me, unless a letter comes before I seal this that may alter the direction. Happy am I that the Granville tent is pitch'd on the peaceful plains of Calwich, and not amongst the bloody warriors: how miserable should we be at this time were it otherwise than it is! The distress abroad makes my heart ache every hour of the day; God only knows where it will end. We may fear the worst as we deserve it, but I hope *ten righteous men may be found that will yet save the city*: and so I leave this melancholy subject to regale myself with *the Violet, the Primrose*[1], &c., who have not been a little refreshed by the "*Pearly Dewes*," and I see my brother and the cousin Fo. at the head of the females well pleased and pleasing. I know no more of bishoprics. The camp has drove all thoughts of the church out of statesmen's heads for the present, but had *the one* been better regarded, perhaps *the other* would not have been in the *deplorable way it seems* to be in at present.

This is Holly Mount, not HOLY-mount, and does not belong to the Deanery, but is a *hired place* the Dean has taken till a Deanery-house is built.

I believe, indeed, Cuz Fo. and you have many a motherly conversation that has set Violet a gaping, but I hope to see the day when she can pay you in your own coin; though I know *so few* men *worthy of her*. I don't know what to wish about it. You have not mentioned my favourite bower at the end of the pond. I hope it flourishes? and where is the tent pitched now? Has my brother got a housekeeper that pleases him? If wishes could bring us together, either you and your company would be here or I with you. I *dreamt* last night my brother was with me at

[1] The Honourable Anne Granville and her sister Grace, Mrs. Foley.

Delville, and oh *my happiness!* I hope the Fair Maid of Honour keeps up her intimacy with Lady Middlesex; if she does I should think it might be in her power to get Violet a promise of the next vacancy for Bed-chamber woman: Mrs. Herbert now, I suppose, quits that post. We shall not be at all pleased with Lord Kildare [2] if he marries an English woman that will make him live in England: he has forsaken a very pretty cousin of his, to whom he addressed himself before his father died, and gained her affection. His father's ambition was not satisfied with such a match, though no manner of objection could be made to Miss O'Brian, who is *very pretty*, and like my cousin Foley—*so like*, that I met her once at an assembly in Dublin, and followed her from room to room to have the pleasure of looking at her. My Lord Kildare [3] at his death, they say, made his son promise *not* to marry her, *not* knowing how far they were engaged to each other; and the young man *very basely* did *not* tell him, for as *he was a good man* it is thought he would not have insisted on his breaking his contract, which he has done, and my Lady Kildare has made her a present of a thousand pound, a *poor recompence* for the loss of the man she loved, the first Earl of the kingdom with the greatest estate.

The Dean wishes so much to see the Maid of Honour well married, and is such an encourager to matrimony, that he will hasten to England with all expedition to perform the office for Miss Granville at the

---

[1] Grace Boyle, only daughter and sole heiress of Richard Viscount Shannon.

[2] James, 20th Earl of Kildare, married February 7, 1746, Emilia Mary, daughter of Charles Duke of Richmond and Lennox. His lordship was created Viscount Leinster in Feb. 1746; Marquis of Kildare in March, 1761, and Duke of Leinster, November 26, 1766. He died November 19, 1733.

[3] Robert, 19th Earl of Kildare, died February 20, 1773-4.

shortest warning, since she does him the honour to prefer him.

I had a letter yesterday from Mr. Stanley, apologizing for Mr. Monck; who told him I wrote him two letters, which had exasperated him very much; but, that he always intended " *making me a present*" of *the dishes with the basons*, which he is ready to deliver to my orders. I will take them as I think them *my own*, but cannot accept them "*as a present;*" I shall desire them to be sent to my brother's house.

Lady Sarah Cowper to Mrs. Dewes.

Haynes Hill, near Twyford, Berkshire.
July 25th, 1745.

MY DEAR MRS. DEWES,

Perhaps it may appear very unreasonable to you that I should already expect an answer to my letter, I who am so lazy myself, and have so little right to demand an exact correspondence from my friends; but you have been so indulgent to me, that by hearing nothing of you I can't help fearing something disagreeable has happened; that you, or some of your family, are not well, or have some other grief, and there is no end of imagining all that may be; but if you are well and happy, it will be kind to let me know it, because I am really uneasy for you. My letter may indeed be lost; I should be sorry for that, too; it was a long, incoherent account of all I had heard of the battle at Fontenoy, and it fill'd five sides of paper, and I should not be pleased to have it fall into *other hands*. I am now with Lady Anne, and propose staying here all the summer. I am

well myself, but she continues in "a low way," such as I
am not satisfied with, though she makes no complaints;
her nerves will probably never recover the shock of the
fit, and all to be hoped is, that with proper care she may
never have another.

The public affairs are not in a way to raise our spirits,
and that we have no army news from Flanders is come
to be a comfort, for there is no reason to hope success,
and a great deal to fear if the Allies should be attacked.
The news of a great victory on the Rhine is sunk to
nothing, and the election of an emperor seems to be
deferred. I hear from town they have made rejoicings
for our success at Cape Breton; it is said to be a very
valuable acquisition, and that is some comfort in these
bad times.

I will stop here and not venture another long letter
till I know if you received the first, and if you were
not tired with it; that is a fear I have just thought of,
and in reason should take place of the others I mentioned; but I find those that regard you take faster hold
on my imagination than that which would only mortify
myself. My sister desires humble service to you; I beg
my compliments to Mr. Dewes, and that you will name
me to your children, and try to make them understand
that there is such a person in the world who never saw
them, and yet who is sincerely anxious for their welfare.

I am, my dear Mrs. Dewes,

Your very affectionate

And obliged humble servant,

S. COWPER.

[1] Taken from the French in June, 1745.

Mrs. Delany to Mrs. Dewes, at Welsbourne.

Holly Mount, 26 day of July
(A day I love most truly,
And celebrate most duly,) 1745.[1]

My dearest sister, many happy returns may you see of this day to bless your family and friends! My heart overflows with warm wishes and with gratitude for the treasure of friendship this day procured me. This is a subject (were I to indulge it) would carry me from all others, but words are not wanting at this date to express the mutual happiness we have enjoyed together, and we have each of us felt it beyond what words can express.

To-morrow we go to a place called Ballyculter, where one of the Dean's curates lives; he is to preach on Sunday at that church, and in the evening we return again: it is about eight miles off. I hope we shall get home to my dear Delville by the 20th of August I had yesterday a letter from Lady Chesterfield, who says, "*I hope to see you soon in Ireland, which will be a great pleasure to us,*" and as they are to be in Dublin by the latter end of August, it would not look well in us to run away without waiting on them, and I would willingly give my Lord Chesterfield an opportunity of knowing D.D., which cannot be but by their spending a *quiet day* together at Delville, where we shall not entertain them as a royal pair, but in a private quiet way. This will keep us till the middle of September, and as Michealmass "*riggs*" (or winds) have an ill name, we think it best to defer our journey to October, which generally gives us calm pleasant weather —so pray God send us a happy meeting!

Yesterday we had seventeen people to dine with us, and

---

[1] 26th July. Ann Granville's birthday

as this house is not bigger than Bradley, you may think we were well-stuffed. D.D. and I shall dine to-day tête-à-tête, and we drank your health this morning in whey and tea. The lovely weather we now have gladdens our hearts, I hope you partake of our sunshine as you did of our rain. I have been very busy this week at my painting, and shall next week I hope finish my picture of the old Duke of Ormond after Sir Peter Lely, a picture *that has (and will)* cost me a great deal of pains.

I must end as I begun, with wishing my dearest sister every felicity this world can afford. I am with the utmost tenderness and fidelity, ever yours,

M. D.

Mrs. Delany to Mrs. Dewes.

Holly Mount, 10 Aug. 1745.

I hope your ramble will do you good. So much good company, I think, must have been a rare cordial to *the Hermit.*[1] I find his domestics are *not right yet*, nor can they ever be in good order till he has a wife to manage them, for *men* are *no judges of domestic affairs; we* were designed for *that purpose*, and *have* the talents that *are fit for the purpose.* What you tell me of Lady F. S. is very odd, I don't know what authority she had for what she said, but I believe Lord G. has more of Lord C.'s confidence than *she* has. I must transcribe six lines of Dr. Barber's on D.D., that he sent me last post.

> Let others gain from power a titled name,
> Unconscious of the noble rights to fame!
> On thee the mitre could reflect no light,
> Where learning, genius, virtue, taste unite;
> Circling thy head with glory's brightest rays;
> Viceroys can neither give nor damp that blaze.

---

[1] Mr. Granville.

Your account of poor Lord North's[1] family has made my heart ache; but Providence, who sees fit to send him these severe trials of his resignation, I don't doubt will support him.

I am to dress and dine abroad, at Mr. Bayley's, seven miles off. I am sorry my mama talks of leaving you; I know how loth you must be to part with her; and if *all* my friends are divided when I come to England, my visits must be so too, which will allow me but *little time* to stay with *each*. I have had a letter from my brother since his return home, and have heard lately from Welbeck and Southampton—all pretty well. My brother is much pleased with Welsbourne, and wishes his own house may be as good a one.

Mrs. Delany to Mrs. Dewes, at Welsbourne.

Holly Mount, 17 Aug. 1745.

My dearest sister's charming packet with her own letter, Mrs. Chapon's, and Lady Sarah's, came safe to my hands and gave me great pleasure and entertainment. I had made a proposal to Sally which *I feared* she would not accept of, but she is very reasonable in the affair, and I hope she is in a way of having her son Hal taken off of her hands for some years: she had mentioned being anxious about his education, and yet not being able to maintain him in any of our universities. The Dean said *if his parents* would consent to his entering the college of

---

[1] Lady North died in April, 1745.

Dublin as a sizer (which in Oxford and Cambridge are called servitors) he would take care he was treated with a particular regard: they are here upon a much better footing than in England, and have all the advantages of learning, and the same chance for a fellowship, that those have who enter as gentlemen-commoners; and I offered to maintain him till he had some other provision. This *they have consented to*, if Mr. Tracy does not succeed in a thing he has in view for him, which to be sure will be better, which is getting him into the East India Company. How extremely well written Lady Sarah Cowper's letter is! she has an uncommon strength and clearness in her manner of expressing herself. I am glad she has renewed her correspondence with you; if she bestows on you what she withdraws from me I can forgive her neglect, though *since* my *being married* she has shown a negligence that has mortified me extremely. But my own dear sister's love and goodness is permanent, and makes me happy beyond expression; it doubles all my joys, and lessens all my anxieties.

If we find on our return to Dublin (which I hope in God will be on Wednesday next?) that we shall not be able to go soon to England, we will defer it till spring, which is a better time than sailing in the short cold days. The Dean has been so much perplexed here and embarrassed with his troublesome curate, and had such a hurry of business on his hands, that it was impossible for him to leave this place sooner. When we first came we were in hopes of being in England by this time; people who are free and disengaged from any duty may be punctual in the execution of their schemes, but otherwise it is impossible.

I had on Tuesday sixteen people here at dinner, on Wednesday ten, on Thursday twenty-two; and yesterday we dined abroad eight miles off, and have only this one day to pack up; and glad—very glad—shall I be to see again my pleasant dwelling at Delville. The Dean thinks you are in the wrong to tease yourself about your little boy's not loving his book, and you should be cautious not to give him a distaste to it by pressing him too much, for he is young enough to be indulged another year.

Did you ever read Ockley's History of the Saracens?[1] It is a most extraordinary and interesting history. What a chastisement did the Xtians bring upon themselves by their neglect of their duty!

Mrs. Delany to Mrs. Dewes.

Delville, 24 Aug., 1745.

Again I am returned to my dwelling. This place is now in perfect beauty, and the weather has been so fine that every hour of the day I could spare from business and meals has been spent in the garden, chiefly in *Pearly Dewes'* bower, where one of our tame robins welcomed us home, and flew to the Dean's hand for the bounty he used to bestow. But I have my hands so full of business at present that I much fear I shall not be able to make my letter so long so I wish to make it. Just as I came to this place I was interrupted by com-

---

[1] Simon Ockley, a learned divine and eminent Orientalist, born at Exeter in 1678. In 1711 he was chosen Professor of Arabic at Cambridge, and died in 1720. He wrote a "Life of Mahomet," "Sermons," &c., and "The History of the Saracens," which is the most important of his works.

pany; they have hardly left me time to fill this side, but I will scribble hard.

I hope you had an opportunity of going to the races; it is pleasant sometimes to mix in a gay crowd; especially if the constant course of one's life is of the sober tranquil kind; it gives a little exercise to the spirits, that is not amiss. I was much amused with your account of dear little Court's gallantry; I am very glad he shows already so much politeness: *politeness is the polish of virtue,* and it ought not to be neglected. Is not three years old *very young* for breeches? I know it is *the fashion,* but I should imagine the spring a better time for changing his dress than the latter end of the year. I have not seen the Prince's song on the Princess, but if it is to express his affection towards her I shall be *greatly offended* with the *burlesquers.*

I am very glad you do *not expect me* till spring, for as it is impossible for me to leave this place before October, I think it would be *safer* and better not to go till April. I am come home to a hurry and have found many things to settle in my household that all housekeepers are sometimes troubled with—servants, accusations that must be cleared and are very teazing; though I don't *torment* myself with those affairs; but as our family is large, and consequently expensive, it requires both *my care and attention.* We left Holly Mount on Sunday. After church at Down we went to Mr. Forde's at Seaford, which was some miles on our road towards home; there we dined and lay that night. The next

---

[1] Mathew Forde, Esq. of Seaforde, in the county of Down, married in 1724 Christian, daughter of John Graham of Platten. Mr. Forde, married, 2ndly, Jane, widow of Sir Timothy Allen, and died in 1780.

morning we out at seven, and lay at Newry. The next day baited, dined at a place called Castle Bellingham, one of the prettiest places I have seen in Ireland, but the weather so bad I could not look about me at all. Lay that night at Dunleer at Mrs. Hamilton's; Miss Mary Forth was gone to town. Got home to Delville about 7, and was charmed to see it look so gay and spruce. Had the pleasure of finding Mrs. Green here ready to receive me, and my pussy Tiger knew me and caressed me mightily. I had a letter yesterday from Miss Granville; our little cousin Foley has been, I find, dangerously ill, but is recovered. The yatchs are to go this day for my Lord Lieut', so in a few days I suppose we shall have them. I design to make my first visit in an *Irish stuff manteau and petticoat*, and a *head* the Dean has given me of Irish work, the prettiest I ever saw of the kind; he has made me also a present of a repeating-watch and a diamond ring; the diamond is a brilliant, but such gems are only valuable when they are testimonials of a kind and affectionate heart; as such to me they are inestimable.

You have heard that the Bishoprics are settled; Cork to Clogher, the Bishop of Dromore to Cork, and Dr. Marley (a *worthy and ingenious man*) to Dromore.[1]

The following letters appear to have been written by an old retainer of Mr. Granville's, then a waiting-woman of Mrs. Donellan's, to her friend at Calwich.

---

[1] Dr. Robert Clayton, Bishop of Killala, and afterwards of Cork and Ross, translated to Clogher in 1745. Dr. Jennet Brown, Bishop of Dromore, translated to Cork and Ross. Dr. George Marlay created Bishop of Dromore.

Aug. 26, 1745.

Indeed, friend Martha, you are very ill-natured not to let me hear a word from you. If my eyes had not been so weak that I can scarce see the penn in my hand, I wou'd have writ before now, for I neither know whether the sowe has piged, the turkeys hatched, nor how many chickens you have rear'd. Has the otters eate all the fish? how many young swans have you? I did dream last night that all the ducks were flow'd away; is that true? And tel me, I beg and pray, and that soon, what is become of master; is he well? is he buryed in mortar? or does he sit all day long humdrumming at the what do you call it? May be he is gone to Ireland, and then God knows what is become of him? I long to hear; I fear I shall not live to see him any more, for I have had a bad sumer. Mrs. Donnellan has been very ill, but, thank God, is better. We have had good weather; it is a little mended. How has yours been? We have had ten days fine, which has got the corn in about London. We have had very great rejoicing for the taking of Lewisburgh,[1] but you will see all that news in the newspapers, and I am too blind to write any more but to give my love to everybody that I know at Calwich, and I hope my good old friend Martha will believe

That I am most sincerely
Her friend and well wisher,
Mrs. Anne sends her love. A. G.

---

[1] The town and fortress of Louisbourg surrendered to the English on the 16th June, 1745, after a siege of forty-nine days.

A. G. at Fulham, to her friend Martha at Calwich.

Indeed, my good friend Martha, it has been a deadly while I have taken to answer your kind letter; but what can a body doe with one eye, and that a very bad one. More over, my hand shakes like any aspen leafe, and I have not been well all sumer. I have a pain in my shoulder on one side, and a pain in my elbow on the other; much pain and very lame of my knees, and ankcles; when I walk, it is like an elephant, without bending a joint. O how I grunt and groan night and day! I will take my oath I wou'd rather be an otter than an old woman; but you do not know what it is to be old! You are capering about in your fine cardinals, and things, like a girl of twenty. I suppose you are about geting a young husband. I was told so, and much good may it doe you, if he gives you a hearty thrashing now and then. I wish you wou'd tell me who he is; write me word what his name is. But I hope this affair do not make you forget the dear piggs, and turkeys, and geese, and ducks; send me word if they be in good heart and thriving. And what is master doing? Is he smothered amongs the lime and bricks? or has he got his work done, and laid himself down upon the gazy hill, to take breath a little? This furious hott weather—I never felt such in my life. Tel him, that is, if he have out lived it, that I have thought forty times to come to Calwich, and live in the river amongst the otters, and lye titely with them and try whether they or I should eate the most carps; and I believe I should have come, if a thought had not changed in my head, that

there might come at once a hundred about me, and eate
me up, in stead of a perch. You know I am a little
slimikin thing, not unlike a perch or an eel, both which
they like, and might easily mistake and pick my bones
in a moment; so I chous to stay, and be broyled at
Fulham. But I have been so taken up with your
intended marriage, and my owne history, that I have
not said a word of Mrs. Donnellan, who is nearer my
heart then any other thing, even the King, his owne
self I do not love half so well! Aske master if that be
not saying a great deal, and tell him, as he remembers
he left her much out of order in London, that she
grew worse every day till we came to Fulham. At
that time she was scarce able to get on horse back:
however, she did, and rid every day, with which she
mended considerably til the violent hott wether came,
which made it impossible for any body to ride, the heat
and the dust was so powerfull. She has not been on
horse back near a month, and is not so well, very restless nights, and her cough bad. Thank God, yesterday
the weather changed, and brought us some rain, not
before it was wanted, for this part of the world was quite
burned up; no grass to be seen, but the corn extreme
fine, and ready to reap. If it please God to send us a
good harvest we shall have great plenty of that. How
has the season been with you? Have you any fruit?
We have not as much as curans fitt to make a little
wine with. Well, I wish you wou'd let me know what
master is doing. Has he finished his house, done all he
has to doe, and got rid of his workmen? Surely, I
thought, he wou'd have been in London before now, and
have got a new gown on purpose, thinking to see all the

prime youth of Staffordshire review'd in Hyed Park, with Colonel Granvile at the head of them—such a day! So I went; but when I found it was the Norfolk Militia, how was I mortifyed, though they were fine men, and very fine officers! But what did I care for them? I wanted to have seen master! and now they tell me your militia are not yet raised. Good luck! good luck! What is it you mean, to be so doul? I realy believe in my heart master do not care if the French coms and eate us all up alive. Is there not flat boats—I know not how many thousands—ready to come every day? and when they once set out they will be with us as quick as a swallow can fly, almost; and when they land we have no body to fight them, because you *will not rais* your militia. For my part I dare not go to the Thames, for fear they shou'd be coming; and if I see one of our owne boats leaden with *carrats*, I am ready to drop down, thinking it one of the French. I have not one word of news, but that it is grown cooler to my great joye. Mrs. Donnellan is got on horse back again, and I hope it will doe her good. She sends master her most kind compliments, and I hope he will accept of a thousand sincere good wishes of mine, which coms to him heartily. Mrs. Donnellan remembers you kindly, and I hope dear Martha will believe that

    I am, her true old friend,

        A. G.

My service to Mr. Nathan, tho' I never saw him when he was in town. Mrs. Anne sends her compliments to you and him.

If the writer of this letter had lived in these days (1860) she would have been *better satisfied* with the reviews in Hyde Park, and have believed she might have approached the Thames, without fear of being carried off in " the flat-bottomed boats" of the French! Besides the amusement afforded by the quaintness of these epistles, there is an evident sincerity and a devotedness towards her old "*Master*," which is very pleasing, and does infinite credit to the writer.

Mrs. Delany to Mrs. Dewes, at Welsbourne.

Delville, 7. Sept. 1745.

My dear sister's letters of the 20th and 24th of August came to me together. I had the pleasure of hearing from Gloucester that my mother got safe there and that Miss Nanny Viney accompanied little John home. I have got a picture of you hung up in my bedchamber of Mrs. Irwens's doing, by that she begun at Bath and her memory together; it smiles upon me and gives me a sort of melancholy gladness, for it really is like you.

I am glad you and Sir Anthony[1] correspond; when Mr. Dewes is in London let him visit him as often as he can. So near a relation ought not be neglected, especially now he is a lonely man and growing in years. Now it is time for me to say something of that which is near both our hearts—our meeting. The insurrection in Scotland has made it at this time *unsafe to cross the seas, so that till that* commotion is stilled it would be imprudent to venture; and my brother seems to think it would be rather prudent on other accounts to defer our voyage till spring.

I have as yet only seen my Lady Chesterfield on her public days: I went to her on Tuesday morning. She asked to see me soon again, so I went on Friday morning with the Dean, who could not go sooner. Her days

---
[1] Sir Antony Westcomb.

are Tuesdays and Fridays mornings for company; at night on those days are the drawing-rooms, and every Friday a ball. There has not been yet a night drawing-room, so I have not been presented to his Excellency; but on Tuesday next I shall make my first appearance in an Irish stuff mantua and petticoat. Lord Chesterfield said he was "very glad to have an opportunity of being personally acquainted with the Dean, of whom he had heard and read with so much advantage."

I have this week been very busy at work to finish my *branch*[1] for my portico in my garden, but it is not yet accomplished. Domestic affairs must interpose for some time and company. Coll. Brown is in Ireland, and came to see me; but I was abroad, and the Dean is gone to ask him to dine here. My house is now furnished very completely. Is it not strange, my dear sister, that you and I should dwell in houses that *neither of us have seen*—that I should be *unacquainted* with *your home* and *you with mine?* but I hope in God this will not last long.

Lady Sarah Cowper to Mrs. Dewes.

Sept. 10th, 1745. Haynes Hill.

Your letter, my dear Mrs. Dewes, gave me a great deal of pleasure. I was at first a little startled by what you say of your illness, but a second reading makes me suppose it of a sort which it is to do good to the world, and I hope no harm to yourself, and if this is the case, it is not right to be sorry for it. My sister and I are both much obliged to you for the invitation and encourage-

---

[1] For a chandelier made of shells.

ment you give us to try the medicinal waters in your neighbourhood. I should like the journey so well for one reason, that I could willingly undertake it for that alone, if other considerations did not make it an impracticable scheme: at present all parties of pleasure are threatened to be disturbed by rackets at home. I won't repeat what I hear of them, you may if you please read it in the letter I inclose, and must beg you to send to Mrs. Delany, for I don't know how to direct to her, and have only the frank this goes in.

I wish I could be as easy and unconcerned as a few happy people, that either seeing better or worse than the rest of the world treat the invasion and rebellion as a phantom and an imposition. Indeed the attempt seemed so wild and rash, that at first I was one of the unbelievers, and while some denied positively that the Pretender's son was in Scotland, there seemed so little reason for his going there almost alone, and without any foreign force at hand to assist him, that I thought it a false alarm; but now that they give up the point so far as *to confess he is there*, I can no longer agree with them in *being easy*. If it is true that the French design only to draw our troops from Flanders, and facilitate their conquests abroad, and that the kingdom of England, and the present government may however be safe, I am sure at least that the unhappy wretches already drawn into rebellion, and more that may follow their example, must be sufferers. The distress must fall somewhere, and all humane people will have some share in it.

You ask me if there is any certain account of Ingoldsby. I hear he has been tried by a court martial, acquitted of cowardice, but found guilty of disobeying orders, and suspended during the general's pleasure; that this mild sentence was occasioned by the Duke's generous compassion for him, from regard to former services, and to his own intreaties for mercy, which he begged in the most abject manner. He made no defence, unless it can be called one that he denied having seen Lord Bury[1] who carried him two messages, and when Lord Bury reminded him of the place and other circumstances, he owned the whole. Some of his friends say he has an illness, which is indeed a sufficient excuse for all the errors a man can be guilty of, and it is pity it was not sooner known; but I think the insinuation in the paper he published, by which he plainly endeavours to fling the blame upon the Duke, is such an instance of ingratitude as is hardly pardonable, if the account is true; I can only say for it, that what I write you, came from an officer who was present, and adds that he will be permitted to sell his commission.

To the wishes I have made Mrs. Delany, one circumstance was wanting, that the love, peace, and content you say attend you, may have no interruption, and that Welsbourn may be the place where you may enjoy those blessings with each other! I am my dear Mrs. Dewes,

Your very affectionate and obliged
humble servant,
S. Cowper.

---

[1] George Keppel (Lord Bury), afterwards 3rd Earl of Albemarle, was an aide-de-camp to William Duke of Cumberland at the battle of Fontenoy, and with him at Culloden in the following year, and brought to London the despatches announcing the latter victory. He commanded in chief at the reduction of the Havannah.

Mrs. Dewes to Lady Sarah Cowper.

Welsbourne, 17 Sept. 1745.

A thousand thanks to my dearest Lady Sarah Cowper for letting me see and convey to my sister the great delight of your letter, and such letters are nowhere to be met with. The enclosed I received this post, and take the liberty of sending it to your Ladyship to shew some of my sister's thoughts and employments. I grieve I may not hope to see you and Lady Anne; I flatter myself she is pretty well, as you did not mention her in your last letter.

The account you are so good to send of the public danger and distress gives me great pain, for though I hope the rebellion in Scotland will soon be stopped, yet the misery that must be the consequence to some families is mournful to reflect upon. I have no intelligence so good or so particular as your Ladyship's, therefore shall be infinitely obliged by hearing as often as writing is not disagreeable to you, though I have a more tender concern in that request, and must add with Jemima,

"But of yourself speak much,
Speak very much, and still speak on."

Your tenderness will be alarmed at my mourning paper, and I mention the cause of it the last, because the subject of it truly affects me from the sorrow poor Mr. Dewes is in for the death of his mother. She was a very good woman, and an extremely kind parent. Mr. Dewes has rewarded her care with perfect duty and affection; and had the satisfaction of receiving her last breath in blessings to himself and his children. Her pious prayers

I hope will be answered; but they filled him with a melancholy which I fear will not soon be removed, though *reason and good temper* govern all his actions. He is at present with his brother, where the good old lady lived and died; and that son has the greatest loss, for she was both his nurse and housekeeper, and he is an infirm old bachelor. These subjects and misfortunes fill the mind with gloom and heaviness, and would make life insupportable, were it not for the hopes of passing through it to a more happy place, where all our sighing and tears shall be done away, and where friends meet to part no more. But, alas! I have so many attachments to this world, and my tender chains increasing every day in my little boys, that I must endeavour to support the earthly cares I am encompassed with, and wait with patience a dismission from them. As I cannot turn my pen to any pleasing subject, it would be cruel to add more than that, I am, in all events and circumstances, my dear Lady Sarah Cowper's

Most obliged and most obedient
humble servant,
A. Dewes.

My best respects attend Lady Anne Coliton. I hope Mr. Poyntz and all his family are well.

Mrs. Delany to Mrs. Dewes.

Delville, 3 Oct., 1745.

As I thought my dearest sister might have some alarm for her friends on this side of the water during our wars and rumours of wars, I have written to you three posts together, that you might know we are very quiet, and I hope likely to continue so, if the good news that came express yesterday to our Lord-Lieut! be true, of the rebels defeat in Scotland. Ireland has been formerly a place of great disturbance and confusion on these occasions, but not for many years; people in general are very well affected towards the present Government, and even the papists who are not in number what they were, seem to know their happiness in a quiet possession of what they have, so that had England been so unhappy as to have struggled under a civil war, we should have been the quietest part of his Majesty's dominions. At present the storm seems to be abated, and I hope in God, the next news we have from England will be of its being entirely quelled. When I consider how great a calamity a civil war is, we cannot be too thankful that a timely stop is put to it. Many lives already have been sacrificed to it; but as these sort of distresses cannot subside at once, I think now I cannot hope to see you till spring and calm weather and times invite me over, so I must sit down patiently to bear what is not in my power to order otherwise.

I expect a visit this morning from Lady Chesterfield; she said she would come the first fine day. My shell lustre I wrote you word I was about, was finished ten days ago and everybody liked it. 'Twas a *new whim* and shows the shells to great advantage. I had fixed it up in my portico, which is dedicated to the Duchess of Portland; but the damp weather made the cement give and I have been obliged to bring it into the house, and it now hangs in my work-room and shows to more advantage. My present work is finishing some drawings for my book, and as soon as Lady Chesterfield has made her visit I shall set about painting again, but I don't care for interruptions when I am at that employment; my first work will be to give my mother's picture one more painting over—I don't like it yet.

I believe I wrote you word Mrs. Green was in the house with me; her company is really what I like, and it is a great satisfaction to me to show her all the kindness that lies in my power; as saving a little money now on first setting out may make their circumstances easy for the rest of their lives.

Mrs. Delany to Mrs. Dewes.

Delville, 8 Oct. 1745.

As your letter was dated on the day of the engagement in Scotland I don't wonder you mention so calmly the affairs in agitation, but before this you have had various accounts. My mind is now much better satisfied, for if it please God to give us success we are now very well prepared for the rebels, the Dutch troops and our own being landed and the Duke by this I suppose returned home. We have reason to fear a chastisement, as I believe there never was more impiety in the world than at this time; but I hope there may be "*ten righteous men found*" to save the city, and that our next accounts from England and the North will bring us the comfortable news of all danger being over. There has been such a run on one of our bankers that he has been obliged to shut up, but they say in the end nobody will lose by it: we have luckily no concerns there, but tenants won't pay, and it is made at least a pretence for not paying money.

I don't think it likely Lord North should marry Lady
W.; but don't wonder where there is such an intimacy,
there should be such a report. If he does marry again (as
I think it very likely he should), I don't know any one
so fitted to make him and his family happy as our Violet.
Her *discretion* and *goodness of temper* would make her
a jewel in a family so mixed as they are. He knows her
very well, and all her good qualities and has frequently
mentioned her to me with great esteem, but it is to be
feared he may be taken by some blooming thing that
will marry him for his fortune and *to make a show*, without
considering how truly valuable he is for his religious,
virtuous dispositions. Donellan says in her last letter
to me that our young cousin and her great friend at
Court have quarrelled; that it is an ugly story and much
talked of; 'tis thought *jealousy* is the foundation, but
gives me no hint *who the jealousy is about*. If you know
anything give me some account. Delville salutes Welsbourne most affectionatly.

Mrs. Delany to Mrs. Dewes.

Delville, 15 Oct., 1745.

We are very impatient to know what is doing in the
North. I thank God here we are very quiet, and hope
the packets when they come will bring us the comfortable
news of the rebels being dispersed; but I dread our
being further engaged in a civil war, and think our last
accounts were *no way satisfactory*. Various are the reports; the last was that Edinburgh was burnt to ashes!

Last Friday was the King's Coronation. I went to the
Castle morning and night. There was a ball, but *no good*

dancing; and I hope *for our credit* Mrs. Fortescue will come and grace the balls. Mrs. Chenevix, the Bishop of Killaloe's[1] wife, and I have agreed to go to the Birthday in Irish stuffs. Lady Grandison[2] and Lady Betty Mason are come to Dublin, which I am very glad of; it is a great pleasure to meet with an old acquaintance. Lady Grandison is an agreeable woman and was always very obliging to me. Next Friday I go to Court with Miss McDermots; Lord and Lady Chesterfield have heard their story, and are prepared to receive them with distinction, which indeed they very well deserve. I have had a good deal of Mrs. Clayton's company, she is in good spirits; their house is very magnificent, but *more for show than comfortable living.* I would not give my sweet Delville for it, no, nor for *any palace I ever yet saw.*

Mrs. Delany to Mrs. Dewes.

Delville, 22 Oct., 1745.

Besides the desire I have of hearing from my particular friends, it is impossible at this time not to wish to hear how public affairs go on. All things here continue very easy and quiet, the militia perform duty every day, and we are in a posture of defence to repulse the enemy

---

[1] Richard Chenevix, appointed Bishop of Killaloe in 1745, translated to Waterford the same year.

[2] The Honorable Frances Carey, daughter of Anthony Viscount Falkland, married John Villiers, 5th Viscount Grandison and 1st Earl. Lady Elizabeth Villiers, their eldest daughter married, in 1739, Aland John Mason, Esq., M.P. for Waterford; and 2ndly, General Charles Montagu Halifax. Lady Elizabeth Mason was created Viscountess Grandison, 10 April, 1746, and on the death of her father, 14 May, 1766, was advanced to the rank of Countess Grandison.

if he is daring enough to attack us. We are in no
danger unless things grow worse in England, and I own
I am under no apprehension that a ragged, ill-disciplined,
and irregular body of men, though pretty numerous, should
stand long against our forces when they have once met;
unless Providence designs to chastise us for our impiety,
which, indeed, is to be feared. To drive from my
thoughts unavailing fears, and divert my mind from
thinking too much of my disappointment this year in
not going to England, I employ every hour as much as
possible. I have been sorting my mosses and ores, and
am going to new arrange my shells, and to cover two large
vases for my garden: my painting has lain dormant
some time, having been in expectation of their excellencies every morning; and I did not care to be found
in a litter; and Shakespear and the harpsichord fill up the
evenings. These are *my drams*, and such as refresh without
intoxicating; but I believe my spirits would flag even with
these amusements, did they not give so much pleasure to
D.D.; his approving of my works, and encouraging me to
go on, keep up my relish to them, and make them more
delightful to me than assemblies, plays, or even an opera
would be without he shared them with me. *Eager* as I
am in all my pursuits I am *easily checked*, and the least
disapprobation or snap, from the person I wish to oblige,
in thought, word, or deed, would soon give me a distaste
to what was delightful to me before ! I hope this does
not proceed from pride, but from a disposition in my
heart that will not suffer me to enjoy any pleasure that I
cannot communicate.

Yesterday we were honoured with a visit from our
Viceroy and Queen; they sent over early in the

morning to know if we were disengaged, as they would breakfast. To work went all my maids, stripping covers off the chairs,[1] sweeping, dusting, &c., and by eleven my house was as spruce as a cabinet of curiosities, and well bestowed on their Excellencies, who commended and admired, and were as polite as possible. They came soon after eleven in their travelling coach, with only two footmen; Mr. Bristol (Dash's uncle) and Mrs. Chenevix[2] in the coach with them. They were first carried into the drawing-room, examined every room in my apartments above, delighted with the situation, liked the furniture, but were impatient to see my own works; upon which the Dean conducted them into the Minerva, where I had two tables covered with all sorts of breakfast. When breakfast was over they made me play on the harpsichord, which I did with a very ill grace. When that was done we went into the garden and walked over every inch of it; they seemed much surprised with the variety they found there, and could not have said more civil things had it been my Lord Cobham's Stowe! They staid till near two, and my Lord Lieut' and the Dean had a great deal of conversation, which I believe was mutually agreable; we are going this morning to Court to return thanks for the honour they did us, and the hour calls upon me to dress.

To day we dine at the Bishop of Clogher's, to morrow at Lord Grandison's. Last Friday I went to Court with Miss Dermot, and dined with Mrs. Hamilton.

---

[1] These "*chairs*" were doubtless her own marvellous chenille embroidery of flowers from nature.

[2] Mrs. Chenevix, wife of the Bishop of Killaloe, afterwards Bishop of Waterford.

Mrs. Delany to Mrs. Dewes.

Delville, 16th Nov., 1745.

I have received two letters from my dearest sister, with an account of Mr. Dewes's illness; your last dated 1st Nov^r, by which I find I have lost one I should have had between these two. What wretched beings should we be without that consoler—Hope!. That cheering ray darts through the darkest cloud, and I have felt its kind influence so often that I reverence it like a guardian angel, and had I been a heathen I should certainly have made it my deity and worshipped at its shrine. 'Tis that has supported me under the *great disappointment* I have had of not seeing my dear friends in England this winter, that carries me joyfully on to the spring and to the happy time so much wished for by us both. I could not help apprehending that your care and concern for Mr. Dewes would hurt your spirits. Nothing is more affecting than to see the person one loves dejected. The nature of his disorder I am afraid has made him so; though I am sure his regard for you at all times, but especially now, will make him exert himself to the utmost of his power, and ought to make him consent to have the best advice for his health, which is of so much consequence to your happiness. I say nothing of the rebels, for we are here much in the dark about them; but it is impossible not to be terrified till we hear of their total defeat.

Pray have you ever read the four sermons by Swift that were published last year?[1] They are very fine and worth

---

[1] According to Dr. Johnson, Dean Swift gave up mental labour in 1736, though some works previously written were subsequently published. In 1741, he was placed under legal guardians and personal restraint; and after years of raving, alternating with speechless fatuity, he died in October, 1745.

the reading. Have your read Bishop Sherlock's sermon on the rebellion? It is charming. There is just published a humorous pamphlet of Swift's, I think called "Advice to Servants;" it is said to be below his genius, but comical—I have not yet seen it. Surely I wrote you word a month ago of his death.[1] It was a happy release to him (I hope), for he was reduced to such a miserable state of idiotism that he was a shocking object; though in his person a very venerable figure, with long silver hair and a comely countenance, for being grown fat, the hard lines, which gave him a harsh look before, were filled up.

I have had a letter from the Duchess of Portland, and am sorry to find her spirits are very low.

Sir Thomas Robinson is at Barbadoes and Harry Chapon going to Jamaica.

Mrs. Delany to Mrs. Dewes.

Delville, 23rd Nov., 1745.

The arrival of the packets hath in some measure relieved my anxiety on Mr. Dewes' account. I hope by this time he is perfectly well, and that you are on the wing for Gloucester. The sooner you are settled there the better, for every week adds depth to the roads.

I don't wonder you should leave your boys with regret, but one of them at such a time will be as much as your spirits will well bear. Court is of an age not to be left with servants, besides his pretty prattle will be a vast entertainment to you and a delight to my mother. Last Sunday, at eleven o'clock in the morning, Mrs. Greene was brought to bed of a plump little boy;—it was very lucky the nurse-keeper was in the house,

Yesterday I went both morning and evening to the Castle, with Mrs. Marley.¹ There was a full Court. Lord and Lady Chesterfield dined at the *Bishop of Clogher's* last Wednesday. Nobody lives with more state and show than *they* do: fine house, fine furniture, fine clothes, and every fine thing; but I would not change my estate with them, for they are so much engaged in the hurry and grandeur of the world, that they have not now any time to enjoy the more rational pleasures of friendship and conversation.² Poor Miss Mary Forth has been extremely ill but her disorder not known; I am much concerned for her; she is a most sensible and valuable creature, and has been greatly hurt by her attendance on my friend *Mrs. Hamilton*, and seeing all *her* troubles and sickness, I believe has been the principal cause of her own present disorders.

Never were people so earnest after news as we are, and yet no news can we hear that may be depended on. The taking of Carlisle by the rebels is the last we have had; some lament it, others more politic say it will prove a trap to them. Pray God send us peace! but it seems removed far from us. I have not heard from my brother Granville a great while. Is it not a shame to say I hope he is *not engaged* in my Lord Gower's regiment? Should I not have a more martial and public spirit? If giving up my own life would save my country from ruin I think I could do it, but to hazard a dear friend's at an un-

---

¹ Mrs. Marley, wife of the Bishop of Dromore.
² This is the first comment upon the Bishop's and Mrs. Clayton's proceedings after Mrs. Delany's return to Ireland, and clearly proves that she has had reason to believe them both changed for the worse in the twelve years of her absence.

certainty I cannot bear, and I hope in God *he is safe* from any such hazard. You have not mention'd him lately.

I was going in all haste to have a new fruit wall built, but it must now be deferred till spring. The lawn before our house, where our sheep are to feed, will be finished soon, and will be a great improvement to the view before that part of the house. I am deeply engaged in copying the Duchess of Mazarin's picture; yesterday I finished painting the face for the second time. I have copied in large one of the sketches of Dovedale that I took when we were there together. How many tender ideas did it raise whilst I was drawing it!

On the Princess of Wales's birthday there appeared at Court a great number of Irish stuffs. Lady Chesterfield was dressed in one, and I had the *secret satisfaction* of knowing myself to have been the cause, but *dare not say so here*; but I say, "I am glad to find my Lady Chesterfield's example has had so good an influence." The poor weavers are starving,—all trade has met with a great check this year.

Mrs. Delany to Mrs. Dewes, at Gloucester.

Delville, 30th Nov., 1745.

This folio I hope will find my dearest sister well recovered after the fatigue of her journey and her dear boy; and our dear mama happy with her well beloved guests, and my letters will find the way after you; O that I cou'd at this instant be as easily convey'd! Mr. Duncomb's letter that came by the × post came very expeditiously. When you are brought to bed I beg I may have an account sent me by × post and by the other also, for fear one should miscarry. Mrs. Green had an extraordinary good time; she says she expected to have felt a great deal more; I was surpriz'd at that, for I always thought whatever apprehensions were, pain always far exceeded them. I pray God it may be so with you, on his mercy and goodness I rely, and that only can support my spirits at this time.

I very sincerely rejoice, and so does the Dean, at Mr. Dewes's recovery; we have both felt a great deal of pain on his account. I could wish if his feverishness is gone off, that he would take Dr. Bave's bitters; I believe I sent you the receipt: they have done great service to many people to whom I have recommended them.

I am glad the fair little boy was so well before you were obliged to leave him. I think you have exerted the motherly authority very heroically, and I don't doubt but he will bless you in time for the *little smart*,[1] he has received from your hands. You have more merit in such a case than the generality of mothers can have, because you have more tenderness almost than any human creature.

I congratulate you on the finishing your curtains, and

---

[1] This was no doubt an allusion to that very wholesome instrument of correction, in the hand of a judicious parent—a small legitimate *real birch rod*, the disuse of which in the present age, from the maudlin sentiment of those who consider themselves so much wiser than Solomon, has led to correction by all sorts of petty tortures, bad for body and mind; and has conduced very much towards gluttony, by the substitution of the punishment of privation of food, or the change of children's diet to what is most disliked, as well as other equally injurious penances which fret the temper, under the mistaken idea that the reasoning faculties of children *can be exercised before they are formed*, and that the instantaneous and efficacious, though harmless, smart of a few twigs of birch is beneath the dignity of a mother to apply or a descendant of Adam to receive.

think it a *vast work accomplished* for a person engaged with such a family of children. I like the character of your wise neighbour, and hope to hear of an increase of his wisdom.

The Bishop of Waterford died yesterday morning, and before noon the bishopric was disposed of to Chevenix, Bishop of Killaloe, and the bishopric given to Dr. Syng, Archdeacon of Dublin,[1] and the Archdeaconry to Dr. Pocock (the traveller), chaplain to the Lord Lieutenant. Now I know the rage boils, and that even *you* almost say bitter things, but the present Bishop of Waterford is a very humble and honest man, he has a family of children and no fortune; and I only wish that bishoprics were generally as well bestowed; Killaloe is *not worth a wish* and much less any regret.

We were invited to dine at the Castle yesterday, and were received with great politeness and good humour; nobody there, but ourselves: as they said they "wished to have us alone, that they might enjoy our company without interruption." My Lord Chesterfield was in high spirits after dinner, which was small and very good; coffee was then set on the table, and the Dean and my Lord Lieutenant fell into a very entertaining and agreeable conversation, chiefly of poets and poetry. There is

---

[1] Charles Este, Bishop of Ossory, was translated in 1740 to the bishopric of Waterford, in which he was succeeded, 1745, by Richard Chevenix, Bishop of Killaloe, and Nicholas Synge, Archdeacon of Dublin, was made Bishop of Killaloe.

[2] It is worthy of remark that Mrs. Delany never considered it beneath the refinement of her taste, or the superiority of her understanding, to comment upon the dinners of her friends, and often to give details—not those of an epicure, but those of a gentlewoman whose daily duty of household superintendence at home made her observant of what was right *or* wrong elsewhere.

no entertainment equal to that of hearing two very ingenious men talk on agreeable subjects. We stayed till near seven, and came home well pleased with the entertainment of the day, and not at all mortified with the good fortune of others. The Dean has always one happy and never failing satisfaction in his own way of thinking— which is a firm conviction that all things are ordered by a wise Disposer, who knows best what is good for us.

The bell rings for church, this being St. Andrew. If I can add a few lines I will.

A. G. to her friend Martha, at Calwich.

Dec. 12th.

Indeed, my good friend Martha, you send me so many fine presents, that I shall blind myself with thanking you, or what will be almost as bad, kill myself with eating them. Such a turkey! O how monstrously I did eate, and to be sure it lasted me more meals than one; though I did give Mrs. Donnellan a bitt. She sends her compliments to master, and desires you will tell him that he is sadly wanted in town, and upon my word I long to see him more than I will say. We have terible cold weather; I have been half froze. I realy think I shou'd not have lived last week if you had not sent me the good turkey to eate, it kept the frost out of my stomach. I honor Toby for killing so many ratts, and I am rejoyed to think the fox is killed; I wish you could kill ten more, and then the skins would make me a gown. But can you tell me how you catched him, for *here* is the greatest devil of a fox at present hanging about St. George's and Westminster that was ever known anywhere; he destroys every thing he comes near, beast and bird; some people think he has brought to his den the very king of beasts; he does not kill them all, for he could not eat so many, but he *makes them destroy one another!* He has a cunning way of drawing them all about him, and they say he has a kind of glittering dust in his brush that he shakes when they are near him, and the dust flies into all their eyes, and from that time they do nothing but devour and eate one another, and he does not forget to make them bring tit-bitts and good morsels to put in his own maw. He has been hunted these two or three winters furiously, traps and gins of all sorts set, but he has not yet been catched. Now, dear Martha, if you can put me in a way how to catch him I wou'd cut off his tail and put an end to his shaking that cursed shining dust about, and pull out both his eyes, then you and I wou'd carry him about for a shew, we shou'd get a power of money by him at sixpence a piece. I am told there is not one county in England where he has not sent some of his own breed to, and has given them some of this more than accursed dust, with which they do more mischief than any beast alive has ever done. Maybe it is one of them you have killed for fear it shou'd burry his brush deep in the earth for fear of this same dust; and have a care of your own eyes, and I beg master will take care of his, for they say it may do Christian's eyes harm as well as others.

The King of Prussia is well, and going into winter quarters: he says *he will knock all their heads together* in the spring, and *I hope he will.*

I have no news. My duty to master, and tel him I prodigously wish he wou'd come to town this bad weather. I hope you will take care and keep yourself warm this winter. Mrs. Donnellan is remembered to you, and I am.

Dear Martha, sincerely yours,

A. G.

In Mrs. Donellan's handwriting.

Gran had just finished this scrole when Mrs. Donnellan was informed that Mr. Granville had been very ill, but was better. She sent immediately to his house to enquire, but his servant knew nothing of it, so that she is in hopes it is not true; however she shall be very glad to hear either that he has not been ill or is better, if the report is true, and she desires friend Martha will make her kind compliments to him; and she hopes if he has been ill, that he will come to town, as soon as he is well enough to venture, and she shall beg to hear how he does, as she shall not be easy about him till she does. *Gran* was unwilling to send her letter till she heard more of him, but Mrs. Donnellan thought if he was pretty well it might divert him, and was an opportunity of sending both wishes.

December 12.

The Editor has not found any clue by which to identify the writer of these curious and entertaining letters. That she had been in the service of Mr. Granville is evident, and that she wrote to a person in his service, and residing with him at Calwich, is also clear. But there is a humour, and an interest in public affairs, and a vein of irony, which, considered with orthography, which is very little inferior to that of the gentlewomen of the time, indicates that she was one of that useful and respectable class which has disappeared with the century—of clergymen's or poor gentlemen's daughter, who, well qualified in all domestic matters served or "took service" as a housekeeper or "gentlewoman's woman," and when there was no company and she was not engaged in the business of her calling, assisted her mistress in ingenious works, and did nothing without her knowledge and sanction.

Mrs. Delany to Mrs. Dewes, at Gloucester.

Delville, 21 Dec., 1745.

Many flying reports we have had of the entire defeat of the rebels, but there is no stress to be laid on ship news; besides the rumour of one day is contradicted by the next. I have answered all your letters; never was one more welcome than that which brought the account of my brother's being with you at Gloucester. I had terrified myself extremely on his account; I could not think of him surrounded by those desperate rebels without fearing the worst that could happen; but your letter happily relieved me from my anxiety.

I don't find that the troubles of the times have given any check to gay doings in this part of the world. The castle is crowded twice a week; plays, assembly, and drums, are as much frequented as ever. I must own this may be a right policy to keep up the hopes of people, but I am surprized that their spirits should hold out; and I cannot but think, under the terrible apprehensions of losing our liberty and our property, it would be more becoming to *abate* our diversions, especially as we have reason to think that the great irreligion and luxury of the times have brought our present calamities on us; though (I hope in God) we have no apparent reason to fear that the rebels will succeed in their attempts. We already feel, and must still feel more the sad effects of only an attempt, for expenses have been very great, and it will be a considerable time before those wounds can be healed. The distemper amongst the cows about London [1] is a sad distress; I hope it has not reached the country.

I wrote you word last Saturday that I was to have a rare rout. I had two tables for dinner, ten persons at each table; my hall is as large as my parlour, and boarded, so I thought it best to have one of the tables placed there, and I desired an aunt of Mrs. Green's to do the honours for me, which made the affair very easy. Mrs. Green sat in my bedchamber to receive her company, and everybody was gay and well pleased except young Mrs. Agar, the daughter to my Lord Castledurrow [2] (whose son, Mr. Flower, married Miss Tatton), and she poor woman was taken ill at dinner, and in danger of miscarrying: I urged her *to stay* as much as I could, as I really thought she run a vast hazard in going home;

---

[1] The distemper here alluded to amongst the cows, was a violent inflammatory fever, attributed to the wetness of the season. It prevailed in 1744 in the south of France, Savoy, and Italy, and afterwards commenced in Sweden, Norway, Denmark, and Great Britain. The receipt made use of in Sweden was considered very efficacious, and printed at Stockholm, in the King's printing office, in November, 1745. It was composed of snakeweed, camphire, valerian, elecampane, lovage, laurel berries, the root of angelica, carline thistles, agaric, and roots of masterwort. All these ingredients, in various proportions, were to be reduced to powder and mixed with 16¼ ounces of common salt. It was to be administered to each cow fasting, on toasted bread, which was to be sprinkled with as much as could be taken up with the thumb and finger.

[2] William Flower, created in October, 1733, Baron of Castle Durrow, county Kilkenny. He married Edith, daughter of the Hon. T. Caulfield, and had a son, Henry, who married Miss Tatton, daughter to General Tatton, and a daughter who married in July, 1741, James Agar, Esq., of Ringwood, county Kilkenny.

but home she would go, and the day after she miscarried, but is in a fair way of doing well.

Last Monday the Dean and I went to the rehearsal of the Messiah,[1] for the relief of poor debtors; it was very well performed, and I much delighted. You know how much I delight in music, and that piece is very charming; but I had not courage to go to the performance at night; the weather was so excessively bad, and I thought it would be hazardous to come out of so great crowd so far, that is my kind guardian thought so for me.

The great folks at the Castle continue to show great favour, but we pay them little attendance, no more than not to be remarked as backward. Everybody is to appear on the Prince of Wales's birthday in Irish stuffs, as they did on the Princess's: I have not yet bought mine. My new housekeeper promises very well, and I have got a pretty young cookmaid[2] that dresses meat incomparably well, as far as we go, for we keep a plain table.

I have desired Mr. Stanley to pay Mr. Dewes twenty-four pounds, fourteen of it to be disposed of as usual, and ten pound for Mrs. C. on H's account, indeed I meant it for him, but my money was not paid time enough before his sailing. The Dean's kind love and wishes attend the "pearly Dewes."

---

[1] The Messiah was first performed in Dublin on the 12th of April, 1742; when Mrs. Cibber executed her airs so pathetically that Dr. Delany is said to have exclaimed as he listened, "Woman, for this, be all thy sins forgiven."

[2] This is not to be understood to mean a cook with a pretty face, but a clever person in her business.

Mrs. Delany to Mrs. Dewes, at Gloucester.

Delville, 4 Jan., 1745-1746.

Your letter of the 29th of Dec. came smiling to make the new year open with a fair and promising aspect. It is impossible, if we ever make any proper reflections, not to have the heart truly sensible at this season of the year of the many blessings we enjoy which demand our most grateful praise and thanksgiving.

A thousand thanks for all your kind wishes, which are returned by D.D. and me to the utmost. As I write constantly to you, I don't address a letter particularly to my mother, which I hope she does not think disrespectful or unkind, for my affection and duty for her are more than my words can express, but I know when she has any letter to answer it is a trouble on her spirits, though when you are unable to write yourself I know her goodness will indulge me at that time.

The ugly rebels have been this year a public and *private* plague! Had it not been for their proceedings we had in all probability been now together; though when the hour comes so much wished-for of my setting foot on English ground, I shall *then* rejoice that I was kept so much longer in Ireland amongst them. I cannot express what a joy and satisfaction my brother's being at Gloucester has been to me; I know how happy his company makes you all, and the dread I had on my spirits when I imagined him a prey to the rebels is relieved. I find the town is resolved to provide a young wife for

Lord G;[1] surely he is not such a Jew as in the midst of such a variety to confine his choice to his own tribe? He has not before been *famous* for his *love of cousins!*

The Dean has had a bad cold, which he caught by reading damp books; during which time I was so gracious as to indulge him with my English room, which is very warm when the wind is easterly. We lived four days in it, our quarters are now enlarged. I have now finished my three and thirtieth drawing for my book, and am reduced to the fruit of my imagination. I have made one landscape after my own whim, which is a favorite of the Dean's. But his partiality takes [*She should say may be suspected to "take"* (in the Dean's hand)] place of his judgment.

We have almost finished Sir Thomas Hanmer's Shakespear; our next study is to be the Life of the Admirals,[2] which they say is very entertaining. I hope soon to have Letty Bushe here.

Mrs. Barber, the painter's wife, is brought to bed of a boy; they have now two boys and a girl. Since the very cold weather we have taken to our old sports of hunting the fox and puss in a corner, which warms us better than a great fire. I have sent you a grey stuff such as is the present mode, and the Dean has taken the liberty to send my mother a brown one. They go with a cargo of goods, and a merchant has undertaken to send them all safely.

---

[1] Lord Granville, whose attentions to his cousin, the Maid of Honour, were before mentioned.

[2] The Lives of the Admirals and other eminent British Seamen; by J. Campbell, LL.D. A voluminous historical, biographical, and political writer; was born at Edinburgh, 1708; died at London, 1775. This work passed through three editions in the author's life.

To-day Dr. Pocock dines with us. On Monday I am to
have Mrs. Hamilton's four sons and two daughters to
choose King and Queen, which will make the young
things happy.

Mrs. Delany to Mrs. Dewes.
Delville, 11 Jan., 1745-6.

My dearest sister's letter of the last day of the old year
delighted my eyes last Tuesday. I hope you went through
all your Xtmas routs without taking cold, or being too
much fatigued. It is a time that custom has given up to
mirth, and as far as cheerful society and hospitality
goes it ought to be continued. I have not had much
of it here. We are too near the metropolis for that sort
of living; especially this winter, when everybody is
engaged in a more public way of diverting themselves.
I have withdrawn myself from these sort of engagements,
and find more pleasure in the quiet enjoyment of my own
amusements at home than a crowd can give me; and it
is very happy that as our season of life changes our taste
for pleasures alter. In the spring and summer of life
we *flutter and bask* in the sunshine of diversions—it is
true we run the hazard of being tamed and seldom
escape it; in the autumn and in the winter of life we by
degrees seek for shade and shelter, and if we have made
a good and prudent gathering of fruit and harvest, we
may then have the full enjoyment of them, as long as the
great Author and Giver thinks fit.

My eyes have continued very well; and I have painted,
and drawn, and read, and work'd, and done everything
with them without any return. I am very glad you

have had Sally in good spirits; I suppose she has left you before this. I take her rebuke, which I well deserved; and will write to her very soon. I spoke to Mr. Barber about copying Lady Stanley's picture; and as soon as I receive my brother's commands will set about it. Pray let me know if he would have the little Cupid and the whole copied *just as it is*.

Last Twelfth-day I invited Mrs. Hamilton's little family to choose King and Queen. The eldest daughter about nineteen, three boys, the eldest thirteen, and a little girl not yet five, a most delightful entertaining child. She was Queen, and entered into the part as well as Garrick could have done. I sent them home loaded with plum-cake, and in fine spirits. Last Tuesday we dined at Lord Grandison's: Lady Betty Mason has lost her third child, and has now only a little boy four months old. Our nursery goes on finely. Yesterday arrived our ingenious Letty: she has brought good health and fat sides, and I am very happy to have her; she has spread before me some of her drawings that she has done since I saw her, and they are charming. I lent her some prints of Claude Lorraine, that she has copied to great perfection; and now we shall paint and draw and chatter together as fast as our hands, eyes, and tongues can go."

My spirits rise as the sun grows brighter, and though it must be some months hence, I hope in God this will be a year of our meeting. I think it best to inform you and my brother about the time we propose seeing England; that you may contrive your affairs to the best advantage for our being as much together as possible. The Dean cannot leave Ireland till he settles his accounts, which will be in May, and about the middle he will be quite at liberty.

That too is the safest season for crossing the sea, and if we stay till then we may spend a whole year in England. I have not yet finish'd the Duchess of Mazarin; the cold weather and dark days kept me very idle. I now am in full employment. To-morrow the Bishop of Clogher and Mrs. Clayton dine here.

I hope by the accounts we have had lately of the rebels that they will no more molest us. Our Duchess, I suppose, is at Whitehall before this; She has been much affected by the troubles of the times; Lady Wallingford was with her at Bulstrode. We have just finish'd Sir T. H.'s Shakespear.¹ It is a very complete edition. I have been tormented all this morning in looking for two guineas' worth of tickets for a lottery of books, and cannot find them; and with Bushe's chattering and showing me her drawings, has run away with my morning.

Mrs. Delany to Mrs. Dewes, at Glocester.
Delville, 18 Jan., 1745-6.

I am now under some distress for poor Mrs. Greene; her pretty little boy, I am afraid, is in a very dangerous way. Dr. Barber has attended him constantly, and this morning desires the assistance of a man-midwife to consult with. Mrs. Greene is greatly afflicted, she is of a quiet affectionate disposition and not apt to complain, which makes grief prey upon her more sharply; we had all grown very fond of the little boy; it is an exceedingly pretty child; but I hardly think he can recover.

---

¹ Sir Thomas Hanmer published a corrected and illustrated edition of Shakspeare's dramatic works, in 6 vols., 4to.

Next Monday we are all prepared to appear at the Castle in Irish stuffs; I have bought a *sprigged* one. Some are made very costly, which *I think foolish*, for when they mix much silk they are not so useful, some are so silly, they tell me, as to have them sprigged with silver; by the by, I hear we are like to be disappointed; for Lady Chesterfield has been much out of order with St. Anthony's fire, and yesterday was not well enough to see company.

I believe I wrote you word that my ingenious Letty was come to me, and I am very happy in her company; her good sense, her good humour and liveliness, make her an agreeable companion for all ages and all seasons. I have often lamented her not having made some acquaintance with you, and she does the same; sometimes she talks of making England another visit, and if she does I hope you will meet, for I am sure you must like one another. O provoking! this moment am I interrupted by company, and must finish.

Mrs. Delany to Mrs Dewes, at Gloucester.
Delville, 25 Jan., 1745-6.

I hope the old saying on St Paul's day will not be verified this year. We have already been grievously afflicted with wars, and the wind now blows most vehemently, and most vexatiously, for it blows full against the packets. Four will be due to-morrow. I am as ignorant of what you are all doing, and how you are, as if you were in China, and if the packets when they come in do not bring me word of my being richer by a nephew or niece, I shall be baulked. Since I last wrote to you, we have been in frights for the little boy here, but he is now very well again, though so ill two days, that we gave him up for gone. We are all fond of the little thing, and it is a very pretty baby.

Our great Lady has been so ill as not to see company a great while; she did not appear on the Birthday, so there was no morning drawing-room, but a ball at night, and my Lord Chesterfield did the honours. It was prodigiously crowded, and all the ladies were dressed in Irish stuff, and never looked finer or more genteel: except five or six who wore silk, and they were *not* distinguish'd to their honour. The men were not so public-spirited as the ladies—most of them were in their foreign finery.

Last Sunday Mr. and Mrs. Vesey, (Mrs. Handcock that was), Miss Handcock, and Mrs. Marley came to dine with us; I found them in my garden when I came from church. On Monday I went in the morning to see Mrs. Hamilton. I am making some little brackets such as Mr. Bateman's, but instead of gilding them I *cover them with shells*; I design to have eight of them for my closet, to hold little pieces of China. Letty is now drawing some beautiful landscapes in the Indian book Mrs. Mead gave me; she drew four in it last year. Her good sense and good humour make her a very desirable companion, without considering the embellishments that enliven the whole. She seems pleased to be here, and is always ready to listen when I want to talk of my English friends, which is no insignificant quality with me. We have finished Shakespear and have begun the History of the Naval Forces of England, which promises us very good entertainment. On Tuesday last I went to hear Deborah performed, for the support of one of the infirmaries. It is a charming piece of music, and was extremely well performed; we have a woman here, a Mrs. Storer, who has a very sweet and clear voice, and though she has *no judgment* in music, Dubourg manages her so well in his manner of accompanying her, as to make her singing very agreeable.

We dined that day at my Lord Grandison's. All the conversation at present is about the poor Bishop of Ossory's[1] loss; she (his wife) died last week of a fever, much lamented by everybody. She was *sister* to Miss O'Brien, who was so ill-treated by my Lord Kildare: she was very pretty and very young. On Wednesday we dined at Mr. Monck's, Lady Bell very civil, and the same *Miss Notable* as ever. On Thursday Mr. Barber's child was Xtned, and we spent a merry day there: I think I told you they have a house joining to our kitchen garden. Yesterday we spent the whole day at home, and I am as glad of a pretence so to do, as I have *formerly been* of going to a public place. The change in *my Ministry* has been for the better. Apropos, the great folks on the other side of the water, we are told, are changing, and some day Lord Gr. is to be Principal Secretary of State. What say you? I am *quite easy* about the matter; we shall ask no favour (let who will be in power)—for ourselves I mean. Did I write you word we had got a new terene?[2] the Dean invented it, and I drew the draught; it is very well executed, the chasing is mighty well done: it holds six quarts, and has a very light look. My next work will be to make a nine-pin alley, which I have undertaken to do; we have a little odd nook of a garden, at the end of which is a very pretty summer-house, and in the corners of it are houses built up for

---

[1] Dr. Michael Cox, Bishop of Ossory, 1743, translated to Archbishopric of Cashel 1754, died 1779.

[2] Query Tureen.

blowing auriculas; it is upon the whole of a triangular form, long and narrow, much like this scratch.

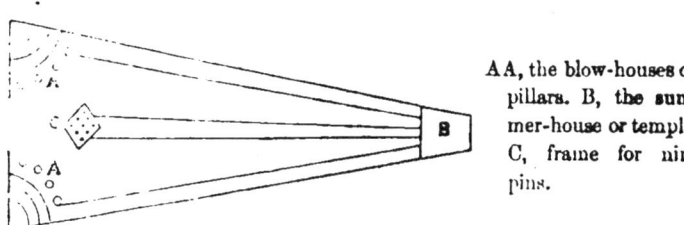

AA, the blow-houses on pillars. B, the summer-house or temple. C, frame for nine pins.

The walls to be covered with evergreens, and room enough for borders of flowers. It was originally designed for a nursery for flowers, but the walls are too close, it is very near the house, and will make a special nine-pin alley, which I think a *very merry exercise*. We had thoughts of having a bowling-green before our house in the garden front; but the hill, which descends gradually to the brook, looks so natural and pretty as it is, that it would be a pity to make it level: and so we determine to keep it a lawn, and to have sheep.

The following lines will explain the saying of "*St. Paul's Day.*"

"If Saint Paul's day be fair and clear
It does betide a happy year;
But if it chance to snow or rain,
Then will be dear all kinds of grain:
If clouds or mists do dark the sky
Great store of birds and beasts shall die;
And if the winds do fly aloft,
Then wars shall vex the kingdom oft."

"These prognostications are Englished from an ancient Calendar; they have likewise been translated by Gay. who enjoins:

Let no such vulgar tales debase thy mind,
Nor Paul nor Swithin rule the clouds and wind."

Mrs. Delany to Mrs. Dewes.

Delville, 1 Feb., 1745/6.

We have lately had very sharp weather, frost and some snow; but the sun has shone between whiles, and the verdure of our fields gives a cheerfulness to our prospects in the midst of winter that I never saw in any other place. The spring appears in my flower-garden, but I am afraid the frosty mornings will nip the forward things. I am less concerned at any defect that may happen there this year, as I hope to spend the blooming season in England. D.D. and I talk every day of our intended journey; when he sees me in a sighing way, he then as a cordial *begins upon that subject*, and it never fails answering his kind intention.

Last Monday we dined at Mrs. Frank Hamilton's; the Bishop of Clogher's people were there and Miss Forth; on Tuesday we dined at Dr. Clarke's in the College, and met Mrs. Forde's family; and on Wednesday we dined at Mr. Bayley's, our neighbour at Holly Mount. Three days together spent abroad is being a downright rake, but the sobriety of my own dwelling is much pleasanter to me than all the flirtations of the world; though the society of it, I will always keep up to the *best of my power*, as it is a duty incumbent on us to live sociably, and it is necessary to keep up good humour and benevolence in ourselves, or the qualities of the heart contract and grow useless, as our limbs would do without any proper exercise. On Thursday we kept home and fast; the Dean, his niece, and the servants went to church; I had a little cold, and had Bushe, and we staid at home. I have repeated more that once how happy I am in her company; she is in very good health and spirits, and at this instant is singing most melodiously.

We have had some news by way of Belfast that is by no means satisfactory. If what is told us of Gen. Hawley [1] be true he is as worthy an officer as Cope, and we are *very unfortunate* in our generals. The History of the Admirals is very entertaining. The Dean has given me a charming book of prints after Raphael; they were designed for the History of the Bible, engraved (etched I should say) by a famous Italian. When shall I be so happy as to show you all my pretty things? I want that part to give me a perfect relish to them, but that I fear is a great way off. You have a young charge that will not for some time permit you to bestow that happiness, but my brother, I hope, who has *neither wife nor children to confine him*, will not refuse me a joy that he can so easily confer, and I hope before the month of May expires I shall make my demand in person. My fingers ache with cold, and were not my heart very warm I could not have held my pen so long.

---

[1] Lieut.-General Henry Hawley, Governor of Portsmouth, and Colonel of the Royal Regiment of Dragoons, died unmarried at his place near Portsmouth, 24th March, 1759, aged 80. In his extraordinary will he directed that "as there was now a peace and he might die in the common way, his carcase might be put anywhere; that there was to be no more expense than if a poor soldier was to be buried from the hospital; "that the priest was to have the fee, and the carpenter to be paid for the carcase box." Lord Mahon says he was an officer of some experience, but destitute of capacity, and hated by his own soldiers as well as his enemies for his violent and vindictive temper. He had two gibbets erected in Edinburgh for the rebels who might fall into his hands, and several executioners to attend his march.

Mrs. Delany to Mrs. Dewes.

Delville, 8 Feb 1745-6.

Last week was a rich week. I had a letter from our Duchess, one from Donnellan, and one from Sally. No miser ever view'd his treasure with half the delight that I read over my letters; they are my cordials when my spirits droop,—a specific against spleen; it is well for me that the Dean so well understands and feels the little cares and anxiety that belong to affection, otherwise I should sometimes try his patience; but he is so far from condemning me that he is *ready to join with me* in every mark and testimony of love to my friends. Your first letter (of the 3rd last) was dated 14 December, meaning I suppose January, with an account of the Foleys passing through Gloucester. I have had a letter from Miss G. since her arrival at Windsor. She expresses great pleasure in having seen you, and gives me a very particular account of your looks and of little Court; she says he is the most entertaining child she ever met with, and *very like you in his manners*. When I read that part of her letter I cried out, "*Dear little rogue!*" to the surprize of the company, who were very civil and silent whilst I was reading my letter, and much diverted at my sudden exclamation. I hope this will find my brother still with you. I am sure you are happy together, and I share it at this distance; I am vexed I should have sent my brother's linen unmade, but as I wrote to him above three months ago for his directions and received none, I concluded he would rather have them made in England. If you have another boy I fancy you will call it *Bevil*, if Mr. Dewes has no particular inclination to some other name.

Mr. Barber will copy Lady Stanley's picture¹ according to my brother's orders. I suppose he remembers both the hands are in. The Cupid will not do by any means, as it will look but like a little fly, so reduced. We are greatly impatient to hear from Scotland. I heartily wish the Duke of Cumberland may put a final period to the rebellion, but it is impossible not to be anxious, for the hazard he runs in heading an army that has behaved themselves so ill. His presence and conduct I hope may animate them with a martial spirit; the men seldom fail when the leader is an hero. The Duchess of Portland says nothing of Lord and Lady Andover;² so I fancy the report of their parting may be false; I wish it were true, for he is unworthy of her goodness.

Your last letter was dated 27th January, and came to me in seven days. Could our letters always make as swift a passage, it would be charming. I am glad to find there is so sociable a spirit in Gloucester. See what it is to have *an agreeable man* amongst you!

I hope before May, *peace may be within our walls*, but if the commotions of war are confined to Scotland, our seas between Dublin and Chester will be safe enough, and I don't at present apprehend there will be any reason to defer our journey. Yesterday I went to the Castle to pay my

---

¹ Lady Stanley's picture was painted by James Houseman, or Huysman, born at Antwerp in 1656, and died in London, 1696. Houseman painted both history and portraits, in which last he was a successful rival of Lely; and among the beauties at Windsor is the portrait of a lady equal to Lely's. Houseman also painted the altar-piece in the Queen's Chapel at St. James's. He excelled in the representation of Cupids.

² Mary, second daughter of Heneage, 2nd Earl of Aylesford, married William Lord Andover, son of the 4th Earl of Berkshire and 11th Earl of Suffolk.

compliments to Lady Chesterfield, who has had a very long confinement with St. Anthony's fire; she looks very ill. I was dressed in my Birthday poplin, and looked very fine. To-morrow we are to have a houseful of our northern neighbours, and on Monday we dine at the Bishop of Clogher's. Mrs. Clayton is to have a drum in the evening and we are invited to it. Their house is very proper for such an entertainment, and Mrs. Clayton very fit for the undertaking. She loves the show and homage of a rout, has a very good address and is still as well inclined to all the gaieties of life as she was at five-and-twenty; the Bishop loves to please and indulge her, and is himself no way averse to the magnificence of life.

The agreeable and ingenious Letty sends her very kind wishes and humble service to you. I shall have a great deal of her handywork to show you; she is so good as to draw almost every day for me, and has inspired me with landscape-drawing out of my own pate; I have invented three which the Dean is very fond of.

Mrs. Delany to Mrs. Dewes.

Delville, 13th Feb. 1745-6.

The Dean has subscribed to some philosophical lectures, and they are to be three times a week for six weeks, which with my other employments will fill up my time pretty well; but no occupation shall interfere with my devoirs to my absent friends. I dedicate a certain portion of my time to them, and make my other engagements as much as possible subservient to that.

I don't wonder my brother is a favourite at Gloucester.

He is so sociable in his disposition, that it makes him an acceptable companion, and I own his having been so long there has been a vast comfort to me, as I know how great a satisfaction it must have been to you and my mother. I am mightily pleased with your account of Master Jemmy Viney, I hope he will be a blessing to his mother.

I don't wonder at the reports at Gloucester about our *widow friend*; I shall have a joke or two with her, by way of payment; pray tell her that, with my very kind service to her and her family; and when you write to Sally let her know that my Lord North, at my request, has written a letter to Mr. Trelawney, the Governor, to recommend Mr. Harry Chapon, which I hope may prove of great service to him, and he should be advised to wait on the Governor as soon as possible; I think to write a letter to him that he may show the Governor to testify his being the person recommended. Last Monday I was at Mrs. Clayton's drum, which was *very magnificent*; her apartment is very fine, and she had a great deal of good company. D.D., Bushe, and I dined there, and staid till near nine. To-morrow I go to the Fair Penitent[1] to see our three famous actors together. Garrick[2] performs the part of Lothario, Sheridan[3] Ho-

---

[1] The Fair Penitent, a tragedy by Nicolas Rowe. He was born 1673, and died 1718.

[2] David Garrick, born 28th February, 1716, died 20th January, 1779. He twice visited Ireland. A short poem in his praise, called "The Stage," is dated Dublin, 14th February, 1746, and printed in the *Gentleman's Magazine*.

[3] Thomas, third son of Dr. Thomas Sheridan, was born at Quilca, near Dublin, in 1721. He was educated at Westminster School, and Trinity College, Dublin; which university he suddenly quitted; after having graduated M.A , and turned actor, in which profession he obtained some celebrity. He died 14th of August, 1788. He was the father of the celebrated Richard Brinsley Sheridan.

ratio, and Barry[1] Altamont. Sheridan I have not seen; my brother has; he is here in great reputation. Barry is the handsomest man and figure altogether that ever I saw upon the stage, and a promising actor. The ingenious Letty and Mrs. Green go with me. Next week Esther is to be performed; the rehearsal will be on Tuesday. To-day we dine at Lord Grandison's, and a strange *gibble gabble* woman has plagued me all the morning; I never was more nearly provoked to be rude in all my life. I crammed her with chocolate and plum-cake, and then sent her packing, but she has robbed me of what is not in her power to restore—*a good hour of my time.*

Have you heard anything lately of Sir T. Hanmer? it

---

[1] Barry was the son of a silversmith, and born in St. Warburgh's parish, Dublin, on the 20th of February, 1719. He determined to try his success on the stage, and accordingly in 1744 he made his debût on the Irish boards, in the character of Othello. He afterwards played at Cork with equal applause, and thence returning to Dublin, made one of that galaxy of talent which drew such full houses in the summer, that it was very common to say, that a person had *died of a Garrick, a Quin, or a Barry fever*. In 1746, he came to London, and was engaged at Drury-lane, where he performed both in tragedy and genteel comedy with much approbation. After having for some time divided the applause of the town with Garrick, Barry removed to Covent Garden, in 1749; when a decided competition took place between the two great actors, each playing against the other their principal characters with various success. The grand struggle made by both, was in the part of Romeo, in which the majority agreed in awarding the palm to Barry. He died Jan. 10, 1777. The admirers of Garrick were in the habit of allowing Barry every physical and denying him every mental qualification. They sneered at him as "the whined-toned lover," "the elegant automaton," &c., but there is no doubt, "in the softer scenes of dramatic woe, conjugal tenderness, and agonizing distress, Barry was Garrick's master." Victor in his History of Theatres, (1761,) states that, on January 20, 1745-6, he went over to Ireland, and when he arrived in Dublin, he found "his good friend Mr. Garrick" at the Theatre Royal, with Mr. Sheridan as sharers and adventurers, and Mr. Barry engaged at a salary by the proprietors. There were several tragedies, in which Victor had the pleasure of seeing these three performers appear together, as in the Fair Penitent, Garrick acted Lothario, Sheridan Horatio, and Barry Altamont; and he adds his belief "that he was much envied that happiness."

is reported here that he is dead, and it has stopped D.D.'s writing to him till he knows whether the report be true or false. Yesterday after prayers, it being very bright and a dry hard frost, the Dean and I walked to see Mrs. Barber, a good mile from hence; the wind was in our back and very pleasant, but we did not wish to *face* so keen an enemy, and returned in the chariot.

I am much obliged to my *courtly* nephew for remembering "*Aunt Delany.*"

Mrs. Delany to Mrs. Dewes.

Delville, 28 Feb., 1745-6.

I am more obliged to my friends at Gloucester than I can express for the good news they have constantly sent me of my dearest sister's being so well, and as little can I express how happy and thankful it makes me. I have this moment received a letter from Mrs. Viney, dated the 19th instant (which I think was your ninth day); she tells me you are better than you have ever been yet, and that my niece[1] eats paps purely. It will save some trouble *if you can* bring her up by hand, and since she is naturally so stout *I believe it may perhaps be done.*

I gave you or my mother an account of my being engaged in philosophy, besides which I have three oil pictures in hand. I am copying an angel for the Dean after a Guido, finishing a half-length of the famous Duchess of Mazarin for Miss Bushe, and must give my mother's picture (*I have copyed for you*) another painting, it does not content me. I am extremely pleased with the phi-

---

[1] Mary Dewes, only daughter of Ann Granville, Mrs. Dewes.

losophy lectures, but am cruelly disappointed. I hoped to have been made a *very wise woman* by them, but alas! they only serve to show me my own ignorance. I am surprized that knowledge should make anybody vain; I think it rather serves to humble the mind; since to those who have drank deepest of the draught of knowledge there must remain so many things unaccountable. I went to *school* this morning and had not time to write till this moment, and it is now six o'clock.

The Bishop of Clogher and his family, and Mrs. Fortescue and her sister, dine here. Last Tuesday I went to the Castle to present Mrs. Green. I was there morning and evening. It was ball-night, and I was heartily tired before I came away. Lady Chesterfield is to have music once a week; *nobody invited,* but those that used to go on the private evenings may go. I have had a hint given me to go the first night, which will be to-morrow I believe.

Pray have you heard anything of Will Cull since he left us? I am much afraid he is gone astray. I charged him to go directly to Gloucester, but as you have not mentioned him in any of your letters I suppose he has taken some other road. I have had the good fortune (I hope) to provide for a brother of my poor George's, a very ingenious clever young man; as the Bishop of Clogher has lately lost his gentleman, and upon my recommendation has taken Mr. George, who will have a very happy life, for they are very good to all their family, and it is a profitable place.

Mrs. Delany to Mrs. Dewes.

Delville, 8 March, 1745-6.

I thought my joy was full on my dearest sister's account, and that it could not rise higher, having been so constantly and kindly informed by my good and obliging friends at Gloucester of your being as well as I could wish; but when I received my dear mama's letter yesterday with your own nine precious lines in it, I found a new joy spring up in my heart, for which I give you ten thousand thanks: though another line would have converted my pleasure into pain, lest the writing of it might have proved prejudicial to you.

I am very glad my niece Mary takes so well to her food: I don't see why it should not rear her up as it did me: I wou'd have her like me in every thing that *is worthy* of your regard, but to endear her *equally to me*, I wish most heartily she may resemble my own dearest sister. You remember Madame de Sevigné: Mary must be *my Pauline*.

After a silence of many months, and receiving two very kind and entertaining letters from Mrs. Duncombe, I have this day wrote to her. I gave you an account of my morning employments, and how busy I am. The philosophical lectures please me extremely; I have gone through nine. On Monday next it is to be on optics; which I am told is the most entertaining of all. Last Wednesday the Dean and I were invited to the Bishop of Clogher's to a musical entertainment, made for my Lord and Lady Chesterfield; no ladies were invited but performers—Lady Freak,[1] Miss Maxwell, and your

---

[1] Sir John Redmond Freke, Bart., married Miss Brodrick. He died 13th April, 1764, when the title became extinct.

humble servant, but I was excused; the other ladies played and sung extremely well. Lady Freak has a great hand and genius for music, but has had few advantages in learning; Miss Maxwell has been very well taught. Mr. Dubourg played the first fiddle, and played better than ever I heard him: the concert was very agreeable, and everything ordered well and handsomely. Lady Chesterfield says she never heard so good a performer as Dubourg.

Mrs. Delany to Mrs. Granville.

Delville, 15 March, 1745-6.

MADAM,

I am under the highest obligation to you for your goodness in giving me so particular an account of my sister; I thank God most heartily that she is so well, and congratulate you again and again on the blessed occasion.

I could with great pleasure to myself address a long letter to you, dearest madam, as conversing with you every way is a most particular pleasure to me; but as writing is troublesome to you, I will not load you with a letter to answer, but go on to thank my dearest sister for her most delightful lines in your last letter, dated the 2nd inst.; first assuring you of the Dean's humble duty, and that I am with the tenderest affection, dearest madam,

Your most dutiful daughter,
and most obedient humble servant,
M. DELANY.

To Mrs. Dewes, in same letter.

Now my dear sister for you. Notwithstanding the bad weather, we have gone every other morning to the philosophical lectures, which have entertained me extremely; next Monday will be our last. I have not been at the Castle a great while. I think I wrote Mrs. Duncombe word of a concert of music we had at the Bishop of Clogher's, for the entertainment of my Lord and Lady Chesterfield, which was very agreeable. Last Tuesday Mr. Bristowe, an uncle of Miss Dashwood's, dined here; he is a great virtuoso, understands all the *virtus* to perfection; he is much delighted with Delville. Mr. Barber has just finished another picture of me in enamel, which Mr. Bristowe says, is better done than any he ever saw of Zincke's, indeed I think it very finely enamelled; and I hope it will bring him into good business. Lord Massareen[1] sits to him on Monday, and Mr. Bristowe has promised to prevail, if possible, with Lord and Lady Chesterfield to sit to him, and that will bring him into fashion; he is very industrious, and deserves to be encouraged; his wife is a very pretty prudent young woman: they have a comical little girl of three years old, not pretty, but a smart girl, and he proposes to make her a mistress of his art, as soon as she is capable of learning. This is the Dean's birthday, and I expect a good deal of company. What say you in your part of the world of public affairs? I think the rebels threaten to teaze us *some time longer*; if good weather comes, I hope the Duke will be able to deal with them as they deserve.

---

[1] Clotworthy, 5th Viscount Massareene, who was created, in July, 1756, Earl of Massareene. He married, first, in March, 1738, Anne, eldest daughter of Richard Daniel, Dean of Down; who died 27th March, 1740, and he married, secondly, 25th November, 1741, Elizabeth, only daughter of Henry Eyre, Esq., by whom he had several children.

Mrs. Delany to Mrs. Dewes.

Delville, 22 March, 1745-6.

I am very sorry that my brother has been so subject to colds this winter. I had a letter from him by the last packet. I want to know if he expects us at Calwich for our first resting-place, that *was* the scheme of last year, but if his affairs call him to London this spring, it may not be convenient to him to return so soon as the middle of May, which is the time we hope to be able to leave this place: I have written to him to-day to know. I am willing to settle our route as nearly as I can soon, not to leave it till the last moment, as I shall have a great deal of business on my hands; for I must *see* all my fine furniture and pictures well papered, and I have a new inventory to make of my household goods, and two drawers of papers to look over and separate in order. I hope my house-keeper is one I can trust; she is a sober woman and does everything required of her extremely well, and I shall take Betty Woodal and Margaret with me.

We have met with a sad disappointment in our coach; when it came home it was so little, and such indifferent work, we could not keep it. We have bespoke another, and hope it will be finished by the time we want it. We have bespoke it with the top like a landau, for lightness, but every other way a coach.

I rejoice that *my little girl* thrives so well. I am sorry her nurse can't stay with her; I should think it would be better for you to take the child home with you now, for you have room enough at Welsbourne. I am afraid the cold weather has affected my mother: it has been extremely sharp, but now, thank God! it is very fine, and I have begun my morning walks. I was two hours (almost) in the garden this morning before breakfast. The sweetness of the air, the singing of the birds, and the charming prospect made it appear like an enchanted place, after having been buried in snow and chilled with nipping frost for a fortnight together; we have had about a week of good weather.

I beg my dearest sister will not alarm herself about our voyage, for I hope in God before our day of leaving this place the rebels will be beat off the field. We design taking the Government yacht, which is a very safe pretty vessel, the captain a skilful sailor, and supplied with many hands. The Castle folks talk of going the middle or end of next month, so I hope they will not interfere with our schemes. I am very sorry Captain Cole is dead; I am afraid he will be a loss to his family, for I think he had some place or pension: the Duchess did not name it to me, I suppose she thought she had. I heard from her by the last packet. I want to know how Sir Tony behaved amongst you; did he make you a long visit? I sent to enquire after his health in London, he was gone to Bath. I am glad Lady G. Spencer¹ behaved herself so obligingly to Mr. Dewes.

Mrs. Delany to Mrs. Dewes.

Delville, 29 March, 1746.

My little "*Pauline*" is (though unknown) a great favourite already, and you may command every thing from me that can be of service to her, but you are so well furnished with materials to make her a complete valuable

---

¹ Lady Georgiana Spencer, daughter of Lord Granville.

woman, that you will want no foreign aid; however, I hope we shall lay our wise heads together about her many and many an hour: in the mean time feed her and dance her well, for that is all can be attended to at present. You say you "wish her at Longford;" I did not know you meant to send her there.

On Monday the Dean goes to my Ld Lieut^t to ask leave for the yacht to carry us over; we cannot have it till the middle of May. The Dean had a letter from his steward in the country yesterday, who was to have come to settle accounts the first week in May, but he cannot come till towards the latter end. D.D. is very good, and takes all the pains he can to be at liberty as soon as possible; indeed he loses no opportunity of indulging every wish of my heart. Our garden is now a wilderness of sweets. The violets, sweet briar, and primroses perfume the air, and the thrushes are full of melody and make our concert complete. It is the pleasantest music I have heard this year, and refreshes my spirits without the alloy of a tumultuous crowd, which attends all the other concerts. Two robins and one chaffinch fed off of D.D.'s hand as we walked together this morning. I have been planting sweets in my "Pearly Bower"—honeysuckles, sweet briar, roses and jessamine to climb up the trees that compose it, and for the carpet, violets, primroses and cowlips. This year I shall not smell their fragrancy, nor see their bloom, but I shall see the dear person to whom the bower is dedicated, I hope, and I think I shall not repine at the exchange. To check my joy when I think of our meeting, the odious rebels come across my mind. What say you of them in England? I pray God keep us from a civil war! *If we can keep them in Scotland*, that is from setting foot on English ground, I don't apprehend they will spoil our scheme for going to England this year. The bell is just going to ring, and I must make myself ready for church.

Mrs. Delany to Mrs. Dewes.

Delville, 5 April, 1746.

I am most truly thankful that you are so well, and have a little female infant to exercise your own good judgment on; which will want little assistance, for I think you are guarded against the errors of *mistaken fondness* towards your children. I thank you for the *right* you have given me over my "*Pauline.*"

I am very glad you like the poplin, and the Dean is very proud my mother approves of hers. I have got one for Mrs. Viney and for each of her daughters, which I will send to England by the first opportunity. I desire their directions, who they shall be consigned to. I can't undertake to bring them as they are prohibited, but a person skilled in those affairs has undertaken the care of them.

Last Tuesday the Dean went to the Castle to ask leave for the yacht to carry us over, which is granted. My Lord Lieutenant goes from hence on the 15th, when the yacht returns. Lady Pendregast[1] has the first promise and we the second; so that supposing the wind should be as fair as our wishes, we shall not be able to leave Ireland sooner than the middle of May, at which time, please God, we

---

[1] Anne, daughter and heir of Sir Griffith Williams, Bart., married Sir Thomas Prendergast.

shall set sail for England: oh how my heart leaps! I had a letter last post from my brother; he says he is soon to go to London, and will return and meet us at Calwich whatever time we name. If it would be more convenient to him for us to meet at Welsbourne, I believe you would not object to it; but if it is to be at Calwich, my dearest sister, will you not be there? how can I bear to live on English ground, within a few miles in comparison of our present distance, and not see you? We design bringing over with us a light four-wheeled chaise we have, besides our coach, that when we have a mind to make any little excursion, it may be ready. We have some thoughts of taking a flight for a fortnight to London before winter.

Yesterday I was put into a sad fuss by my housekeeper being taken very ill; she is fat and short-necked, and complained so violently of her head that I feared an apoplexy; but Dr. Barber had her bled and vomited immediately, and she is now in a fair way of doing well. She would have been a great loss to me, as she is I think an excellent servant, and one that I may trust with the care of my house in my absence.

Lady Betty Mason is made Viscountess Grandison in her own right; they all dine here on Monday.

Mrs. Delany to Mrs. Dewes.

Delville, 11 April, 1745-6.

I proposed indulging myself with a long letter to my dearest sister this morning, and lo! I am reduced to one quarter of an hour: how provoking! Now everybody is going out of town, the sun shines, and they come in swarms to take leave and *bask in our sunshine*, which the smoke of Dublin will not allow of. I was last night the greatest of rakes; went to take my leave at the Castle, was crowded to pieces; did not come home till twelve o'clock, fatigued to death; slept well and refreshed myself with walking half an hour after breakfast; then came in, prepared all my materials for a folio sheet, and was no sooner settled at my desk than in came Mrs. Forde and her family, and are but this moment gone. I find it is in vain to propose writing a long letter now, so don't expect it. When we meet, which I hope in God will be some time next month, we will make ourselves amends with talking. O pleasing happy hope!

The Dean is now making all the dispatch he can in his garden, to leave things in some regulation. I must do the same in my house, but have not yet begun about it.

I am enraged at the Goth of a man who so barbarously broke up the Roman pavement. Cannot you procure some of the fragments? I fancy one might piece them together. Miss Bushe is much yours, and at this instant painting with all her might, whilst Mrs. Green is talking, squawling, screaming, and making more variety of noises than ever were made by human voice, to her boy, who is really a most lovely child.

Mrs. Delany to Mrs. Dewes.

Delville, 28 April, 1746.

I told you a long story about an invitation, but it was all a mistake and misunderstanding, which has occasioned me no small hurry, for on Monday morning Mrs. Chenevix (whom I went to see) told me that the Lord Lieutenant designed dining with us on Wednesday, and held himself engaged. We were to dine at the Bishop of Clogher's, and just as we sat down to dine the Bishop of Waterford came, and told us that his Excellency would dine with us the next day. I immediatly dispatched a messenger to Delville, with a note to my housekeeper, to tell her she must prepare the dinner for next day of seven and nine, and a dessert, and I was obliged, as soon as I had dined, to go to the Castle, and ask Lady Chesterfield, but she had refused the Primate and therefore could not come to me, which she seemed sincerely to regret. The Dean went that evening to my Ld L. to know at what hour he would dine, and to desire him to bring whom he pleased. Lord Lieut: said he feared he had made some mistake about the day; but he was glad to seize the first day for the fear the wind would change. Home we went at eight, and it cost me about an hour or two thinking; but my dinner turned out very well, the particulars of which, if you think it worth your while, you shall have when we meet. He came at three, said he had reserved us for the bon bouche, was extremely civil, agreeable, and cheerful, and staid till nearly eight.

This has been a week of hurry with me indeed. On Thursday I went to the music for the benefit of the Hospital of Incurables, which was crowded—the piece performed was Alexander's Feast; and yesterday went to see the Beggars' Opera. We have had glorious news from Scotland. I hope, in God, the affair of the rebellion is now at an end, and that we shall meet in peace. All these gay doings have interrupted my painting, and I much fear I shall hardly have time to finish what I meant *to bring with me*, for it must have some time to dry before it is packed up. I told you Lady Pendergast has the next turn of the yacht, which will be some time next week, and I believe we shall allow it to take another trip with Lord Blessington¹ before we shall be ready; for till the middle of May it will be impossible for us to think of moving, and it may be the latter end. The Dean proposes to bring over his chaise as well as the coach, and I suppose at Warwick we can at any time hire a set of horses; and we shall bring over three of our own, which will serve for visiting in your neighbourhood.

You must forgive the Dean's having ordered Mr. Langhorne² to send in a little wine to your cellar at Welsbourne, by way of *hanselling a new place.* He humbly begs my mama will not think it necessary to write him a letter for such a trifle as he sent; it would make him blush, and reproach him for the liberty he took in sending her so mean a present; he is sure she is so good as to accept of it as a small mark of his remembering her with the utmost gratitude and respect, which he shall ever do, joined to a tender affection; and I am to say as much from him to you. I had a letter last post from my brother; he is doubtful whether he shall be able to be as soon at Calwich as we hope to be there, so I believe at last we shall steer our course to Welsbourne. O how my impatience increases!

The following letter from Dr. Delany to Mr. Granville explains that between the date of this letter (April 26th) and May 27th, Mrs. Delany had been seriously ill; the tone of the letter also

---

¹ William, 3rd Viscount Mountjoy, was created Earl of Blessington on the 7th December, 1745.

² Wine merchant, in King Street, St. James's Square, London.

proves that nothing but the fact of her being the sister, of the one and the wife of the other, prevented a breach, as Mr. Granville evidently had never overcome his annoyance at her marriage.

Dr. Delany to Bernard Granville, Esq., at Calwich.

Delville, May 27, 1746.

Sir,

I am under great concern that Mr. Monck's account of your sister's illness, reached you sooner than her own; but indeed it was her own fault, or rather the fault of her tender affection for her friends. I would have written to you by the same post that Mr. Monck wrote to the Duke of Portland, but she would not suffer me, because she thought you might be too much alarmed, and she had reason to hope that her own account of her health by the succeeding post would prevent that uneasiness to you. The truth is I thank God, she never was in danger, nor attended by more than one physician, Dr. Barber, who had attended her on all other occasions, and is much in her esteem, and confided in for his skill and knowledge of her constitution. To him I added a surgeon, of whose skill and friendship to her and me I was well satisfied; and though they both assured me there was no danger, yet I thought that so invaluable a life should rest upon the most solid supports that skill could supply, and therefore I ordered them to hold a consultation with Dr. Robson and Dr. Barry which I suppose gave occasion to the report of her being attended by four physicians); these perfectly agreed in the method in which Dr. Barber had treated her, and therefore I chose not to alarm her by the appearance of those strange physicians. I thank God she is now well, and I trust in God will long continue so, a blessing to her friends and the world, and to one who honours her above everything on this earth, and is, for *that reason* and every other that can create esteem to truth and virtue,

Your most faithful and most obedient
Humble servant, PAT. DELANY.

The yacht was sent off Sunday, and we hope in God nothing will hinder us from hastening to our friends in England as soon as it returns.

A long interval here occurs of five months, during which period Mrs. Delany was with her family, and during which time Sir Antony Westcomb wrote to Mrs. Dewes the following letter—

Sir Antony Wescomb to Mrs. Dewes.
August 17th.
(Believed to be 1746.)

MY DEAR COUSIN,

I have the favour of yours of the 4th instant, and likewise the bacon (as you call it), but before I eat it it shall be a ham. Your direction on the basket was *quite wrong*; you must direct for me, in Holles Street near Cavendish Square, or at the Smyrna Coffee House in Pall Mall. I am exceedingly sorry I cannot have the pleasure of seeing my dear aunt, but I hope I shall have that satisfaction before I die. I am full of ailments, and withal so weak, that I cannot get into nor out of bed without help; and to complete all, either by a strain or other accident, I have got a contraction of the nerves of my right thigh, with a lump at the upper end, not at all agreeable. If this should continue I am afraid my intended journey into Warwickshire will be defeated, for I can hardly bear the coach a mile. Tell my aunt that I use oil of earth-worms with opodeldoc to endeavour to dispel the lump, but hitherto without any visible effect, and that if she knows of anything that will do to let me know it. I am afraid I have tired you sufficiently with my impertinence, for which I heartily ask your pardon, and am

  My dear cousin's
   Most affectionate humble servant,
     A. Wescomb.

Mrs. Delany to Mrs. Dewes.

Cornbury, 30 Oct. 1746.

How impatient have I been for an hour to fly to my dearest sister, and tell her what my heart suffered when I left her happy mansion, which contains a treasure, whose value strengthens with every year, as every year (whether absent or present) gives me fresh proofs of its worth. But now I have found that hour I am at a loss for expression; gratitude, tender affection, and sorrow that I must leave you, give me such a hurry of thought and flutter of spirits that I can say nothing upon the subject, but that I love you most tenderly, and am truly thankful to you and Mr. Dewes for the many favours received at Welsbourne. I assure you that D D. joins most heartily in all I say, and we hope our dear, sensible little nephew remembered all his messages; and now I must quit a subject that is too affecting to us both, and proceed to tell you what steps we have taken, and are to take.

First, many thanks for sending the keys which my loggerheads left behind them. The road to Shipston was heavy, and bad enough; from thence to Chippingnorton pretty well: there we had a good inn and dinner. We left Chip. at four, and got to Cornbury by half an hour after five, where we were expected, and immediatly conveyed into the apartment allotted for us,—which is so neat and so elegant that I never saw anything equal to it. It consists of two large rooms and a bedchamber: the first room is hung with flowered paper of a grotesque pattern, the colours lively and the pattern bold and handsome. (that is the Dean's dressing-room); the next room is hung with the finest Indian paper of flowers and *all sorts of birds,* (that is my dressing-room); the ceilings are all ornamented in the Indian taste, the frames of the glass and all the finishing of the room are well-suited; the bedchamber is also hung with Indian paper on a gold ground, and the bed is *Indian work* of silks and gold on white satin; the windows look into the park, which is kept like the finest garden, and is a Paradise. The great apartment above-stairs is very fine: the room we sit in after dinner is 48 foot long and two and twenty wide; the walls are covered with whole lengths of Vandyke,[1] and so are two large rooms besides that belong to the Duchess of Queensberry's apartment. I have not time to describe the house more minutely, but upon the whole I think the house the *most comfortable and pleasant fine house* I ever

---

[1] Walpole says, "At Cornbury there are portraits of all the royalists, and regicides, and illustrious headless."

saw, for it is not only magnificent and elegant but *convenient* and *rational*; it resembles its master, and is both strong and genteel, nothing can be more agreeable than his behaviour. After we had been a few minutes in our rooms, a servant came to know if we would give his lord leave to wait on us: he came immediately, and said many pretty things, seemed much pleased at our coming, and then led me upstairs to the Duke and Duchess of Queensbury, Lord Charles Douglas,[1] (the youngest son), and a Mr. Young and Mr. Macky, two Scotch gentlemen, friends of the Duke of Queensbury. Her Grace is *most gracious* and *entertaining.*

The lord of the place will not let us go from hence till Saturday, and though it is as agreeable as a place can be, since I have left my dearest sister I am impatient to get to Bulstrode, but a lameness in one of our horses obliged us to discharge the set we had from Coles, and we could not conveniently have any from Oxford till tomorrow morning. We sent John Ward, William and the chaise on to Bulstrode, where I suppose they are by this time, to give notice we should not be there till Monday night; and have appointed John Ward to meet us tomorrow at Woodstock, and by him I shall send this letter.

Lord Cornbury[2] looks thin and dejected, but strives to exert himself for the entertainment of his company. We meet at breakfast between nine and ten, which lasts near two hours intermixed with conversations; when over, the

---

[1] Lord Charles Douglas, youngest son of Charles, 3rd Duke of Queensbury died in 1756.

[2] Bolingbroke addressed his "Letters on the Study of History" to Lord Cornbury, and he was complimented by Pope in the passage, "*Disdain, what Cornbury disdains.*"

coach is ready for D.D. and me to tour in the park, and to see my lord's improvements, the rest of the company ride. I never saw any spot of ground more beautiful than the park. I have taken a sketch of one part, which was originally a stone quarry, and is now improved into the wildest prettiest place you can imagine—winding walks, mounts covered with all sorts of trees and flowering shrubs, rocks covered with moss, hollows filled with bushes intermixed with rocks, rural seats, and sheds; and in the valley beneath a river winds and accomplishes the beauty. We return home at two and spruce out, dinner at half an hour after two; the afternoon—coffee, sauntering, conversation comes on, and tea; my drawings produced, many civilities are uttered, and the whole ends with a pool at commerce, which brings us to our hour of supper; and we go to our separate apartments at eleven. Yet such is my state of mind at present that I cannot half enjoy it, and in the midst of what is really agreeable I feel a want that cannot be supplied, and when the clock strikes nine, how do I want my dear little sexton to summon us to prayers! and how do I want my dear sister!

Ever yours, M. D.

Mrs. Delany to Mrs. Dewes.

Bulstrode, 7 Nov., 1746.

In the morning Lady Primrose[1] came from Windsor to make us a visit, which made our dinner late; and Mr. Robert Harley[2] and his nephew came to dinner.

---

[1] Hugh, 3rd Viscount Primrose, married, in 1739, Miss Drelincourt, daughter of the Dean of Armagh.

[2] Robert Harley, Esq., M. P., brother to Edward, 3rd Earl of Oxford. He died unmarried in 1774.

Unavoidable chatter and tea have run away with most of the afternoon; but I will make the most of my few minutes. You can decypher my scrawls let them be ever so bad, but I must chide you for making so many acknowledgments for trifles. Only repeat our old favourite song, and that speaks for us both: "*All friendship is a mutual debt,*" etc. I want to know where I may send to Sarah Smith when I go to town, which I believe will not be till the first week in Dec^r, for Miss Granville comes here the beginning of next week and will stay the rest of the month, and I don't care to go whilst she stays. We went to see her yesterday.

The Duchess of Portland was so considerate as to make a visit to the Duchess of Norfolk,[1] who is in the neighbourhood, that we might have the freedom of a tête-à-tête, and Lord Inchiquin[2] was so provoking as to come and interrupt us, but I had a little *wise* discourse with her; Cuz Fo. comes to her the beginning of December, and stays till after Xtmas. Lady Wallingford left us this morning, and on Monday Mrs. Montagu comes for a week. Our dear Duchess, I think, looks very well; she is grown much fatter; but is the same kind good creature she ever was. The children are all much grown and improved, and Lord Edward a charming boy; he speaks very few words, but makes signs and shows a great apprehension of every thing. Mrs. Elstob is pretty well, and enquired very much after you. *Monsr de Poivre* is so good-humoured and courteous that he may be called *Monsr de Miel.*

---

[1] Edward, 9th Duke of Norfolk, married, 6th November, 1727, Mary, daughter and co-heir of Edward Blount, Esq., of Blagdon, Devon.
[2] William, 4th Earl of Inchiquin.

My new night-gown met me, and is a very pretty new fashioned silk—green and white.

You were not quite misinformed about Lady Emily Lenox[1] and Prince Lobkowitz; he *was* in love with her and made proposals of marriage, but the Emperor would not consent for some foolish reason of state. I did not hear that Lady Emily was any way engaged to him, and every thing is agreed on between her and Lord Kildare, and my Lady Kildare[2] (the mother) is come over to go the wedding. Prince Lob: was in England last year. Once more adieu.

---

[1] Emlia Mary, second daughter of Charles, 2nd Duke of Richmond, married, first in 1746-7, to James, Earl of Kildare, afterwards created Duke of Leinster; and secondly to William Ogilvie, Esq.

[2] Mary, eldest daughter of William O'Brien, 3rd Earl of Inchiquin, widow of Robert, 19th Earl of Kildare.

CHAPTER VIII.

Mrs. Delany to Mrs. Dewes.

Pall Mall, 15 Jan. 1746-7.

My lodging consists of one parlour (staircase is light and easy) and a drawing-room, a size larger than what I had in Clarges Street: tapestry hangings, crimson stuff damask curtains and chairs, and tolerable glasses between the windows. The bed-chamber backwards, new and clean; crimson and yellow *flaring* hangings of paper, and a bed of the same materials as the curtains in the dining-room; but it looks into a pretty garden, and over the Prince of Wales's into the park, which is cheerful and pleasant. The two pair of stair rooms and the garrets all very tolerable. The rent four guineas a week; the situation is next door to the Cocoa Tree, which is the direction to me. Foley and Gran come to town to-morrow.

Yesterday, out of my great prudence, having had the headache two days with the bustle, I was let blood.

I opened my door to everybody yesterday, and had Mrs. Clayton, Mrs. Donnellan, Miss Brown, Duchess of Portland, Mrs. Montagu, Lady Cath. Hanmer, and Miss Deering, the Duchess of Queensbury, and the Duke of Portland. Mr. Bateman and Mr. Southwell, and the Maid of Honour. To-day I dine with the Claytons, in the afternoon go to Lady Sunderland. To-morrow I go to St. James's to pay my devoirs with the Duchess of Portland; dine at home; in the afternoon go to the Duchess of Norfolk, who is ill and confined; to the Countess of

Kildare, (who is come from Ireland to her son's wedding) and finish at the Duchess of Queensberry's, who is to have *a hurricane.* On Saturday I propose sitting quiet. On Sunday I go to Carlton House to pay my salutations to their Royal Highnesses, and in the afternoon to Mrs. Montagu. I go to-morrow in my Irish green damask and my worked head; on the Birthday, which is on Tuesday next, in a flowered silk I have bought since I came to town, on a pale deer-coloured figured ground; the flowers, mostly purple, are mixed with white feathers, I think it extremely pretty and very modest. Thus far was written yesterday; my head is dressed but I wait for my mantua. Mrs. Cob has promised to bring it by twelve; she is I hope well married; her husband seems to have sense, and has promised me to be very kind to his wife. (*This is by the by*). Lady Sunderland looks ill, but is better. Her son Sutton is as tall as my brother; he is going immediately to Oxford, and promises very well; Miss Sutton is, as she always was, an agreeable young woman. Many enquiries, after you were made, many services sent.

I was, as I proposed, at Court yesterday, and was presented and most graciously received. The King asked me how I liked Ireland, the Duke did the same. I dined at home, and in the afternoon my brother came; he looks grave, and lives much at home, though he is much courted for his company abroad. At six I went to the Maid of Honour's, and found *the Nosegay*[1] together. Mrs. Foley looks very well after her journey.

I hope Mr. Chap. can hold Senington,[2] with his other livings. Has he a house there, or does he continue

---
[1] The three sisters Honourable Ann and Elizabeth Greville, and Mrs. Foley.
[2] Query *Sevenhampton ?* near Andover's Ford, Gloucestershire.

at Cheltenham? I must send my little Jacky a pair of stays, and his sister;[1] let me know what size I must bespeak. Lady Sarah Cowper is so happy (so very happy) as to have her sister in town with her; she has had a fever, and ever since a lurking feverishness, for which she now takes tar water. After my visit to *the sisters* I went with the Duchess (of all the Duchesses), to the Duchess of Norfolk, who stays at home and sees everybody, and from thence to the Duchess of Queensberry's rout, where I saw much finery. My eyes at first were dazzled with the prettyness of the scene, but half an hour was enough. However I had the Duchess of Portland, and we sat together almost all the time we staid; there I saw Mr. Keck and Lady Susan.[2] I came home at half an hour after ten to my own good companion, who always receives me with smiles. Miss Granville came home soon after me, and when a little chat was over we retired to our apartments.

Gran likes her apartments mightily, and Mrs. Foley has made her a present of a very handsome suit of clothes for the Prince of Wales's birthday.

This morning I am to go to the Duchess of Queensberry's to see her work and painting; dine at home with our cousins and my brother; in the afternoon I proposed staying quietly, but the Duchess of Portland will have me and all my company come to her; I oppose, but believe she will yet get the better. To-morrow I am to be presented at Carlton House. I like Sarah Smith very much; she is nimble and quiet, civil and very handy.

---

[1] Lady Anne Colleton.
[2] Lady Susan Hamilton, eldest daughter of James, 4th Duke of Hamilton, married Anthony Tracy Keck, Esq., of Great Tew, county of Oxford, and died June 3, 1755.

Mrs. Delany to Mrs. Dewes.

Pall Mall, 21 Jan. 1746-7.

I must now communicate to you all my transactions since my last journal, which I believe ended with my having been at St. James's and at the Duchess of Queensberry's rout. On Saturday Whitehall; the Duchess inveigled away all my company, and I followed. Sunday I went to St. James Chapel at eight, came home, dressed and went to Carlton House at three with the Duchess of Portland: I was presented, and so was the Dean; who was also spoken to by their Royal Highnesses very graciously. Dined at the Duchess of Queensberry's; nobody but her Grace, the Dean, and myself; she was extremely civil and entertaining. At seven the Duchess of Portland called me to go to Lady Kildare; not at home. Went on to Hanover-Square: Mrs. Montagu there; drank tea; she went on to other visits; I staid till nine o'clock.

Monday I spent the day at Whitehall settling our Queen's jewels, and yesterday we made our appearance at Leicester-house. The Duchess of Portland was in white satin, the petticoat ruffled, and robings and facings. She had *all* her fine jewels on, and looked handsomer than ever I saw her look in my life, and in my eyes outshone in every respect all the blazing stars of the Court. There was not much new finery, new clothes not being required on this Birthday. They curl and wear a great many *tawdry* things, but there is such a variety in the manner of dress, that I don't know what to tell you is the fashion; the only thing that seems general are hoops of an enormous size, and most people wear vast winkers to their heads. They are now come to such an extravagance in those two particulars, that I expect soon to see the other extreme of thread-paper heads and no hoops, and from appearing like so many *blown bladders* we shall look like so many *bodkins stalking about.* I never saw a greater crowd than at Leicester-house. The reigning beauty I think among the very young things, is Miss Carpenter,[1] Lord Carpenter's daughter; and since Lady Dysart was fifteen I have not seen anything so handsome; but the prize of beauty is disputed with her by Lady Emily Lenox. She is indeed " *Like some tall stately tower*;" the other is " *some Virgin Queen's delicious bower.*" We dined at Whitehall. Lord Bateman[2] dined there; he is excessively thin, polite and modest in behaviour. In the afternoon I called upon Cuz Fo; made a visit to the Percivals and Lady Westmoreland, who is confined with the gout.

Coming out from her house, as soon as I got into my chair, the chairmen fairly overturned it,—*fairly* I may say, for not a glass was broken nor was I the least hurt; I own I was a little terrified, and Lord Westmoreland hearing a bustle at the door, *found me topsy turvy.* He insisted on my getting out of my chair, which I did, drank a glass of water, sat half an hour in his library, and went on to Lady Frances Carteret; found her at home ill of a cold; she enquired much after you and your fine children: we are to dine there on Friday next. Today we dine in Bond Street, to-morrow at Mrs. Vesey's. Miss Granville went with us to the Birthday in a white satin with brocaded flowers, and my brother's present of

---

[1] Alicia, daughter of George, 2nd Lord Carpenter, married first, Charles, 1st Earl of Egremont, who died 21st August, 1763, and secondly, Count Bruhl, Minister from Saxony. She was Lady of the Bedchamber to Queen Charlotte.

[2] John, 2nd Viscount Bateman, succeeded his father in 1744. He was Master of the Buckhounds, and M.P for Woodstock.

a Brussels laced head, and I hope my Lord Weymouth will add another hundred pounds a year to her income, and then she will be in very easy circumstances.

Poor Mrs. Littleton,[1] has left a most disconsolate mother, and an afflicted husband; she was happy in this world, according to our notion of happiness, and was an agreeable and deserving woman, which makes her much lamented. My concern is for the unhappy survivors, for I hope she has found a more certain and more glorious happiness than can be our portion here, but they have lost that which cannot be made up to them in this world. Her own great imprudence it is thought occasioned her death.

Lord North has been here twice, and I have most unluckily been abroad. Master Brownlow[2] has had the small pox, and Miss Charlotte is inoculated from him, so that at present he is shut up from many of his acquaintance. I hope now the bustle of the Birthday is over I shall have leisure to spend more time with her than I have.

Just as I came to this place, in came Mr. Handel, and he has prevented my adding any more. Violet's kindest compliments: she is a very agreeable person in the house. The Maid of Honour was so fatigued at the ball, that as soon as she had danced her minuets she fainted away, but she is now well again. "The Allegro" is a *drawing*, I have imagined in imitation of Mr. Handel's *Let me wander*, etc., and I have brought in all the images as well as I could. "The Penseroso" is in embryo.

---

[1] Lucy, daughter of Hugh Fortescue, Esq., of Filleigh, county Devon, who died January 19, 1747, and wife of Mr. Lyttelton, who succeeded his father in the baronetcy, 1751.

[2] Brownlow, son of Lord North by his second wife, Elizabeth, daughter of Sir Arthur Kaye. He was born July 17, 1741, and was successively Bishop of Lichfield, of Worcester, and of Winchester, and died July 12, 1820.

to a barrel of oysters of Billingsgate, Mrs. *Swift of Fleet Street*, Mrs. *Parsons of Bishopgate Street*, Mrs. *Plummer in Leadenhall Street*, Mrs. *Selwine in Sackvile Street*. At first she could not tell what to make of such a *rigmy-role*, but at last fixed it on Greene and the Duke.

Sir Charles Mordaunt[1] made me a visit the day before yesterday; he says his daughters are to be in town next month. Mr. Stanley and twenty fiddle faddles have turmoiled me all the morning; but I must tell you before I conclude that I have got a provision *I hope* for Mrs. Drake. Poor Mrs. C. is to be boarded in the country, and as the Duchess of Portland wanted some trusty person to attend her, I thought of Mrs. Drake, and wrote to my mother to know if Mrs. D. would undertake it for twelve pounds a year, which she does readily, and is much pleased at the provision. Mrs. C. is never outrageous; it may rather be called a total loss of memory than madness, though she is as incapable of doing anything for herself, as if she was in the strongest frenzy.

A period of four months ensues after this letter; and the next date is Chester, in May of the same year, when the Dean of Down and Mrs. Delany were once more on their way to Ireland.

Mrs. Delany to Mrs. Dewes, at Welsbourne.

Chester, Sunday, half-an-hour after eleven, (*May*.)

Had our wheels been as heavy as my heart when I left Welsbourne we should have made a tedious journey.

---

[1] Sir Charles Mordaunt, of Massingham in Norfolk, the 6th Baronet of the family. He was member for the county of Warwick, and died in 1778. His first wife was a daughter of Sir John Conyers, by whom he had two daughters; he married secondly, in 1730, Sophia, only daughter of Sir John Wodehouse, by whom he had two sons, John, who succeeded him, and Charles.

mob under your chin if you please. Scotch caps are all the mode and worn by all ages; they are put on with a couple of pins, and that is a great recommendation for any dress.

Last Saturday I went to the play; it was the Funeral,[1] which I think an entertaining play, and the new farce of Miss in her Teens,[2] composed by Garrick; *nothing can be lower*, but the part he acts in it himself (Mr. Fribble) he makes so very ridiculous that it is really entertaining. It is said he mimics *eleven* men of fashion—Lord Bate—n, Ld Her—y, Felton Her—y, some others you don't know, and our friend Dicky Bate—n, I must own the latter is a *striking likeness*; but do not name to any body these people, for I don't love to spread such tattle, though I send it for your private amusement, and that you may not be ignorant of the ways of this world. I went with the Duchess of Portland, who is very well, and charged me with her "kind love to Pip." Sunday dined at Whitehall, and met my brother in the afternoon. Yesterday went to Sir Luke Schaub's to see his pictures, which are now in better order than when I was in England before; he has got a very good house in Old Bond Street. In the afternoon I was engaged to Lady Mary Colley, to meet Mrs. Donnellan and Clayton; to-day they dine with me, and I stay at home the rest of the day.

The Duchess of Portland was saying one day no one had invited her to a drum, upon which I sent her ten cards in feigned hands,—from *Mrs. Guzzle in Swallow Street, Mrs. May of Bloomsbury, Mrs. Winter of Snow-hill, Mrs. Alestub of Brewer's Street, Mrs. Sprat*

---

[1] The Funeral, or Grief à-la-mode, a comedy, by Sir Richard Steele.
[2] Miss in her Teens, a farce, by Garrick; produced in Dublin during his second visit to Ireland.

to a barrel of oysters of *Billingsgate*, *Mrs. Swift of Fleet Street, Mrs. Parsons of Bishopsgate Street, Mrs. Plummer in Leadenhall Street. Mrs. Selwine in Sackville Street.* At first she could not tell what to make of such a *rig-my-role*, but at last fixed it on Greene and the Duke.

Sir Charles Mordaunt[1] made me a visit the day before yesterday; he says his daughters are to be in town next month. Mr. Stanley and twenty fiddle faddles have turmoiled me all the morning: but I must tell you before I conclude that I have got a provision *I hope* for Mrs. Drake. Poor Mrs. C. is to be boarded in the country, and as the Duchess of Portland wanted some trusty person to attend her, I thought of Mrs. Drake, and wrote to my mother to know if Mrs. D. would undertake it for twelve pounds a year, which she does readily, and is much pleased at the provision. Mrs. C. is never outrageous; it may rather be called a total loss of memory than madness, though she is as incapable of doing anything for herself, as if she was in the strongest frenzy.

A period of four months ensues after this letter; and the next date is Chester, in May of the same year, when the Dean of Down and Mrs. Delany were once more on their way to Ireland.

Mrs. Delany to Mrs. Dewes, at Welsbourne.

Chester, Sunday, half-an-hour after eleven, (*May*.)

Had our wheels been as heavy as my heart when I left Welsbourne we should have made a tedious journey.

---

[1] Sir Charles Mordaunt, of Massingham in Norfolk, the 6th Baronet of the family. He was member for the county of Warwick, and died in 1778. His first wife was a daughter of Sir John Conyers, by whom he had two daughters; he married secondly, in 1730, Sophia, only daughter of Sir John Wodehouse, by whom he had two sons, John, who succeeded him, and Charles.

So many tender attachments as I have there makes such a separation very severe; but in our stages through this world we must feel the alternatives of grief and joy. To leave a friend one loves must at all times be most painful; if anything can render it less so it is the consolation of such a friend as bears me company, who *not only* thinks it reasonable for me to grieve for leaving inestimable friends, but *himself* sincerely *grieves too*.

He is gone to church, and by mistake I am not; they neglected bringing me word, as D.D. ordered them, when the bell rung, and I am now too late. We arrived on Friday at Castle Brumidge between ten and eleven, through excessively bad roads; there dined on bacon and eggs, roast fowl and broiled fowl, I swallowed meat and drink and *something else*, for *few, very few words passed*.

Next day (which was yesterday) dined at Newport, lay at Whitchurch: could we have met with a fresh set of horses there, had come on to Chester to avoid travelling on Sunday; but the perverseness of our coachman was such that he would neither be ready early enough any morning nor go one mile further. Thank God we arrived here at ten this morning safe and well, without any bad accident, but the obstinate surliness of our coachman. Mr. Coles has used us ill, and pray let him know it; two of the horses were too young to work, and the man that rode postilion had never been postilion in his life. Mr. Lawe with our pair of mares made as much expedition as we did. I have promised the coachman if he delivers this letter, or sends it to you as soon as he returns, that you would give him something. Lady Kildare did not go till last Thursday, the wind being contrary; the yacht is expected in this tide, and in all probability we shall set sail to-morrow morning. Dr. Cobden and his lady are gone in a ship they found ready; they *drove* themselves from London to Chester, and left their maid to come in the stage coach with their portmanteau! The maid is come, but no portmanteau, she swears it was delivered to the stage coachman, the man swears he did not receive it, the trunk can't be heard of yet, and if not found the man will be sent to Newgate. It is really a vexatious affair. All our things are safely arrived. I left word with Betty Smith that, upon second thoughts, I would not have Lord Sandwich[1] sent in less time than a fortnight; it had best be thoroughly dry.

We are to dine at 1, and at 3 set out for Park Gate; by that time I hope we shall have some account of the yacht—I will not seal my letter till then. D.D. is clearly of opinion we might have performed our journey to Chester in two days with ease had the horses been such as Mr. Cole promised him they should; or even as *they were* had he not expressly commanded the coachman to the contrary. I believe there never was born so provoking a man as the coachman, but thank God we have done with him, and are safe at Park Gate. I send this by the postilion, who seems to be the honester man of the two. Adieu, my most dear sister, the yacht is not yet returned, and not expected till to-morrow afternoon: I shall not be sorry to rest a day. We have a quiet clean lodging, and are both very well.

---

[1] One of Mrs. Delany's paintings.

Mrs. Delany to Mrs. Dewes.

Park Gate, 19 May, 1747.

'Tis cruel my dearest sister to have lost so many precious hours; for *here we are still*, and *may be some days longer*, as the yacht by accounts this morning had not sailed out of the Bay of Dublin yesterday, and the wind is now against her; but we could not foretell that, for had the wind been favourable, the yacht had waited for us, instead of our waiting for her; we keep up our spirits as well as our present disagreeable circumstances will allow: I compare it with what I suffered when I was last going to Ireland, and think myself happy. D.D. reads to me whilst I work cross-stitch, or cut letters,[1] and exerts his good-humoured cheerfulness to keep up my spirits. We walk out twice or thrice a-day. Park Gate consists of about 50 or 60 houses in an irregular line by the water side; the river Dee runs from Chester, but is not navigable farther than to this place. A few ships lie before us, and continually people passing and repassing, which is some amusement. The strand opposite to this house is about four miles over, and on the other side is a large tract of mountainous land, (Flintshire,) but very rich and finely cultivated. The fields behind the houses are pleasant to walk in, but the strand before the houses rough

---

[1] Almost every thing Mrs. Delany did is marked with her cypher, and in innumerable instances cut out in coloured paper. The "*letters*" here alluded to are probably cyphers to be used when wanted. On one occasion, while waiting a long time for fair weather to embark at Park Gate, and having exhausted her materials for employment, she saw a painter going to repaint the sign of the inn; she immediately proposed to pay him the price he was to receive, and to do it for him, which she did with his paints and brushes. Mrs. Delany related this story herself to the Editor's mother; the sign was (she believed) a Swan.

and stony. *What rare amusement should I have* did it produce any shells! but alas here are none but ordinary dirty cockles and mussels. About a mile off is a little village called Nesson; we walked to it yesterday in search of adventures, but met with none; came home at nine hungry to our supper, and slept very well after it. Our books are almost read through, and I am afraid we shall not meet with any in our neighbourhood, except the minister of our parish will be so charitable as to supply us. He is to make us a visit this afternoon, and perhaps his wife will also come, his name is Mapletoft.

In our walks this morning we were much amused in finding a variety of fine caterpillars, but I can't say any uncommon sorts except one, which some inhuman foot had crushed to death, with a head as green as an emerald, and the body shades of browns and gold colour. Another great pleasure to us, was hearing and watching the lark singing, as he soared, hovering, wavering, and fluttering from side to side as he varied his strains, and at last dropped down to the grass to meet his mate. How many natural and exquisite delights daily poured down on us from heaven, are daily lost upon us for want of a leisure moment to attend to them, or a heart sufficiently grateful to acknowledge them, of which this instance of the lark is at once a fine emblem and proof.

I think now I have given you a true and exact account how we are situated, and how we have past our time.

Mrs. Delany to Mrs. Dewes.

Delville, 26 May, 1747.

I hope my dearest sister has received all my letters regularly, and then she knows that we have had (I thank God) a very good journey and safe voyage, and are arrived at our own dear villa; where if I could be so happy as to receive and entertain those friends that have so kindly received and entertained me in England, I could not envy (were I the most envious of creatures) any being upon earth. But I must not indulge a thought so much out of my power; I will endeavour to be thankful for the blessings I enjoy, fully convinced how unworthy I am of them, and not presume to think I have any pretensions to be possessed of more.

Your most welcome letter of the 15th May gave me very different sensations of pain and pleasure; every little sentiment and circumstance was delightful to a heart so affectionately devoted to you as mine is. Your visit to the nursery, the manner of the children's accosting you, your going to my room and closet, all that I had formed to myself, and followed you step by step! I feel the truth of what you say, that we "ought to make our friendship *contribute to our happiness, and not our woe*;" and since we must be separated, let us make that distressful circumstance as light as we can, by communicating our thoughts and manner of life; when we cannot purchase an original, we must content ourselves with the best copy we can get. Apropos, all my pictures, china, &c., have come safe and well, and I don't doubt but those that you have taken care to send after

me, will do the same, I hope when you opened my box you looked at the plants and birds.

Lady Sarah Cowper's letter touched me extremely; I have returned it to you. I don't know what to make of her disorder, and think it must be much increased to confine her all the summer in town. Don't send Lord Sandwich till quite dry.

We were invited to dine on Friday with the Fordes, and went, and in the evening I called upon the two Mrs. Hamiltons and Miss Forth, and found all well. But Mrs. Forth Hamilton is now under an anxiety I am sure you will feel for—her two children were inoculated last Friday morning. I hope they will do well, and that joy may restore her to a happy state she has not known for some time.[1] Saturday I spent at home unpacking and beginning to settle. We had the pleasure of finding house and gardens in perfect beauty; and Mr. Greene has added three beautiful young deer to my stock with a milk white face; my swan is well; Tiger knew me, and I have a very fine thriving colt and calf. On Sunday went to church, had a table-full of old acquaintance, in the afternoon went to church again, and found ladies at home on my return. I have breakfasted and drank tea in an afternoon in my garden twice; *Pearly Bower* in high beauty, and I have not failed paying my daily homage to it. The robins have *not* yet welcomed us, but one chaffinch has, and hops after us wherever we go. Yesterday Mrs. F. Hamilton walked here by 8 clock and

---

[1] It must be remembered that inoculation for small pox was at this time resorted to partially and often ended fatally; and the misery that parents endured in deciding upon having it done, may well be imagined, although aware it was giving their children a greater chance of life than if caught naturally.

staid till 2, and my Mrs. Hamilton spent the greatest part of the morning with me. I had company all the afternoon—people you don't know, so that I have not had a quiet day since I came home. Bushe desires her *baisemains*. As soon as I get my receipt-book I will send you the isinglass cement.

Mrs. Delany to Mrs. Dewes.

Delville, 6 June, 1747.

The drawing-box and book and everything contained therein are arrived safe, even to the very nightcaps. I have been so lucky in my journey home, as not to have had anything the least rubbed, broken, or damaged. I suppose you *looked* at my Lady Abbess?[1] It is really like, though by no means a good likeness. It was prettily and kindly done; but how without a magical wand it could be so soon finished I cannot conceive.

I am glad you have got the letter from Park Gate, with the verses; the race of coachmen and postilions are a faithless generation; never more shall we bring coach or horses over. They are a great expense, and the damage they receive by the voyage, and the *great trouble* attending them at the *Custom house* is so teazing, that I should never wish to be so embarrassed again in a country where those conveniences *can be had* for money. I thank God the Dean and I have been perfectly well since we came home, and have enjoyed the sweets and sunshine of Delville as much as some rainy days and a great deal of company would permit. Yesterday we spent the whole

---

[1] Honourable A. Granville.

day (but an hour at dinner, and that was partly) in the garden, for our *kitchen-grate was down*, and a new one putting up, stoves making, and a boiler placing, so that we could have nothing conveniently drest at home: we sent our mutton and chicken to Mr. Barber's house at the end of the garden, and had it drest in his kitchen, and eat it in his dining-room, which looks into Carlingford garden. His wife and children are gone further into the country for a little while. Mr. Barber came home when we had half dined, in a great hurry, to burn some of his enamels, little thinking to find his house full of company, which occasioned some mirth amongst us. As soon as we had dined we adjourned to the Beggar's Hut, and had coffee there. Just as it was over, Mrs. Clayton called on me to go to Lady Orrery's,[1] who lives about half a mile from hence; she was not at home; we returned to Delville, and drank tea in the garden.

You are very kind in inquiring after Smith; she was very sick at sea, but well again as soon as landed; she is much delighted with Delville, and (as much as she has seen) with Ireland. *She* and *my housekeeper* take to one another extremely; and I hope I am now settled with honest quiet domestics. Fribble behaves himself very well, and Thomas will make I believe, in time, a very good butler. I should have mentioned to you my pretty birthday present before but that I thought D.D. had told you what it was. It was a pair of 3-drop amethyst earrings, set round with diamonds: I shall wear them on Tuesday next, (the *9th of June,*) with the pearl necklace; we have invited all our good friends,

---

[1] Margaret, daughter and sole heir of John Hamilton, of Caledon, Esq., was the second wife of John, 5th Earl of Orrery.

the Barbers and Mr. and Mrs. Greene, to make merry with us that day, and have got my pretty ninepin alley in order for their entertainment. I wish poor Dowager Barber could make one amongst us; but alas! she scarcely ever rises out of her bed, though I think on the whole she looks and is better than when I left her last year.

Mrs. F. Hamilton's children are in a very fair way. Bushe is gone to spend the day with them, and we dine with Mr. and Mrs. Lawe. I made yours and Mr. Dewes's compliments to him, and he begs a thousand acknowledgements to you for all favours, particularly the meath,[1] which was of great service to him. I am much obliged to Miss Holyoak for her kind remembrance of me.

The Fables were bought of Mr. Dodsley in Pall Mall; he won't scruple changing one of the volumes I am sure. Miss P.[2] was married at St. James's Chapel, as you know by this, on the 20th of May. So now, adieu. Did I not tell you I had hopes of having *my* Mrs. Hamilton with me for ten days or a fortnight, whilst her house is new painting? D.D. talks of going to the North soon: and if he does not stay long I shall be glad to be excused the journey.

Mrs. Delany to Mrs. Dewes.

Delville, 13 June, 1747.

I must begin this letter with making an apology for D.D's negligence of the enclosed letter, which he supposes (for he has quite forgot) was given him at Gloucester for my mother, and the short stay he made at

---

[1] Query mead.
[2] Mary, daughter of Brigadier-General Price, married, in May, 1747, the Honble. and Revd. Edward Townshend, fifth son of Charles, 2nd Viscount Townshend.

Welsbourne and the hurry he was in made him not recollect it at a proper time. He asks my mother a thousand pardons, and hopes you will intercede for him, and present his and my humble duty.

It was a great pleasure to me to hear of my brother's being with you, and of his being well; I have not heard from him since I came to Ireland. I don't wonder he was pleased with Wroxton, his good taste must make him like it; but if he only breakfasted there, he could not have time to see all its beauties.

I am glad Mr. Dewes wedding[1] is over, and his trouble and care at an end. I had a letter from Cuz Foley two packets ago, with an account of Father Foley's being in a dangerous way; I imagine by this, he is either dead or recovered, for he could not last long in the way he was in when she wrote; she gave an account of his illness with her usual good-nature, and seemed to be much affected with the melancholy scene. I pity poor Miss Foley, though I believe the old gentleman's peevishness, which has *so grown upon him of late*, will make his death less grievous. Mrs. Worsenham[2] was grown weary of the tedious winters at Stoke, and has taken a house at Worcester, which I think is a lucky circumstance. *My* Mrs. Hamilton has promised to spend a fortnight with me here. I believe she will come to me the week after next. Pray have you been with Lady Anne Coventry and given her the vase. I am to-day to have the Bishop of Clogher, Mrs. C. and niece, Mr. Donnellan, his lady and daughters, Mr. and Mrs. Marley. Bushe is with me, and Mr. and Mrs. Greene; and we are to have in the evening

---

[1] This must have been the wedding of a ward of Mr. Dewes.
[2] Query Mrs. Wolstenholme, mother of Mr. Foley's third wife.

a large party at nine pins. I have made my alley very spruce, and sown in the borders some of the flower-seeds I brought with me from Welsbourne.

And now I have a sad tale to tell you. My fine cow, who had just brought me a fine calf, died yesterday, just in the same manner as Fair Face; she was well at seven in the morning and grazing, and before eight, she was found fallen into a ditch, and died before night, very much swelled. The wise folks think it was some poisonous thing that she had eaten; we had her buried, skin and all, and her skin cut cross and cross, that nobody might be tempted to dig her up. I hope it was nothing infectious, for thank God this country has hitherto escaped the sickness among the cattle.

Last Wednesday the Archbishop of Dublin, Dr. Cobbe,[1] and Mrs. Cobbe, Mr. and Mrs. McAulay, dined here, and on Thursday we dined at McAulays.

D.D. hath been engaged these three days past to hear the examinations at the college for fellowships, which they say are the most learned of all the university examinations. I have not yet been able to settle to painting; I propose beginning next Wednesday, but I have a terrible long train of visits to return. Yesterday in the afternoon, in the midst of the broiling sun, I left my shady *Pearly Bower* to make visits. What a mortification! but civilities must be paid, and something given up to support society.

Yesterday morning I for the first day since I came worked four hours at *my Quilt*, and Mr. Greene read to us. Bushe painted, and Mrs. Greene made a night-gown

---

[1] Charles Cobbe, Archbishop of Dublin from 1742 to 1765. He was previously Bishop of Kildare.

for the little boy. One day next week we are to go a house-warming to her. Mantua-makers and housekeeper, &c., call me away.

I suppose you have seen Mr. Littleton's[1] verses on his wife, but least you should not, I add them, for I think them very pretty *and just*.

> Made to engage all hearts, to charm all eyes,
> Though weak magnanimous, though witty wise,
> Polite as all her life in courts had been,
> Yet good as she the world had never seen.
> The nobler fire of an exalted mind
> With gentlest female tenderness combin'd.
> Her speech, was the melodious voice of love,
> Her song the warbling of the vernal grove,
> Her eloquence was sweeter than her song,
> Soft as her heart and as her virtue strong.
> Her form the beauty of her mind express'd,
> Her mind was Virtue by the Graces drest.

If you have not read his letter to Mr. Gilbert West on St. Paul's Conversion, I beg you will, it is one of the finest things I ever read in my life.

Mrs. Delany to Mrs. Dewes, at Welsbourne.

Delville, 20 June, 1747.

How my vagabond letter came to be put into the Maidstone bag instead of the Kineton, I can't imagine.

---

[1] George, the eldest son of Sir Thomas Lyttelton, of Hagley, in Worcestershire, was born in 1709. In 1741, he married Miss Lucy Fortescue. On her death, about five years afterwards, he wrote a monody, considered the best of his poetical productions. In 1747 he gave the world his Observations on the Conversion of St. Paul. He wrote also *Dialogues of the Dead, History of Henry II.*, &c. Mr. Lyttelton held many important offices in the Government, and was created Lord Lyttelton, November, 1757. He died August 22, 1773.

I am glad at last it was so fortunate as to find a safe harbour.

I am very glad my brother hath made the tour of your neighbourhood, it is a very pleasant one. But you have not named Sir Charles Mordaunt, which makes me fear he is not yet well enough to come home. I am very sorry Mr. Sherwood has had a return of his disorder. I trust, without my making frequent repetition of ye same, you will do me and D.D. justice with all your neighbours. Poor Mr. Fortescue's death was very shocking. I am sorry Mr. Dewes has had so many interruptions and calls from his own home; I suppose he will be obliged to go to London soon.

Last Sunday I spent at home, as I generally do. In the afternoon came some ladies of the neighbourhood, and Dowager Lady Kildare; on Monday Bushe and I made visits in Dublin, furiously drest out in all our airs! I caught a little cold, and kept at home quietly all Tuesday; four gentlemen of the college came and dined here, and not one day have I yet sat down to dinner with a less addition. On Wednesday two friends of Bushe's, and old acquaintances of mine dined here—Mrs. Preston and Mrs. Dillon, two sisters, and two young she Dillons. Mrs. Dillon went by the name of "*Beauty divine*" when I came first to Ireland; fifteen years have faded her bloom, but not ruffled the sweetness of her countenance, which is still pretty. Mrs. Preston is plain in her person, but a sensible, friendly, good woman; I have promised to make her a visit of a few days this summer when D.D. returns, it lies in his road from the North, and I shall meet him there. On Thursday morning I painted. I am now copying " Lady Johanna Thornhill," and have King Charles 1st *again* to copy for D.D., and the promise of a fine one from our Lord Primate;[1] he and his sister Mrs. Stone, and the Bishop of Derry,[2] and Mrs. Barnard, (another sister of the Primate's) dine here to-day. *You love a bill of fare,* and here it is.

First Course.		Second Course.	
Fish.		Turkey Pout.	
		Salmon Grilde.	Pick. Sal. and Quails.
Beef-steaks.	Rabbits. Soup. and Onions.	Little Terrene Peas. Apple Pye.	Cream. Mush-rooms.	Terrene.
Fillet Veal.		Crab.	Leveret. Cheesecakes.
		Dessert.	
	Blamange.	Raspberries and Cream.	Almond Cream.
	Cherries.	Sweetmeats and Jelly.	Currant and Gooseberries.
	Dutch Cheese.	Strawberries and Cream.	Orange Butter.

I have scratched it out very awkwardly, and hope the servants will place my dinner and dessert better on the table than I have on paper. I give as *little hot meat* as possible, but I think there could not be less, considering the grandees that are to be here: the invitation was "to *beef stakes,*" which we are famous for. Thursday afternoon produced a visit from the Duchess of Manchester,[3] Miss Hervey, and Mr. Phipps. The Duchess, I think, looks just as she has done for ten years—a fine figure, well drest, speaks little, but rather easier, and more than she used to do. Various conjectures were made about Miss Hervey's looks; she was pretty, but pale and wan, 'tis thought she is married, though it is kept a secret. Has not

---

[1] George Stone, Primate of Ireland, Archbishop of Armagh from 1747 to 1765. He was previously Bishop of Derry.

[2] William Barnard, Bishop of Derry from 1747 to 1768.

[3] Robert, 3rd Duke of Manchester, married Harriet, daughter and co-heir of Edmund Dunch, Esq.

the Duchess of Queensberry's appearing again at Court surprized you? I suppose it was to thank the King for giving her son leave to raise a regiment in Scotland? I have sent your ring by Mrs. Dillon, who sets sail to-morrow for England, directed to Mrs. Donnellan, and have desired her to give it Mr. Dewes if in town, or send it to Mr. Clifton. I hope you will have it safe. I would not have such rare favours lost.

Yesterday we spent a very pleasant day in the country with Mr. and Mrs. Lawe at their bleach yard, 9 miles off, near the famous salmon leap of Leixlip.[1] They have a pretty cabin there, and gave us some fine trout caught out of their own brook just at their door, that were excellent, and many other good things. I wished you there, it was so new a scene; and the men at work laying out the cloth, &c., on the grass full in our view was very pretty; the machine for rinsing the clothes is very curious. The happiness and good humour of the Master and Mistress, and the industry going forward was an agreeable and rational entertainment. Mr. Lawe drank your health, and talks every time I see him of your civility and your charming children. As we returned home we called at Mr. Conolly's house at Leixlip, and walked in his gardens; they are on the top of a hill that winds round the river Liffy, laid out into fine large grass walks well planted, and set with all sort of forest trees

---

[1] Leixlip Castle was erected by Adam Fitz Hereford, one of the Anglo-Norman conquerors. Its antique towers, mantled with ivy, rise above the surrounding trees and river. Immediately adjoining Leixlip is the salmon leap, where the Liffey, falling over a ledge of rocks, forms a beautiful cascade, up which the fish at certain seasons are seen to spring. The tower of Leixlip is in the county of Kildare, and situated on the river Liffey, about ten miles from Dublin. Near Leixlip is Celbridge, where Vanessa died.

and flowering shrubs; openings here and there that show the river so far below you that it is almost horrible. A winding path and steps by degrees carry you down to a winding terrace by the river side above a mile long; every step there shows you some new wild beauty of wood, rocks, and cascades.

Mrs. Delany to Mrs. Dewes.

(*Believed to be July* 11*th*) 1747.

How negligent and forgetful was I not to send Mr. Dewes the above note before, and now I suppose he is in London. My mother is *very good* in forgiving the Dean for keeping Miss Viney's letter so long; he is thoroughly sensible of all her indulgence to him, and we both beg our most affectionate duty.

I suppose there will (till privilege of Parliament comes in again) be a general stagnation of correspondency. For my own part I write to no body for *constant* but to *you* and the *Duchess of Portland* and *Donnellan.* I had a letter last post from Cuz Fo., and find Father Foley is much better. I am much obliged to my dear little Court for desiring I should have Finch, but to *make him easy* pray let him know I have got two cows still. I thank you, my dear, for your good accounts of *Pauline*, but I am better pleased to hear of her sense and sprightliness than of her *beauty*; though I hope she will not want as much of that as is necessary to give a *pleasing impression—not* a rapturous one, for that may prove more to her *unhappiness* than *happiness*. How can that strange Sir H. persist in his unreasonable design on the fair Catherine? His excuse is dotage! I hear a very good account of Mrs.

Lambert, the Duchess of Portland has been there and much pleased with their behaviour to one another. How goes on Mr. Dewes's *daughter*[1] *with her marriage?* We are very busy in settling all my drawers of shells, sorting and cleaning them. I have a new cabinet with whole glass doors and glass on the side and shelves within, of whimsical shapes, to hold *all my beauties.* One large drawer underneath for the register drawer, and my little chest of drawers I have placed in my closet within my bedchamber, from whence I send you this letter. How blest should I be could we have a tête-à-tête in it with you! it is calculated for that purpose, being retired from all interruption and eaves-droppers. On Monday next we dine at the Primate's and in the afternoon I shall visit grandees (so that will be a whole day lost) with Mrs. Hamilton, which I cannot help. The Dean goes away for a month at least; he has just bought a pair of mares, young and good serviceable animals, but not so handsome as Jackson and Nancy.

I have written to Lady Sarah Cowper, but have not heard; writing is I fear troublesome to her, for which reason I will be moderate in my demands on her. She used to write to me once a month, but now I would compound for once a quarter; she has starved me into that compliance.

An interval here occurs in the correspondence, which is accounted for by the death of Mrs. Granville, whose illness must have been very short, if indeed she had any illness, as she died in August, and Mrs. Delany sends a message to her mother in the above letter, without the slightest allusion to any indisposition. Mrs. Delany and

---

[1] "*Mr. Dewes's daughter*" must have been a goddaughter, and ward of Mr. Dewes.

Mrs. Dewes were so devotedly attached to Mrs. Granville, that the letters which passed must have been very painful on this occasion; and it is most probable that finding on re-perusal they only renewed their grief, that both sisters destroyed them. The oral tradition which must be authentic (as it came immediately from Mrs. Delany herself to the Editor's mother) is that Mrs. Granville died on her knees in the *act of saying her prayers*, and that she had often expressed her wish that she might thus die; the stool at which she was kneeling is still preserved, and Mrs. Delany said it was always used by her mother for that purpose. It is high, the legs are black like ebony, of a curious ancient form, and it is covered with needle-work, the pattern of which is still perceptible. The letters of Mrs. Delany which are preserved *recommence* two months after Mrs. Granville's death, and for some time are more a diary than a correspondence; but as they contain an exact picture of her daily life in Ireland with her associates there, and are intermingled with records of circumstances, they could not be omitted without destroying so many of the links in the chain of her existence as would frustrate the object of this work, which is to trace her from her earliest years to her death under all the varied scenes in which she so admirably adapted herself to the duties of the present time, enjoying to the uttermost everything in her power that could worthily be enjoyed, and contributing to the happiness of all around her. The following diary (letters) will therefore follow in their proper order.

Mrs. Delany to Mrs. Dewes.

Delville, 6 Oct., 1747.

I have had the joy and satisfaction of hearing you had passed your ninth day very well, and I am much obliged to your kind nurse, Miss Nancy Viney, for the good account she sent me.[1] The morning has been fair, and

---

[1] It appears, from this acknowledgment of a letter from Miss N. Viney, that Mrs. Dewes was at Gloucester, where she must have remained after her mother's funeral for her own confinement.

ANN GRANVILLE,

Mother of M.rs Delany.

painting; I should have done it this, but poor Mrs. Barber was so very ill, Mrs. Nuens[1] could not leave her. I have had an account from Mrs. Kena, at Chester, of her having sent on board one of our merchant-ships the case with Lord Sandwich's picture.

We are going to be very busy in settling the library. The Dean has made an addition at the end of it of a sort of closet, to which you ascend by one step; it opens with an arch, five foot and a-half wide; there is to be a window at the end which is east, and on the south side, opposite to the south window, there is to be looking-glass representing a sash window, which will reflect the prospect, and prevent the cold of the north: it is to be all stucco, and adorned with pilasters, a table in the middle for writing and holding papers, and only convenient room left for going round it and for seats. The old part of the library is 32 feet long, and about 11 wide; it holds a great many books, and when finished will be very pleasant; the prospect from the new window charming. How often shall I wish for you to help me to settle the books—an employment you always were fond of; here you would meet some that would amuse you very well. The addition is 12 ft. square.

Have you ever met with Mons[r] Saurin's[2] History of the Bible, with cuts done by Picart, Houbraken, and others; it is esteemed a very learned and curious book. I never saw it till last week that I found it in the library,

---

[1] Mrs. Nuens used to grind Mrs. Delany's colours.
[2] James Saurin, a very celebrated preacher, born at Nismes, 1677, died 1730. He published several works; amongst others, Discourses, Historical, Critical, and Moral, on the most Memorable Events of the Old and New Testament: Haye, 1735-39. 6 vols., fol. There is also an edition in 11 vols., 8vo.

but the cuts are not so fine nor so laborious as those in Physique Sacré.

Do you remember the story of Madame de Gondez?[1] I have been reading it again lately, and am extremely pleased: what a fine delicate character is Disenteuils! 'tis a story that furnishes a winter's evening conference very agreeably, the many pretty and uncommon characters that are in it, and the charming sentiments. The Fairy Tales (of which we have borrowed eight volumes) have their share of entertaining us. Don't you think we are well occupied? The mind is sometimes not disposed to attend to things of consequence, and may be amused by trifles.

Miss Bushe desires particular compliments; Miss M. Hamilton desires I will let Master Dewes know she will answer his letter; she has (she thinks) written a first copy of a very good one, but her mama thought fit to burn it, and she is afraid she shall "never write so good a one again."

Mrs. Delany to Mrs. Dewes, at Gloucester.

Delville, 13 Oct, 1747.

I am very sorry good Mr. Dewes should have anything to disturb and distress him, and in the infirm way Mr. Dewes is in, I should fear a fever might be fatal. Where is *Mrs. Holyock*[2] *and her daughter?* I am glad the little Bevil is well, and the rest of your fair flock. Miss

---

[1] La Comtesse de Gondez, 1727, by Margaret de Lussau, a romance writer of some eminence, born in France 1682, died 1758.

[2] Mary, the only sister of Mr. Dewes, married, John Holyoake, of Morton Bagot, Esq, in the county of Warwick.

Viney I reckon has been very happy in having her uncle with her. The Bishop of Clogher and Mrs. Clayton are come to town; I went to see them yesterday morning.

Yesterday Dr. Carmichael,[1] the Bishop of Down[2] and his sister, dined here; Dr. Car. and his lady are two good-humoured prating people, who were in raptures with Delville; they gave me a long account of my *sister Granville*,[3] who lives within two miles of them in Buckinghamshire, she is very well, fat, and handsome. Her mother and brother Dick Rose are dead, Tom just married, and they give him the character of a very honest good humoured man, his sister lives with him, and is neither "*mad*" nor "*married*," though *both were reported of her*. I will send you two pounds of knitting thread the first opportunity; I hope the pictures from *Newenham* to Dublin will come safe. I suppose my brother will mourn the *old mourning, I shall*, as I am at such a distance; I have put my own maid and housekeeper into mourning, and D.D. has put his own servant out of livery into mourning, though it is not now a general fashion, but as it is a mark of respect D.D. thought it right to do so, and we are now of a time of life to indulge the *dictates of the heart* more than the *reigning fashions*.

I shall *pity poor Mrs. Viney extremely* when you leave Gloucester, and that house desolated that has been so great

---

[1] Dr. William Carmichael, second son of James, 2nd Earl of Hyndford. Dr. Carmichael was appointed Archdeacon of Bucks in 1742. He married in August 1734, Mrs. Godschall.

[2] Dr. John Ryder, Bishop of Down from 1743 to 1752, when he was promoted to the Archbishopric of Tuam, and died 1775.

[3] The widow of her brother Bevil, whose marriage has never been alluded to in any letter in the Editor's possession, and which marriage was undoubtedly against the consent of the family; all that is known is that her name was *Rose*.

a comfort to her, it *will be sad*; and I own I feel my tenderness towards her greatly increased since the mutual loss we have had. I wish Sir Anthony may be prevailed on to do something for *poor Patty*.[1] I used to allow her one guinea a year I will now allow her two. Mr. Wise,[2] I believe, is in easy circumstances enough.

Mrs. Delany to Mrs. Dewes.

Delville, 20 Oct. 1747.

I was not at all surprized with the account your last letter brought me, for as soon as I heard of your Mr. Dewes's being sent for I thought it most likely it should end as it has done. I am truly sorry for any affliction that can befall my good brother D.; though this is what he must have been prepared for, and had more reason to have expected sooner than not. The unhappy unhealthy way Mr. Dewes had been in for years, and the little comfort and enjoyment he had of this world, with the consideration of the happiness so good a man must enjoy in the next, I hope will have their due weight as soon as the first melancholy scenes are over.[3]

I am glad my brother Granville designs to go to town so soon; Calwich is too solitary in the winter for one of his turn of mind, or indeed for *any single body*. We were born for some society; it refines our manners, it keeps up our good humour, and without it we should grow

---

[1] Probably an old (Wescomb) pensioner of Mrs. Granville's.
[2] Probably an old servant of Mrs. Granville's.
[3] Court, the eldest brother of Mrs. Delany's brother-in-law, died at this period.

rusty and intractable. I suppose Sir Ed. Stan.[1] was out of town at his country-seat when you wrote to him about being gossip. If Mr. B. does not make good his promise to Miss V. he has done her a great deal of wrong: it is cruel to feed up any one with hopes and not gratify them, especially one who has a strong relish to worldly affairs.

Your account of the D. and Dss of D. is very surprizing; after so many years of love and friendship, and so many children grown up, all affectionate and fond of one another, it is a madness not to be accounted for. This morning I was delighted with seeing the rising sun as I lay in my bed, rising above a tuft of trees that face my window. Our garden is still in high beauty, our elms as green as ever, and the evergreens are in perfection. We have a great number of holly trees in our evergreen grove, and they are now full of red berries, and look very rich—Why are you not here to see them?

D.D. is going this morning to the Castle to ask the Ld Lieut^t to breakfast here; he said he designed coming, and I think it best to settle the day.

I think black bombazeen will do very well in a sack. I have one in a manteau and petticoat which I wear when in full dress, at home a dark grey poplin, and abroad, undrest, a dark grey unwatered tabby: I shall make no more dark things; after three months black silk is worn with love hood, and black glazed gloves, for three months

---

[1] Sir Edward Stanley, Bart., ancestor of Lord Stanley, of Alderley. He married Mary, only daughter of Thomas Ward, Esq., and died in 1755. Sir E. Stanley has been frequently mentioned as "*Ned Stanley*" before he succeeded his brother Sir James Stanley in 1746.

more; your mourning must be the same for Mr. Dewes of Mapleborough.[1]

I am very glad the Duchess of Leeds[2] is so well and has a son.

Mrs. Delany to Mrs. Dewes.

Delville, 28 Oct. 1747.

I hope Mr. Dewes will find all affairs well and in an easy way, and as he always shewed his brother great friendship and kindness on all occasions that he has returned it in the best manner he could. On Tuesday the Dean went to the Castle to ask my L^d L^t to name a day for breakfasting here. Thursday was named. On Wednesday we dined at the Bishop of Down's and met Dr. and Mrs. Carmichael; in the evening I went to my kind friend Mrs. Hamilton, who is as much attached to you as it is possible for one who does not know you personally.

I made but a short visit in Anne Street, from thence made formal ones, and appointed Bushe to meet me at Lady Tullamore's[3] (who keeps Wednesdays) that I might carry her home with me, for I had a mind to give her an opportunity of seeing Lord Harrington,[4] and she has for some time given up going to the Castle. Thursday very

---

[1] These directions about mourning are curious, and prove that "*grey poplin*" and "*grey unwatered tabby*" were considered deeper than black silk.

[2] Mary, daughter to Francis, Earl of Godolphin, married in 1740, to Thomas, 4th Duke of Leeds. *Their* only surviving son, Francis Godolphin, 5th Duke, was not born till the 29th January, 1751.

[3] Charles, 2nd Baron Moore, of Tullamoore, married in 1737, Hester, daughter of James Coghill, Esq.

[4] William, Earl of Harrington, Lord-Lieutenant of Ireland, September 13, 1747.

luckily proved a fine day; I had breakfast prepared in the drawing-room; the L.L^t came, with Sir John Cope[1] and the Captain of the Guard in waiting, at half an hour after eleven; the Dean met him at the street-door and I at the bottom of the stairs; when he came in the drawing-room and saw Miss Bushe, he asked me if he had ever seen that lady? I told him her name, and that her ill health would not allow her to pay her respects to him at the Castle, upon which he very politely saluted her; he seemed much pleased with the place. The Dean was in good spirits, and exerted himself to entertain him, so that it made the time pass easy and agreeably. He walked into all my rooms on that floor, commended everything, and said he must see the garden. About one we walked into the garden but Sir J. Cope whispered me and begged I would *not let him* walk much, for he had not ventured to walk at all since his coming to Ireland; he walked as far as to see the compass of the garden, and then we insisted upon his returning, which he did; when he came back we conducted him to the Minerva, and he seemed very glad of a seat. He was much amused with the medley of gimcracks that it contains, and at half an hour after two left us.

In the afternoon I carried Miss Bushe home, and brought back Mrs. Forde and her daughter. We have been under some concern for poor Rupy Barber, who has had a most desperate sore throat, but is recovered. He was two days so bad he could neither swallow, nor speak to be understood; but *fig-water* has cured him. Yester-

---

[1] Sir John Cope, Bart., M.P. for Hants in four successive parliaments, in the reigns of Queen Anne, and in that of George II. He died at Bramphill, Hants, in December, 1749.

day we dined in town with Mr. and Mrs. Preston, great friends of Bushe's. She met us there, and in the afternoon we all made a visit to Mrs. O'Hara, a clever, sprightly, little, old lady, sister to Lord Tirawley, who has his wit with the addition of a very good heart. She visited me this summer, I was not acquainted with her before. Lady Grandison and her son are well; she has now lain in a fortnight and the family are in great joy. She has had four children, and *none alive but this boy*.

This evening I go to town to make my compliments to my Lord Lieutenant for the honour he did us There hath not been a drawing-room since he was here, for last Friday (the usual Castle-day), was a festival that nothing could put by, and that always occasions a prodigious rout and confusion at the Castle—the anniversary of the Irish rebellion. There is open house kept that day, and a vast dessert, and after the dinner is over the common people are let in *to carry off all that remains* both of dinner and dessert; you may imagine what a notable scramblement it occasions.

Mrs. Delany to Mrs. Dewes.

Delville, 22 Dec., 1747.

We have a melancholy scene now before us, that has affected the Dean and me very sensibly, and I fear will you. Poor old Mrs. Barber has struggled for six weeks past with a disorder that I doubt must prove fatal to her; her children, *as they have great reason*, are in the utmost distress. Poor Myra (who is in a deplorable way) and the youngest son Lucius Barber, were entirely maintained by her and Betty Woddal, who has the care of Myra. I am sorry to send you so affecting an account of an old friend, that has given us both a great deal of pleasure, and who had truly many amiable qualities, but it is certain she will have a happy release from a painful life, which for some years past she could have no great enjoyment of.

In return for your account of Mr. Creswell I can send you two stories that will match it pretty well. One is of a young lady, youngest daughter to a Captain Johnston here, a very pretty girl just sixteen, who ran away on Friday night with Sir Robert King, a vile young rake of a considerable fortune in this country. They went off on Friday night; the father pursued and overtook them on Saturday morning, held a pistol at the knight's head, swore he would shoot him through the head if he did not instantly marry his daughter, which rather than die he consented to do. A parson was ready and called in, but Sir R. K's servants rushed in at the same time, gave him a pistol, and an opportunity of escaping, which he did, and left the forlorn damsel to return with her father. They all appeared at church in Dublin on Sunday morning, and the girl appears at all public places as unconcerned and brazen as if she had acted the most prudent part in the world.

The other story is indeed much more notorious and shocking. You don't know any of the people, so I shall not name names, but a gentleman's daughter who has for several years borne an extremely good character, about twenty-six years of age, has managed her father's house with great prudence, and always shewn a great tenderness for him on all occasions, has gone off with the schoolmaster of the parish, a clergyman who has been married several years, and his wife a very good kind of woman! He *now says* he never was married to her, and accuses her with carrying on an intrigue with the lady's father and brother that has run away with him! These are sad strokes in a family! how much less *is the death* of a dear friend to be lamented than such wicked conduct!

Yesterday morning I expected Lady Kildare and Mrs. Vesey to breakfast with me, but Lord Kildare would not let her venture so far. We dined at Mrs. Forde's, who is now happy, having in her house eleven children and grandchildren; I called on *my* Mrs. Hamilton, and found her and the rest of our set together, and all well. Bushe comes to me to-morrow to spend her Xtmas. I am very sorry to find by the papers, that our cousin Foley has lost his place in Parliament.

Mrs. Dewes to Mrs. Delany.

Welsbourne, Wednesday, 10th Feb., 1747-8.

I have been really fretting all this week that my dearest sister should be uneasy by not receiving the packets she expected. I am sure were the art of writing unknown my loss would be infinitely greater than yours— I mean in regard to our mutual letters. How happy am I to have my thoughts correspond so exactly to yours as they have done of late, though it is natural that the *same cause* should raise correspondent ideas, and our hearts have been very equally affected by the late sad occurrence; but indeed I agree that it would be as cruel as it is vain to wish our dear friend here again, though *in some hours of weakness I own I do.* I hope you never will suppress any thought when you are talking to me, for that unreserved freedom between us has constituted the greatest part of our happiness, and more happiness surely two friends never felt than we have done, and I am persuaded shall continue to enjoy till the great and sad separation— *far be that fatal hour!* I must again repeat my desire that you will never suppress one of your thoughts nor actions, especially *those you most delight in;* which I love to hear, as they are not only a joy but an example to me; for though Solomon says it in a different sense, "as iron sharpeneth iron," &c., yet it will hold in this, that the good actions of those we love excite in us *the desire of doing like them.* To show this, though in a small instance: the morning I received your last letter (which was Monday) Mr. Dewes was going to Mapleburrough, but desired the pleasure of reading your letter before he set out, and he enjoyed it for almost an hour. He then said, *"There never was in the world a person so excellent as Mrs. Delany in every respect of mind and person; and the Dean too, how good! that poor gardener! to make his last moments so comfortable to him:"* and then he said to me, "You won't forget to let clothes be made *for the poor child at Niniveh you said was in so sad a condition."* Now was not that design quickened by the consideration of your ways? therefore *scruple not* to repeat them continually. Mr. Dewes has a truly charitable and good heart, and you will esteem him greatly for his late conduct in regard to his brother's will, or rather his designs; for the will was so plain that Mr. Fitzakerly, our present greatest lawyer, said *that only was to be followed;* but though Mr. Dewes *asked council,* he followed the law of kindness *only,* both to the memory of his brother and in regard to the persons that may have lost some advantages by his death.

Mr. Dewes, I am sure, as well as myself, shall always think ourselves obliged by the kind notice and advice you give in regard to our children, but *I fear* he will not consent to a public school, he is so fearful of the bad ways and vices they have there to encounter; and besides, is really afraid of the hardships and severity they are to undergoe *much more than I am*, for I own I am ambitious to have them excel and make a figure. His chief objection to Abingdon school is that he has heard Mr. Woods is passionate, but Mr. Head, who was his scholar, spoke very much in his favour, so I hope to prevail to have one there. Does not the Dean think it will be better to have them at different schools? I have a notion that going together, as they are so much of the same age, whichever excels may raise an emulation, and prevent the love I wish to subsist between them; now when they meet as strangers at breaking-up times at home they will naturally be fond of each other. But this is a point I can't well determine upon, the Dean can better advise us; Bunny is fully as quick in learning as Court, but does *not love* it, and is very *heedless*, and he has a naturall artfulness that is *generally commended* in children, but I take great pains to break him of it. Pauline is not yet so genteel as Jackey because she is very fat, but she bridles[1] very well. Court is greatly alarmed at

---

[1] Qy. "*Bridles*." This expression alludes to that sort of carriage which is now (unfortunately) almost unknown. It may therefore be necessary to explain that one of the first lessons in deportment at the period this letter was written, was to hold up the head on entering a room, and to keep the chin in, which is expressed by "*bridling*," and then having curtseyed at the door, to advance deliberately towards the person who had the first claims to greeting; to shut low

your intelligence about Miss Hamilton, and asked many questions who and what was "the Primate," and says "a bishop should not be so wicked."

I am sure your "*Angel*"[1] is heavenly, as all your works are. I am glad the things are arrived safe: you put too great a value upon the trifles I have in my power to return for the greatest obligations. I am glad you like the engraving; it was done by Ingley the jeweller, whom you must remember at Gloucester; he is very ingenious but horridly idle, and drinks. Indeed the variety of things that has lately passed through my head and heart had made me entirely forget that you had ever mentioned the lining of the bed, which appears ungrateful, though you are too just to give it that turn; I have no pattern of the lining, and am really almost angry that you are so good and kind, but I shall not think to make it up till you come to give your directions, though I had rather it were ready to receive you, when you next make us happy; I wish you would send me a little bit of the size and sort of fringe you think will do, for perhaps I may have some by me; I believe it must be plain, for all others are so tedious; I am sure the short apron[2] will be charming.

A gap here occurs in the Correspondence. The next letter is from Lady Dysart on the occasion of her sister's marriage to the Marquis of Tweedale—four months after the date of this letter.

---

gradually, and to rise slowly and gracefully. Girls were always made to curtsey in the *first position*, because if there was any unsteadiness in the knees and ancles, it would be immediately detected,—the hands were folded and kept to themselves, and butting, bobbing, and rushing about with outstretched palms was unknown.

[1] A copy after Carlo Dolci.

[2] The short apron here alluded to is probably one still in existence, with purple violets and leaves designed from nature, and embroidered in coloured silks on a fawn-coloured lutestring.

Lady Dysart to Mrs. Delany.

New Burlington Street, June 28th, 1748.

I was long in expectation of a letter from dear Mrs. Delany, which I now acknowledge. I am much pleased with Mr. Barber's works, particularly the head of Calista, which he told me was for you, and *I think* preferable to any of Zincke's pictures; I will recommend him as much as lies in my power; at present the town is so empty that I can do him but little service. Lady Geo. Spencer has long promised me her picture, and I will have it by Mr. Barber, but she says I must stay till next winter. I thank you for subscribing in my name for the Irish *(illegible)*; the half guinea shall be payable upon sight. I think my sister Fanny[1] to all appearance happily established; the Marquis is a sensible reasonable man, and quite her lover. He has £4000 a-year in Scotland and two houses— one of them, I am told, is a very fine place; my sister has £1200 a-year jointure rent-charge. He has given her a very fine pair of brilliant earrings, one drop, a girdle buckle, and five stars for her stays; her clothes (she was married in) were white satin flounced, with a magnificent silver trimming all over the gown and petticoat; she had besides a white and gold with colours, a pink and silver sac, a brocaded lutestring gown and petticoat, a white satin sultane with embroidered robings of natural flowers, and a pink and white sprigged sultane. I have now told

---

[1] Lady Frances Carteret, daughter of John Earl Granville, married, April 1748, John, 4th Marquis of Tweedale. Horace Walpole mentions having met at Gosfield, when on a visit to his friend Mr. Nugent, in 1748, "the Marquis of Tweedale and his new Marchioness, who is infinitely good-humoured and good company, and sang a thousand French songs mighty prettily."

you *all her clothes;* her lace was fine and well chosen, her best head was point. The Marquis has the house in Grosvenor Street where Sir Robert Ride lived: they don't go to Scotland this year.

I have not painted anything since the St. Catharine you saw, I was too ill last summer to undertake a picture. I went to Tunbridge, which did me service, but I have never recovered my strength since that illness which was very near putting an end to me. Mr. Philips is in town, and I have been to see him, he has a paralytic disorder, and is much broke. I don't think he will ever be able to return to Ireland and claim his picture: but remember you are *one in my debt,* and I should choose to have it *your own.* I beg my compliments to the Dean, whom I hope to see a Bishop, for he would do honour to their bench; but I am of opinion, that—

> *A genius* in the reverend gown,
> Will *help* to keep its owner *down.*

I hope it will not be always his case. My time has been divided between Ham and this place since the beginning of May. We gave a great entertainment at Ham, and Lady Georgina[1] gave one at Wimbleton, to the Marquis and his lady, and the company that were at the wedding, sixteen in number. I hope to hear from you—I *won't say* when you have *nothing better* to do, for you have so many ingenious ways of employing your time I *should have no chance.* I have left Whitehall against my inclination, Mr. Treby would not let or sell it. I live in the house in New Burlington Street that Governor Worsley built,[2] where

---

[1] Lady Georgiana Spencer, (afterwards Lady Cowper,) sister of Lady Dysart and Lady Tweedale.

[2] Henry, second son of Sir Robert Worsley, and great uncle of Lady Dysart, was Governor of Barbadoes, in 1721. He died unmarried, March 16, 1727.

Sir Robert Worsley lived; it is a more convenient house than that I left, though not so pleasantly situated. I fear I have tired you. Believe me most sincerely, dear madam,

Your affectionate and faithful
Humble servant,
G. DYSART.

A month elapses after this letter before the Correspondence of Mrs. Delany recommences at Clogher, and it appears that the Dean and herself had been making a tour of Irish visits.

Mrs. Delany to Mrs. Dewes.

Clogher, 2d August, 1748.

According to our design we set out from Clonfede (Q^y) Dr. Clarke's on Monday the 1st of August at eight o'clock; passed through very jumbling roads, narrow and winding but not dangerous; the country as we went along pleasant, but not so finely improved as what I have sent you an account of in my last giant letter. From Dr. Clarke's to Callidon, where Lord Orrery lives, is ten miles, we sent our compliments, but did not call on him, designing to have waited on him and his lady in our return; from thence to this place is fourteen miles. We got here by dinner-time, found the Bishop and his Bishopess very well, in good spirits, and glad of our company. I am very happy to find my brother had been with you; it is what I was pretty sure he would do,—he never fails in *essential points* of kindness. I must tell you I was so silly, upon not hearing a great while from him or hearing where he positively was, as to take it into my head he would surprise me at Clogher; I could not help indulging so far a hope about it, as to feel a disappointment at not finding him: I confess this was *very foolish*, but *not unnatural*.

This house is large, and makes a good showish figure; but great loss of room by ill-contrivance within doors. It is situated on the side of so steep a hill that part of the front next the street is under ground, and from that to the garden you descend fifty stone steps which is intolerable, and in hot weather such as we have had, a fatigue not to be endured. The garden is pretty; a fine large sloping green walk from the steps to a large bason of water, on which sail most gracefully four beautiful swans. Beyond the bason of water rises a very steep green hill covered with fir; in the side of it Mrs. Clayton is going to make a grotto, the rest of the garden is irregularly planted; the Bishop is very busy, and I believe will make it very pretty. The company in the house with them, besides ourselves, are—Miss Brown, Mr. Burgh, a clergyman, a very agreeable gentleman-like man, Mr. Brown, a nephew of the Bishop's, and a Mr. and Mrs. Sandy, who always live here and take care of all their affairs in their absence. We came on Monday, dined, walked about, and chattered; on Tuesday, Mr. and Mrs. More and their two daughters dined here—they live about seven miles off: he is a great planter and improver, has a large estate, his house is bad, but the country about it and situation very fine. On Wednesday, in the afternoon we went to Longford's Glinn, which is about two miles from hence. We went in the coach to the opening of the glen; it is a charming awful scene, but as you have the poem that describes it very exactly I shall not attempt a description of it: I have taken a sketch or two, but I am afraid I shall not be able to do justice to the original. I looked for mosses and herbs, but found no new sorts, part of the verdure is very fine. I gathered four sorts of fruit—raspberries, cranberries, strawberries, and nuts, of which there are great plenty, the raspberries were particularly high-flavoured. I was resolved to send you *something* that grew in the glen, and have enclosed a piece of moss. The glen put me in mind of part of Matlock, but more retired, and the water that runs through is a little bubbling brook instead of a river; the one looks as if frequented by human creatures, the other by nymphs and fawns. I returned home so thoroughly fatigued by scrambling amongst the rocks and briars, and by my great attention to every different view, that I could hardly hold out to supper. I waked on Thursday well refreshed, and in the evening it was proposed to eat a syllabub about a mile off. For the frolic's sake, it being no coach road, we agreed to go, three ladies, on what is called here a truckle car (what they makes use of for carrying goods), drawn by one horse and the wheels *not three foot high*; and one was prepared for that purpose, well-covered with straw, upon which with some difficulty we settled ourselves. As we were going through *the town* (which *entre nous* is not quite so considerable as *Welsbourn*), I found my legs, which hung over the side of the car, sliding nearer and nearer to the ground, and down I jumped: Mrs. Clayton did the same, and behold our axle-tree was broken! The Dean and Miss Brown were in a chaise before us, and the Bishop on horseback. You may imagine this little adventure made some sport for us. No harm could happen to us, and we sneaked home on foot, not a little ashamed to be so exposed in *the midst of the city of Clogher!* The rest of the day past in laughing at one another, drinking tea, and walking in the garden. Upon inquiry we found it would not be greatly out of our way to return back by my Lord Orrery's, so we chose to make him a visit and return back to this place, which we did. We went on Friday, and got there by one. Lord Orrery is *more agreeable* than he used to be; he has laid aside the ceremonious stiffness that was a great disadvantage to him. He is very well-bred and entertaining; his lady, (whose fortune was near 3000 pounds a year), is very plain in her person and manner, but to make amends for that she is very sensible, unaffected, good-humoured, and obliging. I spent the day very pleasantly: it is a fine place by nature, and they are both fond of the country; she delights in *farming*, and he in *building and gardening*, and he has very good taste. They have a lodge about a mile from their house, where they spend most of their time; it has all the advantages of water, wood, and diversified grounds: and there the new house is to be built. Nothing is completed yet but an *hermitage*, which is about an acre of ground—an island, planted with all the variety of trees, shrubs, and flowers that will grow in this country, abundance of little winding walks, differently embellished with little seats and banks; in the midst is placed an hermit's cell, made of the roots of trees, the floor is paved with pebbles, there is a couch made of matting, and little wooden stools, a table with a manuscript on it, a pair of spectacles, a leathern bottle; and hung up in different parts, an hourglass, a weatherglass and several mathematical instruments, a shelf of books, another of wooden platters and bowls, another of earthen ones, in short everything that you might imagine necessary for a recluse. *Four little gardens surround his house—an orchard;* a flower-garden, a physick-garden, and a kitchen-garden, with a kitchen to boil a teakettle or so: I never saw so pretty *a whim so thoroughly well executed.* We returned on Saturday, met the Bishop's family at Mr. More's, halfway between this and Callidon. Yesterday went to church twice—the Dean preached; walked in the evening round Castle Hill, "*for royal Ergal's palace famed of old;*" it is very high, and a fine meadow around the sides of it, where we sat an hour on the haycocks, refreshed by the fragrancy of the hay and the sweetness of the air, till the setting sun warned us to bend our footsteps home. This is Mrs. Clayton's birthday, and we are to have a ball and monstrous fine doings; but I must prepare to do all the honour I can to the day, and am called away to dress. To-morrow we go to Dr. Madden's, fourteen miles off, in our way to Mr. Preston's, where we hope to be on Thursday next, and in ten days after that at home; adieu.

Mrs. Delany to Mrs. Dewes.

Swinton,[1] 18 August, 1748.

I received my dearest sister's letter dated the 26 July the day before I left Clogher, which gave me an account of your not having been well; but hope your next letter will give me the satisfaction of knowing you are quite well. If upon bleeding you found your blood was thick, I wish you would take hartshorn for some time every day, and take care of yourself,—your family as well as

---
[1] The residence of Mr. Preston.

myself claim that from you as you value their happiness.
As soon as I return to Delville I will send you the
song on the Gardens. Pray, did I not leave with you
the 8th vol. of Swift? I know I intended it. I think
the Wises were very silly to let a shower of rain prevent their coming to Welsbourn. I want an account
from you of Miss Graves; the last time I saw her I
thought her extremely altered. What manuscripts did
I promise? I have led such a fluttering life of late
—no wonder they should be jumbled out of my
head.

My last letter ended with an account of great preparations for the celebration of Madam Clayton's birthday: there were eight couple of very clever dancers,
and Madame and I divided a man between us and made
up the ninth couple *by turns*; at eleven we went to
supper—a sumptuous cold collation. At twelve the fiddles
struck up again, and every lad took his lass to "*trip it on
the light fantastic toe.*" D.D. and I took that opportunity
of walking off to our own apartments, as we intended to
set out early the next morning, and soberly took our rest
whilst the jovial company danced briskly away till past
two o'clock; the Bishop always goes to bed at ten, but
that night he sat up till eleven. The next morning we
left Clogher at eight, where we had spent eight days very
agreeably, and went to Dr. Madden's,[1] (fourteen miles from
Clogher). *He is a very remarkable man*, and to give you

---

[1] Dr. Samuel Madden, born in 1687 : he was an Irish clergyman and a Dean, and held the living of Drummully. He founded a society at Dublin in 1740 for the improvement of the arts, similar to that which was afterwards established in London. In 1744 he published " Boulter's Monument," a poem ; and a play entitled " Themistocles," and died 1765.

a just portrait of him would take up more time than is
allowed me at present. He has a very prating wife, who
would pass for the grey mare, and *makes a boast of that
which a wise and reasonable woman would not.* They
have six daughters and five sons, all grown up men and
women; fortunately for my head the *major part* were gone
to a ball, for *they are* themselves a concert of *trumpets,
French-horns and bagpipes.* The place is pretty; a very
fine wood of all sort of forest trees, planted by Doctor
Madden just by the house, surrounded by a fine river. He
has been a great planter and benefactor to his country on
many accounts, and a great encourager of the premiums
and charter-schools: we lay there one night. The country
from Clogher to that place very pleasant; from thence to
Virginia a very dreary country, but to make amends the
finest roads I ever travelled. The next morning, from
Virginia we went to Kells; dreary enough still, where
we dined. But we passed by a fine lake, with several
beautiful islands, twenty-five miles from Clogher. There
my good Letitia met me in Mr. Preston's coach, she looks
well and sends you many kind wishes: we dined together
at Kells, and came to this place by 7 in the afternoon.
This place is the *quintessence of cleanliness and neatness*; but
I cannot tell you more particulars at present but that I am
well pleased to be here, and to be so near dear Delville,
where, please God, we shall go on Friday next.

Mrs. Delany to Mrs. Dewes.

Delville, 20th August, 1748.

My dearest sister will not be displeased to receive a letter from my own peaceful bowers.

I thank God you are so well again, and hope you will have no return. You know so well my heart, that to say I am cheerful when I am not so would not pass with you. *I own I have felt on the return of this month*[1] *all that you express*, and at the same time conclude as you do, after many tender and grateful reflections, that we ought to rejoice at our dear and valuable parent's present happiness; which by continually reflecting on must entirely by degrees get the better of that self-love which makes us lament our own loss in her. I thank God I find that happy effect in part, and believe your strength of mind, and true resignation to the divine will, will perfect it in you in a much higher degree. All your news was welcome, and if it were not all quite new your manner of telling it makes at least *as entertaining* and something *more intelligible* than the magazine. I desire you will not imagine I have any intelligence but from yourself; if you do I shall be kept in ignorance of many things I like to know. How shocking was Dr. Broxholm's[2] end! and how much I pity his poor wife!

I will send you the account of the caterpillar as soon as I am settled enough to get it transcribed. I am

---

[1] Mrs. Granville, her mother's death.
[2] Horace Walpole says:—"You have seen in the papers that Dr. Broxholme is dead. He cut his throat. He always was nervous and vapoured; and so good-natured, that he left off his practice from not being able to bear so many melancholy objects."

much obliged to you for Mr. Merrick's[1] verses, which are very good in more senses than one. I shall be glad to see his works when they are published; if they are to be by subscription, pray subscribe for me. I am afraid I shall not be able to do any knotting for you, for very unthinkingly I sent you all the knotting thread, and shall not be able till next year to get the right sort. What is —— going to Bulstrode for now? I wish it may not embarrass our friend the Duchess, for as her M. is now with her, it will not be in her power to take so much notice of ——— as she would otherwise do, and that may mortify her extremely. I am afraid the last letter I answered of her's was not to her mind, but *I must be sincere*, especially with those I love, and she has such *high* notions for her daughter as I am sure will not answer. She asked my opinion about making interest *for a place at Court*, and I hinted rather at her putting her out to some *good service*, though I don't think the girl has had an education for that, but it is very hard to advise where our judgments are so different. I am very glad you have got Mrs. Norcliff home again,—she is a valuable neighbour.

I wrote you word of our progress as far as Mr. Preston's of Swainstown, seventeen miles from hence. Mr. Preston's first wife was sister to *my* Mrs. Hamilton; she left him three sons, now grown up pretty sensible young men, the eldest and youngest in the army, the second a clergyman just in orders—they were all at home. Mr. Preston is an

---

[1] James Merrick, M.A., an English divine and poet, born 1720, died 1769. He published poems on sacred subjects: viz., the Benedicite paraphrased, the Lord's Prayer paraphrased, Nunc Dimittis paraphrased, Balaam's Blessing on Israel, a Hymn, the Trials of Virtue, the Ignorance of Man, Verses written originally in Persia—Oxford, 1763, 4to.: and many other works.—*Watts's Bibliotheca Britt.*

old prim beau, as affected as a fine lady; but a very honest man, obstinate in his opinions, but the pink of civility in his own house, which is as neat as a cabinet, and kept with an exactness which is really rather troublesome. The present Mrs. Preston, who has been married to him about seven years, was daughter of the Bishop of Meath (Lumbard), is a most sensible, agreeable, conversable woman, plain in her person, but in her manners genteel and friendly, an excellent good woman, and a great friend of Bushe's, whom I found there, and left in very good health. They are in a very pleasant neighbourhoood, and "live very elegantly" (*as Sally says*). Lord Mornington's (Dangen) is six miles from them, where I was to have gone last Wednesday, but a little disorder, occasioned by eating too many cherries, obliged me to come home.

Swainstown is in the county of Meath,—a flat country, and all corn, which though of benefit to those who have estates there, does not afford the traveller such *pleasant scenes* as lands better wooded and varied by hills and dales. The river Boyne runs through part of it, and wherever it flows beauty attends its banks, which are indeed very fine. Mr. Ludlow has a seat near it, and three miles from Mr. Preston's, called Ardsalla. The house a good one, with some good pictures, the gardens fine, and laid out a great deal in the old taste, with high cut hedges and straight walks, but the part next the river is in a wilder way, planted with scattering trees, and pretty seats to take different views of the winding of the river. I was extremely delighted with one part of the garden, which was designed by D.D., a place that was formerly a stone quarry, dug down so low that the rocks as you walk at the bottom are a considerable way above your head, and are so well crowned with trees of all kinds that they hover over you as you walk, and shade you entirely from the sun. Little plantations of trees and flowering shrubs in different forms adorn the walk as you pass winding along; nothing can be wilder or more romantic. I am afraid I do not give you a right idea of it. But when I came home, notwithstanding all the variety of fine and pretty things I had seen, I thought Delville looked enchantingly pretty! I found my house as clean as if the fairies had swept it, and all my domestics and neighbours rejoiced at our return; the sight of poor little Tommy Greene was a renewal of the concern we had felt for the loss of his valuable mother,[1] and the little creature was so transported at my coming home, that it was moving to see the silent pleasure he had, for he could not speak, but hugged and stroked my arms, and would not stir one minute from me, as if directed to beseech my protection and make up in some measure his loss. His father (a most disconsolate man) is gone the circuit, and returns this week.

I found all the Barbers well; and *Quadruple Alliance*— (Mrs. F. Hamilton, Miss Forth, and Miss Anne Hamilton,) dined and spent the day with me on Thursday, and we drank tea in the new part of the study. Yesterday morning they breakfasted with me, with the agreeable addition of *my* Mrs. Hamilton, and staid till near three. My orange-trees come on finely; there is but one that has failed, and four of them bore prodigiously. All my plants and flowers have done very well, that is, all that came up

---

[1] This is the first allusion to Mrs. Greene's death, which must have taken place during the periods when the links in the correspondence are incomplete.

before I went into the country, except the tuberoses, and they promise but indifferently. On Monday the Dean begins about his chapel; he makes an addition for the communion-table to stand in *clear of the aisle*, over which is to be a round gothic window. When that is completed, he has promised to build me a kitchen out of doors, and that which is now my kitchen to be turned into a room for my maids, that they may have *no call upstairs* but when they are about their *business there*. My flower-garden, which is now just under my eye, is a wilderness of flowers, the beds are overpowered with them, and though the enamelled look they have is rich and pretty, I believe it will be advisable to have the different sorts of flowers appear rather more distinct. And now I must take leave of you, having many domestic affairs to enquire into, and some more letters to write. The Dean is mightily pleased with Mrs. B.'s letter, and has great compassion for her, but fears her *constitution* has so great a share in *her disquiet*, as will baffle all endeavours to satisfy her scruples.

The Correspondence does not appear to have been preserved for nearly two months after the date of this letter.

Mrs. Delany to Mrs. Dewes.

Delville, 15 October, 1748.

Last Monday we set out for Dangan, Lord Mornington's, and were excessively pinched with the cold, for a colder day I never felt; but we were soon warmed by a kind welcome and good dinner. Lord Mornington is now the same good-humoured, agreeable man he was seventeen years ago, when I made him my last visit, but his family much improved. You know Mrs. Fortescue—she was always a favourite of mine; her pretty husband was abroad, which I was sorry for, as he would have been an agreeable addition to our society. Miss Wesley[1] did the honours of the table, for her sister is confined to her chamber; she was so ill last year that they sent her to the Bath, she has not been returned above six weeks. My godson, Master Wesley,[2] is a most extraordinary boy; he was thirteen last month, he is a very good scholar, and whatever study he undertakes he masters it most surprisingly. He began with the fiddle last year, he now plays everything at sight; he understands fortification, building of ships, and has more knowledge than I ever met with in one so young. He is a child among children, and as tractable and complying to his sisters, and all that should have any authority over him, as the little children can be to you.

The place is really magnificent; the old house that was burnt down is *rebuilding*. They live at present in the offices; the garden (or rather improvements, and parks, for it is too extensive to be called a garden), consists of six hundred Irish acres, which make between eight and nine hundred English. There is a gravel walk from the house to the great lake fifty-two feet broad, and six hundred yards long. The lake contains 26 acres, is of an irregular shape, with a fort built in all its forms;

---

[1] Frances, second daughter of Richard, 1st Lord Mornington, who married in 1750, William Francis Crosbie, Esq.

[2] Garrett, only son of Lord Mornington, born July 19, 1735, afterwards created Viscount Wellesley and Earl of Mornington. He was father of Arthur, 1st Duke of Wellington.

there are islands in the lake for wild fowl, and great quantities of them that embellish the water extremely. I never saw so pretty a thing. There are several ships, one a complete man-of-war. My godson is governor of the fort, and lord high admiral; he hoisted all his colours for my reception, and was not a little mortified that I declined the compliment of being saluted from the fort and ship. The part of the lake that just fronts the house forms a very fine bason, and is surrounded by a natural terrace wooded, through which walks are cut, and variety of seats placed, that you may rest and enjoy all the beauties of the place as they change to your eye. The ground as far as you can see every way is waving in hills and dales, and every remarkable point has either a tuft of trees, a statue, a seat, an obelisk, or a pillar.

The weather was stormy all the time we were there, but I took a small sketch or two, though I performed my operation like the witches—*in a whirlwind:* and I had so little opportunity of examining the whole disposition of the place, by reason of the bad weather, that I can give you but an imperfect notion of it. How great a satisfaction is it to see so fine a place in the possession of a man so worthy of it! The maiden aunt, Mrs. Sale,[1] that has lived with her nieces ever since their mother died, is a quiet easy woman, who neither adds to nor checks any mirth. Mrs. Fortescue has a beautiful boy about five years old, a jolly girl a year younger; she is very fond of them, but discreet in her management. We left them yesterday morning not

---

[1] The wife of Richard Lord Mornington was Elizabeth, eldest daughter of John Sale, LL.D. and M.P. for Carysfort.

without great solicitations that we would stay longer; but D.D. was wanted at home by his workmen, and I don't care to stay long abroad; I found the little boy very well at my return, and rejoiced at seeing me again. We came home by Lucan, and called there at two o'clock in hopes of finding Mr. and Mrs. Vesey at home, and dining with them, when the butler told us they were gone to dine in Dublin; well then we had nothing to do but go to the public-house at the end of their avenue, concluding that Miss Handcock was gone with them. The woman of the public-house honestly owned she had nothing for us, *not even a little bacon*; this was a cruel disappointment at that time of the day, so on we went towards Chapel-Izod, a famous place for entertainment, about four miles farther; but luckily we were called after with Miss Handcock's compliments, who desired we would return and eat a bit of mutton with her, which we did most gladly; and no wandering, starving hero or nymph in a forlorn wood, ever relished a fairy repast better than we did a good substantial shoulder of mutton and potatoes; and no part of the entertainment was more agreeable than the pretty kind manner we were received in by our charitable hostess. We got home by seven. The latter end of next week Mr. and Mrs. Vesey[1] and Miss Handcocks come here to shelter themselves for some days, their house is full of work.[2]

Another period of three months here intervenes in the Correspondence.

---

[1] Mrs. Vesey was the youngest daughter of Sir Thomas Vesey, Bishop of Ossory, and married first, William Handcock, Esq., of Willsbrook, county Westmeath, and secondly to Agmondisham Vesey, of Lucan.

[2] The end of this letter is wanting.

Mrs. Delany to the Duchess of Portland.
Delville, 14 Feb., 1748-9.

I have deferred some posts writing to my dear Lady Duchess that I might give an account of my commission. I have got the *six suits*, which I think very good, and hope your Grace will approve of them, and that they will wear well. I did not buy them of the same merchant you had the last of, and must pay the carriage of them. As soon as they are delivered to you be pleased to give me notice, and directions how I shall draw upon you for the money. They come to £41 2s. Irish, which is £37 18s. Eng. The tea napkins are bespoke, and I will bring them with me; they will be about two shillings a napkin; I could not meet with the quantity wanted ready made, the price on each suit is marked, Irish money.

As to my dearest friend's wish about my phiz, it should be accomplished were it in my power; but it is given up by the whole college of painters to be an impossible face to draw *like*, as there is *no settled countenance* to copy! but *ill-conditioned* muscles, that grow crabbed and cross at the time they ought to be in the best humour! Add to this a *muddled complexion, deep lines and furrows*, which time has bountifully and amply displayed, and for the size of the person belonging to that same face—*it is a porpuss grown*.[1]

---

[1] This humorous description of herself is completely contradicted not only by tradition but by the pictures still existing of Mrs. Delany. Her complexion was so wonderfully fine that her blush was described to the Editor by her own mother as brilliant to the last year of her life, and as easily called forth by any sudden emotion, as in a young girl of fifteen, and she never was represented or described as fat.

I am glad, and so is Bushe most sincerely so, that the Lady Mayoress[1] found such favour with your Grace: it has given a new spring to her pencil, and she has begun and almost finished such a set of *pantines* as will be worthy a place in your cabinet of curiosities. She has done the Duke and Duchess, Don Quixotte, Sancho Panza, Maritornes, and is going on to the Laughing Cook and Dorothea; but proud as I am of contributing to your store of rarities, I don't know whether I shall be able to give you up my *Puppet Shew!*

Well now, my dear friend, I begin to feel the pleasure of our meeting, and every day I do something towards my journey; though we cannot set forward till the latter end of May. Mrs. Vesey offered me her house in London, but D.D. would not have it, because it is such a distance from Whitehall. I wish I could get a house in Spring Garden; I have not yet done anything to your toilette-boxes; I have got a little good white at last, but fear the effect will not be pretty: however I will do something by them, if you will forgive my spoiling them. I wrote your Grace word that I thought Hayman[2] the best master I knew of, but am not sure he will teach. My *poor dear Goupy, are you gone?* I am sure you have left nothing like you behind you—so modest, quiet, civil, honest, and an *incomparable master!* forgive this eulogium, but my heart would vent itself, and your Grace *knew* his worth. I find by the newspapers, that the Bishop of St.

---

[1] An allusion to some drawing by Miss Bushe, sent to the Duchess of Portland.

[2] Francis Hayman, born at Exeter in 1708, died 1776. He was the best historical painter in the kingdom before the arrival of Cipriani. He furnished drawings for editions of Congreve's Works, Pope's Works, Newton's Milton, Hanmer's Shakespeare, &c.

Asaph[1] is married, may I take the liberty to beg your Grace would assure him of mine and the Dean's best wishes for his happiness! If the lady has equal merit to him (which I hope she has), he must be a happy man. Now because I have not time, I am so perverse as to want to turn over, but it is Lent and a time for mortification, and I will indulge myself no longer.

Mrs. Delany alludes in this letter to her expectation of soon being in England, which was realized, and was probably the cause of an interval of some months in the correspondence, during which time the following letter proves that she had been with her sister at Wellesbourn, and had then made a pilgrimage to Gloucester for reasons she herself best explains.

Mrs. Delany to Mrs. Dewes.

Glocester, 1 July, 1749.

Yesterday I received my dearest sister's letter, and am glad you are determined to sit quiet this sultry weather. As for our meeting at Gloucester, it would have been *too much* for us *both*, and Mrs. V. takes the not coming in the *true sense*. Though I have suffered in my spirits by coming here, I have acquitted myself of a duty I owed, and find a satisfaction in my mind for having done it, and a quiet and uninterrupted enjoyment of my dear sister's company at my *return* to Welsbourne, will compensate for the melancholy hours I must spend in this place, where so many objects put me in mind of our great loss. But I will say no more on this subject, though my heart is easier for having said so much. I hope my dearest sister has now no

---

[1] "Married, the 31st Jan., 1749, Right Revd. Dr. Robert Drummond, Lord Bishop of St. Asaph, to Miss Henrietta Orell, a 30,000*l*. fortune."

pain in her side, but I fear the *excessive heat* will increase it—and surely hotter weather was never felt, except that one memorable day we spent together at Mayfield.[1] Now for the journal. I found all here well except poor Nancy, who seems to me in a very bad way; our first meeting was what you may imagine it to be, and the first object that struck my eyes was a *new tomb*, and that put my spirits into such a hurry that I could not get the better of it for some time, nor had I courage to venture yesterday to church morning or evening, or to go out of doors but into the garden. I set Mrs. Viney to the harpsichord, and I was much pleased with the improvement the girls have made. Miss Viney really sings well, and Harriot surprised me with her playing; I think she will make one of the *best players I ever heard* on the harpsichord: they are agreeable well-behaved girls, and Jemmy a pretty modest lad.

Mrs. R. came yesterday in the afternoon, and the Bishop of Gloucester, who enquired much after you, and expressed concern of your not being perfectly well: we dine with him on Monday. What a strange *inconsistent* letter is this, my dearest sister! rambling like my poor fluttered head; and yet I think I find myself well composed to-day, and I intend going to church; for there is, after all, but *one method* that *can compose* the mind properly—which is, performing our duty to the best of our capacity, and praying for grace to sustain us under all trials. Mrs. Viney has begged so hard that we would stay till Thursday, that we have yielded to her solicita-

---

[1] Mayfield, near Calwich, in Staffordshire.
[2] Dr. Martin Benson, Prebendary of Durham, made Bishop of Gloucester, 1734, died 1752.

tions: we shall hardly leave it till Monday or Tuesday. Don't expect us; we will come as soon as possible. On Thursday we propose going to Cheltenham. I am sure you know and believe that the dear little boy shall have all manner of care taken of him; he will be no sort of trouble to us, but a great entertainment. And now adieu. God bless you!— A thousand kind services and wishes attend you from hence. I think I feel rather more impatience to see you now than when I landed at Park Gate. Once more adieu.

Mrs. Delany's visit to Gloucester to see her mother's tomb, and to comfort her old friend Mrs. Viney, was another among the numerous instances of the deep feeling she possessed, and of the principle of duty which she ever followed. A journey to Gloucester from Wellesbourn was no trifling expedition in those days; and it was evident that there was no one at Gloucester who individually gave her any pleasure—their value being merely that of association. Her sister was absent, her mother was dead, but she did not rest until she had visited the grave of one she so much honoured in life, and administered consolation to the old surviving friend, whose desolation she had before commented upon, while her own sorrow was so recent. The good Dean accompanied her, and as usual participated in her sorrow as he ever did in her joys, and showed that invariable sympathy which first won her regard, and afterwards secured her attachment.

Mrs. Granville was buried in a tomb outside the cathedral at Gloucester, but within the iron railing of its inclosure, and near the walls of that sacred edifice, where it may still be seen standing alone, with the following inscription: "Here lies interred the body of Mary Granville, daughter of Sir Martin Westcomb, Baronet; relict of Colonel Bernard Granville, who passed a long widowhood in this city, leading a most exemplary life, doing all the good to her poor neighbours that her income allowed of."

Mrs. Delany to Mrs. Dewes.

Birmingham, 17 Aug., 1749.

MY DEAREST SISTER,

How painful it is to leave you, though I have the flattering hope of our meeting soon again; but I left you not well and I shall not hear of you this age. You were excessively good in sending me word this morning you had had a good night. Our little Pauline did not rest very well: I saw her and gave her my blessing. Were you out with me to-day?

Now a word or two of our notable expedition to Birmingham. The first part I suppose Frank has acquainted you with, and my running away with him to Stratford, where he got us the horse we wanted for Bennet: well, on we drove, hooping on very restive horses, and Mr. Shackle came roaring that we had killed his cattle. All his unreasonableness a letter can't contain, nor this skewer of a pen write, but thus it has ended : we have sent a messenger to Calwich to notify to the squire that we cannot be with him before supper-time, and have amused ourselves here as follows:—we sent for Mr. Priest to tell him of Shackle's impertinence, and after dinner walked to Vauxhall, a good mile from hence. The garden is very neat and pretty, with a handsome bowling green and seats in several parts of the garden ; in one of them we drank tea, eat bread and butter, and Rhenish and sugar. In our way home we stumbled among a crowd, enquired. what was the matter, was told a methodist preacher was going to hold forth in the street. We stopped a good while in hopes of being edified, but our patience would not hold out till sufficient quantity of mob were gathered for a congregation, so home we came, Mr. Priest with us, to our mutton-broth and roast pigeons (but not such mutton and pigeons as Welsbourne produces). We are to have four horses and a postilion to-morrow at the door by 5 to carry us to Calwich: we dine I don't know where. The landlord here has promised to send this to Stratford to Mr. Bot on Saturday.

Mrs. Delany to Mrs. Dewes.

Calwich, 19 Aug., 1749.

I wrote to my dearest sister on Thursday night at Birmingham with an account of all that had past from the time of my leaving Welsbourne. We accommodated matters with our imposing coachman Mr. Shackle (by-the-by a very great rogue) and set out next day from Birmingham at 6 with four horses and one postilion; dined at Ousley Bridge, were met by Richard Hall near Uttoxeter and got to Calwich before 8: the joy of seeing my brother made me soon forget all the disagreeable part of my journey. My brother says, that you may not lie two nights on the road, that his chaise shall meet you at Abbot Bromley and bring you here, and your own chariot may rest and come on the day after. I hope you will be able in your answer to this to give us some notice of the time of your coming.

I will tell you nothing about Calwich but that I am delighted with it, and have sauntered about all this morning. When we were at dinner at Ouseley Bridge, a little boy about Bunny's age (but not such a boy) peeped in, and there being some jelly of currants on the table I fancied the child had a mind to it and sent them to him, and presently after Mr. and Mrs. Kinnersley[1] came to thank me for my kindness; they enquired much after you, and desired their compliments. I have been so silly as to forget franks. I must beg the favour of you to get *a dozen or two* for me from Sir Charles Mordaunt; you will find paper in the middle drawer of the walnut table in my closet: a dozen will do if I am to see you soon.[2] I don't know but you will find a few of the Duke of Portland's in the drawer with the paper.

The verdure here is in high beauty, and we saw great quantities of new corn in the haggards as we came along through Staffordshire. I found a letter from Miss Granville with a receipt for you, but I hope you will never have occasion to make use of it. Mrs. Kinnersley told me that her little boy who was with her had two years ago so violent a fever that nobody thought the child could recover, and that he was reduced to so great weakness as not to be able to stand alone for a considerable time after it: since his recovery he has had better health than ever he had, and so will, I hope, our little Mary. I have great dependance on asses' milk and exercise, which I hope in God will perfectly restore her, and I shall be glad to hear of your having both been on horseback.

---

[1] Thomas Kynnersley, of Loxley, Esq., county of Stafford, an officer in the navy, married Penelope, only daughter of John Wheeler, of Wootton, Esq.

[2] Franks were never dated at the period of this letter, but the ladies provided themselves with packets of half sheets folded and signed by members of either House of Parliament, which lasted for months, and on which they wrote themselves whatever address was required.

Mrs. Delany to Mrs. Dewes.

Calwich, 25th Aug., 1794.

Many happy returns of this day [1] may my dear brother and sister Dewes enjoy! I not only speak for myself but for all here, whose kind service and wishes attend you very affectionately. I doubt this second distress about your children will make you negligent of yourself and give all your attention to them. As to your coming here, it is unnecessary to say what pleasure it will be to us all, but don't let any indulgence to us make you do what may give you uneasiness. It is hard to give up such a joy as your company, particularly to me who cannot always be in the way of having such a happiness; but it would be cruel to press you to come, unless you can do it with perfect ease to yourself. After the fatigue of body and mind you have gone through the change of air, the sweetness of Calwich, and the satisfaction of our being all together, will refresh your spirits and be of great service to your health. But if that is not to be, I will come to you as soon as possible, and I know nothing will keep you from us, but you or your children's illness. Mr. Dewes did very right in opening D.D.'s letter, and you in opening mine; do the same by any that come to your hands that you think will give you any intelligence you wish to have.

We have had very pleasant weather since our being here, except last Tuesday; when we had the most violent tempest of thunder, lightning, rain and hail, that ever I remember to have seen or heard. It began about 5 in

---

[1] 25th August, Anne Granville's wedding day.

the afternoon and lasted till 4 in the morning. The thunder and lightning never ceased; it abated about half an hour and then came on with greater violence again. We had three claps that shook the house—it was like the going off of a cannon at the window. I thank God no damage was done, and though I was startled at the loud claps, I was much less terrified than I have been formerly at much less storms.

On Wednesday the Okeovers and Doxeys dined here, and the heiress Miss Nichols; she is a fine lively girl, but wants a *good deal of modelling*. To-morrow Mr. and Mrs. Kinnersley dine here. This afternoon we go to Snelston. I have had no letter about the nurse for Mrs. Foley. The Duchess of Portland got safe to Welbeck; I had a few lines from her yesterday. You must bring Jenny's mare, for my brother agrees with me and other physicians that riding is *absolutely necessary* for you, and you ought not to neglect it a day. Don't forget a bundle of franks. Can you conveniently bring my green and white linen sack,[1] it hangs in the painting-room, if you can't it is no matter.

Mrs. Delany to Mrs. Dewes.

Calwich, 4 Sept. 1749.

I shall think the time long till Thursday next, and hope in God then to receive comfortable news of you and your dear children; I shall then be able to judge if

---

[1] Linen gowns of all descriptions were constantly in use in those days, and it is surprising that they have not been revived, as the texture is so superior to cotton. They were printed like chintz, and also dyed in plain colours and in stripes.

there can be any hopes of your coming here (though I greatly fear not), and then I shall fix my time of returning to you. To have lost so much of your company on so sad an occasion is grievous; and I am convinced, from too frequent experience, that to be absent from a dear friend at the time of sickness or distress is more painful than being with them, as it is attended with a constant suspicion of things being worse than perhaps they have really been in every particular. D.D.'s illness last week prevented our going to Okeover, but we think of going next Wednesday; and Loxley we intend taking on our way home and staying there a day or two.

As to the shells[1] I hope you have not sent them, as they will come too late for me to do any work with: had you brought them and we had all worked together it would have been delightful, but that scheme is now over. Sickness and sorrow will attend us on our journey through this vale of tears; and if we are so blest as to have intervals of health and joy we ought to be thankful. But when I am lamenting your tenderness of constitution, and pain on your children's account, to balance that I consider your strength of mind and happy fortitude on all occasions. I view these melancholy scenes as so many trials of your virtue, and this is a consolation not to be met with from any other consideration; and reconciles me even to your distresses.

I hope when Lord North comes into this neighbourhood he will come for a day to Calwich, as my brother would be extremely glad to see him here, though he says

---

[1] Mrs. Delany made a grotto at Calwich, which the Editor well remembers seeing as a child. It was entirely lined with shell work done by herself and her sister.

he shall be afraid of his drawing him in to do a great deal more, but he has a great opinion of his fancy and judgment. Is Miss Wheeler Mrs. Mills?

After this letter Mrs. Delany returned to Wellesbourne, where she remained till the second week in November.

Mrs. Delany to Mrs. Dewes.

Oxford, Sunday morning, 9 o'clock.
12 Nov. 1749.

No post went out last night: it goes to-night at seven, and I cannot let it go without sending my dearest sister a journal of the heavy hours that have passed since I left her. We got to Euston about one, were delayed half an hour on the road by the car *wheels breaking*, no overturn, but Smith was forced to be hoisted up behind Bennet *without* any pillion, and James came wabbling on with the broken equipage, his *Fribbleship* much ruffled. I feasted at Euston on your good provision, but not very hungry: we staid about two hours. About three miles from Oxford we had like to have lost one of our *forewheels*, but fortunately saw our danger before any bad accident. The coachman pretty soon repaired the loss, and we arrived at Oxford about six. We sent for Mr. Viney, but being weary and low-spirited we did not care for any other company: he is much pleased with his plum-cake, and obliged to his little friend for it; this morning we are very well. D D. and Viney are gone to eight o'clock prayers—I am preparing their breakfast for them, and at ten shall go to University Church: after that will resume my pen.

Mr. Cleaver preached a very ingenious and proper discourse on the great advantages of being well acquainted with the Scriptures: it was nearly an hour long. From thence we went, escorted by the *Great Shaw*,[1] to see several of the colleges. He asked very particularly after you, and hopes you forgive his taxing you with being scribe to *the letter*; he now has found out a hand like it, who he is sure must be the person that sent it, and would show it me, but his wife coming soon into the room prevented my asking to see it. I fear I shall not be able to add any more to this; Shaw, his wife, daughter, and Mr. Viney dine here, and in the afternoon Lord Lewisham[2] and Mr. North[3] drink tea. Dinner is on table.

Bulstrode, 13 Nov. 1749.

Upon examination I found that this letter will reach you as soon from hence as it would have done from Oxford, so I brought it on to add the sequel of my journal.

The young men drank tea with us as expected. Much disappointed Lord Lewisham was that I would not stay

---

[1] Dr. Thomas Shaw, born 1692, died 1751. A great traveller in Egypt and the Holy Land and Africa. In 1740 he was nominated principal of St. Edmund's Hall, which he soon repaired, and restored from a ruinous state by his munificence. He was also made Regius Professor of Greek at Oxford. The work of Dr. Shaw, which has been translated into the French, Dutch, and German languages, is the best that has been written containing an account of the Algerine and Tunisian states. His geographical researches threw light upon the ancient and modern state of Numidia. In the course of his travels he collected nearly 600 plants, of which 140 were newly discovered, besides an immense number of minerals and medals, many of which he presented to public institutions.

[2] William Viscount Lewisham, born in 1731, succeeded to the Earldom of Dartmouth on the death of his grandfather, 15th December, 1750.

[3] Frederic, son of the 1st Earl of Guildford, born 12th April, 1732, and afterwards the well-known Prime Minister, Lord North.

long enough to visit his rooms; they staid till near eight. We kept Jemmy Viney to eat mutton broth with us; went to bed early, and rose at half an hour after five, breakfasted at nine at Tetsworth, dined at twelve at Wickam, got here at half an hour after three; but what was my vexation when upon enquiring after the Duchess, found she was gone to London, Lord Titchfield had a feverish disorder, and she and the Duke were gone off with Babess to town, and they did not know when they were to return; *and for my consolation here was Lady Bell Monck!* I can't say I entered the house with a very good grace, but at last I was brought to myself by the caresses and obliging behaviour of Lady Betty and Lady Harriot, and a messenger is just come to say Lord Titchfield is pretty well again, and I hope the Duchess will return on Wednesday. My spirits were so sunk on leaving my dearest sister that I could not all the way raise them till I saw the walls of Bulstrode, and then the thought of surprizing the Duchess a day sooner than she expected cheered and revived me. We had a very pleasant journey. Whenever you hire horses let it be from the man we had ours of in Oxford; we had excellent cattle, and the civilest best humoured coachman and admirable driver that ever was hired, his name is Thomas Robinson. Lady Bell occupies the yellow apartment, Babess has the ground room, and we have Lady Oxford's apartment.

Mrs. Elstob is pretty well, and Mr. Achard in good spirits.

I left the Irish notes for Mr. Dewes on the harpsichord.

Lord Guernsey[1] is to have Lady Charlotte Seymour for certain. Have you had any account from Coventry of the two boxes of shells?

Mrs. Delany to Mrs. Dewes.

Bulstrode, 14 Nov. 1749.

Lord Titchfield is much better—his fever quite left him; but as he is to take physic to-morrow, the Duchess don't care to leave him till the day after, but begs of us to come to town and settle our affairs, that I may not be obliged to leave her when she comes to Bulstrode. I suppose we shall return together on Friday or Saturday. The enclosed came from my *nephew's mistress*[2] last post. I hope he will be in good spirits to answer it.

Yesterday morning, after breakfast, we all sallied forth to walk. We fed all the animals, such as bantams, guinea-fowl, pheasants, peacock, ducks, drakes, widgeon, teal, and an animal that is neither monkey, fox, nor squirell, but something of each creature, very harmless and tame, kept in the flower-garden, and has a hard name which I can't remember; it is larger than a great cat. In the evening we had tea at the usual time, and worked till supper; after supper played at cribbage—Lady Bell and I against our husbands; and in our last game we had in

---

[1] Heneage Lord Guernsey married, 6th October, 1750, Charlotte, daughter of Charles, 6th Duke of Somerset. He succeeded his father in the Earldom of Aylesford, 29th June, 1757, and died May 9, 1777.

[2] Miss Mary Hamilton, who kept up a correspondence as a child with Court, the eldest son of Mrs. Dewes. Miss Hamilton married, 1763, the Rev. Nathaniel Preston, of Swainston, county Meath.

playing a 15, a *pairoyal*, a double *peroyal*, a *second peroyal*, and an *end game*, which was 27. To-morrow morning we propose setting out as soon as it is light, and now I am called to tea, and shall not be able to write again to you till Monday.

Mrs. Delany to Mrs. Dewes.

Bulstrode, 20 Nov. 1749.

I shall now proceed to tell where I have been, and what I have been doing since my last letter. On Thursday morning we got horses from Uxbridge, and went to town in our chaise, Smith on a stool at our feet. We stopped in Park Street at our brother's, who did not expect such visitors. He was glad to see us, and we to see him; he looked well but complained of a cold in his head. He would have had us dine with him, but I was obliged to go on to Whitehall, as the Duchess of Portland was in doubt about our coming, and had been so good as to offer us rooms there; so on we went, found the Duke at home, Mr. Lambert with him; Mrs. Lambert and little boy very well. D.D. went to dine at Mrs. Percival's, to enquire if Donnellan had got us a house. It was near three: I dressed myself, and by that time the Duchess came home; Babess was gone to her sister. I dined with the Duke and Duchess at the Bishop of St. Asaph's. Visited Lord Titchfield, and drank tea with him in the afternoon; he has been very ill, but is well again, only a little weak; he is a charming boy and learns faster than his master desires he should; goes into the 4th form as soon as he is well enough to return to school. I left him at 7, and went to Whitehall with a bad headache. Babess came home soon, and Lady Bute[1] followed, and then the Duke and Duchess. I went to bed as soon as I had supped; and between nine and ten, D.D. and I set out a house-hunting, and after much fatigue met with a very pretty little house in St. James Place, that we have taken: and what pleases us both extremely is that there is a very good bed-chamber, a large dressing-room (or drawing-room if you please), a little room for a servant, and a light closet within the bed-chamber, which we hope my dearest sister will make her apartment before the first of March. Lent begins and oratorios in February; and what additional *harmony* your conversation will be I leave those to judge who know *how well we accord.*

I am at last relieved from the perplexity I was in about a certain person's coming to town to me by D.D. who has very kindly asked Miss Granville to be with us till you come to town, which she has promised to do, and as I mentioned that to Mrs. Viney (when she spoke of her daughter's coming) as a thing likely to happen, I think it will put a stop to that affair very well, and I hope not give her any offence; for I have so great an esteem for her, that it would grieve me to disoblige her. Poor Betty Granville is in a very dangerous state of health—a constant cough and pain on her chest, no appetite, no sleep, though they give her laudanum, and Babess is in a miserable way about her. Lady Bell Monck is here; they were to have left us to-morrow, but a violent creek has seized Mr. Monck's neck, and he can't stir. The Duchess is very well, and very sorry she had not the pleasure of seeing you, but as things have

---

[1] Lady Bute, daughter of Lady Mary Wortley Montagu, wife of John Earl of Bute.

happened it is well you did not come as you proposed, for Lord Titchfield's illness, kept her a whole week in town, and it would have been a mortification to her. I am so much pleased with Lady Betty and Toz that I must again repeat that I never saw two such agreeable girls of their age in my life—so civil, lively, humble, and conversable; they are doatingly fond of the Duchess, never so happy as in her company, and at the same time in such awe that they watch every motion and look to observe if she approves of what they say and do.

All the talk at present is about Lady Mary Cook[1] and her strange Lord. She has been cruelly treated by him and his father (who perhaps will see what I write of him, for he examines all letters that pass): he will reap but little satisfaction from that employment, and, like listeners, hear no good of himself. There was a great meeting at Westminster Hall last Friday, where she was produced in Court, lead in by my Lord Cook; she petitioned for leave to see her relations, lawyers, and physicians, which was granted: what next will be done nobody knows, but a modest woman is much to be pitied who undergoes what she must do if a trial comes on.

The Duke and Duchess go to town next Friday, and return on Monday: I shall go with them to settle all particulars about my house. I saw Miss Sutton and her brother Dick on Friday morning (after we had seen houses) at Mr. Percival's. Our chaise took us up there at half an hour after eleven; we called on my brother, his cold better, and he abroad. We then drove away to

---

[1] Lady Mary Campbell, daughter and co-heiress of John Duke of Argyll and Greenwich, married, in 1747, Edward Viscount Coke, only son of Thomas Coke, Earl of Leicester.

Bulstrode, and got here at half an hour after three, expecting the Duke, etc., would be here soon after; but a messenger came to tell us that their coach *broke down* in Westminster as they were coming out of town, so they did not come till Saturday. Now we are rummaging and sorting shells, and making preparations for a thousand works more than we shall have time to finish. Could you any way contrive to send me 12 or 14 of your cleaned mussels, those that look transparent; I will faithfully repay you.

Mrs. Delany to Mrs. Dewes.

Bulstrode, 26 Nov. 1749.

I am now, I assure you, as well as you can wish me to be. I had promised the Duchess of Portland to go to town with her as last Friday, but was so prudent as to let her go by herself, though I really had business besides the pleasure of being with her: she and the Duke return to-morrow to dinner. Yesterday Lady Bell Monck was dying with a gouty cholic, and she scared us all; however it is all over now, and she only complains of a violent soreness where the pain was. Mr. Monck has been confined for a week past with a swelled face, and Mr. Achard with a cough, so that we have been a house of invalids. L. B. M. is a sad check upon our pleasures; they have named three different days for going away, and yet they are here, and I fear will be as long as we stay in the country, which is truly a mortification; the Duchess behaves herself in the most obliging and proper manner that can be towards her, but it is much thrown away, however, it becomes her so to do, though *her pearls* are unregarded. Babess and the Gracelings have shewn me much affection and tenderness, and we have had much enjoyment of one another since my confinement to my room. Lord Titchfield is very well again, and goes to school tomorrow; the Duchess charges me with kind love to you.

I thought you would be disappointed in Gaudentio.[1] I know it did not charm me; D.D. told me before I read it that there "was little in it," and unluckily for Gaudentio I had just been reading Clarissa, and it must have been an extraordinary book that would have been relished after that! "Tom Jones," in his married state, is a *poor thing*, and not written by Fielding. Lady Mary Cook fainted away when she was brought into Westminster Hall; she is at present in her vile husband's custody, and now confined in a little dark room up two pair of stairs; she is in a very bad state of health: her mother, sisters, lawyers, physician, and Lord and Lady Bute (her near relations) are permitted to see her now by order of the Court. How much happier is *your Nanny Ward* than Lady Mary Cook with all her riches. I don't find she has by her conduct *in any way* deserved such tyranny; the worst I have heard of her is that her temper is not good.

Have you not heard of the second box of Irish shells? Mr. Barber writes me word he sent them the beginning of last month, directed to Mr. Old in Coventry, as I desired he would; if that is gone too, I shall think

---

[1] The History of Gaudentio di Lucca, published in 1725. Mrs. Barbauld speaks of it as "the effusion of a fine fancy and a refined understanding;" and says that "it is attributed to Bishop Berkeley."

some envious sea nymph watches an opportunity of seizing a treasure belonging to her own regions, jealous of our rivalling her with her own productions. It will be a little discouraging if we meet with this second disappointment. When Mr. Harley comes I will remember the sedan chair; he is not expected till the week before Xmas. Dr. Shaw comes here next week for a fortnight. Poor Dr. Young is in great trouble; his daughter-in-law, Mrs. Haviland,[1] (the lady he recommended to me in his letter,) is dead, it is said she died suddenly in her coach between Drogheda and Dublin. If you hear of any reports of a disagreement between Lord Anson[2] and his Lady you may contradict them—*there never has been any*; she is a little coxcombical, and affects to be learned, which may sometimes put him out of countenance; but Lord Anson is a most generous, good-natured, amiable man, and he deserved a wife of more dignity. Lady Wallingford has been extremely ill, but is better. She is in a wretched state of health, and so is our cousin Betty Granville; she went in the morning to the Princess of Wales' birthday, but looked so pale and faint that both the Prince and Princess desired her not to come at night, but to take the best care of herself she could. Mrs. Foley proposes being in town the 9th next month; *Mrs. Stock* leaves her, and has taken a house in Cleveland Court.

Dr. and Mrs. Tomlinson are to be in London this

---

[1] Lady Elizabeth Young had two daughters—the eldest married the Hon. Mr. Temple, son of Lord Palmerston, and died of consumption at Lyons; the youngest, Caroline, married Major Haviland, with whom she went to reside in Ireland.

[2] George Lord Anson, the celebrated naval commander, married Lady Elizabeth York, daughter of Philip, 1st Earl of Hardwick.

wiuter. My brother is very well, and Donnellan. Smith desires humble duty; I can't guess what you mean by "*the Duchess' tickets*," unless some of her visiting tickets, which are stampt, slipped accidentally into your letter. Could you procure a slip, or root more properly speaking, of Mr. Sherwood's fine dark polyanthus, and send it in a pot of earth packed up in a basket to be left at Gerrard's Cross, directed to the Duchess of Portland? I don't know whether this is a time for removing them.

Lady Nassau Pawlet[1] is mad; she says she will murder her daughter (a girl about nine years old, her only child), for she killed her brother! Lady Nassau's two sisters—Lady Gower[2] and Lady Leicester,[3] Lord Cook's mother—are so much taken up with persecuting poor Lady Mary Cook, that they have no thought of their unhappy niece.

Mrs. Delany to Mrs. Dewes.

Bulstrode, 4 Dec., 1749.

I had a letter last post from my brother; he is very well. I know nothing of Sir Tony, but suppose if anything extraordinary ailed him my brother would have mentioned him. Your wish has at last prevailed, and we are free from all *inters*, but not till last Friday, so now

---

[1] Lady Isabella, daughter of Thomas, 6th Earl of Thanet, married Lord Nassau Pawlet, brother to the Duke of Bolton.

[2] The Lady Mary Tufton, a daughter of Thomas, 6th Earl of Thanet, was born in 1701. She married, 1st, Anthony Earl Harold, last surviving son of Henry De Grey Duke of Kent, April 17, 1718, and on his death became the third wife of John, 1st Earl Gower.

[3] Lady Margaret, daughter of Thomas, 6th Earl of Thanet, married July 2, 1718, Thomas Earl of Leicester.

our têtes-à-têtes and works go on **swimmingly**. I have begun to put on the shells on the lustre, and hope it will be finished in less than a fortnight: we could do nothing whilst some company were in the house who were to be treated with ceremony! Poor Babess's apprehensions for her sister increase—she went to town this morning. One day last week (Friday, I think) she had a letter from one of the Maids of Honour to say that she supposed she did not think Mrs. B. G.[1] so ill as she really was, and that she was grown a great deal weaker and none of her complaints removed. This terrified Babess extremely; she was for going instantly to town, but we prevailed on her to stay till to-day; she is excessively fond of her sister, and has indeed not only been a kind sister, but has acted the part of a tender parent.

Did I not say that Lady Margaret was *not* grown in proportion with her sisters? she is pale, and quiet in her manner; she is a sensible little girl, but not of a strong constitution I believe. Lord Edward is a sweet pretty boy, but not so forward at his book as his brother was at his age. Lady Mary Cook's match was made by my Lady Gower. I am sorry Lord North has had the gout, I *never can congratulate* anybody upon having so severe a companion. When does he go to London?

I did not tell the Duchess of your drawer for shells till I received your commands so to do. She says she must have just such another for that purpose and *twenty others*; but a material thing is wanting, which can neither be borrowed nor purchased—a thing we seldom know the true value of till gone; and every hour that

---

[1] Mrs. Betty Granville.

strikes ought to put us in mind how fleeting it is, though it is that which, if well and rightly employed, will make us happy everlastingly!

When you send to Snitsfield pray present my humble service to Lady A. Coventry, and let her know that I have not been unmindful of the book of shells I mentioned to her, but there is not one to be had at this time; the bookseller I had mine of says he expects some over from France soon, and has promised I shall have the first that comes, which I will take care to send to Lady Anne Coventry by the first opportunity. I shall send you some oranges for orange wine as soon as they are good, I give you notice now that you may have your sugar and vessel ready. My house is in *St. James's Place*, the landlady's name *Lynch*.

I think the fringe of the valance and bases should be the same depth as that on the bottom of the curtains. *The great* Dr. Shaw arrived here this day in excellent spirits. The strange odd creature I named is a Java hare.[1] Let me know instantly by what carrier I shall send down the oranges. There is great bustling in London about the Westminster election: if Lord Trentham[2] should carry it, which it is thought he will not, he will *pay dearly* for it they say.

A few days ago the Duke of C— went with some ladies in his coach to see the election, and the mob took them for foreigners, called them French —— and was going to pull them out of the coach, but on their vowing they were English they let them alone.

---

[1] There are two water-colour drawings, by Mrs. Delany, of the Java hare.

[2] Lord Trentham was opposed for Westminster, in December, 1749, by Sir George Vandeput.

Mrs. Delany to Mrs. Dewes.

Bulstrode, 10 Dec., 1749.

I am glad you have seen the bride folks, and that Mrs. Mills is as lively as Miss Wheeler was: I hope she will be able to communicate some of her spirit to her husband, and he some of his gentleness to her, and that will make a mutual amendment; though for the course of this world, and the cares she may have to go through, her stock of spirits may be very necessary! I desire you will make her easy about the payment of the money; when it is quite convenient to her will do or me. I think you are much in the right not to put the glass into your chariot till you have something better to see than dirty roads.

Last Thursday the Duchess of Portland went to Eton to meet Lady Andover; Babess went with her to lie that night at Windsor, in order to meet Mrs. Foley at Slough next day; she complained a good deal that morning, and had had no sleep for some nights. The Duchess came back to dinner without Lady Andover, she was in hopes of bringing her home with her. Babess said she would come to us yesterday, and the coach was setting out for her, when her servant brought me a letter with an account of her having been so ill she could not go to meet her sister nor return to Bulstrode, but to-morrow the Duchess and I propose fetching her. I don't wonder she should be ill; the constant anxiety she is in about her sister is enough to wear her away. She went to town last Monday to see her, and returned on Tuesday; she found her not worse, but not the least better. Next Thursday the coach goes to town to fetch Lord Titchfield home for the holidays. I design going up in it, to settle all particulars about my winter-quarters, and to see poor Betty Granville and Mrs. Foley, who is come safe to town, and her children. Lady Mary Cook is so ill, that it is thought she can't live; she is confined to a very dismal, ill-furnished room *up two pair of stairs.* I have not yet met one man who does not pity her and detest her tyrant; I should have an ill opinion of the humanity of that man, that could justify such cruelty; if she dies, she has been as much murdered by the severe usage she has met with, as if she had been poisoned. I am very glad you have got Miss Hine[1] with you; she seems to be a good kind of young woman. If she knows how the *crokand* sugar used to be done at Mrs. Norcliff's, I wish you could prevail on her to teach Sally how to do it. You have been very good to Sally; I am sorry she should have added to your number of sick folks, for you have been sufficiently tormented with sickness.

I think of your kind intention towards St. James's Place with the greatest pleasure; if it can be conveniently and agreeably accomplished it will make D.D. and me extremely happy. I have not yet finished the lustre; your mussels have been of great use, but I hope in ten days' time it will be done and hung up in its place; it promises to be very gay, and the Duchess likes it extremely. I have made her six baskets: she

---

[1] "Miss Hine" must have been what in these days would be called "a governess," but the subsequent allusion to her knowledge of confectionary in the place she had previously been in, proves that a practical acquaintance with different branches of housekeeping was then naturally to be expected in a governess.

likes them so well and finds them so convenient, that
if I have time I must make her a few more. The
great and mighty Shaw has been very entertaining and
comical; I gave him your message about the shells;
he says he has none, or they should be much at your
service. I was afraid last night I had forfeited all his
grace and favour, he told us a very droll story of his
journey to Sir Thomas Littleton's,[1] and of his having a
most ridiculous toss out of the chaise; he was thrown
head foremost upon the board over "the leathern apron,"
as he called it, but catching fast hold of one of the
horse's tails, he saved himself from falling farther;
but being a little unwieldy, it was some time before he
could be raised from the place. This happened just as
he stopped at Sir T. Littleton's door, all the ladies and
gentlemen ready to receive him; a jerk in the stopping
of the chaise suddenly caused this downfal. His
humorous way of telling this accident, and the idea
that struck us all of his figure in such a posture, you
may believe raised a great deal of mirth amongst us;
and the Duchess insisted upon my making a drawing of
it, which I did. She was so much diverted with it, that
she would show it Dr. S. I was against it, but she
earnestly begged, and I consented, as I had done things
of that kind by him before, and he always took it with
good humour. This did not succeed so well, and he
walked off gloomy, which really vexed me; but Mr.
Achard told him the concern I was under, and that the
drawing was destroyed; he then would not confess he

---

[1] Sir Thomas Lyttelton, Bart., M.P. for the county of Worcester, father of
George Lord Lyttelton. He died September 14, 1751.

had been angry; said that it was absurd to suppose he should take anything ill of me, and when we met at supper, he was as merry and good-humoured as ever: so "all's well that ends well."

Lord North passed by yesterday, and sent in a message with an excuse for not calling, but he was lame and obliged to go on. I was a good deal shocked last Thursday with an account that Bennet had had a fit. It was certainly an apoplectic fit—he had one twenty years ago; I hope it will give him a serious and proper way of thinking. He was the person who made the disturbance at the Sun at Cheltenham; he was blooded, is to have a blister and other medicines by way of precaution.

A Rebus sent me.

What in every tavern you usually see,
In what the wrecked sailor would willingly be,
Or the stone that has built half the churches in town,
Is the name of an amiable friend of your own.

Could Mrs. Viney send the Duchess a root or two of the bee-flower? The polyanthus, she will be extremely glad of.

Mrs. Delany to Mrs. Dewes,

Bulstrode, 17 Dec. 1749.

On Friday I went to town in the Duke of Portland's coach, that went to fetch Lord Titchfield. D.D. and I set out from hence at nine, got to my brother's at half an hour after twelve, just asked him how he did, and as we were to meet at dinner at Cuz Foley's I staid but a little while with him. Thence to Mrs. Percival's, saw

Miss Sutton and Mrs. Percival, but no Mrs. Donnellan. By this time it was two o'clock; the Dean walked away to Paul's Church-Yard and I took a chair to do business; went in the first place to Mr. Dufour's, the famous man for paper ornaments like stucco, bespoke a rose for the top of her Grace of Portland's dressing-room, where the shell lustre is to hang, which was finished last Thursday, (had been just twelve days in hand, this by way of digression). From thence went to settle with my new landlady. She not at home; and there I staid near three quarters of an hour, at last she came, and very courteous: and for five guineas a week goes out of the house and leaves it free.

It was half an hour after 3 before I got to Mrs. Foley's, where I was to spruce myself up a little before dinner. Mrs. Foley looks very thin, and I fear B. Granville's illness affects her a good deal, though she has better spirits about her than Lady Abbess; Mrs. Foley and I went in the afternoon to drink tea with her. The physician that now attends her has had her blooded, and blistered on the arm and the pit of her stomach, and with all these operations she has not lost her strength, which gives me hopes that her youth will at last get the better of her complaints. I called for a quarter of an hour on Lady Wallingford, who looks wretchedly, and has been in a great deal of danger.

D.D. and I met at Whitehall on Friday evening, before 9; we supped on sprats and very luckily met the box of shells Mrs. F. Old sent me from Coventry, but it does not make me amends for the box lost, for this contains only trumpery sorts, none that are fit for anything but common grotto work. We returned to Bulstrode on Saturday with Lord Titchfield and Dr. Shaw, who went to London for a few days on business. As you forgot to enclose my Pauline's measure, she cannot possibly have her coat before Xmas. I will observe your directions about the materials; I think it time enough for her to be dressed in silk.

The Duchess would with great pleasure make you a visit were it in her power; but she hopes to have the pleasure of seeing you in town this winter, and sends you many kind services and wishes, a volley of which were let off as I just now came from the tea-table and saying I was going to finish a letter to you.

Mrs. Delany to Mrs. Dewes.

Bulstrode, 22 Dec. 1749.

As next Monday, my usual day for writing, is Xmas day, I will not put off answering your last letter, and the Duchess finds so much employment, that I have little time for writing. I have finished the lustre[1]—I believe I told you so before—and it has been a *great work*. I have begun a pair of candlesticks,[1] for her, but fear I shall hardly finish them, as not a flower is yet made. I had a letter from Mr. M. in answer to one I writ to him at Welsbourn about Mr. Clifton: he delivered my letter to Mr. Frankland, who said many obliging things of me,

---

[1] "*The lustre*" and the "candlesticks" were made of shells. Mrs. Delany excelled in shell work, and attained to such perfection in it, that she executed cornices of the most beautiful designs, which were formed of shells, which when painted or coloured over appeared like the finest carving, but for smaller objects like the *lustre*, &c., they were left in their natural colours, which, arranged by her unerring eye, had the most beautiful effect, and united the brilliancy of the colours of enamel with the inimitable tracery and harmony of nature.

and how much he valued my recommendation; that he would do all that lay in his power, and in the meantime begged his acceptance of a twenty pound note!—was not that pretty? indeed something more, for it was great liberality. I watched the eclipse, but was more pleased at the thought that your eyes were at the same instant placed on the same object than with the eclipse; I believe it was not much above a *third* part of the moon. I know nothing more about Lord Trentham than what the newspapers say. Lord Guernsey will not be married very soon; I have not heard that the day is fixed.

Lord Titchfield is a fine boy, and learns surprisingly quick, but I do not think him quite *so agreeable* in his manner as his two eldest sisters, who are so modest, so civil, and so good-humoured that you would be charmed with them. The Duchess keeps up her authority amongst her children as she used to do, and they watch every motion of her eye. Yesterday we carried home Miss Granville; she had some affairs to settle before she went to London. Betty continues in the same way, has still the pain in her chest and no voice. Her sisters are much to be pitied, who suffer as much in their mind as she does in her body.

The Duchess, &c. send you many loves and services.

CHAPTER IX.

JANUARY, 1750, TO DECEMBER, 1750.

Mrs. Delany to Mrs. Dewes.

St. James's Place, 16 Jan. 1749-50.

A long letter should have followed my short dab to my dearest sister, if time and opportunity would have given me leave. But you know, and will know I hope again, that the first coming to London occasions much hurry and interruption. I cannot forgive Mrs. J. stuffing into your chariot, and being so airy as to give you cold; I beseech you not to be so complaisant, and I still owe her a grudge for some precious moments she robbed us of. Lord Harrington does not go, at last, to Delville, at which I most heartily rejoice; the Lord Chancellor [1] has prevailed with him to go to his country house at Merion. The day after I came to town I dined at Mrs. Percival's, which was last Thursday (on which day I wrote you to tell you we were safely lodged—Sally, trunks, and all.) I spent the whole day in Hanover Square, called on the Maid of Honour in the

---

[1] Robert Jocelyn, Esq., appointed Lord Chancellor of Ireland, September 7, 1739, created 29th November, 1743, Baron Newport, and 6th December, 1755, Viscount Jocelyn; and died Oct. 25th, 1756. His son was created Earl of Roden.

ing; she is indeed in a melancholy way. On Friday morning I had mercers, &c., and all that train. Donnellan, Fred. Montagu, and Mrs. Montagu, then dined at Whitehall; visited Lady Bell Monck in the afternoon, and finished with Mrs. Foley, who is as well as can be, but does not go out.

Saturday morning, full of business, dined at Foley's; my brother met us, who is very well, and in good spirits. In the evening went to Betty Granville, finished at Dash's, and met our Duchess. Sunday went to early church at St. James' Chapel, dined at Montagu's, made Lady Wallingford a visit by the way, who looks wretchedly, but is better than she was. The evening I spent at Donnellan's, met Mrs. Southwell and the Duchess. D.D. was to have been of our party, but has got one of his troublesome colds; he would make me go yesterday to the play with the Duchess. In the morning I had Mr. Carr and silks, and have bought a rich satin for a sack, as near the colour of the ribbon we bought together as I could get it, and a purple and white flowered silk. Then in came the Bishop of Gloucester, who staid an hour; after him, General Dalzil;[1] then Mr. Montagu, Mr. Achard, Mr. Hill, and Lord North; so that with difficulty I was dressed by three quarters after 3 : dined at Whitehall, and as I said before, went to the new play, "Edward the Black Prince,"[2] which entertained me

---

[1] A descendant of the celebrated royalist general Sir James Dalzell, Dalziell, or Dalyell, of Binns, Bart., who raised the Scotch Greys, and never shaved his beard after the death of King Charles I. His beard-comb is preserved as an heir-loom; it is twelve inches in breadth, and has teeth six inches deep. There were several military officers among his descendants, probably the one above-named was James Dalyell, who in 1763 was killed in America.

[2] Edward the Black Prince, (never before acted,) "was played for nine nights,

very well, though it is rather a dull play; but the story, or rather incident, is so interesting, and Garrick acts it with so much spirit, that I liked it very well. The Duke of Portland is here; Miss Thornhill just coming. D.D.'s cold not better, I stay at home all day. In the afternoon comes Donnellan, Miss Sutton, and the Duchess of Portland. I can add no more. My brother dines with us; he complains a little but he looks well, and makes me happy, and when my dear sister comes my happiness will be complete.

Mrs. Delany to Mrs. Dewes.

6 Feb. 1749-50.

Yesterday I went to Brompton with Miss G. Lodgings are taken there for the Maid of Honour, who is so much worse than when I last wrote that I think there is no manner of hope of her recovery.[1] They call it a consumption, but it is of a singular nature. The pain on her breast is constant and violent, and at times she is so oppressed that if not instantly bled they say she would expire, and yet it is *not an asthma.* The physicians *talk learnedly* about her, but, in truth, though they all give her *up as irrecoverable,* they don't well know what her distemper is. Pray God give them all consolation!

Now as to your coming to town, pray come as soon as

---

commencing January 6, 1750, at Drury Lane." Some parts were said to be well written, but on the whole it was dull and declamatory; and the character of "the Black Prince too uniform, too cold and tame for such an actor as Garrick."

[1] Mrs. B. Granville, the Maid of Honour seems to have been one of the most marvellous instances of vitality *in spite of* human art that ever existed; she survived till 1790! Forty years after this letter!

you can, for Lady Ab. has no intention of returning to me again. I should have been very glad to keep her a fortnight longer, but if Brompton agrees with Betty they will stay on for some time; if not, and an end is soon put to her sufferings, her sister designs going directly to Windsor. D.D. insists on your coming the latter end of this month at farthest, for oratorios begin the 2nd of March, and I challenge you to go with me; and if the dear child is well and you can get Mrs. Peters, I hope you will comply with his request. I beg you will answer this as soon as possible. What joy it will be to me if I may expect to see you within this fortnight. I shall not forget the 11th February.[1] I pray God many returns, and that you and the dear child may enjoy it, attended with health and happiness of every kind!

I have this morning had a visit from Mr. Bayley, who begs his humble service to you. He has expressed so much gratitude to you and our dearest departed friend,[2] that it has (though a satisfaction to meet with so grateful a mind) raised a tender recollection that is rather more than my spirits can at this time well bear; but as I think it wrong to indulge what may prejudice one's health, I intend going about this morning to see fine pictures and dine at Whitehall, where I shall meet the Duchess of Queensbury, and spend the evening with Foley.

---

[1] The birthday of Mary Dewes.   [2] Their mother, Mrs. Granville.

Mrs. Delany to Mrs. Dewes.

St. James's Place, 20 Feb. 1749-50.

I bless God that my dear little girl has missed her ague; I suppose you will repeat the bark plasters to Mary's wrists before the usual time of the ague's returning, which is generally in eight days, and till that is over I don't expect you should fix your day at all; only let me know within a week of the time that Miss Granville may remove to Lord Weymouth's, where she intends going as soon as you are determined to come: she would go sooner, but I will not suffer her; but to make her stay easy, I have assured her that you will not defer coming one day on her account. Indeed I believe she will soon be released from her painful and miserable attendance on poor B. G., who is now reduced to the last weakness; she was so ill last Saturday, the pains on her breast and at her heart so strong, that from 7 in the morning till two at noon she was in the utmost danger; the physician that constanly attends her, Dr. Monsey[1] was in the house with her, and says he thought she was expiring several times—she had several fits of strong convulsions. Unfortunately that was the day fixed upon for the Xtning of my goddaughter, Miss Mary Foley.[2] The hour appointed was 12, to meet at Mrs. Foley's; the Duke of Portland godfather, the Duchess, proxy for Lady Mansel,[3] who was

---

[1] Dr. Monsey, physician to Lord Godolphin, who lived at Gogmagog Hill, near Cambridge.

[2] Mary, second daughter of Thomas (afterwards Baron) Foley, married Richard Clerk, Esq., of Kingston, county Oxford, and died in December, 1844.

[3] Sir Wiliam Mansel, married Amy, eldest daughter of Sir Biohard Cox, Lord Chancellor of Ireland.

very ill. At 11, just as I was going to dress, a messenger came from Brompton to let me know B. G. was so extremely ill, and that I was desired to go there immediately, the Dean gone out, and I knew not where to find him. so I took a hackney-coach, called at the end of Stratten Street, and sent to consult with Mr. Foley, who intreated me to come to the Xtning and not say anything to Mrs. Foley *till it was over.* I then went on to Brompton, found poor Babess in a miserable way, Dr. Taylor and Sir Edward Hulse [1] sent for. I told her the necessity there was of my going to the Xtning, and that I would return again as soon as it was over. I got home as fast as I could, much discomposed as you may imagine, and not at all in a condition to see Mrs. Foley; so I sent a note to her, to say I had been detained by business, and begged the gossips would meet me at May Fair Chapel, where the child was to be Xtned, and then I consulted with the Duchess how I should break the sad news to Mrs. Foley—as we then imagined the poor Maid of Honour *could not outlive the day.* It was agreed I should tell her that she had taken a medicine which had ruffled her very much, which was *in fact true,* and that Babess begged of me to come; this alarmed her immediately, and she intreated me to return to her sister, which I did, and found things rather better. She (that is Betty) grew easy towards evening; I then left her to go to Mrs. Foley.

---

[1] Sir Edward Hulse, Bart., eldest son of Sir Edward Hulse, M.D., first physician to his Majesty George II.

Mrs. Delany to Mrs. Dewes.

St. James's Place, 1 March, 1749-50.

Indeed my dearest sister's motherly tenderness and patience has been tried, and my own disappointment is also your disappointment.

B. G. continues in the same languishing state, always in pain, but gains no ground as to strength; she was blooded two days ago, and they talk of bleeding her again to-morrow. I expect our Duchess to drink a tête-à-tête tea with me, and then we go together to the Duchess of Queensbury.

To-morrow oratorios begin—Saul, one of my beloved pieces—I shall go. The new play written by Mr. Whitehead,[1] Lord Jersey's tutor, is now acting, and much applauded; it is too tragical for me: it is called The Roman Father, written on the plan, as I understand, of Corneille's *Horace*. Lord Titchfield is pretty well, though still confined to his room.

I am glad you have got Mrs. Peters. Poor Mrs. Lambard has buried her son; she is ready to lie in, and I hope will have another, as it will be of consequence to their fortune. My brother is well, and so is Sir Anthony. Mrs. Southwell is recovered of a very bad fever. The present talk of the town is of an affair between Lord Hervey and Lord Cobham. Lord Hervey was at a drum of Lady Cobham's; he held his hat under his arm, the inside upwards; Lord Cobham laid

---

[1] The Roman Father. A tragedy by W. Whitehead. Acted at Drury Lane 1750. Founded on the combat of the Horatii and Curiatii. Mason says " it is an improvement on Corneille."

a wager with Mr. Nugent of a crown that he would spit in Lord Hervey's hat, *and did*, asking Lord Hervey pardon for doing it, and telling him the reason, upon which with the utmost composure, Lord Hervey offered him his hat to win as many crowns as he pleased; but next morning sent Lord Cobham a challenge.[1]

An interval of two months here occurs in the correspondence, during which period it appears by the following letter, Mrs. Dewes was with her sister in London, till within two days of Mrs. Delany's return to Ireland.

Mrs. Delany to Mrs. Dewes.

7 o'clock, 4th May, 1750.

I thank you, my most dear sister, for the happiness I enjoyed yesterday, and am most thankful for the happy hours we have spent together this year, and hope we shall have a cheerful return of them. Yesterday was a day snatched out of the shade: but I fear the fatigue was rather too great for you, and your exerting your spirits in the kind manner you did, hurt you.

---

[1] Horace Walpole gives a different version of this story, viz., that Lord Cobham laid a bet of a guinea with Mr. Nugent, that he would commit this "absurd brutality," and that "Lord Hervey would not resent it," Lord Hervey with great temper and sensibility asked "if he had any further occasion for his hat?" "Oh, I see you are angry." "Not very well pleased." Lord Cobham took the fatal hat.

Mrs. Delany to Mrs. Dewes.

Chester, 6 May, 1750.

I had a very good night, I thank God, at Newport. We set out at 6 precisely, drank a cup of warm whey, and breakfasted at a place called Hernehill. We got to Whitchurch by one, dined on salmon, mutton, and chicken. We came to this place by eight and drank tea; we were much fatigued. Most of our way was dragging through *hot* sands; otherwise the roads were everywhere very good, and we have reason to be very thankful, not having met with any bad accident. I am very well, and just come from St. Peter's Church. I have hardly any remains of my cold. The yatcht left Holyhead last Thursday with Mr. Fox and Lady Caroline[1] and Mr. and Mrs. Ellis.[2] The weather is so fine and temperate that, in all probability, it will be at Park Gate to-night, or to-morrow morning early, so that we may go off with the evening tide. We propose leaving this for Park Gate to-morrow at nine.

If we are delayed a day or two, which I hope we shall not, it will be pleasanter to be near the sea-side and green fields than penned up in a hot dull town. I won't seal this letter till to-morrow morning: by that time I may have some account to add of the yacht, or Dr. Barber, who is expected every hour. I found a letter

---

[1] Henry Fox, Esq., Secretary-of-State, married, in 1744, Lady Georgiana Caroline Lennox, eldest daughter of Charles, 2nd Duke of Richmond. In 1763 he was created Baron, and his wife Baroness Holland in 1762.

[2] The Right Honourable Welbore Ellis, afterwards created (1794) Lord Mendip, married Elizabeth, only daughter of Sir William Stanhope.

from him. He thinks himself extremely obliged to you, for the honour you have done him in desiring him to take Welsbourne in his way. He had not seen Dr. Clerke when he wrote, who is to be his conductor, and could give no answer but that if it depended on him he should most gladly wait upon you. I found the box of shells here, much shattered, and have sent it to Whitehall.

Mrs. Gordon, the lady that entertained us here last summer, and was so agreeable as we walked on the walls, has drunk tea with me, and is sensible and entertaining. She has one daughter, now at the Bath, that she doats on and commends in a pretty modest manner. She talked of her daughter and I of my sister, and have promised that whenever you come to Chester you will make her a visit. We breakfast with her to-morrow before we go to Park Gate.

Mrs. Delany to Mrs. Dewes.

Delville, 18 May, 1750.

I had an intention of writing to you last post but —impossible—shoals of impertinences made it impracticable. A year's absence makes it so necessary to have a thorough inspection into everything, and I am settling my family in a different way from what it was formerly, which obliges me to be Mrs. Notable, and to do much more than I ever did in my life, and I hope it will agree with me; and own that the bustle of it, (which once I should have thought better executed by a servant than myself,) has been of service to me, as it has occapied every moment and left me the less leisure to think of *some moments,* the recollection of which are yet too tender to dwell upon. Smith takes to her new employment very cleverly, and when once I have *fixed her* in the *method* I like, I shall return to my *less necessary,* but more pleasing employments of painting, &c.

I must take up the journal still, and then you will be more exactly informed of all I do than by any other way of relating it. On Tuesday morning, the two Mrs. Hamiltons, Miss Bushe, and Miss Anne Hamilton came here—all well, and made many enquiries. We dined at home that day, and spent most of it in looking over our house and gardens, and find everything very well; the garden in excellent order. Wednesday, we dined with *my* Mrs. Hamilton, spent the day there; Thursday, with Mrs. Forde; yesterday, with Mrs. F. Hamilton; to-day, with Mrs. Clayton, and I have had Lord Grandison, Mr. Mason, Mr. Curry, Lord Mornington, Mr. Fortescue! It is almost two and I not dressed for dinner, and you are to pay for this strange dab, for send it I will, that you may know we are very well, never in better health.

Mrs. Delany to Mrs. Dewes.
Delville, 22 May, 1750.

I was interrupted in my last journal by a train of visitors; had time to dress and get to Mrs. Clayton by a little past three, staid with her till near seven, made a visit or two in my way home, and had just a moment's daylight to run into my garden and see two fine myrtles set—the one given me by Mrs. Hamilton, the other, Miss Bushe. Sunday went to church twice;

neighbour visits in the afternoon; at 7, D.D. and I went to see Mrs. Barber. Yesterday morning I had *my* Mrs. Hamilton from nine to one to myself, which was, I believe, a mutual pleasure; then came in the Bishop of Derry, Mrs. Barnard, and their son, and then Dr. Stopford and his lady; all left us to a tête-à-tête dinner at 3. At 5, Mrs. Helsham and Mrs. Roberts came; went away soon after six. I settled my shells on the outside of my cabinet; the inside will take up more time than I can spare at present. I have found my house in pretty good order, and the garden *is Paradisaical.* Oh that my dearest sister could see it with as much ease as going to Stratford or Warwick! and yet with *such* a passage as *we had* from Park Gate to Dublin, the voyage is not so formidable an affair as it appears to be;—for we dined at Park Gate on Sunday at one, and the next day at Delville at 5!

After all the bother and rout I made about my *portable garden* it is lost; the box can nowhere be found. I gave it in charge myself to the captain of the ship that brought it over, (it did not come with us,) and he knows nothing of the matter. Our fruits and flowers have been much hurt by the easterly winds; it is now so cold that a fire is comfortable, though the sky is clear and the sun bright, and *my prospects* in great perfection; Tiger is perfectly well, and our little robins as familiar as usual. The greatest damage I have sustained in my absence is my shell lustres falling to pieces, and most of my crayon pictures *mildewed*; but as they are the works of an author of no very great value, it gives me no very great concern. To-day Mr. Frankland and his daughter dine with us; to-morrow we call at eight o'clock on Mrs. F. Hamilton and Bushe to go to Bray, ten miles off, to see Miss Mary Forth, who is there drinking goat's whey, and next month goes to Bristol. Mrs. F. Hamilton, to my great satisfaction, does not go to England with her son; she is terrified with the Eton rebellion,[1] and other prudent reasons joined have determined her to stay here. Mrs. Clayton and the Bishop, and Miss Brown, went yesterday towards Clogher, and we are preparing for the North as soon as we can pack up what will be necessary for us.

On consideration, my scheme of staying at Delville this summer will not do: as it is on my account that D.D. is absent a whole year it would not be well in me to let him go to the North without me, and I should not be easy to have him there alone. Next Friday we dine at Chapel-Izod, a house belonging to the Government, lent to the Bishop of Derry—a sweet place, about two miles beyond Derry; and Saturday we are to dine at Lord Grandison's.

I had a letter yesterday from Donnellan; she tells me the Maid of Honour goes out every day in a coach, seems in good spirits, looks wretchedly, and the Duchess has a very bad opinion of her. I own I *cannot* think she will recover, but may linger a great while; I hope, in God, she will make a proper use of the time given her. D.D. went at 6 to see my Lord Chancellor at Merion, six miles off. I am at a great loss for franks now. I can get none here, and if I enclose it to Sir C. M. he may be at Cheltenham, and to send them roundabout to Bulstrode is tedious; however, this letter shall go that way. I have got the *harp-shell*, and will send the prints of the gems by the first opportunity.

Mrs. Delany to Mrs. Dewes.

Delville, 29 May, 1750.

What depends on the weather we must bear without repining, but when our loss arises from the negligence of messengers we may justly be angry. How little do those *stocks of posts* know the hearts they torment by their carelessness. You can easily imagine how little time I have had at command since my coming to this place. D.D. dined in Dublin at Lord Grandison's, and left Bushe and me to a tête-à-tête in my closet. I got a cold by a succession of company last Sunday, who drank tea in my garden; the last company was the Duchess of Manchester, Lady Arabella Denny,[1] Mrs. Fitzmorris, who staid till very late, and the wind north-east. I was taken ill that night with a pain in my head and sore throat, and was blooded on Monday, took physic on Tuesday, repeat the same to-morrow, and shall not attempt writing. But my good and agreeable Letitia, who now makes me happy in her company, will add a line or two, to let you know how I do.

Tuesday, 5 o'clock.—I am so well to-day, my most dear sister, that I could, with pleasure, and no sort of inconveniency, write you a long letter, but my kind nurses will not allow it; so that pleasure I must postpone till next post.

Continued by Miss Bushe.

With true pleasure I can assure you, your amiable and worthy sister is pure well, and as cheerful as she

---

[1] Arabella, second daughter of Thomas Earl of Kerry, married Arthur Denny, Esq., of Tralee.

can be separated from so dear and deserving a friend as yourself. The talk is of you hourly, an indulgence to herself, and great pleasure to one who has reason to think so advantageously of you as I do. Dear Mrs. Dewes, do think of seeing Ireland and *a group of people* ready to receive you cordially, and amongst them some whimsical characters, that, *when* the day lowers and the air is heavy, will help to cure spleen. Since I began this, I have been mostly thinking how I shall say what I ought, or what I think on your pretty token of remembrance; but I am so bungling at expressing, though indeed grateful at heart, that I will only assure you I shall always keep and value it as you should wish a person to do, who is, with truth and great esteem,

Dear madam,

Your most obliged and faithful servant,

L. BUSHE.

P. S. I beg you may constantly think that, to the best of my capacity, Mrs. Delany shall be *nursed* and *entertained*; all indeed she has now, thank God, any occasion for.

Mrs. Delany to Mrs. Dewes.

Delville, 2 June, 1750.

I hope my letter by the last packet gave my dearest sister no uneasiness but what must naturally attend on account of a friend's having been ill, and not raised any fears of my being still out of order, for I assure you the information I sent was strict truth, and I am now, I thank God, as well as ever I was in my life. I have taken Salt Polyckest and Cheltenham waters. D.D. whose apprehensions are in proportion to his tenderness, sent for Dr. Quin. Monday is my business day. I have read over your letters since my confinement, (which was but from Monday to Friday), and they have been my *castor, pearl cordial,* and *sal volatile*. How kindly did you remember the 14th of May.[1] I enjoy too many blessings not to be very thankful for the return of that day; with earnest prayers that I may be worthy of the attention and love of so many valuable and dear friends. Your not receiving my second letter from Park Gate was very vexatious; because that could have saved you some pain. I gave you an account in that of a letter I had written to Mr. Richardson[2] of the books D.D. ordered him to send you, and desired you would let him know where Eagles, the Keinton carrier, puts up in London. As you read Clarissa, when you object to any particular expressions *let me know* the *page* and the *line*. I am very glad you have taken your building in hand, and enlarged your scale so as to give you all the conveniences you want; and I think you are in the right not to put up the bed till you have done your building. I am sorry the church service is not settled to your mind. I think Sir C. M. has been unreasonable. I have

---

[1] Mrs. Delany's birthday.
[2] Samuel Richardson, the son of a Derbyshire farmer, was born in 1689. He was brought up as a printer, and carried on that business for many years in Salisbury Court, Fleet Street. In 1740 he published his "Pamela," in 1749 his "Clarissa," and in 1753 his Sir Charles Grandison. In 1760, he bought "a moiety of the patent of law-printer." He had a country house at first at Northend and afterwards at Parson's Green, where he exercised great hospitality. He died July 4, 1761.

had all my acquaintance at my door, but D.D. would not let me see anybody till yesterday, that Lady Grandison, and Lady Meade[1] came in the afternoon. To-day the Veseys dine here. I am in debt to the Duchess of Portland and Mrs. Donnellan. I don't know where to direct to my brother, but at a venture shall send my letter to Park Street, till he informs me where to find him.

Mrs. Delany to Mrs. Dewes.

Delville, 8 June, 1750.

MY DEAREST SISTER,

Covered with dust and wearied with the toils of cleaning and new arranging my cabinet of shells, throwing out rubbish, adding my new acquisitions, all which has been the work of yesterday and this morning to the present hour of one—(and which could not have been accomplished without the good assistance of my Mrs. Hamilton and Bushe, who have toiled like horses) —to refresh my body and mind I am retired to write to the sister of my heart, to thank her for her last charming letter, and to assure her that I continue in as good health as her own heart can wish me.

We have not yet fixed our time for the northern journey, nor can we, having everything to provide of furniture for the house we go to. Sometimes in the midst of my enjoyment of the garden it makes me sigh to think that my fruits and flowers, which I with care

---

[1] Catherine, widow of Sir Richard Meade, Bart., and daughter of Henry Prittie, Esq., married secondly, Henry Cavendish, Esq., who was created a Baronet, in 1755, and was the ancestor of Lord Waterpark.

and pains have planted, will be gathered by others. Not that I am such a churl as to *grudge* my friends, or even my acquaintance, the produce of my garden, but I wish only to have the pleasure of bestowing them myself and of having some share of them: then, on the other hand, when I consider how much good D.D.'s presence must do in the North—and I hope *I may* in a small degree do some—I think of my journey cheerfully, and set about preparing for it *manfully!* That expression does *not suit the occasion*, for if *the men* were to go through all domestic bustle as we are obliged to do when we acquit ourselves properly, they would think themselves *somewhat obliged* by the trouble we save them!

This day se'night we dined at the Bishop of Derry's, Chapel-Izod; Mr. Franklin and his daughter dined there, and Sign^r Pasquali,[1] who plays very neatly and with a good taste on the fiddle. Sunday we always pass at home. Monday, Mrs. F. Hamilton passed the day with me. Tuesday, we went (D.D., B., and I) to Lucan to breakfast; D.D. went to Leixlip, two miles further, to see the Primate, and Mrs Vesey carried Bushe and I to Carrtown to see Lady Kildare and Lady C. Fox; nobody at home but the Dowager; dined with the Veseys. Wednesday, I travelled all over Dublin shopping, bespeaking paper for hangings, linen for beds, and a thousand things too tedious to be here inserted. Thursday, D.D. went to Dublin by 7, and attended the

---

[1] Pasquali, (Nicolo,) an Italian violin-player and composer, was first known about the year 1743, in London, where he then resided. He afterwards settled at Edinburgh, and continued there as a teacher to the period of his death, which took place in 1757. He published several musical works, overtures, &c.

college examinations for fellowships; sent a *how de's*
to Mrs. Fortescue, just brought to bed of another son,
and to Miss Wesley who is to be married as soon as her
sister's month is up. Visited Mrs. Smith of the North,
Mrs. Helsham, Mrs. Burghs, Lady Meade, and Lady
Blessington,[1] four of the five at home. This morning
before nine came Mrs. F. Ham. Mrs. Forth, Miss Anne
Hamilton, and the two young Hamiltons; we have
breakfasted and walked all over the garden, and I have
stole away to finish my letter, with a promise (this
being a *jubilee day*) of playing to them on the harpsichord as soon as I have done. To-morrow, Dr. Mathews
and his family and Mrs. Marlay dine here; Tuesday,
Mr. and Mrs. Ellis and Mrs. Agar;[2] Wednesday, Capt.
Forde and his lady, Mr. Knap and his lady; Thursday,
we dine three miles off, at Mr. Cavendish's and Lady
Meade's, with whom Mr. Mount lives. All you have
heard of the Miss Gunnings *is true*, except their having
a fortune, but I am afraid they have a *greater* want
than that, which is *discretion!*

Mrs. Delany to Mrs. Dewes.

Delville, 18 June, 1750.

I cannot yet settle to any of my favourite employments; all the time I can spare from necessary affairs
is taken up at home or abroad. Last Sunday Dr.

---

[1] Anne Boyle, younger daughter and eventually heiress of Murrough Viscount Blesington, married, 23rd November, 1696, William Stewart, second
Viscount Mountjoy. Their son was created Earl of Blesington in 1745.

[2] Henry Agar, Esq., of Gowram Castle, married, May 29, 1733, Anne, only
daughter of the Bishop of Meath. Their eldest son was created Viscount
Clifden, and the third son, Charles Agar, was Archbishop of Dublin, and
created Earl of Normanton in 1806.

Mathews and his two nieces dined here, and Mrs. Marley. Between church and dinner I had a visit from the Dowager Lady Blessington and her two nieces, Miss Dugans. After dinner came Lady Meade, (Sir Richard Meade's widow) and her daughter. Monday I was very busy all day preparing and ordering blankets, &c., for the North. Tuesday, Mr. Ellis and his lady and sister dined here; he is one of the Lords of the Admiralty, and married, against consent of her friends, Miss Stanhope, daughter to Sir William Stanhope—a vast fortune: she is very plain, quiet, and rather dull in company. He has a good estate, and is a pretty sort of man: I think her friends were unreasonable in their resentment; but I believe she deceived her father, and promised him she would not have him at a time she was absolutely engaged. She was left young without a mother, and I fear, had not an example from her father that would instil or fix right principles in her mind.

D.D. was much delighted with Bunny's attention to what he reads, and bid me call upon him, when I wrote an answer, that he might explain the text for him; which I shall do presently, but cannot answer for his complying this day with the summons; he is this moment up to his chin in haymaking in the lawn under my closet-window, and the whole house is fragrant with the smell of it.

Thursday we dined at Pickerstown, about four miles off, Mr. Cavendish's and Lady Meade; it is with them Mr. M. is fixed to take care of Sir John Meade, a fine spoiled boy of six years old; Mr. M. looks wretchedly, and is fallen away to a shadow; I fear he will never recover his constitution. He is now in a very easy situation, and much esteemed. He says though Sir R.

Meade has been extremely indulged and little contradicted, that he is naturally good-natured and tractable; and Lady Meade is so wise as to give him full authority over the child: we were 17 or 18 in company, and had a *vast dinner*, and *such* a *vast turbot* as I never saw for size. Yesterday we dined at Lord Chief Justice Singleton's,[1] at Drumcondra, a mile off. Our company were his brother and sister Fowkes (who keeps his house, for he is a bachelor) and their son and daughter, Mr. and Mrs. Foster, and the *grand connoisseur*, Mr. Bristowe. After tea and coffee I walked out with the gentlemen; the ladies not able to be of our party.

Lord Chief Justice is very busy adding to his house and altering his gardens; Mr. Bristowe has the entire direction of all, but I cannot say he has shown so much real judgment as *conceit* in what he has done. In one part of the garden there is a cold bath that opens with an arch like a cave, this is put under my care to adorn and make something of, and I have presumed to undertake it. When finished I'll send you a little sketch of it. I have got *your harp shell*, and will send it you, and the Elizabeth edging, the first opportunity. I am sorry you have not been able to see Lady Anne C.; I am out of countenance when I think of the letter she favoured me with; but my being ill, and the violent hurry on first coming home, delayed it so long, that now I think it would only be impertinent to write; I know you will do me justice, and assure her of my great esteem and good wishes, in which D.D. joins. I am surprized at the many excuses made about Sally Chapone's not

---

[1] Henry Singleton, Prime Serjeant, made Lord Chief Justice of the Common Pleas in Ireland, 1740; resigned in 1753, and made Master of the Rolls.

coming to you; their Cheltenham schemes are past my comprehension, one month's conversation with you would be of more use to her than all she can meet with *there in twelve!* Dr. Barber is at Cheltenham now with the Chapons. I hope this letter will go free, as in duty bound. Mr. Ellis has given me franks for the time he stays in Ireland. I have not had time to write to Mr. Richardson; when I am in the North I may have time. Mrs. Mary Forth sails for England to-morrow; she is going directly to Bristol for her health.

Mrs. Delany to B. Granville, Esq.

Delville, 17 June, 1750.

I hope this letter will find you enjoying Calwich.—Happy should I have been to have had you here; at this moment D.D. is very busy making hay.

I am glad the Foundling Hospital was so full, and carried on with such decency; I am sure it pleased our friend Handel, and I love to have him pleased.[1] I am sorry Lord W.[2] did not see Lady Abbess;[3] I fear it mortified her, for she really loves him, and any appearance of slight or indifference towards her I know will hurt her.

We have not yet fixed our time for the North; I believe it will be about a fortnight hence—it cannot be

---

[1] On Tuesday the 1st, and on Tuesday the 15th of May, 1750, the oratorio of the Messiah was performed, under Handel's own direction, at the Foundling Hospital, for the benefit of the Institution. On these, and on subsequent occasions he played upon the fine organ which he had presented to the chapel of the hospital.

[2] Lord Weymouth.

[3] The Honourable Anne Granville.

sooner; I have been very busy in cleaning my new shells, and arranging them in my cabinet, and adding those I brought with me,—and now they make a *dazzling show.* I have got a good cargo of grotto shells for you, and will send them to Chester; let me know how they shall be sent from thence to Calwich. I spent a very agreeable day at Lucan with the Veseys; they are improving it greatly—it is really a very sweet agreeable place and well-planted. Did I write you word of my disappointment about my *travelling-garden?* Not a plant saved, all jumbled to pieces; so I shall no more attempt such difficulties, but must content myself with what I can raise from seed.

Yesterday we dined at Pickerstown, at Mr. Cavendish's, who married Sir Richard Meade's widow. It is a flat, but pretty enough; to-day we dine at Lord Chief Justice Singleton's at Drumcondra. He has given Mr. Bristowe *full dominion* over house and gardens, and like a conceited connoisseur he is doing *strange things,* building an absurd room, turning fine wild evergreens *out of the garden, cutting down* full grown elms and *planting twigs!* D.D. has no patience with him, and I shall be under some difficulty to-day to know *how* to commend *anything,* which is what I wish to do. I am called upon to dress. I have the pleasure of Miss Bushe's company with me at present; but we part when I go to the North. D.D. best wishes and humble services attend you, and we both beg our compliments to your neighbours.

I am, my dear brother,
Your most affectionate and most
Humble servant, M. DELANY.

Mrs. Delany to Mrs. Dewes.

Delville, 22 June, 1750.

My garden is at present in the high glow of beauty, my cherries ripening, roses, jessamine, and pinks in full bloom, and the hay partly spread and partly in cocks, complete the rural scene. We have discovered a new breakfasting place under the shade of nut-trees, impenetrable to the sun's rays, in the midst of a grove of elms, where we shall breakfast this morning; I have ordered cherries, strawberries, and nosegays to be laid on our breakfast-table, and have appointed a harper to be here to play to us during our repast, who is to be hid among the trees. Mrs. Hamilton is to breakfast with us, and is to be cunningly led to this place *and surprised*. I think Mrs. Dewes *flatters me* extremely in saying Pauline is like me; I hope she will be better every way. As to the lustre there is no way of repairing it, but the crayon pictures *I have recovered*. I don't pity you at all with your present companions—bricklayers and carpenters, &c.; I think them a pretty amusement, and will provide you with much future comfort and convenience. I delivered your message to Mrs. Forth, and were the season of Bristol not so far advanced she would accept of your agreeable invitation, but she is obliged to make all the haste she can to drink the waters; I most heartily wish they may be of service to her,—she is a valuable woman, and a true Xtian. I am glad you have seen Lady Anne Coventry; I wish she and *Sproser* could change situations; the 15 guinea shell was the tender-shell'd nautilus; Lady Anne *has one* of the kind.

I congratulate you on the departure of the nurse, and that she gave the little girl so little uneasiness; and I hope Juliana will prove a proper and useful servant. I am glad you have heard from dear Lady Sarah Cowper; Mrs. Hamilton disappointed us, and did not come till twelve; we breakfasted in our new grove at our usual time, for she knows our hours, and we are under agreement *not to wait*. No ceremony subsists between us; it is laid aside, though ceremony is proper to keep those at a distance that otherwise might be troublesome.

Last Sunday I had a good deal of company: Monday, *dined* in my garden—the Vesey family with us. In the afternoon drank tea in my orangerie; company after company till 9 at night. Tuesday, dined at Lady Grandison's; Wednesday, with Doct[r] Clements, an agreeable Fellow of the College. Our party: Lady Ross,[1] Mrs. Hamilton, Mrs. Montgomery (supposed to be his wife, but not owned), a modest, sensible, well-bred woman; we made it a very pleasant day, saw all the varieties, walked in the garden and park belonging to the cottage, came home at 9; Thursday, dined at Mr. Franklin's; Friday, spent the whole day without any interruption at home—worked, walked, talked till dinner, and sat quiet, listening to the harper, till 6; then picked roses—three baskets full. At 7, drank tea in the orangerie; then walked all over our meadows, fed our deer, saw two beautiful fawns and the two young favourite coach-horses eat their oats in the field; stood

---

[1] Lady Elizabeth Kerr, third daughter of William, 2nd Marquis of Lothian, married George Ross, 13th Lord Ross.

by whilst the cows were milking, till it grew so late that we thought it prudent to come home, and I hastened to my closet to finish this letter, because, to-morrow we spend at Lucan, and are to call Mrs. Hamilton at 8, who goes with us, and I shall not have a moment of the day to myself. Thus having given you, my dearest sister, an account of what I have done and what I am to do, I retire, wishing you a good night: the ingenious Letitia is much your humble servant and sincere well-wisher.

Mrs. Delany to Mrs. Dewes.

Delville, 30 June, 1750.

Your letter, my dearest sister, dated the 14th and 16th, gave me infinite pleasure and entertainment; I believe by the account Dr. Barber has sent to his wife of Harry Chapon, that he is in effect agent victualler, for he says "his place is now five hundred pounds a year." I am the more pleased with this news as I think my recommending him by word of mouth to my Lord Gower has been of service to him. I hope Jack will find Jamaica as profitable as Hal has done; and that they will be enabled to make the latter days of their parents comfortable, and provide well for their sisters, who otherwise I think have a melancholy prospect, for all young women bred to idleness, and with a relish to the gaieties of the world, are much to be lamented. I have not heard from Mrs. Chapon since I wrote to her by Dr. Barber.

I am obliged to you for your particular account of the church affair, and hope it will end amicably and to Mr. Dewes's satisfaction; Whyte is a troublesome neighbour and even where he means right, he has so injudicious and snarling a manner of proceeding that he must give offence on all sides. How does poor Mrs. Whyte? I think the Sproser's way of acting with Mr. A. very odd, and do not understand it. You had better have told me who called Clarissa "*fool*," for I have laid it to the charge of several, by turns, and only one is guilty! I hope it was *not* Mrs. Dobson. To call Clarissa *fool*, argues a *weak* judgment in the criticiser.

I shall send you some rags and your shells and gloves as soon as I have an opportunity, but the person I depended upon (Dr. Pococke[1]) went away on a sudden, and your gloves are not yet made. I think the mosaick pattern with cloth work round, will be prettier than the flower pattern for your window-curtains. Have you put up your shell-work over the chimney, and painted it? and how does it look? I am afraid I shall not be able to get any more thread of the sort you used to have, but when I go to the North I will try. I don't know what to do about the pattern for Miss Mordaunt; I am ashamed not to have done it, it sounds so like a trifle, but *I* really *have not time* to do many things that are more necessary to be done: I will enclose you Mrs. Hamilton's fine pattern, and desire when they have done with it to return it. I suppose when you turn your kitchen into a parlour, you will fit the wainscot of

---

[1] Richard Pococke, a learned prelate and traveller, was born at Southampton in 1704. He was educated at Corpus Christi College, Oxford. He travelled in the East from 1737 to 1742, was successively Precentor of Waterford, Archdeacon of St. Patrick, Bishop of Ossory and of Meath, and died in 1765. His "Travels" are full of descriptions, particularly of the curiosities of Egypt and Palestine.

the best bedchamber there, and hang the bedchamber with paper. Whenever you put up paper, the best way is to have it pasted on the bare wall; when lined with canvass it always shrinks from the edges. I have stripped down old stuff beds and sent them to Mount Panther, and in their stead am putting up *blue and white linen* and blue and white paper hangings, this has taken up a good deal of attention, as I am new sashing the room, new setting the grate, enlarging the room, and several alterations that require my overseeing and must be done before we leave Delville, that the rooms may be fit for use by the time we return. My work-room I am going to new model, the wainscot wants new painting, is cracked and has started in some places; the paper I have chosen is pearl colour caffoy paper; the pattern like damask: the pictures look extremely well on that colour, and the crimson damask window-curtain and chairs will suit very well with it.

Miss Hamilton waits with impatience for Court's answer; I hope some time hence they will be able to correspond in French; she understands French very well. We had an account last packet of Mrs. M. Forth's safe landing on Saturday last—a tedious, safe, but sick passage. Bushe is copying a Claude Lorraine. As to Dublin news, all I have heard is of a notable battle, most valiantly fought, between Capt. Carr and *a lady* at the Dublin Vauxhall, the night before last; the gentleman kicked and swore, the lady boxed, and scratched, and swore too (I suppose)—for a woman, that is so well accomplished as to fight in public (for she gave him the first blow), cannot want its concomitant qualification of swearing upon occasion. Though the lady was so stout to begin the onset, the gentleman gave the first provocation by telling her that was not a place for a woman of her character to appear in.

On Monday, Mrs. F. Hamilton, Bushe, D.D. and I went to breakfast at Lucan, left this at half an hour after 7, and called for Mrs. H. at Usher's Key. Found breakfast prepared for us in Mrs. Vesey's dairy, and the table *strewed with roses*; just as we were in the midst of our repast came in Lady Caroline Fox, Mr. Fox, Mrs. Sandford, and Master Fox—a fine rude boy, spoiled both by father and mother; Mr. Fox is a sensible, agreeable man, Lady C. F. humdrum. It rained furiously; so we fell to work making frames for prints. At 2, the supernumeraries went away; we dined in the cold bath—I mean in its antichamber; it was as pleasant as a rainy day could be when we wanted to roam about. The cold bath is as far from their house, as Mrs. Whyte's is from you; the coach carried us, and brought us back to the house for tea and coffee. They are pretty people to be with, no ceremony, everybody does what they please. In the afternoon came Mrs. Stone, with an invitation to us to dine at Leixlip (the Primate's house) on Thursday—engaged to Grandison's—could not go— very sorry. On Wednesday, dined at Mr. Stannard's; very busy all the morning in my garden; Tuesday went to Dublin on business; first to a place called *the World's-End*, where I spent an hour and half in choosing out a set of earthen-ware for the Duchess of Portland, such as yours, and a dozen baskets for Mrs. Montagu, as she desired; then bespoke the paper for hanging my rooms; bought the blue and white linen for my bed; and had just time to dress before dinner. Thursday, the Earl and

Countess of Grandison, the Countess of **Kerry**, Viscountess Grandison, and Mr. Mason dined here; my house and garden very spruce to receive them, and they were very civil in commending everything; the lady is near lying in; I hope she will have a child that will live, she has hitherto been very unfortunate: they staid here till near nine. Yesterday very busy all the morning, taking down and putting by my china and books: in the evening L.B. made some visits in Dublin, and drank tea with Mrs. O'Hara. This morning I need not tell you what I have done—my letter shows. I spent an hour or more in the garden before breakfast; would not breakfast in it because nothing should delay my writing, for fear of visitors. Mr. and Miss Frankland, Mrs. Mountenay, Bishop of Derry, Mrs. Barnard, Mr. Barnard, dine here to-day, and to-morrow we breakfast at Lucan.

Sir Anthony Wescombe to the Honble. Bernard Granville, Esq., at Calwich, near Ashbourn, Derbyshire.

July the 1st, from Blacklands.

Yours, my dear cousin, of the 3^d instant, I received; most people inquiring after you, but I could not satisfy them. Of all your friends there is none left but Charles Hearne, who returns his hearty service. Mr. Luttrell, I have not seen lately. You complain of the heat you had after your arrival. June was rather a cold month till the latter end, and all this month has been the hottest ever known. I hear the thermometer is at eighty degrees. *I am quite burnt up*, and have several shrubs killed in the wilderness.

My apricots fall down by dozens, and my people never dine without a dessert, my peaches and nectarines swell very little yet, plums none ripe, but great appearance of grapes. I have been very unlucky in my melons. I have many plants of cucumbers, and yet I have not had any for use till yesterday; in short, I must call this a bad year for gardens.

I am a litle better of my lameness, and thank you for your kind inquiry about it. I wish good weather to your garden, and that your labours therein may prosper. I am, very sincerely,

 Dear sir,
   Your most affectionate faithful servant,
        A. WESCOMBE.

Mrs. Delany to Mrs. Dewes.

        Delville, 7 July, 1750.

It is not possible to secure a day without interruption. I thought myself secure of this, having refused some parties on purpose not to be hindered; when last night a note came to inform me that Lady Caroline and Mr. Fox, and the family at Lucan would breakfast here, as they were going in a few days to England. I could not put it off, so have set all my best china[1] in order, and prepared everything for their reception; and as they are *people of taste*, I honour them so far as to permit them to breakfast in the library! it has struck eleven, and I hope they will not come till 12.

I felt your vexation and disappointment when Sally

---

[1] Mrs. Delany had a great quantity of very beautiful old China in which she was a great connoisseur.

was with you, for an old affectionate friend as she is one wishes to enjoy without interruption. You may forgive some from your neighbour Sproser for the good turn they did you at that time. I am much rejoiced at the good fortune of young Chapone, and hope he will be enabled to provide for his sisters. I am glad Lady A. Coventry liked the shell work I have sent you by Mrs. Mountenay, (a lady that lives with Miss Frankland), the twelve tea napkins you desired, a little box of odd shells that I think you have not (amongst them the harp shell and two small *whole scollops*), and three old smocks for *cut out work*. I desired the parcel to be left with Mr. Clerke in Jermyn Street, where you may send your commands for them; I fancy *the doctors* will call on you as they return. They are very different men —some *affectation* in one and *whimsical* withal, the other *plain and sincere*.

D.D. has allowed me so much time to prepare for our northern expedition, that I have not hurried much about it, and have now little to do. Bushe is still with me, but goes on Monday next; I wish I could conveniently have taken her with me to the North. We have at last, I believe, fixed our day. We propose setting out next Monday or Tuesday se'night: we go to Seaforde, to Mr. Forde's (two miles from Mount Panther), for two or three days till all our tackling is settled. I am glad Lady Sarah Cowper has bought a house near her brother's, and hope our cousin[1] will know how to value and cherish her worth. I have not heard from my brother a great while; I suppose his removing his

---

[1] The Countess Cowper, daughter of Lord Granville.

hurried him, and though hearing from him is a vast pleasure I am *so used* to his silence that it does not alarm me.

Last Sunday the Veseys engaged us to breakfast and dine with them at Lucan; Mrs. F. Hamilton of our party; her *wit and sprightliness* makes her a good addition on such occasions. D.D. gave us prayers in the chapel, and as soon as they were over we set out in open landau to Luttrell's Town (two miles from Lucan); the road by the river side, on the other hand high banks covered with trees: it is a fine place, and I think I have described it to you in some of my former letters. We dined very agreeably at the cold bath. Monday was a busy morning, spent the afternoon with *my Mrs. Hamilton*. Wednesday, we dined in *great form* at Mrs. Agar's, sister to Mr. Ellis, one of the Admiralty; (he and his lady there.) Thursday, had made a party to breakfast again at Lucan, ditto, party to dine at Castletown, Mrs. Conolly's—which we did; and there also dined the Primate, the Archbishop of Cashell,[1] Lord George Sackville,[2] Mrs. Marley, and as many as made up our dinner company nineteen.

Yesterday was spent in tranquillity at home; and this day may prove so too, for nobody is yet come, and 'tis past 12 o'clock, and a cloudy rainy day; *n'importe,* only bread and butter is spread, and water boiling without mercy. On Monday next we are invited to the

---

[1] Dr. Arthur Price, Bishop of Meath, made Archbishop of Cashell in 1744; died, 1752.

[2] Lord George Sackville, third son of Lionel Duke of Dorset. He assumed the surname of Germaine in 1770, and was created Viscount Sackville in 1782.

Virtuoso Epicuroso, Mr. Bristowe; and you shall know to a pepper-corn what we have to dinner.

I have painters and carpenters now hammering and brushing away; and I have determined about my Minerva, and shall paper it; my cabinet of shells to be removed into the library whilst the room is sprucing up, for fear of my glass doors; the removing it will be a difficult affair, for I don't mean to take down any shells but those that are near the edge of the shelves. Was anything more teazing! almost 3, and no company come, and I have sauntered away the greatest part of the morning looking for them through the telescope, and preparing the breakfast things; there must have been some mistake. I have not entirely lost time though, had I been more settled, you would have had rather a better letter. It grieves me that I have not written to Lady Sarah Cowper: I have tried, but a damp seized my spirits, and I was afraid of raising or increasing a melancholy I fear she suffers greatly from; but I *will write* next post. How can people say we grow indifferent as we grow old? It is just the reverse: the longer we live in the world the more we find how necessary a faithful friend is to our happiness: everything else grows indifferent, the show and splendour and laughter of the world dulls and palls; but the love of our friends brightens and strengthens as our follies abate. No philosophy, no reasoning, can root out that plant if sown with truth and sincerity; and why should it? I have now entered on a subject that fills my heart, and overflows at my pen's end, but have no more time, dinner being ready.

Mrs. Delany to Mrs. Dewes.

Delville, 15 July, 1750.

It is very likely this letter will find the net without the bird; but be that as it may, write I must. On Tuesday next we propose setting out for the North. I am now as busy as a *notable housewife* must be on such an occasion, and the more so as alterations are going on here, as well as preparations for the place we are going to. I have done up a little apartment, hung it with blue-and-white paper, and intend a bed of blue-and-white linen — *all Irish manufacture;* and hope some day to be so happy as to show it to you; but your apartment is allotted in another part of the house. We have had such sultry weather that it has hardly been to be endured; I think it very little short of the memorable day we spent at Mr. Williamson's. I hope you are now enjoying sweet breezes under Calwich trees, and my dear little Mary playing on the grass under your eye; she is too much a jewel to be trusted out of sight, and though the boys are as valuable, you must be a little weaned from them, as their different education must call them from you.

Mrs. Delany to Bernard Granville, Esq.

Delville, 15 July, 1750.

I had the pleasure last packet of receiving my dearest brother's letter from Calwich, and hope the violent heat we have had has made your hay, ripened your fruit, and done you all the good imaginable; but I don't pity you, (though it has been almost intolerably sultry,) who have such trees to shade and such reviving cascades to cool you. I never enjoyed Delville so much as I have done this year, there having hardly been a day that I could not live in the garden from morning till night. I am in hopes, according to my sister's last letter, that this will find you together. Now I have told you how much enjoyment I have had of Delville, I must tell you we are on the brink of leaving it. For some days past I have been sending all sorts of household goods and stores for Mount Panther, and propose leaving this on Tuesday next. D.D. is finishing alterations in his garden, and giving directions for what is to be done in his absence. I am *preserving, pickling*, and papering, &c., &c., &c., &c., and giving directions to my maids; and I have just spruced up a little apartment for you, come when you please. I have a thousand times resolved *never to say a word more on this subject*; it looks like teazing, but I do not mean it so: my heart is full, and wishing to see you in a place where, I thank God, I find myself very happy in *every respect but* that of *not* seeing a *few very dear friends!*

Last Tuesday Mr. Fox and Lady Caroline, and the Vesey family breakfasted here. Lady Grandison was brought to bed the day before yesterday of a son—great joy. I hope it will live, it is the 6*th child* and *none alive*. The present talk of Dublin is of Mr. Tilson's marriage with Lady Kerry[1] last Thursday—nobody suspected it; he is a very lively, gay man, and she rather of the insipid

---

[1] Countess of Kerry.—Lady Gertrude Lambert, daughter of Richard, Earl of Cavan, married first, June 29, 1738, William, Earl of Kerry, and 2nd, James Tilson, Esq.

strain. Miss Hamilton is my confectioner to-day, and is at this time making *orange-flower bread* of my *own orange flowers*, of which I am not a little proud; I am called to assist, but must first tell you that I have sent to Mr. Luke Gavin, merchant at Chester, a barrel of shells, a mixture of all sorts, let them be separated as you unpack them; I have done it in packing them as well as I could, and now I leave you to your works and go to mine. The best of services and wishes attend Calwich from Delville.

I am yours,
M. DELANY.

Mrs. Delany to Mrs. Dewes.
(*Dated " Delville," evidently by mistake.*)
21 July, 1750.

I know my dearest sister wishes to hear if I am safe at my journey's end : thank God we are! We arrived a little fatigued last night; but a good night's rest has refreshed us, and we are both very well. We had intended staying some days with Mrs. Forde in our neighbourhood, not thinking we should find our habitation so fit for our reception as it is; but as there were many things to settle, which could not very well be done without D.D. and my directing them, we thought it best to rest here. We shall dine to-day at Seaforde, and to-morrow at Downpatrick. You who have had the experience of such affairs, can figure to yourself, my present bustle—trunks, hampers, unpacking, hay flying all over the house; everybody scrambling for their things, asking a thousand questions, as " Where is this to be put?"—" What shall we do for such, and such, and such a thing?" However, the hurry is pretty well over, the dust subsides, the clamours cease, and I am hurried away to dress; I am really surprised at Smith's thorough cleverness in going through her work—she has got everything almost in as much order as if she had been here a week.

Mrs. Dewes to Mr. Granville.

Welsbourn, 24 July, 1750.

I hope to have the happiness of seeing you soon, but as Mr. Dewes is now at Mapleburrough I can't fix my day, and he is so desirous of having as much of your company as he can, that I believe we shall come together; and since you are so good to permit me I will bring the little girl, but desire you to mind her no more than the favourites we used to have of another kind, *Fripong, Duff*, &c.; and indeed I don't suffer her to be so troublesome as *they* sometimes were. She is in the whole pretty well, but is subject to a little cough, which I believe your good air will take quite off. I shall leave the boys together to learn French before they go to school, and the maid I took in town seems a sober body, and I dare say will be careful of them, and she has another to assist her. Mr. Dewes is gone for two or three days to set his tythes, which is always a troublesome work.

I have been contriving a Staffordshire oven in my kitchen chimney. I heard yesterday from my sister, who is well. In hopes of seeing you soon I will add no more but compliments as due to and from all friends.

Mrs. Dewes to Bernard Granville, Esq.

Welsbourn, 28 July, 1750.

I thank God I can tell you, my dear brother, that Court is surprizingly mended, and no lameness (which I greatly dreaded) or any inconvenience remains from his fall, only the bruises a little sore; and the poor thing looks sadly in the face, but he is very brisk, and has been abroad. Indeed it is miraculous that he was not killed, and I cannot think of it without trembling, and endeavour to recollect it as little as possible, and hope to banish all melancholy thoughts by the pleasure of your company. Though so many things happen in my family to prevent my designs, *I hope nothing will now* deprive me of the happiness I propose in being at Calwich some day the week after next, which will be about the 9th or 10th of August; I can't fix the day, but shall write again. Mr. Dewes cannot have the pleasure of going with me, for his building will not be covered in this fortnight and he must not leave his workmen, but he hopes to follow me. If I don't hear I shall set out, and take your kind permission of bringing my little girl, who has a little cough still but is otherways well; I propose to have a pair of horses to add to our own, which I believe will draw the chariot with so little luggage as I have occasion for.

Doctor Barber called here on his way to Ireland, and left Mr. Kinersley very well at Cheltenham.

These letters from Mrs. Dewes to her brother are interesting, as showing the very formal way in which Mr. Granville was treated by his sisters; and as it does not appear that Ann Granville ever displeased him, some idea may be formed by her style of addressing him of his power of trying the feelings of Mrs. Delany by cold civility, *after* she *had* offended him by her marriage with Dr. Delany; the ceremonious manner in which he was addressed, would not be at all surprising if there was anything *besides form* in these letters, but there is not; and as the correspondence of the sisters with each other shows *how much* they cared for him, it is evident that Mrs. Dewes would have written more if she had dared.

Mrs. Delany to Mrs. Dewes.

'Mount Panther, 28 July, 1750.

The 26th of this month was remembered, my dearest sister, with every wish the heart could form for your long enjoyment of every earthly blessing; it was not celebrated with song and dance and other external expressions of joy, but with every oblation of true and perfect friendship. We asked our good friends the Fordes to dine with us on that day, but Mrs. F. had a bad cold and could not come, and Mr. Forde staid at home to take care of her, so they sent us three of their daughters and one of their sons, a young cornet; very pretty young people, modest and sensible, especially my favorite, Cherry, who used to spend some time with me, but I am afraid her eldest brother's wedding will rob me of her this summer. He is going to be married to an agreeable young woman, Miss Knox,[1] with ten thousand pounds fortune; the wedding is to be next week, at the young lady's father's, and I hope they will all come together to Seaforde, which will make our neighborhood very lively. Mr. Forde, the father, has done very generously by his son, has settled £2100 a year

---

[1] Elizabeth, daughter of Thomas Knox, Esq., and sister of Thomas, 1st Viscount Northland, married Matthew Forde, of Seaforde, Esq., county Down.

on him; £1000 per ann. at present, and his house at Seaforde furnished as it stands—which is a fine settlement for a man who has six sons and three daughters; but there is one *error* which most fathers run into, and that is in providing *too little* for daughters; young men have a thousand ways of improving a little fortune, by professions and employments, if they have good friends, but young gentlewomen have no way, the fortune settled on them is all they are to expect—they are incapable of making an addition.[1]

I suppose you are at this time at Calwich, though I will not venture to direct this letter there; but as I shall write to-day to my brother, that will give you an account of us and serve till this travels to you. I am glad you have thoughts of taking my Pauline with you; I am sure my brother will be diverted with her drollery, and she will be vastly happy, and I think a *little weaning* her from the boys (as she is growing too old to be their constant playfellow) will do very well. D.D. begs little Bunny's excuse for not answering his question about the verse out of the 137th Psalm; the truth is he was always so busy on the days I wrote my letters that he had not leisure to give me the explanation. The verse is addressed to the people of Babylon, who were then in the height of wickedness. The destroying of the children of vile and wicked parents (whose example might lead them into like errors) was *mercy to the children,* and often God Almighty's chas-

---

[1] The opinion here expressed about "*young gentlemen,*" does not contradict the former sentiments of Mrs. Delany, who was a strong advocate for all young gentlewomen who had not any fortune assisting in their own maintainance by *practical usefulness* in the families of richer persons; though she was well aware that at the rate of remuneration then given, few could save much towards their old age.

tisements were executed by angels sent for that purpose.

I will, the first leisure lazy hour that comes in my way, make a pattern for Miss M. I should accuse myself, who have been above a year and half without writing to Lady S. Cowper, and she the same by me, and longer, and yet I know we love each other, and she has talents for writing which Lady Abbess has not, and is sensible of it; but I know the employment is painful to her. Betty's voice not at all mended, her other complaints better: this account I have from *Mrs. Forth*, who is there—not Mrs. Hamilton; who intends fixing you in Ireland. Mrs. Grierson understood Greek, *not Hebrew*, I believe.

And now to tell you a little of Mount Panther. To begin then: Last Sunday dined at Downpatrick (after church). Mr. and Mrs. and Miss Leonargan, Mr. Bereton, curate of Down, Mr. Trotter, agent to Mr Southwell, dined with us; went to church again at 4 went home at 5, *two hours on the road*, and visits to Lady Anne Annesley and Mrs. Bayley and their husbands made half an hour; tired, supped, talked over the company of the day; went to bed before eleven; up next morn early; routed about the house, found many repairs wanting; sent for smith, carpenter, and cowper; catching showers; peeped now and then into the garden— *excellent gooseberries, currants, potatoes*, and all the garden stuff; *fine salmon, lobster, trout, crabs*, every day at the door. Monday evening went to Dundrum, a mile off, a pleasant nest of cabins by the sea-side, where may be had kitchen chairs, French white wine, vinegar, Hungary water, and capers; *mugs* and *pigs*, of which we bought some. The French white wine is five pence per bottle—

we have not yet tasted it. Tuesday, busy all the morning with carpenters. We dined at our neighbour's, Mr. Annesley; his father is dead, and has left him above £7000 a year. Yesterday, we went in the morning to Holly Mount (5 miles off) to see the Prices, who are in great affliction, having buried a favourite daughter three weeks ago. Came back to dinner, and had for company Mr. Sturgeon, Mr. Mathews, Rev⁴. Mr. Johnson (D.D.'s agent), and his nephew. To-day I propose writing abundance of letters and going again to Dundrum; tomorrow to preach and dine at Down, and so ends *the round O of my journal.*

Mrs. Dewes to Bernard Granville, Esq., at Calwich, near Ashbourne, Derbyshire, by way of London.

Mapleburrough Green, 12 August, 1750.

Last Thursday I brought my three sick children here. I hope this air, which is esteemed very good, will be of service to them, as yet there is no amendment; the weather has been so wet, that I believe that keeps them from mending. Jackey has had two fits of an ague. Mary's cough is very bad, but as she is not feverish I hope she will not be in danger, but I can't help having many fears. The rural quietness of this place would please me very well, had I not set my heart upon being at a much pleasanter place and with my dear brother, whose kind letter I received yesterday, and return many thanks for it. I can't tell when I shall be so happy as to appoint your servant to conduct me through the waters, which I shall willingly encounter, so earnestly do I wish to see you, and I yet hope my little flock will give me leave.

The tenant who has the farm has the worst part of the house; the rest being ready furnished makes it very convenient when we have a mind to be here at any time, or bring the children, and I believe the air is better than Welsbourn as the situation is higher. We *were obliged* to ask leave of Lady Luxborough[1] to come through her grounds, the roads being so bad the other way a coach *cannot come*. She was at the door to receive us, and obliged me to go in, was most profoundly civil, and comes to see me this week; I am not vastly fond of her acquaintance, though she is entertaining, and has made her house and garden very pretty.

The first calf Finch, my favourite cow, (which you gave me,) had was so beautiful I could not bear to have it killed, so gave it to this tenant to breed up, and it is grown a fierce stately bull, and the terror of me and the whole neighbourhood. It tossed his master and gored him so badly two months ago, that they thought he would have died, and he has not yet recovered it, but he *will not* part with the bull, it is so fine a creature; though Mr. Dewes would have given him the value of it for fear of farther mischief; but he is at a distance from the house safe shut up, in a ground only milking times, and then *I am safe shut up in the house*—indeed the rain has kept me much there hitherto. I heard last

---

[1] Henrietta, eldest daughter of Henry Viscount St. John, and half sister of Henry, 1st Viscount Bolingbroke. She married, June 20, 1727, Robert Knight, of Barrels, Esq., in the county of Warwick, who was created an Irish peer, by the title of Lord Luxborough, August 8, 1749, and made Earl of Catherlough and Viscount Barrels, April 30, 1763. Lady Luxborough died in 1756.

post from my sister, who is well at Down and imagines me at Calwich, where I was in hopes to have been; Mr. Dewes brought me here, and then went back to his building. I forgot to bring franks, so you must pay for a long letter.

The constant agues which children suffered from in the last century, and the incessant course of drugs which they imbibed inwardly and outwardly, give cause for wonder that anybody survived *to be bled* when they were grown up, or that having thus survived, that any one ever arrived at old age!

Horace Walpole gives a witty and amusing account of Lady Luxborough in a letter to Lady Ossory, and also to Miss Berry. To the former he states his expectation of being diverted by Lady Luxborough's letters, and his recollection of her "wearing her little wizened husband's picture in her great black bush of hair." He states that "she fell in love with Parson Dalton, (Prebendary of Worcester and Rector of St. Mary-at-Hill, London, who adapted to the stage Milton's Comus), and that they rhymed together, and that he (Horace Walpole) never saw her more till *she revived* in Shenstone's letters, and was a great performer in his ballad of Arcadia, and that he thought these materials of her history promised well for entertainment in her correspondence, considering that she was *sister both* of Lord Bolingbroke and of Hollis St. John." Fourteen years after these remarks he answers Miss Berry's queries about Lady Luxborough, by saying that "she was dead and forgotten, except on the shelves of an old library, or those of his own memory;" that "Lady Luxborough was the first wife of Lord Catherlough before he was an Earl, who was the son of Knight the South Sea Cashier, and whose second wife lived (1789) at Twickenham;" that "Lady Luxborough, a high-coloured black woman, parted from her husband and retired into the country, and corresponded with the small poets of the time, but as there was no Theseus amongst them, it was said that like Ariadne she had consoled herself with Bacchus, although this might be a fable."

This little narrative of Lady Luxborough's antecedents, sufficiently explains why Mrs. Dewes did not wish for her acquaintance, and regretted being compelled to be under an obligation to her.

Mrs. Delany to Mrs. Dewes.

Without date, but evidently Augt., 1750.

I am glad you *detest* the tubs of hoops,—I keep within bounds, endeavouring to avoid all particularities of being *too much in* or out of fashion; youth and liveliness never prompted me to break through that rule, not considering I had graces enough of my own to carry off any extravagance, and now my years and station tie me down to that which has ever been my choice.

I must go back to Sunday, on which day I went with the Dean to Ballee, one of his churches, where he preached, and afterwards dined at Mr. Johnston's, his agent and receiver: there we were stowed up in a very tiny house (but very neat) in a most sultry day, with a table *crowded* with all sorts of good things; our coming home was very pleasant, great part of the way over a fine strand. The place I gave you an account of, where we went to gather shells, is not within a walk, 'tis *two long miles* from hence; next week hope to go again. You have never mentioned Carolan's tunes[1] since you said you had received them, have you tried them? I think some are *very pretty*; *Sir Toby Buck* and *Mickⁿ O'Connor* are *great favourites*. We have the *same*

---

[1] Carolan, the celebrated Irish harper, of whom Walsh says:—"He was the last of our native Irish bards, whose compositions gave celebrity to their author; he died in the year 1738, and with him may be said to have expired what remained in Dublin of that taste for simple and touching melody so peculiar in its character and so long cherished in this country."

harper in the house we had when at Hollymount; he plays very well, and knows a vast variety of tunes; and hot as the weather is the young folks meet here once or twice a week and make up at most three couple, always dance six *or* seven *dances,* and I love to see them mirthful, though I don't *find myself always* inclined to join with them.

The happiest mortal breathing (*if ever they think*) must sometimes feel an alloy to their most enliven'd pleasures. Thursday and yesterday I spent very calmly and agreeably. On Thursday, D.D. and Dr. Mathews went to Downpatrick, Miss Ford (of whom I have given you a character I believe) read to me whilst I worked at my quilt[1] till the gentlemen came home to dinner. In the evening when it grew cool we went to Clough to see Lady Anne Annesley in the chaise, and walked home. Yesterday morning between six and seven we walked (*with our harper*) to Mount Panther[2] to serenade the

---

[1] This might have been either of two quilts, parts of which are still in perfect preservation: the one was an intricate pattern of leaves cut out in white linen and sewed down with white knotting on bright dark blue linen; or it might have been the commencement of another most wonderful quilt worked by Mrs. Delany, and one of the *very few* things she never finished. It appears only to have been done when she had no painting to occupy her, and when old age at last forbad the execution of pictures (either with pencil or scissors) this quilt could not be completed. It is on white linen, worked in flowers, the size of nature, delineated with the finest coloured silks in running stitch, which is made use of in the same manner as by a pen etching on white paper; the outline was first drawn with pencil, each flower is different and evidently done at the moment from the original.

[2] It is difficult to explain how the Dean and Mrs. Delany could walk to Mount Panther at six in the morning, when they were residing there; but the only explanation seems to be that they had gone to a friend's or agent's house for a day or two, taking their harper with them, and leaving Miss Bushe and Miss Forde at Mount Panther, or else that "*Mount Panther*" was written by mistake.

ladies, who were wakened with the music; but the heat was so intense, tho' I walked like an Indian queen with my umbrella over my head; that after taking the tour of the garden with D.D. we all came home in the chaise. All this was performed before our prayer hour, nine o'clock; after that and breakfast we took to our work and book, and only allowed ourselves dining-time and an hour's composure after it, and finished the day as we had begun it, at Mount Panther. We have just finished part of a novel entitled L'Honnête Homme, or the Man of Honour; it is a fine character, but we have left the hero of the story in *so forlorn a condition* that we repent having read it, as we don't hear when the rest will be published. We are now reading Guadentio di Lucca, an entertaining, well-invented story, that pretends to be true.

I have finished a rose, a tulip, an auricula—with their leaves, since my coming here, and a dab of a knot stitch that I began three years ago. I have read (or rather heard read) The Man of Honour, Roderick Random, and the Sieges of Drogheda and Derry.

Mrs. Delany to Mrs. Dewes.

Mount Panther, 17 Aug., 1750.

MY DEAREST SISTER,

I have, I fear, given you great uneasiness by concluding you were at Calwich, for, as you said in your last letter but one that you had fixed your time and had given my brother notice, I little thought of your being retarded by the children's illness; mine, I thank God! is over. I have been two days together to take the air, and am now only cautious to prevent a return of the ague. D.D. sent for Bushe to come to me, but she is transacting an affair of great moment, on which her fortune depends, that made it impossible for her to come. D.D.'s uncommon care of me is not to be described; it is only such a heart as yours that can imagine what it was. I shall not write again till my usual post day, and shall enclose to the Duke of Portland. Your letter directed to Rathfryland came very regularly, but now direct to Delville as usual, for we propose leaving this on the 11th of next month.

Mrs. Dewes to Lady Sarah Cowper.

Mapleburrough Green, August 23rd, 1750.

How excessively good was my dear Lady Sarah Cowper to give me the satisfaction of knowing from her own kind hand that she is pretty well. I am very glad to hear your Ladyship has been prevailed upon to go some journeys, *change of air* being the *best remedy* for most disorders within the reach of human art. What affects our minds can only be removed by that Great Hand that for wise and unsearchable reasons ordains our sorrows, and to Him I ardently pray for your consolation. I have lately received such a miraculous instance of the power and goodness of Providence, that my life is not sufficient to shew forth its thankfulness. Three weeks since I was riding out with my eldest son for a little air, he is eight years old, and has rode a little horse several months, which now threw him; his foot hung in the stirrup, and he was dragged a hundred and forty yards: the footman took him up *for dead.* He was senseless, but, thank God, not a broken bone or sprain; and his bruises (*which were bad*) are now quite well, and he has not the least inconvenience remaining, but jumps and runs as much and as well as ever, and that is perpetually! How I kept my senses and did not fall off my horse I don't know. The cares of a nursery *are incessant;* my two youngest children have very bad hooping-coughs. I have brought them to this place (a house of Mr. Dewes' ten miles from our constant dwelling) to try change of air, but they are not yet better; I wish I had more agreeable subjects to write upon.

My sister Delany has had a bad feverish cold, but she and the Dean both assure me last post she was perfectly well again. I must now rejoice *with* your Ladyship in *Lord Cowper's happiness*—for happiness I think must be mutual in a married state, and Lady Cowper[1] thinks herself *perfectly happy*, expresses the highest affection for my Lord, and is delighted with Lord Fordwich and Lady Caroline, in short is in love with all your family; and as if *all delights* were reserved for my *happy cousin you* have taken a house just by Cole Green, in which she rejoices very much indeed. I believe she is truly worthy of all she possesses, but I can't help envying her a pleasure I have been so long

---

[1] Earl Cowper married secondly, on the 1st of May, 1750, Georgiana, widow of the Honourable John Spencer, and daughter to John Earl Granville. His 1st wife was Henrietta, youngest daughter of Henry Earl of Grantham, by whom he had two children, George Viscount Fordwich, and Caroline, who married, 1753, the Honourable Henry Seymour, nephew to the Duke of Somerset.

wishing for—having dear Lady Sarah Cowper for her neighbour. Being with great affection and respect,
    Madam,
        Your Ladyship's most faithful
            and obliged humble servant,
                A. DEWES.

My letters are directed as usual to Welsbourne. Not knowing where your Ladyship is I take the liberty of inclosing this to my Lord Cowper. I beg my compliments to the Dean of Durham [1] and Mrs. Cowper.

Mrs. Delany to Mrs. Dewes.

Mount Panther, 24 Aug., 1750.

Last Monday we began again our public days, and shall have two more. We propose leaving this place on Tuesday the 11th Sept. Yesterday we dined at Mr. Bayley's; they enquired much after you and your pretty son that they are acquainted with; their daughter is a fine girl, she has begun on the spinnet, and promises to have a good hand. To-morrow we dine at Mr. Price's; and Sunday the Dean preaches at one of his new churches (Bright), and we dine with his curate, Mr. Hamilton; and on Monday is our public day. The last we were fifteen in company. What a surprize, Dr. Meade's being blown up! I thought he had had more sense and prudence; but your virtuosi are strangely infatuated. Your journal, the account of Lady

---

[1] The Honourable Spencer Cowper, Dean of Durham, was the second son of the 1st Earl Cowper. He married Dorothy, daughter of Charles, 2nd Viscount Townshend, and died, *s.p.*, 25th March, 1774.

Luxborough, your farm-house, and all matters relating to you, entertained me extremely; and I hope all my disagreeable letters about my illness came to you at once, that you may know of my recovery as soon as of my being ill. Have you met with the *new System of Fairerie?* It is a small collection of fairy tales in English, humorously told, with pretty sentiments and morals, and quite new; but there is a story or two in the second volume not quite equal to the rest—and a little indelicate. I like "Cornelia[1]" very well; it is better, as you say, than the common run of novels.

Now for Lady Luxborough. I am vastly entertained at your being acquainted with her in spite of your prudence; but I really see no reason why her acquaintance is to be declined. If she leads a discreet life, and does generous and charitable things, she ought to be taken notice of, as an encouragement to go on in a right path, and your conversation and example may be of infinite service to her. She has lively parts, is *very well bred,* and knows the polite world, and you may, I think, divert yourself with her as much as you can, and D.D. says you will only do a meritorious thing in so doing. Dr. Barber has spread the fame of your children all over Dublin, and Mary's *bon-mots* are the talk of the town, and Bushe has abused me for my modesty in not blazing her perfections half enough. Did you write me word that our cousin Proby[2] was going

---

[1] Cornelia, the Vestal, a tragedy, 1750, by Henault (Charles John Francis), President of the Court of Inquests, and Requests of the Parliament of Paris, an eminent French writer, born at Paris, 1685, died 1771.

[2] John Proby, Esq., M.P. for the county of Huntingdon, married Jane Leveson, eldest daughter of John, 1st Baron Gower. Of this marriage there were six children, five sons and one daughter. The eldest son was the Right

to be married to Lady Allen's eldest daughter? He dined with us at Clerke's: Lady Allen settles, at present, £1000 per ann., and another at her death; Mr. Donnellan's son is married to a Miss Nixon, an heiress. I enclose you two of Bushe's last letters for your amusement—full of Dublin chat. And now I must conclude, having but just time to dress. We dine at Mr. Price's, at Holly Mount. Lady Luxborough is well acquainted with Hanover Square Montagu's.

Mrs. Delany to Mrs. Dewes.

Mount Panther, 7 o'clock, 1 Sept. 1750.

Last Sunday we set out at nine from hence, and arrived at Bright church (6 miles off) at a little after eleven. It is placed on an eminence that commands a very extensive view of the sea, the harbour of Killough full of shipping, mountains, hills, and valleys, diversified with cattle, corn, and bog, the solemnity of which last (like a *faded leaf in work*[1]) makes the rest more lively; nothing was wanting to make the prospect excessively beautiful but trees. The church is that which hath raised so much *rancour and malice* in a certain neighbour of ours, and which you have had explained in the letter before—(the discourse on tithes) it is not quite finished within, but when it is, will be a pretty, decent church.

Hon. Sir John Proby, K.B., M.P. for Huntingdonshire, who was created Baron Carysfort, in 1752. He married, August 27, 1750, Elizabeth, daughter of John, 2nd Viscount Allen, and coheir of her brother, John, 3rd Viscount Allen. Their son was the 1st Earl of Carysfort.

[1] This simile naturally suggested itself to Mrs. Delany, as the manner in which she represented faded leaves from nature, in worsted chenille deyed in the remarkable *semi-tints* of Autumn foliage, was unrivalled.

D.D. preached, and with as much spirit as ever I heard him. We were to dine at his curate's, Mr. Hamilton's, half a mile from the church nearer home. D.D. was excessively fatigued (and I hope it was nothing else) with preaching, and could not eat a morsel, was sick and faint, and continued so all the way home, hot and feverish, and had a very bad night; but I thank God he is very well again now, and at this moment watching his workmen, who are putting up new palisades before the house. Wednesday, being much better, he insisted on my going to a fine strand about two miles off, where there are a great many very pretty shells, though none curious: accordingly I went to satisfy him, and, had I been then really easy on his account should have been very agreeably amused.

I don't know whether I told you that Miss Leonargan is with me, and has been about a fortnight; she is a clergyman's daughter, who is a very sensible entertaining man, an old friend of D.D.'s. Mrs. Leonargan is a sensible good woman—they have both kept very good company and seen a good deal of the world. This young woman is their only child; and the greatest advantage she has ever had has been conversing with her parents. In her appearance she is plain, but not vulgar; her manner, from shyness and reserve, a little awkward: she is about 27 years of age, and has, on acquaintance, very good sense, pretty sentiments, loves reading, has read a great deal, reads French into English as fluently as I read English, is humble and obliging, and very smart and comical when she thinks she may be so without giving offence, and a most tender and dutiful child. I knew her a little when I was in the

North before, but she improves very much on better acquaintance, and it is an agreeable circumstances to me to have a young woman in my neighborhood (for she lives at Down) who is always pleased to spend some time with me when convenient, and that I need not treat with much ceremony; I have sent her this morning to Down market for me. Yesterday morning I went to Belville to work a corner of Mrs. Bayley's carpet; they would fain have kept me to dinner and have sent for the Dean, but I feared his being out in the evening and *made an excuse*, and how do you think he served me? why, walked away in *the evening* and made them a visit, while I sat quietly at my work. To-morrow we go to church at Downpatrick, it being the 1st Sunday in the month, but the Dean will not venture to preach; next week will be a hurry. Monday, our last public day; Tuesday, I go to Down to the assembly, and lie at Mr. Leonorgan's; as it would be a mortal offence if I did not make my appearance once there; and that day the new married couple, young Mr. Forde and his bride, come home, so on Wednesday I must make my compliments there. Thursday, spend at Belville, Friday, Fordes dine here; Saturday, pack up and settle household matter; Sunday, preach, and dine at Ballee, another new church, 6 miles off; Monday, finish packing; Tuesday, we shall hoist sail for fair Delville.

Last post I had a letter in very good spirits from my brother, though he expresses great concern at his disappointment of not seeing you at Calwich; indeed I pity him, for I *am sure* he *feels more* on those occasions than his taciturn disposition will allow him to express. I have not had a letter from Bulstrode a vast while, and should be very uneasy but that I know **Lady Oxford has** been there, and the Duchess has no time when she is in the house with her.

I have enclosed you Mrs. **Lawe's case, which is faith**fully and well drawn up, and so singular **and barbarous a** persecution that it is worth your reading. I have just had a letter from Sally, with a petition **from Mr. Ballard** to dedicate his third Century of Illustrious **Women to** me.[1] I confess it is what I dislike **extremely, and have** had a warm dispute with D.D. about it **this morning,** but he insists upon it that I shall consent, **as he thinks** it will mortify the man if I refuse; I dare **say it would** not, and it is much more vexatious to me **to consent—** there is an air of vanity in it that hurts me.

Mrs. Delany to Mrs. Dewes.

Mount Panther, 16 Sept. 1750.

I was at Down assembly, and it put me much in mind of the Gloucester ones that we used to have *before Whitfield's was the fashion*; I paid my compliment, and hope it obliged. I am now in a hurry—I **prepared** you in my last for a short letter this. **Yesterday we** went to Seaford to pay our compliments **to the young** married couple, who came home last **Tuesday; the** bride is a handsome well-behaved young **woman.** To-day we dine at Mr. Annesley's, a mile off, to-

---

[1] "Memoirs of British Ladies, who have been celebrated for their **Writings** or Skill in the learned Languages, Arts, and Sciences. By George **Ballard, of** Magdalen College, Oxford." This work is well executed, and quoted by **Thomas** Park in his edition of Horace Walpole's "Royal and Noble **Authors,"** 1806. Ballard was a native of Cornwall.

morrow the Dean preaches at one of his new churches called Ballee, and we dine at his agent's, who lives close to the church. Monday packing, and company dines here into the bargain, which *is a little troublesome.*

I *can get* some good thread for you—let me know what you would have—7*s.* the pound.

Mrs. Delany to Mrs. Dewes.

Delville, 18 Sept. 1750.

We came home yesterday at 7; set out, as we proposed, on the 11th, lay at Dundalk, a tolerable inn. Next day got to Dunleer, the house where Mrs. F. Hamilton lived when her husband was alive, now inhabited by Dr. Foster and his lady; obliging, good sort of people, ingenious and hospitable. There we staid all Thursday; spent the morning in going to the seaside, about three miles from Dunleer, picking up pretty, odd, seaweed, dined at 3 in the afternoon. Dr. Foster produced some books of fine Italian prints, which were very entertaining. On the road, by way of entertainment, I read a scurrilous, nonsensical book, called Dr. Clancy's[1] Memoires. Delville looks sweet. I have walked all over the garden. Orange-trees thriving, and my deer fat and well-liking. This morning I had a visit from my allies; all well, and glad to get me home again. Bushe can't come to stay with me yet, not till towards Xmas, but I hope she will finish her affairs, which are money matters, sooner than that. Doctor Barber was here

---

[1] The Memoirs of Michael Clancy, M.D., containing his Observations on many Countries in Europe.

this morning; he is charmed with you, your husband, and your children. Rupy Barber and his wife, and Mr. Parker, dined here to-day.

Mrs. Delany to Mrs. Dewes.

Delville, 22 Sept. 1750.

I am afraid my worthy and much esteemed Mr. Richardson will have reason to retract some of the kind things he says of me. I have not yet answered his letter, for my last illness has put me so behindhand in my correspondence, that I don't know when I shall pay my debts.

I am glad Sir Tony is in *a giving humour:* pray let me know what sort of lace? Last Sunday Dr. Barber and his agreeable, gentle, wife dined here; I saw nobody else, except one. (What a fib I was going to tell—I was at church, and *saw a full congregation;*) and in the afternoon Mr. Parker and his sister came, and drank tea, and supped with us. On Monday two Mrs. Hamilton's, Bushe, Miss Hamilton, Mr. Sackville Hamilton, came to breakfast. As soon as that was done, *I set them all to work*; gave each a dusting-cloth, brush, sponge and bowl of water, and set them to cleaning my picture-frames. Bushe undertook cleaning the pictures, and egging them out, whilst the *carpenters and I fixed up the shelves for* my books and china: everybody that popped their head in, was *seized to work*; no idler was admitted; a very merry working morning it was, and my dressing-room is very spruce and handsome. I have pulled my old lustre to pieces, and am going to make one just like the Duchess's. Tuesday we dined at Mrs. Forde's, and found the good old lady pretty well. Wednesday, dined at my Mrs. Hamilton's, met by the other, and L. B., and spent the day very agreeably. Miss Hamilton sung very prettily your favorite songs of the Messiah, accompanied by her brother, Mr. Sackville Hamilton, on the violin: she has a sweet-toned voice and good ear, but wants a little management of it.

Mrs. Delany to Bernard Granville, Esq., Calwich.

Delville, 22 Sept. 1750.

I have been in such a hurry ever since I came home that I have not had leisure to answer my dear brother's kind letter. I have been very well since my leaving the North, though I have no reason to think the place disagreed with me, as I had not been well some time before I went, but I thank God it is all over. The weather is delightful at present. D.D. very busy, topping exuberant branches, transplanting, and giving air to his garden. The trees and shrubs are grown so thick that we are obliged to thin them; I have been as busy within doors; have hung my dressing-room (which was painted olive-colour before) with a dove-colour flock paper, my pictures, books, china, placed as they were before. My room is greatly improved, and I wish you were here at this instant to give me your opinion: how often does that wish rise in my heart? Mrs. F. Hamilton has just finished a little piece of flowers and butterflies for Mrs. H. Hamilton that is *really exquisite*;[1] they

---

[1] The Editor possesses some of Mrs. Forth Hamilton's works in painting and embroidery which she gave Mrs. Delany, which exceed any thing she ever saw

are a pretty set of people that would please you extremely, and are sincere sensible friends. Mrs. Mary Forth is at Bristol, and has found great benefit from the waters; she and our cousins are acquainted, and like one another mightily. I hope you have got your shells? I have had carpenters, and smiths, and all kinds of workmen with me, and some waiting for me now.

I am my dear brothers
Most affectionate humble servant,
M. Delany.

Mrs. Delany to Mrs. Dewes.

Delville, 28 Sept. 1750.

Temperate and pleasant as May! I have just been gleaning my autumn fruits—*melon, figs,* beury pears, *grapes, filberts* and *walnuts*. Walnuts indeed are but just come in with us. I loaded my basket, and filled my hands with honeysuckles, jessamine, July flowers, and pippins, &c. My letter begins like one of Millar's calender months. I pleased myself whilst I was gathering Flora's and Pomona's gifts, in thinking that my dear sister might be occupied in the same way. The garden was truly particularly pleasant to me this day, not having been in it since Monday last. D.D. has not been well, but, I thank God, is this day enjoying his plantations. We were to have had a breakfast meeting of the *allies* at Bushe's on Monday, but was forced to send her an excuse. Wednesday she and

---

of the kind, ancient or modern, for perfection of outline, light and shade, brilliancy and delicacy. She excelled equally in flowers and insects, which she generally represented together.

Miss Forde spent the day here. Yesterday morning the two Hamiltons and Miss Ann, and to-day we are to have Mr. Cavendish and Lady Meade, two Miss Cavendishes, (their mother was one of the Miss Pines, sister to Mrs. Mainwaring,) Sir John Meade (a boy), Mr. Mount his tutor (our old acquaintance), and young Cavendish, who was Captain in the rebellion at Eton. My house is set out in order for them, and I shall not be sorry when the fuss is over. To regale and *compose me*, the Hamiltons have promised to breakfast with me to-morrow, and assist me in sorting shells, for now I am all *whip and spur* to get my lustre revived. I have stripped it of every shell and scraped it to the bone. I have now more choice of shells than when I made it, and hope the second edition will be more correct than the first.

Such a *young woman* as Lady Luxborough was, can never make a tolerable *old woman*, the modesty and awful air of age can no more grace her than the fragrant rose does the bare rock and oozy beach. But though she may not be a *desirable friend*, she is an acquaintance that may sometimes amuse an hour well enough, and make a variety among the actions of the world. Apropos, did I tell you that Mr. Ballard has *picked me out* (a thing unknown to him, but from report of a few partial acquaintances) to subscribe his Third Century to. I am vexed at it, and positively refused, but D.D. contradicted it, and says it will be using the man ill. I hate the sort of compliments an author thinks himself obliged to pay the person he dedicates to; and the poor man will be distressed, for he will think himself *under a necessity* to say fine things; so to ease him of farther trouble, and myself some confusion, I *insist* on your sending the enclosed dedication to him, for I absolutely shall take it ill of him if he says anything in a higher strain; I don't know how to direct to him, or I should have sent it directly to him; I am quite serious, and believe you will enter into my feelings about it.

[*Enclosed.*]

Madam,

I am very much obliged to you for your indulgence in giving me leave to dedicate part of this work to you; and as I am informed you were resolved against addresses of this nature, I will not tire you with encomiums on your family, your person, or your qualifications, as my intention in publishing this book is to raise the mind above the common concerns of this world; and I hope the examples here set before you will animate you to great and good actions, and then your obligation to me will be, at least, equal to mine to you.

I am, &c., &c.

I wish you could write to him and tell him you hear he intends a dedication, and should be obliged to him for a sight of it, and if it is in the common style of panegyrick, send him a copy of this, and say *I desired no other sort of dedication* might be published.

I have not yet seen Mrs. Dillon; she is gone to make a visit to her brother Preston: when I see her I shall most certainly remember you; I hope the Duke and Duchess of Beaufort will make you a visit at Welbourne; they are pretty people; and the Duchess and I are very well acquainted.

You are much in the right to choose the *rock* for our Pauline, instead of the ensnaring *quicksand*. I hope the happy medium may be found for her, and that gentleness of disposition, tender sentiments, and warm affections, will be so tempered and guarded by sound judgment and proper fortitude, as to make her act with honour to herself and family.

Saturday morning.

My company came—not all that I expected; and when they were gone D.D. and I enjoyed a *tête-à-tête* evening. Sir J. Meade is heir to a great estate, a child of six years old, most *unreasonably indulged*—a fine sensible boy, but under *no sort of command.* I had 20 frights for my china, shells and books: his little fingers seized everything with such impetuosity that I was ready to box him; had I been his mama I should have been *most heartily ashamed of him.* With pleasure I recollected that my little nephews would have been much scandalised at his behaviour, and wished them here to set him a good example. His sister, a girl about ten, is already a fine affected lady, knows everything, and pretends to ridicule, such airs! Well, thought I, my Pauline will not be such a forward, pert thing! that's my comfort!

Lady Meade is a well-behaved, handsome woman, *not* bred up with *elegant politeness*, but *civil*, and does not want for understanding: so is it not amazing she cannot see the wrong behaviour of her children, and how insupportably troublesome they are? Mr. Mount is better, and extremely well treated by Mr. Cavendish and Lady Meade, but his task with the young gentleman is a difficult one, though he seems to understand the sort of charge he has undertaken very well. Mrs. F. Hamilton, her son and daughter, walked from Dublin this morning, and we have been this hour past in the garden; she *never* will come into the house till the bell rings for prayers, for fear of *interrupting my affairs.* As soon as breakfast is over, to work we shall go.

The excellent dedication which Mrs. Delany wrote for Ballard to herself was not adopted. The following is his composition, which proves that Mrs. Dewes's intervention was unsuccessful, or that she declined interference.

"To Mrs. Delany, the truest judge and brightest pattern of all the accomplishments which adorn her sex, these Memoirs of Learned Ladies in the 17th and 18th centuries are most humbly inscribed by her obedient servant, George Ballard."

Mrs. Delany to Mrs. Dewes.

Delville, 6 Oct. 1750.

I am now as deeply engaged with "Clarissa" as when I first was acquainted with her, and admire her more and more; I am astonished at the author: his invention, his fine sentiments, strong sense, lively wit, and above all his exalted piety and *excellent design* in the whole. I find many beauties escaped me in my first reading; I was so much interested and run away with by the story, that I did not give due attention to many delightful passages. I am just got to her triumph after his villany: how poor, and despicable a figure does he make upon their first meeting, and how noble and angelic is her appearance and behaviour! The contrast of flagrant guilt and injured though unconquered innocence is most judiciously and beautifully drawn. My heart was almost broke with her frenzy, but that scene afterwards composed and revived my spirits, and made me almost rejoice in her distress; this, and making up my shell-lustre, has taken up every hour

hour that has not been interrupted by company; I will not lay by either till I have finished them. Last Monday I staid at home and gave *full indulgence* to my industry. On Tuesday, went to Dublin to see Mrs. H. Hamilton (received the enclosed for Court) and Bushe, and found the latter unengaged, and brought her home with me. Dined the next day together at Mrs. Forde's. Thursday, made Mrs. F. Hamilton a morning visit, and designed another to my little Tommy Greene; met him on the road coming to me; his father has been at the Bath, and is returning, but I hear little the better for it, for which I am much concerned: he is a worthy man and will be a great loss to his pretty boy. Yesterday Mrs. F. Hamilton and her daughter walked here to breakfast; Master Hamilton was to have been of the party, and has great joy in coming here, but he had not performed his task well, so she left him at home.

I had a letter last post from Mrs. Montagu, she informs me Lord North[1] is made governor to Prince George, with a salary of £1000 a-year, and continued Lord of the Bedchamber to the Prince of Wales: she desires me not to speak of it till it is public, which I suppose it will be before this salutes you. I am extremely glad of this piece of news; so excellent and so agreeable a man must be of infinite service to any youth that is capable of receiving good from precept and example. It was offered, and indeed pressed upon him; it must engross his time very much, and keep him from his favourite Wroxton. I believe the matrimonial report is over, I have not heard anything of it lately.

---

[1] Lord North and Guildford was appointed in 1750, tutor to Prince George, eldest son of Frederic Prince of Wales, afterwards George III.

Mr. L.'s case was not drawn up by the Dean—he saw and approved the beginning of it before he went to the North : there are a few things in the latter part of it that, if he had time, he would have pointed out to be altered I believe. The poor man is unfortunate, and irreparably hurt in his character, though people who know him best seem well assured of his innocence: 'tis well that clean hands and a pure heart can give us consolation under such oppressions.—As Clarissa says; " Heaven *punishes* the *bad*, and *proves* the *best*."

Mrs. Dillon not yet come to town. Lord Donneraile¹ has left Miss St. Leger, (commonly called Sellinger,) near an hundred thousand pounds, to confirm the world that their censures were not without foundation. I heard that Lady Donneraile said she would not go into mourning for her Lord, but I hear she has.

I am going to make a very comfortable closet;—to have a dresser, and all manner of working tools, to keep all my stores for *painting, carving, gilding*, &c. ; for my own room is now so clean and pretty that I cannot suffer it to be strewed with litter, only books and work, and the closet belonging to it to be given up to prints, drawings, and my collection of fossils, petrifactions, and minerals. I have not set them in order yet; a great work it will be, but when done very comfortable. There is to my working closet a pleasant window that overlooks all the garden, it faces the east, is always dry and warm. In the middle of the closet a deep nitch

---

1 Arthur Mohun, 3rd Viscount Donerail, born 7th August, 1718. He married first, 3rd April, 1738, Mary, daughter of Anthony Shepherd, Esq., and secondly, 3rd June, 1739, Catherine, eldest daughter of Viscount Massereene, but died *s.p.*, in 1749, when the honours reverted to his uncle, Hayes, 4th Viscount.

with shelves, where I shall put whatever china I think
too good for common use, but trifling and insignificant
is my *store-room* to what yours is! Mine fits only an
idle mind that wants amusement; yours serves either
to supply your hospitable table, or gives cordial and
healing medicines to the poor and the sick. Your mind
is ever turned to help, relieve, and bless your neighbours
and acquaintance; whilst mine, I fear (however I may
sometimes flatter myself that I have a contrary disposition), is *too much filled* with amusements of no real
estimation; and when people commend any of my performances I feel a consciousness that my time might
have been better employed.

Mrs. Delany to Mrs. Dewes.

Delville, 13 Oct., 1750.

I received the extraordinary sermon, and had not
seen it before, though printed in Dublin; it is a strange,
mad performance, and I am sorry a sober clergyman like
Dr. T. should provoke the poor wretch to treat him
so ill; but a madman's satire goes for little; I wonder
his friends don't confine him, if they can. I hope
as your neighbours S. are grown so touchy, that they
will *quarrel* with their *situation,* and *remove*—unsociable,
idle, inquisitive, near neighbours *are intolerable.* The
good peace-maker is always ready to promote the
happiness of his friends, but natures are not to be
altered; a sullen, surly, captious man, and his wife,
though perhaps not cast in the same mould, yet not
qualified to temper those defects, will ever be ready to

receive affronts, and return them; **what a misery to
themselves and others are such tempers!** I am very
happy that I have no *dangling* neighbours. **I may be
thought too reserved in our village, but I choose rather
to be censured for that, than expose myself to the interruption and tittle-tattle of a country neighbourhood**:
my acquaintance is large in Dublin, and I *never want
company*.

D.D., I thank God, is very well, and busy. He
has laid me in such a stock of billeting, and **fire-fuel
out of his own garden, that I shall not, I believe, want
coals for the whole winter, except for the kitchen, housekeeper's room, and hall.** I have now **eighteen head of
deer**; we killed two bucks this year, that proved as fine
venison for fat and taste as could be eaten: I own it is
disagreeable to me to have them killed, but it is unavoidable, they increase so fast. I am **truly grieved** for
Mrs. Duncombe, for though she is of an age that her
friends cannot hope she would continue long amongst
them, it is sad to think of the **painful course, in all
probability**, she will go through; I shall **be glad to
know what Mr. Pye thinks of her**. Miss Forth is
determined to stay the winter at Bath, and **take another
season of Bristol before she returns home**; all her
friends here made it their request to her. I wish
before she returns she would **spend a week or so with
you**; she would give you great pleasure—s. She has
a *most exalted mind, few men* have *such fortitude*, and *no
woman* can have *more tenderness*.

I have all this week worked most **industriously at
my lustre**; two mornings more will finish **the work**.
Mrs. Hamilton (of Usher's Q.) has began **an imitation of**

carving with shells and pasteboard; to be fixed on the ceiling to hide the pulley, and for the line to come through that holds the lustre, it cannot be finished in a day, and I shall endeavour to prevail on her to spend some time with me here. Bushe is still detained in Dublin on business: my house has not been ready till now for company: I stripped it of many necessaries when I went to the North, and have but just recruited. It is well my good Dean has his garden to relax and relieve his spirits, for now they are much turmoiled with his Tennison lawsuit;[1] it is to come on next term, he prefers his cross bill in a few days.

I am going on with "Clarissa," I thought I could have read it a second time without being greatly affected, but it is impossible. The distress is wrought up so naturally, and there are such strokes of generosity in Clarissa's character, and such tenderness and delicacy in the friendship between her and Anna, that quite overcome me; I am now at her letter of reproof to Miss How for speaking ill of her friends, page 230, first edition.

I believe Donnellan is removed by this time to Hanover Square; she says her mother declines very fast. I am in pain for our dear Bell,[2] in case there is a breaking up of that family. I don't think she would choose to come to Ireland, or that Don. would care to engage her to settle with her, and it is what I could not wish her to do, as I have such a regard for her, and her interests, that I cannot help looking forward *for her*, and having

---

[1] This lawsuit which has only been once or twice slightly alluded to before, lasted for years, and caused great anxiety and expense, in consequence of a claim upon the Dean of Down, by relations of his first wife.
[2] Miss Sutton.

an anxiety for her welfare. *The last private conversation I had with her dear mother*[1] *has made a deep impression;* therein she expressed her anxious desire of seeing her well settled, and *bespeaking* my friendship for her daughter, and as *long as I live,* she shall have it, happy could I be of any real use to her.

The day is so fine now, that I must take a run into the garden, where I have hardly been this week past, the weather has been so stormy. Mr. Greene is come, not better in his health. I went to town to see Bushe, she was gone out with Lady Austin[2] to take the air, and spend the day. From her I went to my Mrs. Hamilton, intending her only a morning visit, but D.D. was with lawyers, and sent me word he was obliged to stay with them till even, so I settled myself down for the day very comfortably with Mrs. Hamilton.

Mrs. Delany to Mrs. Dewes.

Delville, 20 Oct., 1750.

I have worked like a dragon this week at my lustre, and completed it on Thursday. I am now glad the old one was destroyed—this I think prettier, D.D. calls it the *Phœnix:* it was a vast work, every shell dried and sorted, and nobody assisted me, but Mrs. Hamilton one morning made some of the flowers. To-day Mrs. F. Hamilton[3] and her son and daughter come

---

[1] This is the only allusion to the death of Lady Sunderland, which must have occurred when Mrs. Delany was in England—the date the Editor has failed to discover, but her sister, Elizabeth Tichborne died 9th December, 1752.

[2] Sir Robert Austen, M.P. for New Romney, in Kent, married, in November, 1734, Rachel, daughter of Sir Francis Dashwood, Bart.

[3] This was Mrs. Forth Hamilton, born Dorothea Forth, and married to the

to me to stay some time, and she is to earn her bread here, for she has undertaken an imitation of carving for the ceiling where the pulley is to be fastened. Now for the journal; last Monday we dined by invitation at Lord Grandison's; they are in high joy and spirits. The little Mason is a fine thriving child, and I hope will live. Bushe met me there, and there was a Mrs. Wogan,[1] sister to Lord Kilmare, I believe bred abroad, a Roman Catholic; she is one of the largest women of her age that I ever saw; she looks about 30, but has a charming sweet face. She gave me an account of part of her brother's estate in the province of Munster, the islands of Killarney, which are covered with bays, myrtles and arbutus trees; the echoes are so remarkable among the rocks in that river, that people every year go there to try them, and if you fire a gun, the echoes return the sound one after another like the going off of loud thunder; they say one can have no notion of the effect of music there, such as trumpets, French horns and hautboys. I am very desirous of seeing this *enchanted place*, but it lies entirely out of my way. Tuesday I staid at home, worked hard in the morning, and had no interruptions—that was comfortable. Wednesday, went in the evening to Dublin to the Philharmonic concert. We made four visits on our way to the concert—Lady Roos, Mrs. Fitzmorris, Lady Arabella Denny (found her at home) and Lady

---

Honourable Francis Hamilton, a younger son of James, 6th Earl of Abercorn. This was the same lady who painted and embroidered flowers and insects from nature so wonderfully.

[1] Helen, daughter of Valentine Browne, 3rd Viscount Kenmare, and sister of Thomas, 4th Viscount, married John Wogan, Esq.

Knapton,[1] (Lady Vesey that was), then called in Anne Street, drank tea with *my* Mrs. Hamilton, and carried her and her daughter Anne with us to the concert. Was not that *sprightly doing?* Came home safe: D.D. sent Rupy Barber for my guard, and at home by ten o' the clock. Thursday the Bishop of Kildare [2] (Fletcher by name), his sister, Dr. Ledwytche and his lady, and Mr. Greene dined here. I was in the morning so eager at my work that half my company came before I had begun to dress, but it was to put on the *finishing shell* that made me so earnest, and I shewed them my work as my excuse. Yesterday, cold as it was, we set out in our chaise, D.D. and I, and whisked away to Lucan to *breakfast* with the Veseys; it was clear and pleasant, and the autumn scene rich and beautiful, and in no place it appears with more beauty than at Lucan—the banks of the river being covered with wood. We got home half an hour after 3.

Mrs. Delany to Mrs. Dewes.

Delville, 27 Oct. 1750.

I am glad your works go on so well, and am sorry I have no knotting of the sort you want done. I cannot promise too much for you till I have finished a plain fringe I am knotting to trim a new blue and white linen bed [3] I have just put up; as soon as that

---

[1] Sir John Denny Vesey was created Baron Knapton, 10th April, 1750. He married in 1732, Elizabeth, daughter of William Brownlow, Esq., and died 25th July, 1761, when he was succeeded by his son, Thomas, who was created in 1776, Viscount de Vesci.

[2] Dr. Thomas Fletcher, Bishop of Dromore, was translated to the Bishopric of Kildare in 1745.

[3] The Editor has now in her possession a set of covers for chairs made of

is finished I will do some sugar-plum for you; but I
fear you will want it before I can do any quantity : let
me know, and mine may lie by till yours is done, and
send me the sized knotting you want; I have a good
knotting friend also that I can employ I believe for you.
I am sorry what *you* meant a friendly meeting proved a
sullen one; the little *mean tiffs and affronts* given and
taken between people that have professed a friendship
for one another is a disgrace to friendship, let them be
called intimates, but *not friends*. True friendship cannot be tainted by *low suspicions*, and the train of ills
that attends it, but is generous, open, candid, and *delicate*, never listens to malicious insinuations, nor believes
anything to the prejudice of tender affection *mutually
professed*, not judging by others, but by their own observation, and ever cautious of yielding to that without such manifest reason as cannot be resisted. I
am now almost frozen by the fireside, but the weather
though sharp is clear. I am sorry your garden suffered
so much in your absence, it is the fate of all gardens. I

---

linen of the most brilliant dark blue, which she has never been able to match.
They are bordered with a beautiful pattern by Mrs. Delany, of oak leaves cut
out in white linen and tacked down with different sorts of white knotting,
which also forms the veining and stalks. There are constant allusions in these
letters to sending thread for knotting, and to "sugar-plum knotting," which
was used for the most ornamented parts, being highly embossed. Mrs. Delany
and her sister were in the habit of using their knotting shuttles, (as was the
custom of the time,) at those periods of relaxation when the German ladies
use their knitting needles, and the English ladies do nothing; and it is almost
incredible the quantity of knotting in various patterns and colours which was
left by Mrs. Delany, and which still exist, being the remains of the produce
of tea-table leisure hours, although such a large supply was required for the
works which she completed in this peculiar style. Her favourite colour for
the wall of a room or for furniture, was blue in various shades, but either *dark
and bright* or sky blue.

have not indeed reason to complain, ours was well taken care of, and is now very pleasant, though shifting off its summer ornaments. My not going into the garden was owing to the bad weather, or busy works within doors. My lustre is finished, and Mrs. Hamilton very diligent in making the ornament which is to hide the pulley; as soon as that is done it is to be put up, and then I shall take painting in hand. Lady M. is *vulgar* and proud, and thinks that the noise which pleases her may very well be suffered by other people: Mr. M. called here last Thursday; he is pretty well, and always desires his particular compliments to you. I am glad my Pauline so soon made her peace with you, I hope she will very early have such a fear of distressing you, as will make her careful of her behaviour. *The awe* that proceeds from *love*, as the heart is concerned, can never fail; but that which is raised only by the fear of punishment will give way when the spirits are high and they are wound up to a frantic eagerness of doing what they have in view for their present pleasure. Is not that too often seen in human life? where people are engaged in an unprincipled way of living, they gratify themselves though at the expense of their best hopes of hereafter, but the true, well-disposed Xtians, that love as well as fear, though subject to errors and frequently guilty, return, and repent, with grief that they ever offended.

Well, I can't help it, but I wish Mr. Ballard had not thought of honouring me with a dedication. I have not vanity, nor merit of any kind sufficient to be pleased with or worthy of such a distinction. I long to have an account of Sir Tony's present of *old clothes*——So—a violent rap at the door: vexatious! who can it be? (Such cold weather might keep them at home). Who should it be but a mad Councellor Trench, who we are always denied to, but my footman, not knowing him, let him in, and put me in a sad flutter. I have made my escape into Mrs. Hamilton's room, and D.D. has taken him into the garden to set me at liberty. I thank you for your account of Mrs. M's ball; where there is so large a company, it is impossible every one should be matched to her mind, especially where *the partner* is of *more consequence* than *the dancing*. I wonder the Duke and Duchess of B. did not return their visits, though it might happen they had more to return than their time would serve for, but if they could not do all, they could not properly do any. I bless God, my dearest sister, that the earthquake[1] was not felt in Warwickshire, and that no damage has been done where it was felt; surely these frequent shocks are meant as warnings for people to recollect themselves. Happy for those who will consider them in that light: happy every awakening to our duty and to a sense of the infinite mercies of God, and of our own great unworthiness!

Have I not mentioned Mrs. Dillon's distress to you? but you cannot be a stranger to the death of Mrs. Preston, her sister, who went to Bristol to Mr. Pye, and after having taken some of his medicines, wrote word to her husband and sister that she was surprisingly well? the next account was, that of her death; a great shock to all her family and her friends; she is truly

---

On Sunday, September 30th, 1750, a violent shock of an earthquake was felt in Northamptonshire, Leicestershire, and Lincolnshire.

a great loss, as she was an excellent woman, and very agreeable. Poor Bushe is in great grief—she was a sincere and useful friend to her. She stays in town to comfort some that are more nearly concerned, but has not spirits for such an undertaking, and I will get her here as soon as possible. I am very happy in having Mrs. F. Hamilton with me, her sprightly good humour, and ingenious works, make the day pass very agreeably. Yesterday evening we went to a concert to hear a new French fiddler, Morella by name, he has a particularly fine execution, plays with great ease and prettiness, but as it was all *nonsense music* I am not sure I shall like his taste, till I hear him play music *of consequence;* and I believe, on the whole, he has *too many tricks to please us* often. Now we are going to work hard till dinner, and shall take it up as soon as dinner is over, for we are impatient to finish. I should have written more had not the mad Councillor come in.

Mrs. Delany to Mrs. Dewes.

Delville, 8th Nov. 1750.

I don't approve of your walking so far as Loxley and back again before dinner; such long walks never agreed with you, my dearest sister, and I wish you would not try your strength to the utmost: own the truth—had you not a headache next day? I am glad poor Miss Nanny Viney is so happy as to be with you, but much concerned that Miss Viney's hoarseness continues, it is a pity, had it no other effect, that her *agreeable voice* should be hurt. I have received an excellent Berkeley cheese, who am I indebted to for it? I owe Mrs. Viney for a Frogmill cheese I bespoke when last in Gloucester. I hope, *ague fits* are over now, and that you, and the *Dew drops* are all in perfect good health.

I don't know whether Mrs. Richardson is a proper person to find a servant for you; she is a retired quiet sort of woman, who I believe cannot have had any opportunity of knowing of a suitable servant of that sort.

I am a little impatient to know what *treasures* Sir Ant. W.'s box contains. I suppose the clothes are new, though made up, and it would be a *mortal offence* to him were you to give them away! I was much diverted with Pauline's account of Lady Luxborough. I have not yet seen Mrs. Dillon, but now Mrs. L. Bushe is with me I shall go; I am much taken with the young Dillons —they are innocent, agreeable girls. I am truly much concerned for poor Mrs. Duncombe, her disorder is often attended with sad circumstances, and at her age I believe never cured.

I had a letter last post from Babess—she is at Bulstrode: all well there now. I had a letter from Calwich a few weeks ago, my brother very busy planting, and talked of going to town as soon as he had done; he complained of the tedious evenings. I have not heard from Donnellan a great while, Dr. Donnellan is in a very bad state of health. Mrs. F. Hamilton, and Bushe are now with me—I fetched her yesterday; Mrs. H. threatens to leave me on Tuesday, but I will try to keep her one week more, for we are now deeply engaged in some shell carving that is to be placed at the ends of my book-shelves in my work-room. We have been so much taken up, that we have not either gone out or engaged company at home, that we should have *no inters*, only on Wednesday, night we went to the Philharmonic concert, which was agreeable enough, and we design to go to the first good comedy that is acted, and then I think I shall have done with public places for the winter season, till February is over. Yesterday morning, just as we were setting out for Dublin to fetch Mrs. L. B. and Mrs. Montgomery, (a very agreeable woman, and friend of Mrs. F. Hamilton) Mr. and Mrs. Vesey came to breakfast, which delayed us an hour. In our way back from Dublin, we called at Mr. Smith's (*our Chevenix*) to see a pair of vases, which I think the finest, and prettiest toys I ever saw; indeed they are more than toys, and will serve for decanters or ewers very well. They hold above a quart each, are of a very elegant shape, after the antique, made of the Egyptian pebble, lined with gold, set in the prettiest manner, and ornamented with chased gold perfectly well wrought; he got them unfinished, and finished them here; the price three hundred guineas, they weigh an hundred and fifty. So, *madam*, you see, though we are here a poor, despised, and trampled upon nation, we *have our fine things*, and *costly things*, as well—though not quite as common—as in the *superbe Angleterre!* They really are so very pretty that I would rather have them than £500 worth of jewels. I am uneasy I have not heard from Stoke. Mrs. Foley wrote me word of Mrs. Tomlinson's[1] being brought to bed, but not a word since. She is a poor tender thing I am in some fear about.

---

[1] Sarah, daughter of Thomas Foley, of Stoke Edith, Esq., by his 2nd wife, married Boulter Tomlinson, Esq. of Cheltenham.

Mrs. Delany to Mrs. Dewes.

Delville, 10 Nov. 1750.

I am sure your visit at Snitfield was very agreeable. There is something in that old lady[1] so refined and delicate that she looks as if she were in the *milennium state*, part of the earthly mortal state had gone off, and somewhat of the angelic *already* bestowed on her! This reflection leads me to consider if it were not possible for old age to arrive at that sort of perfection, by throwing by all the mere trifling concerns of this life, contracting our wants, and fixing our thoughts on the one thing necessary above all others to make us endure this life and fit us for another. I don't mean by this to give up the innocent amusements of life, or to endeavour at extinguishing, or even lessening, our affections; *one* is necessary to keep up good humour and to make us agreeable to our acquaintance; and without affections, or with lukewarm ones, what wretches should we be! what should we do for society, and how weary should we soon grow of ourselves! But the condition of mind I wish to arrive at is to enjoy all blessings thankfully, to consider every disappointment as a merciful correction, and under great and heavy afflictions to submit with entire humiliation. If old age can be acquired with such a disposition, is it not the next step to perfection, as the millennium is to the completion of utmost blessedness?

I have not yet been able to meet with your answer to Con. Phillips: I have sent to-day to enqure about it. I am impatient to see it after what you have said.

---

[1] Lady Anne Coventry.

You shall know D.D.'s and my thoughts upon it as soon as I have read it. I am glad you keep up your correspondence with our good friend Mr. Richardson. My last reading of his "Clarissa" has given me a higher opinion of his capacity and excellent heart than I even had before, and no sensible, unprejudiced man or woman can read that performance of his with proper attention without feeling the author's extraordinary merit. I think Miss Nanny Viney's being with you must every way be an advantage to her, and a great pleasure to you, because you delight in making every thing happy near you. I am glad to hear all the agues are gone. Mrs. Kendal is a sensible, agreeable woman, but some people, through modesty (not doing justice to their own judgment), are led away by the age or opinion of somebody they are partial to, though *perhaps* not near so competent to judge of what they pronounce upon as themselves; this I think must be Mrs. Kendal's case, or she would like "Clarissa." I never heard of Con. P. having been answered till you mentioned it.

I hope the Newland French woman speaks French well, and if she does she may be a properer servant than a Londoner. I have not read Jo. Thompson;[1] I have heard so indifferent an account of it that my curiosity has not been raised. Last Monday we went to town to see Mrs. Hamilton: Court's mistress[2] is still much out of order with her slow intermitting fever. I am much afraid for her, and never saw a child so altered; I pity Mrs. H., for this is a fine girl, and she

---

[1] The Adventures of Joe Thompson, published in London in 1750.
[2] Mary Hamilton, the childish correspondent of Court Dewes.

is a most tender mother; I am glad you have got the *Tony box.* If the lace is fine, I think Mechlin, though not so showy, as pretty as Brussels. The lustre and the ornaments for the ceiling that encloses the pulley are finished and in their place, and I have given *another* painting to the Duchess of Queensbury; next week I go to work on the Madonna and bambino, for the chapel. Last night I went with my guest, Mrs. Hamilton, to see Macbeth, and was very well entertained with it. Sheridan acted Macbeth very well, the other parts very tolerably done, Lady Macbeth by Mrs. Bland—a very handsome clever woman; acts with spirit, but wants judgment.

On Monday we go to Morella's concert, and then Mrs. Hamilton leaves us; business obliges her to go, or she flatters me that she should with pleasure stay longer with me. We work hard all the morning, and Bushe reads to us in the afternoon; I read till seven and then we play at *puss in the corner* with the children, or dance country dances to a very bad fiddle, till eight—prayer hour, harpsichord after that, and *after supper cribbage* or *commerce*. We *have read* Mr. Richardson's[1] "A Young Painter's Letters from Abroad," which are entertaining, and give a particular account of Herculaneum—the city found under ground, and supposed to have been destroyed in the great eruption that Pliny gives an account of in his Letters; and now we are reading Spence's

---

[1] Jonathan Richardson, a painter and writer on the art, born about 1665, and died May 28, 1745. After Kneller and Dahl's death, Richardson stood at the head of portrait painters in this country. He published several works jointly with his son, and in 1722, "An Account of some Statues, Bas-reliefs, Drawings, and Pictures in Italy, &c." The son made the journey, and from his observations and letters this work was compiled.

Polymetis,[1] that explains several of the most curious paintings and sculptures of the antients; it is written in a very good style and in a very lively clear manner. I fancy you can borrow it from Sir C. Mordaunt, and it would be a good book for your winter evenings.

Mrs. Delany to Mrs. Dewes.

Delville, 17 Nov. 1750.

I have begun a large Madonna and Child for the chapel, which is a great undertaking; I have dead coloured the two faces. Last Monday Mrs. F. Hamilton and I parted at the concert. My heart aches for Mrs. Hamilton, if the child dies it will be a most severe stroke upon her, for though her piety and fortitude are very strong, her nerves will hardly support such a loss long enough to give time for their salutary workings.

Last Wednesday Mr. and Mrs. Donnellan spent the day with us,—they are very good agreeable people. I have a number of visits on my hands, but whilst Mrs. Hamilton is in a distrest way I cannot think of going to anybody but her. I have sent you by Mr. Dubourg, who sailed yesterday, all the knotting and knotting thread I have—it is not a pound, that sort of thread is *not to be bought in London*, and must be bespoke in the country, so that the soonest I could get to send would be a month. The double knotting I have sent will be too fine for you, I fear. Are the curtains done in the mosaic

---

[1] Polymetis; or, an Enquiry concerning the Works of the Roman Poets and the Remains of the Ancient Artists. By Dr. Joseph Spence, 1747, author of Anecdotes, etc.

pattern with the cloth border? I am angry with you
that you sent my letters to Mr. Richardson. Indeed,
such careless and incorrect letters as mine are to you,
should not be exposed: were they put in the best dress
I could put them into, they have nothing to recommend
them but the warm overflowing of a most affectionate
heart, which can only give pleasure to the partial friend
they are addressed to.

I should think resting a few days with you would
make Miss Bushe's journey less fatiguing, but her difficulty will be getting to Chester. From Bath there
are often return coaches that go back cheap, but from
Welsbourne I can't tell how she can be accommodated;
she does not return till Bristol season is over. I had
a letter from Don. last post, she has been ill and much
alarmed about Mrs. Percival. If Mrs. Percival dies
(as her age and infirmities make that event daily to be
expected) Miss Sutton will be at some loss where to fix
till her brother returns from his travels: when he does
they will settle together, and Mrs. D. I fancy, would
choose to fix here amongst her old friends and relations.
As to my dear Bell, how welcome would she be to me,
but her coming to Ireland might *give offence* to some
of her friends, and put her out of the way of settling
in England, though were I to indulge my own inclination, without any other consideration, my dear friend's
daughter should not seek for a home out of my house.
The loss of friends is a painful recollection; what a void
is this life when they are gone! That thought alone,
without considering the infirmities of old age, makes it
by no means a state to be **anxious to arrive at; but if**
Providence sees fit to continue us in this probationary

state to old age, we ought to conclude it is for good and wise ends, and that the afflicting losses we must naturally meet with are but momentary sorrows compared to the joys we shall reap if we submit humbly, as we ought to do. These sort of reflections are called melancholy, but I think them only serious; they prepare the mind and help to fortify it against the day of adversity, and make the blessings we are permitted to enjoy more lively and dear to us. Can you get Lady Anne Coventry's recipe for the rose pattern cross stitch? Many thanks for that of the raisin wine. The Duke of Dorset is to be our viceroy. Bushe and I went last Monday to see Mrs. Dillon and her sister Lady Austen: they are gone to pay a melancholy visit to their brother Preston—are pretty well, and so are the agreeable girls.

Mrs. Delany to Mrs. Dewes.

Delville, 24 Nov. 1750.

I don't fear your prudence in the management of of your children. Love, coupled with fear, are the bands that must confine them to what is right. A wrong and over-indulgent conduct of parents to children is the *greatest cruelty* to them; for if they never meet with contradiction till they are of age to engage in the great concerns of life, how will they be able to sustain the contradictions, disappointments, and mortifications they must encounter in this world? But a perverse, injudicious manner of contradicting and thwarting them, and very severe corrections for trifles, does them I believe almost as much harm as a universal indulgence. Happy are my dear children, who are I hope born to prove the golden mean : it is I am persuaded to a very tender mother, a most self-denying principle to refuse that indulgence, but great the virtue and strong the obligation laid on her *to correct* her child *steadily and properly.*

I am grieved for what poor Nanny Viney suffers, though she has a balm in her mind ready to heal all wounds. How gracious is Providence in making up to us what we love of worldly employments! No one can want consolation that justly attends to his merciful appointments; and when we suffer without having violated his commands (as far as human nature can presume to judge of their own intentions and actions), how great an advantage have they over those whose consciences smite them with having brought God's judgments on them! and a trial of our patience, humility, and resignation, is a happy state, compared to what we must suffer when conscious we are chastised for our evil deeds. Dr. Barber is much obliged to you, and expresses great gratitude to you and Mr. Dewes, we seldom see him, as his lectureship take up three days in the week. The ingenious Letitia is now exercising her fingers on my Indian book.

Have you yet read Mr. West[1] on the Employment of Time? I have not finished it: it is, as far as I have gone, charming. We are now reading Carte's History of the Duke of Ormond. My precious knot of friends in this part of the world send their best compliments. I have been indeed much distressed on Mrs. H. Hamilton's account—but I hope Court's mistress is out of danger.

---

[1] The Employment of Time, in three Essays, published in 1750, was not written by Mr. West, but by Dr. Robert Bolton, Dean of Carlisle, born 1697, died 1763.

Mrs. Delany to Mrs. Dewes.

Delville, Nov. 30, 1750.

I am glad Mr. Richardson has lent you the Lancashire lady's letters; I should be glad to read them again. I thought them written with great vivacity and wit; though against my own judgment as to the catastrophe of "Clarissa." I read them too hastily to say much about them, but I am sure your observation is just as to her obstinacy. I forget who you thought the author of Mrs. Belfour's letters.

I have had letters from my correspondents lately. The Duchess was in London for the two Birthdays; Babess and Dash with her at Bulstrode when she wrote last to me. Donnellan has been distrest about Mrs. Percival, who declines fast; and Dr. Donnellan is in so bad a state of health, that his friends are in great apprehensions for him. Miss Forth is better—at Bath, and Mrs. Hamilton, I hope, will have her fine little girl preserved to her. Bushe is very well and with me, very busy at this time, drawing in my *Indian book*.[1]

Yesterday we were at a charitable music, performed in the round church of Dublin; we had Corelli's 8th Concerto, Mr. Handel's Te Deum Jubilate, and two anthems; I cannot say there was so great a crowd as I wished to see on the occasion. We had promised to breakfast and dine at Lucan this day, and to come home by moonshine, but wind and rain prevented our design. I never heard a fiercer storm than it has been all night, and is but little abated. The first part of this week I have spent chiefly

---

[1] This book is in possession of the Editor. The leaves are of Indian paper, and the drawings are chiefly landscapes, finely finished in Indian ink; most of them by Letitia Bushe.

in painting the *great Madonna;* I have not yet covered my canvass. Last Tuesday we dined at Mr. McAulay's, a councillor learned in the law: there we met the Bishop of Derry, and lady, son, and cousin, and Mrs. Stone, *her* sister. On Monday we are to dine at the Bishop of Derry's. I hope he will have some music—he has sometimes: he has a very good collection of pictures. Mrs. Bernard is a very agreeable, clever woman, well acquainted with the *useful* part of the world, singular in her manner, open in her behaviour, and very penetrating in her judgment: I never met with a woman of quicker parts; she is withal very good and charitable, which crowns the rest.

The Duchess of Portland has given me great satisfaction in her last letter, by telling me that the Maid of Honour is much altered in one particular, in which I feared there never would be amendment—in great *indifference* between her and Lovelace; and the *little woman's* great ease confirms the Duchess in her observation. What friends sometimes look upon as a great calamity often is sent us as a great blessing: if the Maid of Honour's long and painful illness has made a happy change in her mind, her friends as well as herself will be paid for all their anxieties.

I wish I could have assisted you in your time of need with thread and knotting. I am sorry you have been disappointed of the French woman, as beginning French very young, gives a freer and better pronunciation than can be learned when they are older, but as this is an *embellishment* more than any *material* accomplishment, and if (which you can do very well) you teach her the grammar, and how to read, that will do for some years, and when you meet with a servant to your mind, that can save you some part of the attention you now have, take her by all means, for it is too much for you to have the whole care of so many upon your spirits; I hope the boys will be so well next year, that you may put the two eldest to school. Have you read Mr. West on the Employment of Time? I think it charming; he says some pretty things on education; and under the conduct of *Emilia*, I hope my Pauline will prove a Leonora. That child takes up much of my thoughts. *I know* what a world she has to pass through; *how many difficulties* to encounter, *temptations to avoid, afflictions to support*. As a human creature, some of these trials she must prove; but I hope the good education she will receive from excellent parents, their constant precepts and example, will enable her to *fight them manfully*. True religion and a command of her passions will be the best armour she can put on. I look upon it as a great advantage to *our girl*, that her parents are not too youthful, but have also gained a full experience, which enables them the better to perform the great task of forming and bending a young mind to what is right.

I return you Mr. Richardson's[1] letters, and many thanks for the perusal of them; he is a worthy man, and therefore it is an honour to be esteemed and distinguished by him; but I am afraid a man equal to Clarissa will be hard to find! Do you remember our short scheme about one as we went to Birmingham (that day of white melancholy)? Books that are designed to instruct the world in an entertaining way are a hard task, for they must be easy, natural, and polite,

---

[1] The author of *Clarissa*, and an occasional correspondent of Mrs. Dewes.

blended with the strictest moral and religious principles; it is not that in reality they are incompatible, but the corruptions and effeminacy of the fine world is such, that they will not receive and entertain honesty and virtue, unless they *are dressed up* in the most elegant and fashionable attire.

I am much concerned to hear of Miss Viney's hoarseness; it is a thing must not be neglected, and if she does not lose it before spring, by all means she should go to Bristol.

Mrs. Dewes to Bernard Granville, Esq., at his house in Park Street, near Grosvenor Square, London.

Welsbourne, 3rd Dec. 1750.

Poor Miss Nanny has been very ill this week, but we expect Dr. Burgh in his way from Lady Anne Coventry, and I intend she shall consult him.

I don't desire long letters, as I know you don't love to write them, but pray let me know how Sir Anthony does, for I have not heard from him a great while.

I hope you find Mr. Handel well. I beg my compliments to him: he has not a more real admirer of his great work than myself; his wonderful Messiah will never be out of my head; and I may say *my heart was* raised almost to heaven by it. It is only those people who have not felt the pleasure of devotion that can make any objection to that performance, which is calculated to raise our devotion, and make us truly sensible of the power of the divine words he has chose beyond any human work that ever yet appeared, and I am sure I may venture to say ever will. If anything can give us an idea of the Last Day it must be that part—"The trumpet shall sound, the dead shall be raised." It is few people I can say so much to as this, for they would call me an enthusiast; but when I wish to raise my thoughts above this world and all its trifling concerns, I look over what oratorios I have, and even my poor way of fumbling gives me pleasing recollections, but I have nothing of the Messiah, but *He was despised*, &c. Does Mr. Handel do anything new against next Lent? surely Theodora[1] will have justice at last, if it was to be again performed, but the generality of the world have ears and *hear not*. Mr. Dewes is vastly afraid I shall make the boys love music, which he thinks would interfere with their necessary studies, but I doubt they have all good ears, and the little girl really can sing a tune, and he allows me to make her a musician if I can.

I am sorry the Maid of Honour is relapsed. Lord Mansel's[2] death has made a fine widow and heiress. Mr. Dewes and Miss Viney desire their best wishes to you. I heard last post from Ireland: all there are well. Have you read remarks upon Mrs. Muilman's[3] Letter to Lord Chesterfield? It is worth your looking over. I want to see "The Economy of Human Life,"[4] they tell me it is wrote by Lord Chesterfield.

---

[1] Theodora, an English oratorio by Handell, was first performed on the 16th of March, 1750.

[2] Bussey Mansell, 4th and last Baron. His first wife was Lady Betty Hervey, daughter of John, Earl of Bristol, and his second wife, Barbara, widow of Sir Walter Blacket, and daughter of William, Earl of Jersey. Lord Mansell died in 1750.

[3] Letter to the Earl of Chesterfield, by Teresa Constantia Muilman. Published in 1756.

[4] The Economy of Human Life; translated from an Indian manuscript written by an Ancient Bramin: to which is prefixed, An account of the manner in which the said MS. was discovered, in a letter from an English Gentleman now residing in China, to the Earl of ***. Published by Robert Dodsley.

You know poor old Mrs. Kirkham is dead.[1]

I had a bad account of poor Mrs. Duncombe from the Bath last week. She has a cancer in her side, two surgeons attend her, but there are small hopes of her life; Mr. Pie at Bristol did her no service.

Your nephews and niece desire their humble duty, you would think them vastly grown, they are all very well.

Mrs. Dewes, writing to her brother, Mr. Granville, Dec. 19, asks him to allow one of his servants to deliver a parcel to Mr. Richardson, which contained some *manuscript letters* he had sent her to read and which, Mr. Richardson said, "were of value to him."

Mrs. Delany to Mrs. Dewes.

Delville, 10 Dec. 1750.

Last Monday we dined at the Bishop of Derry's (Bernard), Mrs. Stone and Mrs. McAulay of the party. I was very well entertained with looking over the Bishop's pictures: he has a very good collection, by above 200 different masters' hands, original pictures, well preserved, and in good order; not many Italian, but the greatest variety of Dutch and Flemish I ever saw in one collection. It is an agreeable house to go to, the Bishop hearty and good-natured, Mrs. Bernard sensible and clever, and very easy, and besides, a library well furnished with portfolios of fine drawings and prints, with which they seem pleased to entertain their friends. In the morning I called upon Mrs. Hamilton, Miss Mary is recovering very fast. Tuesday

---

[1] The wife of the Rev. Lionel Kirkham, of Staunton, and mother of Sarah Kirkham, Mrs. Chapon.

I sat down to my painting, and Bushe to her drawing. In the evening, when tea is over, we settle to our different engagements; she reads aloud Mr. Carte's Life of the Duke of Ormonde, and I go on with making shell flowers for the ceiling of the chapel. I have made 86 large flowers, and about 30 small ones; I believe I told you this before, and that I tire you with repetition. Wednesday, Thursday and Friday spent alike. We had a pleasant jaunt on Saturday. Went to Lucan to breakfast, found Veseys up to the chin in business, hanging pictures and settling other decorations: all of us engaged in their business, staid to dinner, and till 7 in the evening, came home by a charming moonlight. A comfortable circumstance belonging to this country is, that the roads are *so good and free from robbers*, that we may drive safely any hour of the night. On Tuesday morning next, the rehearsal of the Messiah is to be for the benefit of debtors—on Thursday evening it will be performed. I hope to go to both; our new, and *therefore* favourite performer Morella is to play the first fiddle, and conduct the whole. I am afraid *his French taste* will prevail; I shall *not be able to endure* his introducing *froth and nonsense* in that sublime and awful piece of music. What makes me fear this will be the case, is, that in the closing of the eighth concerto of Corelli, instead of playing it *clear and distinct*, he filled it up with *frippery and graces which quite destroyed the effect* of the sweet notes, and solemn pauses that conclude it. I enclose you a silly nonsensical description of Killarney, the famous Lake and Islands I gave you some account of: I heard it was published, and sent for it for you, and wish it was better for your sake.

Mrs. Delany to Mrs. Dewes.

Delville, 15 Dec. 1750.

I was this morning obliged to work an hour and a half at my picture which by Monday would have been too dry for some softenings that were absolutely necessary, and we dine abroad at Mrs. Forde's, who is an exact person as to hours. Miss Hamilton continues to mend, and will, I hope, soon be quite well.

Your account of poor Mrs. Duncombe I return; but why do I call her *poor?* by this time, in all probability, she is truly rich: yet good and valuable friends are such a treasure to us in this world, that it is hard to give them up, though to their advantage. I hear Lady Westmoreland is dangerously ill. How many friends and agreeable acquaintances shall I have lost within these *seven years!* some indeed were a *grievous affliction,* and all a sensible concern: but we must turn our eyes to the many undeserved blessings we still enjoy, and be thankful. These losses ought to awaken us to a more eager pursuit of those joys that never end.

I am much pleased that you have advanced so far in your work, and sorry I have not been able to give you any assistance; all the thread and knotting I had I sent by Mrs. Dubourg, and hope you have got it by this time. I think you have judged very well for the pattern of your window curtains. I have not yet got the answer to Mrs. Muilman, and am all impatient for it. I have read "The Economy of Human Life," and think it very pretty, all but the chapter on love—and that, if you leave out *excess* in the first sentence, there is no objection to it; *that*, I suppose was to keep up the Eastern custom, but as it is meant for the instruction of Xtians, that part should have been blotted out. I think there are many beauties in the book, and those are chiefly owing to the Proverbs, from which he has taken all his most sublime thoughts.

As to our *belle amie*, engage her to make you a visit the first opportunity she has, and when they have met, you may judge if any steps can be taken to make two very reasonable, good people happy. This week I have had a feast of music. At the rehearsal on Tuesday morning, and last night at the performance, of the Messiah; very well performed indeed, and the pleasure of the music greatly heightened by considering how many poor prisoners would be released by it. You may (Bushe says) write to Mrs. Dillon when you please—she is sure she will be glad to hear from you; her two modest, innocent girls went with us to the Messiah, and asked much after you. We go this afternoon to the Bishop of Derry's, to hear Morella; he conducted the Messiah very well—*surprizingly so*, considering he was *not before acquainted* with such sublime music.

I am happy in Mr. Richardson's approbation; it raises my emulation of being more worthy his esteem. When I am commended by those whose distinction is honourable to me, I am ashamed of every weakness that may hurt me in their opinion. Is there a better spur to good actions than the praise and encouragement of wise and virtuous friends? Not on this side heaven, I am sure.

Mrs. Delany to Bernard Granville, Esq., Park Street, Grosvenor Square.
Delville, Dec. 18, 1750.

I think I have lately been as guilty of laziness about writing as you can be, but though it may have appeared laziness, truly it has been the contrary. Four days in the week I am engaged in painting; I am now copying a large Madonna and Child after Guido, for our chapel. I believe it is an original, but it has been much damaged, and is so obscure in many places, that it is an unpleasant task. I shall have amends made me afterwards by a picture the Primate has lent me of *Raphael's;* I fancy I gave you an account of it. Besides my pencils, I am busily employed in making shell ornaments for the chapel ceiling, but those are my candle-light work. Bushe in the evening reads Carte's History of the Duke of Ormonde to us, and the days that I am obliged to go abroad in are not half so agreeable to me as those I spend at home. I was at the rehearsal and performance of The Messiah, and though *voices* and *hands* were wanting to do it justice, it was very tolerably performed, and gave me great pleasure—'tis heavenly. Morella conducted it, and I expected would have *spoiled it*, but was agreeably surprized to find the contrary; he came off with great applause. I thought it would be impossible for his wild fancy and fingers to have kept within bounds; but Handel's music inspired and *awed him*. He says (*but I don't believe him*) that he *never* saw any music of Handel's or Corelli's till he came to Ireland. I heard him play at the Bishop of Derry's a solo of Geminiani's which he had never seen; he played it cleverly, as his execution is extraordinary, but his taste in the adagio part was *ill suited* to the music. He is young, modest, and well-behaved, as I am told, and were he to play *under* Mr. Handel's direction two or three years, would make a surprizing player. We are so fond of him here, that were it known I gave this hint, I should be *expelled* all musical society, as they so much fear he should be tempted to leave us.

I had a letter lately from Lady Abbess, who tells me poor Betty is worse again; but that in some particulars relating to her conduct with ——, there is such an alteration as gives her great satisfaction. I was so happy yesterday as to hear our friends at Welsbourne are well. How does Sir Anthony? Pray make him our compliments. Dr. Donnellan is come from Inniscarra, and lodges at Clontarff; we are going to see him this morning; I fear he is in a bad way, though his brother, who dined here yesterday, says he is better than he expected to see him. Did you hear of your old friend Mrs. Burgh's death? She is much lamented by her family, but had the pleasure before her death to settle all her daughters; the youngest, Miss Dolly, was married last year to a Mr. Forster, a sensible, clever lawyer, and a very good fortune.

We have many projects in hand; planting, levelling, and railing in the cold-bath field, to let the deer in. You must understand that field is in the midst of our garden. (Alas! I talk to you of it, as if you were as well acquainted with it as I and the Dean most heartily wish you were). I have given you a sketch of it. We seem, in general, well pleased that the Duke of Dorset is named for us: anything, rather than our last V.R., who is detested here.

Well now, my dear brother, it is time to cease my babbling. I hope to hear from you soon. Accept of best wishes for the season, and believe me,
Your most affectionate sister and humble servant,

M. D.

Have you got your shells? Shall I send you more? I believe the best way when you have more, would be to send them by Loughrea to London. Pray make my compliments to Handel. Is *Theodora* to appear next Lent? Compliments to Hanover Square.

Upon consideration, I don't believe the paper you have would suit your bed. But it would *look very handsome in your hall,* give it a finished look—and it is cheaper than painting.

Mrs. Delany to Mrs. Dewes.

Delville, 22 Dec., 1750.

I spent two comfortable hours with Mrs. Hamilton, who is quite happy in the recovery of her little girl: she is now come down stairs, and is as lively as ever, though a little skeleton. I thought it hardly possible she should recover, but I thank God she has! her death would have been a fatal stroke to her excellent mother, whose nerves are ill able to support such a shock. Her eldest daughter is a good creature, and has shewn such a regard to her mother and sister on this occasion, such attention, and been so useful, that it has raised her greatly in my esteem. She is to spend this day with me; if I could transport your*self*, (I mean my dear *sister-self*,) here, you should be here to-day to partake of our musical entertainment. Signor Morella, our present famous performer, and his friend (whose name I know not) that accompanies him, and a Mr. Smith, who plays well on the harpsichord (not the Counsellor), an organist, are to be here before 12, and to spend the day here. The rest of the company are to be Mrs. F. Hamilton, and Miss Ann, Bishop of Derry, Mrs. Bernard, their son and niece. I can't but think if I had the *power* of transporting you hither whenever I wanted you, what *an amazement* your husband, children, servants, and neighbours would be in, and if this thought came into an ingenious head it might be worked up to something droll enough. Miss Forth, if it is possible, will call on you before she returns to us; it is what she wishes to do, were it but for an hour; she is much better. I shall not paint next week, there being so many church days, but shall pursue my works for the chapel of another sort. I am most heartily sorry for poor Mrs. Kendal. I like Newton's Fable extremely. I cannot get the answer to Con. P——.

Mrs. Delany to Mrs. Dewes.

Delville, 28 Dec., 1750.

I thank God I have been very well, but very busy, though the main and most material business of the week I was not able to pursue; for since Xtmas day it has been perpetual rain, and our horses are all ill of the epidemic disorder; the distemper was brought here about three weeks ago by horses from England, and rages everywhere, and several have died of it.

I have just seen the sun rise most gloriously; the reflection of it in the sea and the gilding of the ships and buildings was beautiful. Now the days lengthen I shall grow again an early riser, for I have not *this month* past been up before 8.

I don't think I half answered yours of the 7th. I wish you joy of your curtains being done, and hope you have got my thread by this time: I am sorry to be so little assistant to you in it, but D.D. employs me *every hour in the day* for his chapel. I make the flowers and other ornaments by candle-light, and by daylight, when I don't paint, put together the festoons that are for the ceiling, and after supper we play at commerce, one pool. Our everyday reading is still Carte's History of the old Duke of Ormonde: he is one of the greatest heroes I ever read of, such courage, prudence, loyalty, humanity, and virtues of every kind make up his character, but the sufferings of King Charles the First, though there but in part related, *break one's heart!* I think the periods too long; there is a repetition of facts that might have been avoided; and it is upon the whole rather tedious, but the subject so interesting that it carries one along. Our Sunday reading is the Minute Philosopher.[1] What a work of genius is that! How beautiful the style; and for sense and wit surely nothing can exceed it. I beg you will read it again. I thought it at first reading more abstruse than

---

[1] "The Minute Philosopher," by Dr. Berkeley, Bishop of Cloyne.

I do now; though there are very few pages (I don't know but I may say sentences) but what you will perfectly understand, with close attention. It is impossible for *a minute philosopher*, who has comprehension, to read that book and not become a convert; it baffles all their absurdities with such reasoning and such lively strokes of wit that infidelity must fall before it. The 4th day, that treats of *vision*, is too deep for me in some places; but there is enough clear, even to my understanding, to make it both useful and extremely entertaining. Your observation on old age is very just: it certainly brings many satisfactions unknown to youth, and has thrown by many cares and worldly anxieties; that is *a reasonable* old age,—for when it is not that it is a deplorable state, irksome to the person and ridiculous to the world.

I am sorry poor Miss Viney suffers so much; but the strength and excellence of her mind make up for the weakness of her body, and when Providence sees fit to restore her to her health, she will know how to enjoy the blessing with a higher relish.

I am much concerned for the Maid of Honour. My tenderness for her has increased of late, on my receiving a very satisfactory account of her, and whatever may be the event of her illness, it is a *great comfort* to have her confirmed in a *right way of thinking*. The Prince and Princess have been very kind in their behaviour towards her.

I have not heard from Sally; but my heart feels for her, I pray God her son's good behaviour and success may reward her pangs! To be afflicted at once by the double distress, as a *daughter* and a *mother*, is a most melancholy situation, but her piety will support and comfort her I hope. Poor Mrs. Pointz![1] she has had a great loss; and though not a woman of bright parts, had discernment enough to know her happiness in having such a worthy guide, companion, and friend, and will be much afflicted; and I believe Lady Sarah Cowper nearly as much, for though *she* has before had a much greater loss, I think that does not render the heart insensible to those that are less, but rather, as afflictions naturally increase tenderness of nature, it will make her feel this the more. I fear I shall soon hear of Lady Westmoreland's death; the last account of her I had was of her being dangerously ill.

I have just taken a run along my portico walk into the greenhouse; and send you an orange-leaf and a yellow Indian jessamine of my own raising; I wish they may not lose their sweetness before they kiss your hands.

---

[1] The Right Hon. Stephen Poyntz, formerly preceptor to His Royal Highness the Duke of Cumberland, and at the time of his death steward of his household, died Dec. 17, 1750.

END OF THE SECOND VOLUME.

Printed in the United States
122894LV00004B/4/A